Keys to

COLLEGE STUDYING

BECOMING AN ACTIVE THINKER

SECOND EDITION

Carol Carter

Joyce Bishop

Sarah Lyman Kravits

PEARSON

Prentice
Hall

Upper Saddle River, New Jersey
Columbus, Ohio

Library of Congress Cataloging-in-Publication Data

Carter, Carol.
    Keys to college studying: becoming an active thinker/Carol Carter,
    Joyce Bishop, Sarah Lyman Kravits.—2nd ed.
    p. cm.
    Includes bibliographical references and index.
    ISBN 0-13-170377-3
    1. Study skills. 2. Adult learning. I. Bishop, Joyce (Joyce L.).
    II. Kravits, Sarah Lyman. III. Title.
LB2395.C267 2007
378.1'7—dc22   2005032895

Vice President and Publisher: Jeffery W. Johnston
Executive Editor: Sande Johnson
Developmental Editor: Jennifer Gessner
Editorial Assistant: Susan Kauffman
Production Editor: Alexandrina Benedicto Wolf
Production Coordinator: Holcomb Hathaway
Design Coordinator: Diane C. Lorenzo
Cover Designer: Jeff Vanik
Cover Photo: Getty Images, Corbis
Production Manager: Pamela D. Bennett
Director of Marketing: Ann Castel Davis
Marketing Manager: Amy Judd

Photo Credits, by page number
All photos from *The New York Times* used with
permission. 2, Stockdisc; 11, Dopkeen/NY Times; 23,
Estrin/NY Times; 36, Clark/NY Times; 40, Image Source; 45,
Romero/NY Times; 58, Parley/ © The Fresno Bee, 2006; 74,
DeChillo/NY Times; 79, Yee/NY Times; 87, Fornabaio/NY
Times; 120, Yee/NY Times; 125, Yee/NY Times; 136,
Conrad/NY Times; 154, DeChillo/NY Times; 165,
Houghton/NY Times; 176, Washington/NY Times; 194,
DeChillo/NY Times; 201, DeChillo/NY Times; 215, Michael
Quan; 242, Crane/NY Times; 253, Franco/NY Times; 266,
Chappell/NY Times; 280, Pidgeon/NY Times; 285, Agins/NY
Times; 302, Wilson/NY Times; 320, Dynamic Graphics; 325,
Higgins/NY Times; 346, Muhammad/NY Times; 364,
Crowley/NY Times; 368, Mohin/NY Times; 380,
Muhammad/NY Times; 394, Wilson/NY Times; 397,
Agins/NY Times; 414, Dopkeen/NY Times; 426, Bananastock;
436, Fornabaio/NY Times; 438, Agins/NY Times.

This book was set in Sabon by Integra. It was printed and bound by R.R. Donnelley & Sons Company.
The cover was printed by Phoenix Color Corp.

Pearson Education Ltd.
Pearson Education Singapore Pte. Ltd.
Pearson Education Canada, Ltd.
Pearson Education—Japan

Pearson Education Australia Pty. Limited
Pearson Education North Asia Ltd.
Pearson Educación de Mexico, S.A. de C.V.
Pearson Education Malaysia Pte. Ltd.

10 9 8 7 6 5 4 3 2 1
ISBN 0-13-170377-3

Brief Contents

Contents

PART I KNOWLEDGE, SKILLS, AND PREPARATION   1
WHERE THE FUTURE BEGINS

1 Set the Stage for Success   3
MANAGING GOALS, TIME, AND STRESS

2 Learning Styles, Majors, and Careers   37

KNOWING YOUR TALENTS AND FINDING YOUR DIRECTION

3 Critical and Creative Thinking   75

SOLVING PROBLEMS AND MAKING DECISIONS

PART II READING, UNDERSTANDING,
AND REMEMBERING 119

MASTERING ESSENTIAL LEARNING SKILLS

4

*Reading Comprehension, Vocabulary,
and Speed* 121

READING FASTER AND UNDERSTANDING MORE

5 Studying Textbooks and Course Materials   155

MASTERING CONTENT

6 *Listening and Memory*   195

TAKING IN AND REMEMBERING INFORMATION

PART III NOTES, WRITING, AND MATH   241

BUILDING ACTIVE STUDY SKILLS

7 *Taking Lecture Notes*   243

RECORDING CONCEPTS AND INFORMATION

8 *Effective Writing*   281

COMMUNICATING YOUR MESSAGE

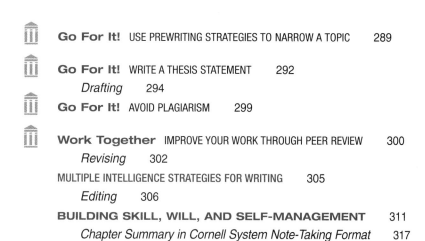

Quantitative Learning   321

BECOMING COMFORTABLE WITH MATH AND SCIENCE

PART IV BECOMING A BETTER TEST TAKER
AND CREATING YOUR FUTURE   363

CHOOSING SUCCESS

10 *Test Taking*   365

DEVELOPING A WINNING STRATEGY

11 *Taking Objective, Essay, and Oral Exams* 395

12 *Moving Ahead* 427

Note: Every effort has been made to provide accurate and current Internet information in this book. However, the Internet and information posted on it are constantly changing, so it is inevitable that some of the Internet addresses listed in this textbook will change.

Foreword

BY THE STUDENT EDITORS

After our first semester, we realized that succeeding in college—or at times just surviving it—required more than diligence and endless studying. It demanded order, ambition, balance, and prioritization. Quickly we realized that hours in the library were only worth minutes if spent incorrectly. Time management, solid study skills, and a direct plan of action were necessary to being a successful student able to maintain a social life and sense of self in a world of books, computers, and calculators. We found these strategies, and more, in *Keys to College Studying*.

Stress was one of the primary difficulties we had to overcome as first-year students. Academic anxiety often filtered into all aspects of our lives. Unless recognized and managed, the stress of college life can be all-consuming and often self-perpetuating. Suggestions in this text helped us deal with this stress and even channel it into productive work.

Being honest about our strengths and challenges also helped us succeed academically. Acknowledging areas that needed extra work was the first step in accomplishing what we never thought possible. Doing well in courses that seemed overwhelming at first gave us enormous confidence that we could succeed again.

As *Keys to College Studying* emphasizes, college is a time for trying your best, working to achieve smaller goals as you strive toward larger aspirations, and being proud of yourself as both a student and a person. We have often considered college to be a vehicle through which we will find a career and attain happy adult lives, but it is also something more fundamental: It is a blank slate, a drawing board, on which we decide what we want and slowly configure how we will achieve it.

We encourage you, when reading this book, to embrace its suggestions on learning and life because the scholastic, social, and personal successes you achieve in college will form the foundation for what you do after you graduate. Being a good student will give you the self-confidence, determination, knowledge, and skills you need to accomplish whatever you set out to do.

Best Wishes,

Student Editors-in-Chief

Lia Mandaglio
LAFAYETTE COLLEGE

Deborah Block
TUFTS UNIVERSITY

Student Editorial Staff

Jon Adler
TUFTS UNIVERSITY

Gibbs Lindsey
COLLEGE OF THE REDWOODS

Frida Matute
GEORGE WASHINGTON UNIVERSITY

Preface

Welcome to *Keys to College Studying*. This second edition takes our first edition focus on study and thinking skills to a new level of usefulness and relevance. We have constructed *Keys to College Studying*, Second Edition, around a central theme: **active thinking.**

This theme provides a context for learning study techniques that offers several advantages. First, the framework encourages you to look at your unique strengths and challenges as a learner and, based on what you understand about yourself, choose and adapt study techniques in ways that work for you. Second, the framework is research-based, focusing on actions that have been shown to improve academic achievement. Finally, the framework empowers you to think and learn independently, in many different academic settings as well as in work and life. *When you know yourself as a learner and know how to think, you can apply what you know to any situation.*

This book empowers you to think actively

Active thinkers are motivated, responsible thinkers who exhibit three key characteristics.

Will: They have the will to learn and an awareness of who they are as learners.

Skill: They can learn and use the skills they need to achieve their goals.

Self-management: They are able to manage themselves and monitor their progress.

Every chapter of *Keys to College Studying* will help you to build your active thinking skills. The theme is introduced in Chapter 1 and reinforced throughout the text. The chart on the following page offers a chapter-by-chapter set of examples showing how chapter topics reinforce and build active thinking characteristics.

CHAPTER	WILL/SELF-AWARENESS	SKILL BUILDING	SELF-MANAGEMENT
1 Values, Goals, and Time	Examining personal values	Goal setting and time management	Coming up with creative ways to manage stress
2 Learning Styles and Self-Awareness	Examining how you learn and relate to others	Matching your learning style to courses and majors	Monitoring how well particular strategies work for your learning style
3 Critical and Creative Thinking	Understanding how you think and examining personal perspectives	Brainstorming, problem solving, decision making	Evaluating the success of problem solving and decision making processes
4 Reading Comprehension, Vocabulary, and Speed	Knowing the internal and external conditions you need for focused reading	Expanding vocabulary, building comprehension skills	Understanding reading purpose and adjusting your focus and pace to fit that purpose
5 Studying Textbooks and Course Materials	Exploring your strengths and weaknesses as a reader	Understanding and using the SQ3R reading technique	Monitoring your ability to retain the material you read
6 Listening and Memory	Knowing your listening and memory roadblocks	Understanding how memory works and building memory skills	Evaluating what techniques improve listening and memory
7 Taking Lecture Notes	Examining what note taking techniques serve you best	Building skills for in-class note taking as well as reviewing class notes	Looking at test scores, evaluating how well your notes work as study tools
8 Effective Writing	Identifying your strengths as a writer and how you approach the task of writing	Developing a strategic approach to writing that includes planning, drafting, revising, and editing	Evaluating your work throughout the writing process, and asking for feedback from others
9 Quantitative Learning	Understanding yourself as a quantitative (math and science) learner	Developing tools for handling math and science classes, textbooks, problems, and tests	Monitoring quantitative learning success and applying methods to improve your work
10 Test Preparation and Test Taking	Pinpointing any specific anxiety you experience around test taking	Learning how to plan an effective review schedule, select the most important material to review, and use review techniques	When you make a mistake on a test, analyzing what happened and how you can avoid the mistake in the future
11 Types of Tests	Knowing which kinds of tests you tend to do well on, and which give you trouble	Building knowledge of ways to handle different types of test questions	Through a semester, monitoring how well your test question strategies are working—or not working—for you
12 Moving Ahead	Getting a clearer picture of your academic, professional, and personal goals	Building skills for handling success, failure, and change	Continually monitoring your progress toward your most important goals

This book provides strategies and resources that help you learn and work

Being aware of how you learn and knowing how to think are necessary foundation blocks on which to build essential study skills. This book respects you, the individual, enough to encourage you to ask your own questions and think for yourself. It offers opportunities to assess your strengths and skills, try out techniques, and evaluate what strategies most effectively move you ahead toward your academic and life goals.

With active thinking as the foundation of this edition, *Keys to College Studying* presents the following learning tools and materials to support your quest for success:

A focus on self-awareness. Chapter 1 gets you on track with ways to understand how you set goals, manage time, and deal with stress. Then, Chapter 2 takes you through two assessments that help you identify your preferred learning styles and related academic strategies. In subsequent study skills chapters, learning styles information is integrated through grids that offer study strategies for each of the multiple intelligences. Chapter 2 will also help you identify those interests and skills needed to develop your academic path, such as exploring a major.

A focus on critical and creative thinking. Chapter 3 helps you develop your thinking skills and understand how to use various strategies to solve problems and make decisions effectively. The techniques you develop as a critical and creative thinker are essential for success in any course, academic setting, or career.

Essential academic skills. The study skills chapters of this text help develop a firm foundation of skills—such as note taking, reading, and test taking—that will serve you in college as well as in your professional life.

Active thinking exercises. The exercises within the chapters and at the end of each chapter encourage you to take an active role in your learning, build teamwork and vocabulary skills, boost test-taking competence, and set goals. At the end of each part, an additional set of exercises reinforces the material: these exercises help forge connections among different ideas and examples and offer a practice session using various types of test questions.

Research help and information. First, this text includes access to **Research Navigator,** a tool consisting of three databases featuring specific collections of both popular and academic writings. *The Prentice Hall Guide to Evaluating Online Resources with Research Navigator,* packaged with this text, describes what is available on these databases and how to use the tool. (If your book did not come with this guide, you should be able to purchase one at your college bookstore.) Access Research Navigator online at **www.researchnavigator.com** using the access code found in the inside front cover of the booklet. Second, an appendix containing the basics about library and online research appears at the end of the text.

This book has changes and additions that make it even more useful to you

From our consultations with students, student editors, instructors, and other experts, we have focused this new edition on what you need to succeed now. Here's what's new:

- Integration of the will, skill, and self-management theme throughout the text
- Goals, time, and stress topics appear in Chapter 1
- New in-chapter exercises—"Go For It" and "Work Together"—and end-of-chapter exercises—"Target and Achieve a Goal," "Get to the Root," and "Make Responsible Choices"
- Revised learning styles material in Chapter 2
- Extensive revision of Chapter 3—the thinking chapter—to clarify what critical and creative thinking are and how they work together within problem solving and decision making
- Updates and significant content revisions in all study skills chapters
- In Chapters 4 through 11, new Multiple Intelligence Strategies grids showing how to apply MI concepts to chapter material to maximize strengths and/or build weaker areas
- Revised chapter summaries in either Cornell system, outline, or think link format reinforce chapter material while building knowledge of note-taking systems
- The Research Navigator booklet, Research Navigator exercises at the end of each chapter, and student access to Research Navigator online

With this book and your own determination, you can build active thinking skills and find academic success

As you work through this course and move forward toward your goals, believe that your skills, your self-knowledge and will to learn, and your ability to manage and monitor yourself can grow and develop. Use this book to develop these characteristics this semester, throughout your college experience, and as you build your future.

Students and instructors: Many of our best suggestions have come from you. Send your questions, comments, and ideas about *Keys to College Studying* to Carol Carter at **caroljcarter@lifebound.com** or call our toll-free number at 1-877-737-8510. We look forward to hearing from you, and we are grateful for the opportunity to work with you.

Acknowledgments

This significant revision has been produced through the efforts of an extraordinary team. Many thanks to:

- Our reviewers, for their invaluable input. **Second edition reviewers:** Charles Scott Kurtz, Southwest Florida College; Sandra Perkins, University of Phoenix; Dianne V'Marie, University of Phoenix Online; Patrick Smith, University of Phoenix Online. **First edition reviewers:** Elaine Wright at the Department of Learning Assistance, Division of Academic Support, University of Southern Maine; and Nancy G. Wood, of the University of Arkansas at Little Rock.

- Our student editors-in-chief Deborah Block and Lia Mandaglio, and assistant student editors Jon Adler, Gibbs Lindsey, and Frida Matute for their insightful comments and hard work.

- Our terrific editor Sande Johnson, developmental editor Jennifer Gessner, and editorial assistant Susan Kauffman for their vision and efforts.

- Charlotte Morrissey for her keen perspectives and assistance on both the editorial and marketing aspects of the text.

- Our production team for their patience, flexibility, and attention to detail, especially Gay Pauley, John Wincek, Alex Wolf, and Pam Bennett.

- Our marketing gurus, especially Marketing Manager Amy Judd; Director of Marketing Ann Davis; and our student success sales directors Joe Hale, Deb Gravely, Brian McGarry, and Connie James.

- Publisher Jeff Johnston; President of Education, Career, and Technology Robin Baliszewski; and Prentice Hall President Tim Bozik for their interest in, commitment to, and leadership with the Student Success list.

- The Prentice Hall representatives and the management team led by national sales manager Brian Kibby.

- Our families and friends, who have encouraged us and put up with our commitments.
- We extend a very special thanks to Judy Block, whose research, writing, and editing work was essential and invaluable.

Finally, for their ideas, opinions, and stories, we would like to thank all of the students and professors with whom we work. Joyce in particular would like to thank the thousands of students who have allowed her, as their professor, the privilege of sharing part of their journey through college. We appreciate that, through reading this book, you give us the opportunity to learn and discover with you—in your classroom, in your home, on the bus, and wherever else learning takes place.

Carol Carter
Joyce Bishop
Sarah Lyman Kravits

KNOWLEDGE, SKILLS, AND PREPARATION

I

WHERE THE FUTURE BEGINS

1

"Nobody succeeds beyond his or her wildest expectations unless he or she begins with some wild expectations."

RALPH CHARELL, NETWORK TELEVISION EXECUTIVE

Set the Stage for Success

MANAGING GOALS, TIME, AND STRESS

s you begin this course, think for a moment about the quote on the opposite page and ask yourself: What do I expect—from this course, from myself this semester, from my college experience? Perhaps you want to build an academic record that will impress prospective employers, or keep your grade point average high enough to declare a particular major. Perhaps you haven't thought about it yet.

Now is the time to set those "wild" expectations of what you can accomplish. Take responsibility for your learning by actively pursuing those expectations, and you will find that your work this semester will serve you far beyond this semester's grades. The academic tools in this book are also life success tools, helping you to continually build skill and knowledge, develop self-awareness, and achieve important goals throughout life.

This chapter will first introduce you to what it means to think and learn actively. Then it will go into more detail about three aspects of self-management that form the foundation for study success: setting and working toward goals, managing time effectively, and dealing with the stresses that often arise through the journey.

> In this chapter you will explore answers to the following questions:
>
> - How can you think and learn actively?
> - How do you set and achieve goals?
> - How can you effectively manage your time?
> - How can you cope with the stress of college life?

HOW CAN YOU THINK AND LEARN ACTIVELY?

I t's Thursday night at 10 P.M. and you've got a test tomorrow morning at 9. You're just now shuffling through a pile of books and photocopied packets, deciding which to prioritize. At the same time you are thinking about how late you can study and still get up on time for the exam and be able to function. Another part of your brain is mulling over whether you can take the time to run out and pick up something to eat and drink to keep you going through the long night. One big question keeps popping up on top of all this mental activity: *How can I stay calm and learn this material so I can get a decent grade on this test? HELP!*

Nearly anyone who is or has been in college has experienced circumstances like these, circumstances that often result in cramming to avert disaster instead of studying to learn. The results—poor retention and stress—undermine the essential goal of your education, which is to remember what you learn so that you can use it in your pursuit of a successful and fulfilling life.

Once in a while, last-minute studying is unavoidable. Almost always, however, the predicament could have been improved—and perhaps totally avoided—by actively thinking through and taking a responsible approach to the test, the course, and the material itself.

What exactly is an active, responsible approach? It means setting goals, making plans, and following through with the end result in mind. Reimagine the opening scenario as an active and responsible student: What might it look like? Here is one effective series of actions:

- At the beginning of the month, you check your syllabus and see that a test is coming up in three weeks on the 22nd.
- You note what the test is on, perhaps clarifying the topics with your instructor or by looking at past tests, and make a list of what materials you will need to study.
- You set up study sessions at various times over the next three weeks, scheduling them around your school and work commitments, perhaps setting aside the most time in the last week before the test.
- You study your materials in a planned and focused way during your sessions, including time to work with others in your class.
- A week before the test, you prepare a "master set" of notes that summarizes key points in your reading materials and notes.
- The night before the test, you review your master set of notes, get to bed by midnight, and wake up in time to eat something before the test. You feel ready to show what you know.

In this scenario, you have not sat back passively and waited for the disaster to loom. You have used your head, taken action, and set yourself up for success.

Claire Ellen Weinstein, an educational psychologist who has done extensive research on learning, describes active students as follows:

> Such learners are diligent and resourceful in their efforts and do not give up easily, even in the face of difficulty. They know that learning is an active process and that they must take some of the responsibility for doing it. [They] actively engage the material and have some sense of when they know it and, perhaps more important, when they do not. When they encounter problems they try to find what they need to solve them, or they seek help from the teacher or classmates. They view studying and learning as a systematic process that is, to a good degree, under their control.[1]

Based on Weinstein's work, the profile of this kind of student consists of three important attributes.[2] Active and responsible thinkers have:

- the **skill** to accomplish their goals
- the **will** and self-awareness to learn
- the ability to **self-manage** and to monitor their progress

How can you use these three attributes to promote the achievement of your own most important academic and life goals?

Build Useful Skills

Learning is a process that demands a set of skills. Active thinkers are good at what they do, largely due to their focus on skill building. To build useful skills, you will:

Know about and use effective study and learning strategies for reading, studying, note taking, listening, memory, writing, research, and quantitative analysis. Chapters 4 through 9 in this text will guide you through a comprehensive range of study skills and help you turn these skills into lifelong habits.

Recognize and use the critical-thinking skills that form the foundation for effective studying. Questioning is at the heart of critical thinking. Active thinkers solve problems by asking questions and searching for solutions. You will explore thinking skills in Chapter 3.

Use resources and technology to aid your studying. These tools include computers for word processing and data analysis, the library for research, and reliable sources on the Internet for research and communication. As the owner of this text, you gain access to Research Navigator, an online service that will help you use libraries and the Internet effectively (for more about Research Navigator, see this chapter's exercise set).

Understand how to prepare effectively for exams to show yourself and others what you know. Chapters 10 and 11 focus on this skill.

Work effectively in a team. Understand that studying and problem solving with others—classmates, team members, and coworkers—is crucial to success. Learning in a group broadens and solidifies knowledge as it builds the ability to work with others. By combining efforts, styles, and perspectives, a group can generate more new ideas and build a more solid knowledge base than an individual could achieve alone. Each chapter of this text contains an exercise for working together that will help you build communication, cooperation, and critical-thinking skills as you work with fellow students to accomplish a goal.

When you work with the students in your classes, maximize team success with these strategies:

- Assign a leader to define and limit projects, set agendas for meetings and projects, keep an eye on progress, motivate team members, and evaluate results.
- Make sure participants have responsibilities and are "part owners" of the team process.
- Set long-term and short-term goals.
- Share the work.
- Set a regular meeting schedule.
- Create study materials for one another.
- Teach one another by making up quizzes, comparing sets of notes, or going through flash cards.
- Open your mind to new ideas, and evaluate ideas based on their quality, not on their source.

Although skills are crucial, they won't do you much good if you aren't motivated to use them. You also need to have the will, or drive, to use your skills.

Develop Self-Awareness and the Will to Learn

Active thinkers are determined to learn, in large part because they understand how they will be able to use what they learn. Their confidence in their ability to learn is supported by a solid awareness of their unique way of thinking and learning. To develop self-awareness and motivation to learn, you will:

Analyze your personal learning styles and pinpoint appropriate study methods. When you know who you are as a learner, you are more able to choose strategies that work for you. In Chapter 2 you will assess your learning style (your way of taking in and retaining information), exploring study techniques that tap into your strengths as well as strategies for improving weaker areas.

Become more confident that you can study and learn effectively. Good students are made, not born; any student who learns the study strategies in this text and makes a point to use them will experience a benefit. Many students lack confidence not because they have no ability but because they have never been taught *how* to learn and study successfully. If you acknowledge that you have the ability to learn, build a repertoire of study skills, and actively put them to work, you will build confidence that keeps you on the path of achievement.

Value effective study skills and strategies and see their connection to life success. Through this book, you will learn all kinds of strategies, from which you can choose the ones that work best for you. As you explore how your skills will serve you beyond the classroom, your ability to value your hard work here will grow, helping you to avoid the "What is the point of this?" feeling that can kill motivation and undermine academic success.

Being able to think effectively is the ultimate goal of your education, because with it you will be able to learn throughout your life—a necessary skill for success in a modern world marked by rapid changes in technology and the continuing growth of information. John Macionis, professor of sociology at Kenyon College, describes how the basic nature of work has changed: "Today, most people . . . work with ideas and symbols in what has become an information revolution. . . . The value of workers today lies in their thinking rather than in their movement."[3]

The final important attribute is to be an effective, responsible, and responsive self-manager.

Manage and Monitor Yourself and Your Learning Process

Active thinkers recognize and implement their role in the learning process. They take responsibility for managing the nuts and bolts of day-to-day academic work and plan ahead for success. To manage and monitor yourself effectively, you will:

Define specific short- and long-term goals and monitor their progress. This involves establishing what you want to achieve, keeping track of your progress, and making adjustments if you veer off a goal path. The next section in this chapter goes into more detail about goal setting and achievement.

Manage your time. Time management allows you to complete work on a reasonable schedule and minimize stress. Later in this chapter, you will read more about how to make the most of your time and plan effectively.

Evaluate how successfully you achieve your study goals. Be receptive to feedback from instructors, employers, and exams, making changes when the feedback indicates that change is necessary. Working well with others and using your thinking skills will help you evaluate effectively and learn from your evaluations.

Take an active, responsible approach to learning. As a college student, you don't have authority figures actively monitoring and shepherding your progress. You are in charge of your education. A responsible approach means basics such as attending class and participating in activities and discussions, completing reading and assignments on time and with the goal of learning the material, and communicating with instructors and fellow students.

One more important component of being a responsible student is maintaining *academic integrity* in all aspects of academic life: classes, assignments, tests, papers, projects, and relationships with students and faculty. The Center for Academic Integrity at Duke University defines academic integrity as a commitment to five fundamental values: *honesty* (a search for truth in work and in communication), *trust* (being true to your word), *fairness* (contributing to a fair academic environment), *respect* (accepting and honoring the opinions of others), and *responsibility* (making fair and honest choices).[4]

Violations of academic integrity—turning in previously submitted work, using unauthorized devices during an exam, providing unethical aid to another student, or getting unauthorized help with a project—constitute a sacrifice of ethics that may bring serious consequences. On the other hand, choosing to value academic integrity builds knowledge, helps develop positive habits and behaviors, and leads others to respect you and your work. Read your school's academic integrity policy in your student handbook or on the Web. When you enrolled, you agreed to abide by it. (See later chapters for related topics—Chapter 8 covers plagiarism and Chapter 10 discusses the consequences of cheating on tests.)

Taking an active approach to your education, as outlined in this chapter and reinforced throughout the book, will prepare you for whatever lies ahead in your coursework and in the workplace. The rest of the chapter prepares you for action by focusing on crucial self-management strategies: goal setting, time management, and stress reduction.

ACTIVE THINKING

SKILL   WILL   SELF-MGMT.

ASSESS YOUR READINESS FOR ACADEMIC SUCCESS

The following statements will help you get an idea of how, as you begin this course, you perceive yourself as a student. For each statement, circle the number that feels right to you, from 1 for "not true at all for me" to 5 for "absolutely true for me."

1. I see the connection between the effective study skills I learn today and my future academic, career, and life success. ① ② ③ ④ ⑤

2. I set effective short- and long-term study goals that will help me manage my workload. ① ② ③ ④ ⑤

3. I manage my time effectively and control any tendency to procrastinate. ① ② ③ ④ ⑤

4. I am aware of what causes me stress and I take steps to reduce it. ① ② ③ ④ ⑤

5. I am aware of my personal learning style, and I choose study strategies that take advantage of my strengths and minimize my weaknesses. ① ② ③ ④ ⑤

6. I understand the components of critical thinking and use critical-thinking skills to get the most from my work. ① ② ③ ④ ⑤

7. I take a systematic approach to reading and studying. ① ② ③ ④ ⑤

8. I am aware of various note-taking styles and techniques and use the ones that help me to best take down and retain information. ① ② ③ ④ ⑤

9. I use listening and memory techniques that work best for me. ① ② ③ ④ ⑤

10. I approach writing assignments with a plan and with enough time to carry it out. ① ② ③ ④ ⑤

11. I know and use the strategies that help me do my best on tests. ① ② ③ ④ ⑤

12. I understand and use a research strategy when doing library or Internet research. ① ② ③ ④ ⑤

Total your answers here: _____

If your total ranges from *12 to 27,* you consider your academic readiness/awareness to be *low.*

If your total ranges from *28 to 44,* you consider your academic readiness/awareness to be *average.*

If your total ranges from *45 to 60,* you consider your academic readiness/awareness to be *strong.*

These questions give you an overview of your starting point. Use your answers to target approaches and solutions in this book that will help you build on your strengths and develop your weaker areas. As you continue through the book and course, keep in mind the areas where you rated yourself lowest, taking special notice of ways in which you can improve those areas. In the last chapter of this book you will have a chance to revisit this assessment and to look at your perception of how you have grown.

HOW DO YOU SET AND ACHIEVE GOALS?

When you identify something that you want, you set a *goal*—an end toward which effort is directed. Actually getting there, however, requires planning and hard work. Think of goal planning as mapping: with a map helping you to establish each segment of the trip, you will be able to define your route and follow it successfully.

Set Long-Term Goals

Start by establishing the goals that have the largest scope, the *long-term goals* that you aim to attain over a period of six months, a year, or more. As a student, your long-term goals include attending school and earning a degree or certificate. Getting an education is a perfect example of a long-term goal.

Some long-term goals have an open-ended time frame. For example, if your goal is to continually improve as a musician, you may work at it over a lifetime, exploring a number of different paths. Other goals, such as completing all the courses in your major, have a shorter scope, a more definite end, and often fewer options for how to get from A to Z.

The following long-term goal statement, written by Carol Carter, a *Keys to College Studying* author, may take years to complete:

> My goal is to build my own business in which I create opportunities for students to maximize their talents. In this business, I will reach thousands of students and teachers through books, the Internet, teacher seminars, and student-oriented programs.

Carol also has long-term goals that she hopes to accomplish in no more than a year:

> Develop and publish one book. Design three seminars for teachers with accompanying PowerPoint visuals and other materials. Create Internet-based materials that encourage student success and use them in student seminars.

Just as Carol's goals are tailored to her personality, abilities, and interests, your goals should reflect your uniqueness. To determine your long-term goals, think about what you want to accomplish while you are in school and after you graduate.

Link Long-Term Goals to Values

People make life choices—what to do, what to believe, what to buy, how to act—based on *values*. Your values are the principles or qualities that you consider important. Your choice to pursue a degree, for example, reflects that you value the personal and professional growth that comes from a college education. Values play a key role in your drive to achieve goals, because they help you to:

- **Build "rules for life."** Your values form the foundation for your decisions and actions. You will return repeatedly to them for guidance, especially when you find yourself in unfamiliar territory.

- **Focus on what you want out of school.** What kinds of skills, knowledge, and attitudes do you most want to build? Your most meaningful goals should reflect what you value most.

Reviewing animal physiology while caring for her son is just part of how this single parent and premed student juggles responsibilities on a daily basis.

- **Choose your major and a career direction.** Values are linked to academic and professional aims. For example, someone who values fitness and helping others may have an academic goal of a degree in exercise physiology and a career goal of becoming a certified physical therapist.

Reaching a long-term goal requires determination and consistent effort. Basing your long-term goals on values increases your motivation. The more defined your values, and the more your goals reflect those values, the greater your drive and desire to reach them.

Set Short-Term Goals

Short-term goals are smaller steps that move you toward a long-term goal. Lasting as short as a few hours or as long as a few months, they help you manage your broader aspirations as they narrow your focus and encourage progress. If you have a long-term goal of graduating with a degree in nursing, for example, you may want to accomplish these short-term goals in the next six months:

- I will learn the names, locations, and functions of every human bone and muscle.

- I will work with a study group to understand the muscular-skeletal system.

These same goals can be broken down into even smaller parts, such as the following one-month goals:

- I will work with on-screen tutorials of the muscular-skeletal system until I understand and memorize the material.
- I will spend three hours a week with my study partners.

In addition to monthly goals, you may have short-term goals that extend for a week, a day, or even a couple of hours in a given day. To support your month-long goal of meeting with your study partners regularly, you may set these short-term goals:

- **By the end of today:** Call study partners to ask when they might be able to meet.
- **One week from now:** Schedule each of our weekly meetings this month.
- **Two weeks from now:** Have our first meeting.
- **Three weeks from now:** Distribute notes from the first meeting; have the second meeting.

As you consider your long- and short-term goals, notice how all of your goals are linked to one another.

At any given time, you will be working toward goals of varying importance. Setting priorities helps you decide where and when to focus your energy and time.

Prioritize Goals

To *prioritize* is to arrange and handle things in order of importance. When you prioritize, you evaluate everything you are working toward, decide which goals are most important, and focus your time and energy on them. What should you consider as you evaluate?

- **Your values.** Considering values helps you establish the goals that take top priority—for example, graduating in the top 25 percent of your class or developing a network of personal contacts.
- **Your personal situation.** Are you going to school and working part-time? Do you have young children? Are you an athlete? Every person's situation requires unique priorities and scheduling.
- **Your time commitments.** Hours of your day may already be committed to class, meetings, or a part-time job. Make sure these commitments reflect what you value, and establish priorities (such as exercise, social activities, and sleep) for the remaining hours.

Academic success requires that you make your studies a high priority, whether you are overloaded with responsibilities or relatively free. If you find yourself missing classes and having a hard time prioritizing study sessions, consider thinking of school as your "job." If you prioritize your academic "job" in the same way you would any other job, you will reap the benefits.

Work to Achieve Goals

After you've spent the time thinking through your goals, practical steps will help you achieve them.

1. **Define your goal-achievement strategy.** *How do you plan to reach your goal?* Brainstorm different paths that might get you there. Choose one; then, map out its steps and strategies. Focus on specific behaviors and events that are under your control and that are measurable.

2. **Set a timetable.** *When do you want to accomplish your goal?* Set a realistic timeline that includes specific deadlines for each of the steps and strategies you have defined. Charting your progress will help you stay on track.

3. **Monitor your progress.** *How well are you moving toward your goal?* Compare your actual time to your planned timetable and your actual steps to your planned steps. Decide if adjustments are necessary.

4. **Be accountable and responsible for moving ahead.** *What safeguards will keep you on track?* Put in place a system of reporting—to yourself, to one or more people close to you, or both—that makes accountability a priority.

5. **Anticipate problems.** *What will you do if you hit a roadblock?* Define two ways to get help with your efforts if you run into trouble. Be ready to get creative with more ideas if those don't work.

Remember, the more specific your plans, the more likely you are to fulfill them. "Effective goals are specific, moderately difficult, but not impossible," says Paul Eggen, professor of Education at the University of North Florida. "Say, for example, you're taking a chemistry course, and there are exercises at the end of every chapter. An effective goal would be to work and understand all the exercises—not at the end of each chapter, but at the end of THIS chapter. That's a much better goal than 'I'm going to get a B in this class,' or 'I'm going to study harder,' or even 'I'm going to study for four hours a day.' The goal of solving and understanding the problems at the end of 'this' chapter is specific, near-term, and easily monitored. And it is psychologically powerful because it puts you in total control."[5]

Through this process, you will continually be thinking about how well you are using your time. In fact, goal achievement is directly linked to effective time management.

HOW CAN YOU EFFECTIVELY MANAGE YOUR TIME?

Everyone has the same 24 hours in a day, every day. Your challenge is to make smart choices about how to use your daily 24. Successful time management starts with identifying your time-related needs and preferences. This self-knowledge sets the stage for building and managing your schedule, avoiding procrastination, and being flexible in the face of change.

Identify Your Time-Related Needs and Preferences

Body rhythms and habits affect how each person deals with time. Some people are night owls, while others are at their best in the morning. Some people are chronically late, while others get everything done with time to spare. A mismatch between your needs and your schedule causes stress; for example, a person who loses steam in the mid-afternoon may struggle in classes that meet between 3 and 5 p.m.

Being aware of your needs and preferences will help you create a schedule that maximizes your strengths and reduces stress. Take the following steps to identify time-related needs and preferences:

Create a personal time "profile." Ask yourself these questions: At what time of day do I have the most energy? The least energy? Do I tend to be early, on time, or late? Do I focus well for long stretches or need regular breaks? Your answers will help you create a schedule that works best for you.

Evaluate the effects of your profile. Consider which of your time-related habits and preferences will have a positive impact on your success at school, and which are likely to cause problems.

Establish what schedule preferences suit your profile best. Make a list of these preferences—or even map out an ideal schedule as a way of illustrating them. For example, one student's list might read: "Classes scheduled on Mondays, Wednesdays, and Fridays. Study time primarily during the day."

Next, it's time to build the schedule that takes all of this information into account.

Build a Schedule

Schedules help you gain control of your life in two ways: They provide segments of time for tasks related to the fulfillment of your goals, and they remind you of tasks, events, due dates, responsibilities, and deadlines. The following strategies are all part of building an effective schedule.

Get a Planner

A planner allows you to keep track of events and commitments, schedule goal-related tasks, and rank tasks according to priority. There are two major types of planners. One is a book or notebook in which to write commitments. Some devote a page to each day, and others show a week's schedule on a two-page spread. The other option is an electronic planner or personal digital assistant (PDA). Basic PDA functions allow you to schedule days and weeks, note due dates, make to-do lists, perform mathematical calculations, create and store an address book, and transfer information to and from a computer.

Analyze your preferences and options, and decide which tool you are most likely to use. A dime-store notebook will work as well as a top-of-the-line PDA as long as you use it conscientiously.

Keep Track of Events and Commitments

Use your planner to schedule and remember events and commitments, especially during busy times. For example, if you see that you have three tests and a presentation coming up in one week, you may have to rearrange your schedule during the preceding week to create extra study time.

Among the events, commitments, and information worth noting in your planner are:

- test and quiz dates
- due dates for papers, projects, and presentations
- details of your academic schedule, including semester and holiday breaks
- club and organizational meetings
- personal items—medical appointments, due dates for bills, birthdays, social events
- names and numbers of people you contact frequently or plan to contact as part of a goal or task
- milestones toward a goal, such as due dates for sections of a project

Don't forget to include class prep time—reading and studying, writing and working on assignments and projects—in your planner. According to one formula, you should schedule at least two hours of preparation for every hour of class—that is, if you take 15 credits, you should study about 30 hours a week, making your total classroom and preparation time 45 hours. Students who work or have family responsibilities—or both—need to be creative, squeezing study time in whenever they can.

Schedule Tasks and Activities That Support Your Goals

Linking the events in your planner to your goals will give meaning to your efforts and bring order to your schedule. Planning study time for an economics test, for example, will mean more to you if you link the hours you spend to your goal of being accepted into business school. Here is how a student might translate his goal of getting into business school into action steps over a year's time:

This year: Complete enough courses to meet curriculum requirements for business school.

This semester: Complete economics class with a B average or higher.

This month: Set up economics study group schedule to coincide with quizzes and tests.

This week: Meet with study group; go over material for Friday's test.

Today: Go over Chapter 3 in econ text.

The student can then arrange his time in ways that move him ahead. He schedules activities that support his short-term goal of doing well on the test, and writes them in his planner as shown in Key 1.1.

Before each week begins, remind yourself of your long-term goals and what you can accomplish over the next seven days to move you closer to them. Key 1.2 shows parts of a daily schedule and a weekly schedule.

Key 1.1	**Sample planner.**

MONDAY	TUESDAY	WEDNESDAY	THURSDAY	FRIDAY	SATURDAY	SUNDAY
9 A.M.: Economics class Talk with study group members to schedule meeting	3–5 P.M. Study Econ Chapter 3	9 A.M. Economics class Drop by instructor's office hours to ask question about test	6 P.M. Go over Chapter 3 7–9 P.M. Study group meeting	9 A.M.: Economics class—Test 3:30 P.M. Meet with advisor to discuss GMAT and other business school requirements	Sleep in— schedule some down time	5 P.M. Go over quiz questions with study partner

Key 1.2   Note daily and weekly tasks.

Monday		March 13
TIME	TASKS	PRIORITY
7:00 A.M.		
8:00	Up at 8 am — finish homework	
9:00		
10:00	Business Administration	
11:00	Renew driver's licens @ DMV	
12:00 P.M.		
1:00	Lunch	
2:00	Writing seminar (peer editing)	
3:00		
4:00	check on MS (Schwartz's office)	
5:00	5:30 workout	
6:00	↳ 6:30	
7:00	Dinner	
8:00	Read 2 chapters for	
9:00	Business Admin.	
10:00		

MONDAY, MARCH 27

8		Call Mike Blair @	1
9	BIO 212	Financial Aid Office	2
10		EMS 262 + paramedic	3
11	CHEM 203	role play	4
12			5
Evening	6pm Yoga class		

TUESDAY, MARCH 28

8	Finish reading assignment	Work @ library	1
9			2
10	ENG 112	(study for quiz)	3
11			4
12			5
Evening		until 7pm	

WEDNESDAY, MARCH 29

8		Meet w/ advisor	1
9	BIO 212		2
10		EMS 262	3
11	CHEM 203 + quiz		4
12		pick up photos	5
Evening	6pm Dinner w/study group		

Indicate Priority Levels

On any given day, the items on your schedule have varying degrees of importance. Prioritizing these items helps you to identify important tasks and to focus the bulk of your energy and time on them. In addition, it enables you to lock in time-specific activities and schedule less urgent items around them.

Indicate level of importance by using three different categories. Identify these categories by using any code that makes sense to you. Some people use numbers, others use letters (A, B, C), and still others use different color pens. The three categories are as follows:

- *Priority 1* items are the most crucial. They may include attending class, completing school assignments, working at a job, picking up a child from day care, and paying bills. Enter Priority 1 items on your planner first, before scheduling anything else.
- *Priority 2* items are important but more flexible responsibilities. Examples include maintaining study time, completing an assignment for a club, or working out. Schedule these around Priority 1 items.

- *Priority 3* items are least important—the "it would be nice if I could get to that" items. Examples include making a social phone call or organizing photos. Many people don't enter Priority 3 tasks in their planners until they know they have time for them. Others keep a separate list of these tasks so that when they have free time they can choose what they want to accomplish.

Go For It! BUILDING YOUR SKILLS

MAP OUT AN IMPORTANT GOAL

Work through your plans to move toward one important academic goal this semester.

First, name your goal. _____

_____

Now map out the short-term actions you plan to take. What will you do to support your goal . . .

Today? _____

_____

This week? _____

_____

This month? _____

_____

This semester? _____

_____

Consider putting this plan to work. As you begin, imagine your success at the end of the semester, and let this image motivate and inspire you.

Use Time-Saving Techniques

The following strategies will help you schedule activities in ways that make the most of your time:

Plan regularly. Spending time planning your schedule will reduce stress and save you from the hours of work that might result if you forget something important. At the beginning of each week, write down specific time commitments as well as your goals and priorities. Decide where to fit activities like studying and Priority 3 items. Keep your planner with you and check it throughout the day.

Make and use to-do lists. Use a *to-do list* to record the things you want to accomplish on a given day or week. Write to-do items on a separate piece of paper so you can identify priorities. Then transfer the items to open time periods in your planner. During exam week and when major projects are due, to-do lists will help you rank responsibilities so that you get things done in order of importance.

Refer to your syllabus. Your syllabus contains instructors' expectations and your ongoing schedule and assignments. The information found there— course schedule, assignments and due dates, test and quiz dates, and so on— will help you schedule and prioritize your study tasks. Check in with your syllabus a couple of times a week to make sure you are on top of reading assignments and quiz and test dates.

Post monthly and yearly calendars at home. Keeping track of major commitments on a monthly wall calendar will give you an overview of responsibilities and upcoming events. If you live with family or friends, create a group calendar to stay aware of one another's plans and avoid scheduling conflicts.

Take advantage of technology. Learn how to access all the information your college and instructors offer online. You can use a computer to download course notes, get assignments, conduct research on the Internet, collaborate with fellow students via e-mail, register for classes, e-mail questions to instructors, and more. Staying connected in this way helps you to maximize efficiency and save time.

Avoid time traps. Try to stay away from situations that eat up time unnecessarily. Say "no" graciously if you don't have time for a project, curb social time if it gets out of hand, and delegate if you find yourself overloaded. In addition, monitor and limit the time you spend surfing the Internet and chatting online.

Use pockets of time. When you have time between two classes or meetings—too short to go home or schedule an activity, but longer than it takes to get from one location to the other—do something useful with it. Carry a textbook or homework assignment that does not require long-term concentration, and when you have extra time, complete as much as you can.

Schedule downtime. Leisure time is more than just a nice break; it's essential to your health and success. A little downtime will refresh you and actually improve your productivity when you get back on task. Even half an hour a day helps. Fill the time with whatever relaxes you—reading, watching television, chatting online, playing a game or sport, walking, writing, or just doing nothing.

Fight Procrastination

It's human, and common for busy students, to *procrastinate*—meaning, to put off difficult or undesirable tasks until later. If taken to the extreme, however, procrastination can develop into a habit that causes serious problems. Among the reasons people procrastinate are:

Perfectionism. According to Jane B. Burka and Lenora M. Yuen, authors of *Procrastination: Why You Do It and What to Do About It,* habitual procrastinators often gauge their self-worth solely by their ability to achieve. In other words, "an outstanding performance means an outstanding person; a mediocre performance means a mediocre person."[6] To the perfectionist procrastinator, not trying at all is better than an attempt that falls short of perfection.

Fear of limitations. Some people procrastinate in order to avoid the truth about what they can achieve. "As long as you procrastinate, you never have to confront the real limits of your ability, whatever those limits are,"[7] say Burka and Yuen. Psychologists call this a "self-handicapping strategy." If you procrastinate and fail, you can blame the failure on waiting too long, not on any personal shortcoming. Procrastination becomes an easy scapegoat for your worries.

Being unsure of the next step. If you get stuck and don't know what to do, sometimes it seems easier to procrastinate than to make the leap to the next level of what you are working on.

Facing an overwhelming task. Some projects are so big that they create immobilizing fear. When persons facing such tasks fear failure, they may procrastinate to avoid confronting the fear.

Avoiding Procrastination

Although it can bring relief in the short term, avoiding tasks almost always causes problems, such as a buildup of responsibilities and less time to complete them, work that is not up to par, disappointment to others who are depending on your work, and stress brought on by the weight of the unfinished tasks. Particular strategies can help you avoid procrastination and the problems associated with it.

- **Analyze the effects of procrastinating.** What may happen if you continue to put off a responsibility? Chances are you will benefit more in the long term by facing the task head-on.
- **Set reasonable goals.** Unreasonable goals can intimidate and immobilize you. Set manageable goals and allow enough time to complete them.
- **Break tasks into smaller parts.** If you concentrate on achieving one small step at a time, the task may become less burdensome. Setting concrete time limits for each task may help you feel more in control.
- **Get started.** Once you take the first step, you may find it easier to continue.
- **Ask for help.** Once you identify what's holding you up, see who can help you face the task. If you are having trouble understanding the assignment, someone else may be able to help you clarify it.
- **Don't expect perfection.** No one is perfect. Most people learn by making mistakes and learning from them. It's better to try your best than to do nothing at all.
- **Reward yourself.** Find ways to boost your confidence when you accomplish a particular task. Remind yourself—with a break, a movie, or some kind of treat—that you are making progress.

Be Flexible

No matter how well you plan your time, sudden changes can upend your plans. Any change, whether minor (a room change for a class) or major (a medical emergency), can cause stress. As your stress level rises, your sense of control may dwindle.

Although you can't always choose your circumstances, you have some control over how you handle them. Your ability to evaluate situations, come up with creative options, and put practical plans to work will help you manage the changes that you will encounter. Think of change as part of life, and you will be able to brainstorm solutions when dilemmas arise.

When change involves serious problems—your car breaks down and you have no way to get to school, you fail a class and have to consider summer school, a family member develops a medical problem and needs you more at home—you can use problem-solving skills to help you through. As you will see in Chapter 3, problem solving involves identifying and analyzing the problem, brainstorming and exploring possible solutions, and choosing the solution you decide is best. Resources available at your college can help you throughout this process. Your academic advisor, counselor, dean, financial aid advisor, and instructors may have ideas and assistance.

Change is one of many factors associated with stress. In fact, stress is part of the normal college experience. If you take charge of how you manage stress, you can keep it from taking charge of you.

ACTIVE THINKING   *Go For It!*   BUILDING YOUR SKILLS

WORK TOGETHER: DEFINE MULTIPLE PATHS TO A GOAL

In a group of three or four, brainstorm goals for building an academically useful skill—for example, leadership, writing, or researching. Write your ideas on a piece of paper. From that list, pick out one goal to explore together.

Each group member takes two minutes alone to think about this goal in terms of the first goal achievement step on p. 13 — defining a strategy. In other words, answer the question: "How would I do it?" Each person writes down all of the paths they can think of.

The group then gathers to share and evaluate the different strategies, working together to choose one that seems effective. Finally, the group brainstorms the rest of the goal achievement process, based on the one chosen strategy or path:

- **Set a timetable.** When do you plan to reach your goal? Discuss different time frames and how each might change the path.

- **Be accountable.** What safeguards will keep you on track? Talk about different ways to make sure you are moving ahead consistently.

- **Get unstuck.** What will you do if you hit a roadblock? Brainstorm the kinds of roadblocks that could get in the way of this particular goal. For each, come up with ways to overcome the obstacle.

At the end of the process, you should have a wealth of ideas for how to approach one particular goal, an appreciation of how many paths you could take to get there, and a conviction that this process will help you find ways to achieve your personal goals.

HOW CAN YOU COPE WITH THE STRESS OF COLLEGE LIFE?

If you are feeling more stress in your everyday life as a student, you are not alone.[8] Stress levels among college students have increased dramatically, according to an annual survey conducted at the University of California at Los Angeles. More than 30 percent of the freshmen polled at 683 two- and four-year colleges and universities nationwide reported that they frequently felt overwhelmed, almost double the rate in 1985. Stress factors for college students include being in a new environment; facing increased work and difficult decisions; social life; and juggling school, work, and personal responsibilities.

Stress refers to the way in which your mind and body react to pressure. At their worst, stress reactions can make you physically ill. But stress can also supply the heightened readiness you need to do well on tests, finish assignments on time, prepare for a class presentation, or meet new people. Your goal is to find a manageable balance. Key 1.3, based on research conducted by Drs. Robert M. Yerkes and John E. Dodson, shows that stress can be helpful or harmful, depending on how much you experience.

Extracurricular activities can provide relaxation and stress relief, as these students have found in their work with the Dynamics, an a cappella vocal group at Skidmore College.

Dealing with the stress of college life is, and will continue to be, one of your biggest challenges. As a responsible and self-directed student, however, you can take steps to handle it. Important stress-management strategies include managing goal progress and time, maintaining physical health, maintaining mental health, and using your school's resource network.

Manage goal progress and time. Every goal achievement and time management strategy you have explored in this chapter contributes to your ability to cope with stress. Remember that stress refers to how you react to pressure. When you set up effective plans to move toward goals, you reduce pressure. When you set a schedule that works and stick to it, you reduce pressure. Less pressure, less stress.

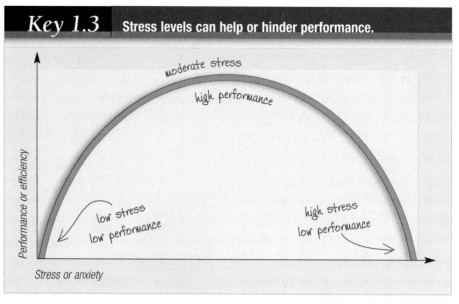

Key 1.3   **Stress levels can help or hinder performance.**

Source: From *Your Maximum Mind* by Herbert Benson, M. D., copyright © 1987 by Random House, Inc. Used by permission of Time Books, a division of Random House, Inc.

Maintain physical health. The healthier you are, the more you'll be able to manage stress. Make your physical health a priority by eating right and building some kind of regular exercise into your routine. Also, don't forget the value of a good night's sleep. Students are notorious for prioritizing schoolwork over sleep, getting far less than the hours they may need to function well both academically and physically. For the sake of your health as well as your GPA, figure out how much sleep you need and find a way to get it.

Maintain mental health. No one is happy all the time, and for most students the college years bring a measure of emotional ups and downs. However, many students experience psychological manifestations of stress (see Key 1.4), and some experience symptoms that lead to a diagnosis of depression or other emotional disorders (see Key 1.5). Make your mental health a priority by recognizing mental health problems, related to stress or other causes, and understanding how to get help. Most student health centers and campus counseling centers can provide both medical and psychological help for students with emotional disorders.

Use your school's resource network. Explore the help available to you and take advantage of it. Advice and assistance from your school's resource

Key 1.4   Many college students experience psychological stress.

In a survey of more than 47,000 students on 74 campuses, the American College Health Association found that:

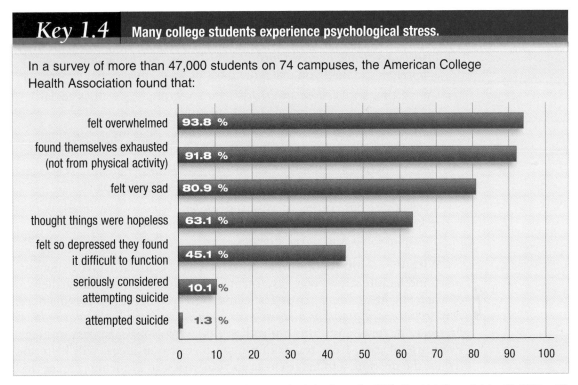

Source: Data from Mary Duenwald, "The Dorms May Be Great, but How's the Counseling?" *The New York Times,* October 26, 2004, p. F6.

Key 1.5   Some students report symptoms of specific mental disorders.

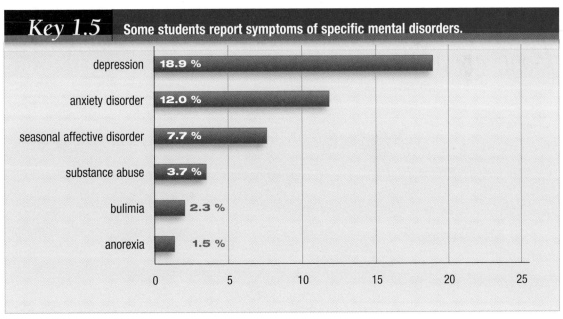

Source: Data from Mary Duenwald, "The Dorms May Be Great, but How's the Counseling?" *The New York Times,* October 26, 2004, p. F6.

network—people, student services, organizations, and literature—can help you resolve issues and confusion, thereby easing your stress.

- *Instructors, teaching assistants, administrators, advisors,* and *counselors* can help you make the most of your educational experience.
- Connecting with *fellow students*—in study groups as well as social situations—can help you cope with all kinds of stress.
- *Student services* such as student health, career placement, tutoring, and academic centers can help you manage the details of student life.
- Getting involved with *organizations and activities* you enjoy is a great way to blow off steam and make connections with people.
- Consulting your *college catalog* and *student handbook* will help reduce confusion; reading *student newspapers* will help you stay on top of news and developments.

With the ability to know your values, work toward goals, manage time, and handle stress, you have the necessary tools to face the challenges of academic life. Even when stress seems to freeze you in place, remember: *Any step toward a goal is a stress-management strategy because it reduces pressure.* In that sense, this entire book is a stress-management strategy. Every useful tool, from test-taking hints to research ideas, will help you reduce the pressure and move closer to your vision of academic, career, and personal success.

"Goals are dreams with deadlines."

DIANA SCHARF HUNT
author and time-management expert

Building Skill, Will, and Self-Management

Monitoring Your Progress

Test Competence: Measure What You've Learned

MULTIPLE CHOICE. *Circle or highlight the answer that seems to fit best.*

1. Active thinkers set the stage for success because they
   - A. understand that they have little control over their education.
   - B. follow the plans that are set out by their course syllabi.
   - C. take responsibility for their work and learning.
   - D. know they can solve every problem on their own.

2. Teamwork strategies include all of the following *except:*
   - A. making sure leaders take on the majority of the work.
   - B. setting a regular meeting schedule.
   - C. creating study materials for one another.
   - D. giving responsibilities to all participants.

3. Long-term goals can be defined as
   - A. goals that you think about for a long time before setting them.
   - B. only those goals that focus on career and family decisions.
   - C. the goals that you will only be able to reach when you are much older.
   - D. the broad goals that you want to accomplish over a long period of time.

4. When you *prioritize* goals, you
   - A. accomplish the same goal first in any given day.
   - B. focus on the most desirable goals.
   - C. arrange goals in order of importance and focus on the most important goals.
   - D. save the most important goals for last.

5. Which is *not* a practical step toward achieving a goal?

   A. Define how you plan to reach your goal.

   B. Set a timetable for when you want to accomplish your goal.

   C. Set up safeguards that will keep you on track.

   D. Abandon the goal for a different one if you hit a roadblock.

6. The purpose of time management is

   A. to make sure you have no downtime that interferes with your study schedule.

   B. to effectively build and manage your schedule so you can accomplish your goals.

   C. to make you conscious of time and how you use it from day to day.

   D. to make your schedule rather than your goals your central focus.

7. It is important to schedule tasks and activities that support your goals because

   A. it will make daily efforts more meaningful.

   B. it will move you more effectively toward achieving long-term goals.

   C. it will bring order to your schedule.

   D. all of the above.

8. Reasons that people procrastinate include all of the following *except:*

   A. a belief that you are only as good as your performance.

   B. a fear of facing your limitations.

   C. confidence.

   D. facing a task so large that it overwhelms you.

9. *Stress* can be defined as

   A. the way in which your mind and body react to pressure.

   B. the panic that some people feel about a test.

   C. anxiety about social situations.

   D. negative emotions.

10. Stress-reduction techniques include

   A. time-management skills.

   B. study strategies.

   C. getting exercise, sleep, and healthful food.

   D. all of the above.

TRUE/FALSE. *Place a T or an F beside each statement to indicate whether you think it is true or false.*

_____ 1. A student with academic integrity has committed to five values: honesty, respect, trust, fairness, and responsibility.

_____ 2. The less specific your plans to reach a goal, the more likely you are to fulfill them.

_____ 3. Body rhythms and habits have no effect on a student's ability to manage time within a particular schedule.

_____ 4. Referring regularly to your syllabus will help you stay on top of test and assignment dates and schedule and prioritize your study tasks.

_____ 5. The majority of today's college students feel overwhelmed; some experience symptoms that lead to a diagnosis of one or more treatable psychological disorders.

Target and Achieve a Goal

Commit to one specific self-management strategy from this chapter to improve your study skills.

Name the strategy here:
_____

_____

Describe your goal—what you want to gain by using this strategy.
_____

_____

_____

_____

Describe how you plan to use this strategy through the semester to achieve this goal.
_____

_____

_____

Building Your Skills

Brain Power: Build Vocabulary Fitness

Here is a selection from the current media. Read the material, paying special attention to the context of the vocabulary words shown in bold type. Then choose the correct definition for each word in the table that follows. Use a dictionary to check your answers. Finally, on a separate sheet, use each vocabulary word in a sentence of your own to solidify your understanding.

In this account from The New Yorker, *Michael Specter discusses the avian flu, detailing its dangers and discussing ways that scientists may be able to prevent its spread throughout large populations.*

> If the **avian** epidemic does move widely into human populations, as many scientists have predicted, it will mark the first time the world has been able to anticipate a **pandemic.** For thousands of years, people have rarely known the causes of their illnesses; they have certainly never been warned that an epidemic—whether smallpox, plague, cholera, or influenza—was **imminent.** Viral genetics has changed that. We can follow the **evolution** of a virus on a molecular level and **gauge** its power. Researchers at the C.D.C. [Centers for Disease Control] have just begun crucial experiments in specially protected laboratories where they will attempt to juggle the genetic **components** of the H5N1 virus. There are two ways to do that. First, the team will infect tissue with both the bird virus and a common human flu virus and see what grows. They will also use the tools of genetics. Molecular biology now allows scientists to break a virus down to its genes; the researchers will **disassemble** H5N1 and mix it in a variety of combinations with human flu viruses. Then they will test the results on animals.

Source: Michael Specter, "Nature's Bioterrorist," *The New Yorker.* February 28, 2005, p. 60.

Circle the word or phrase that best defines each term as it is used in the excerpt.

VOCABULARY WORDS	A	B	C
1. avian (adj.)	relating to apes	relating to birds	relating to Asia
2. pandemic (noun)	widespread disease	limited disease	widespread trend
3. imminent (adj.)	past	coming soon	happening now
4. evolution (noun)	development	increase	growth
5. gauge (verb)	evaluate	describe	measure
6. components (noun)	items	editions	parts
7. disassemble (verb)	divide	take apart	put together

Get to the Root

Every time you learn a Greek or Latin root, you increase your ability to recognize English vocabulary words that include that root and to figure out their meaning. Grow your vocabulary by studying this root and its related words, writing in two more words from the same root and including definitions for both new words.

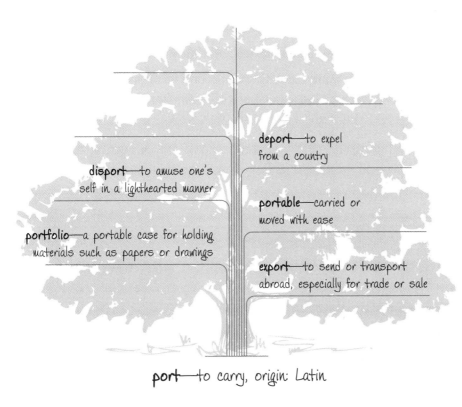

deport—to expel from a country

disport—to amuse one's self in a lighthearted manner

portable—carried or moved with ease

portfolio—a portable case for holding materials such as papers or drawings

export—to send or transport abroad, especially for trade or sale

port—to carry, origin: Latin

Investigate Using Research Navigator

Figuring out how to find useful information on the Internet can be like sifting through an enormous flea market to find the treasures. With this edition of *Keys to College Studying,* you have been granted access to **Research Navigator,** a Prentice Hall tool consisting of three databases featuring specific collections of both popular and academic writings.

The booklet that is packaged with this text, *The Prentice Hall Guide to Evaluating Online Resources with Research Navigator,* goes into detail about what is available on these databases and how to use this tool. (If your book did not come with this guide, you should be able to purchase one at your college bookstore.) You will access Research

Navigator online at **www.researchnavigator.com** using the access code found in the inside front cover of the booklet. In addition, you can find basic research information in the Research Appendix at the end of the text.

Access Research Navigator using the Internet address shown above. Then sign on to the service using your Login Name and Password. Scroll through the subject titles listed for the Link Library. Choose a subject linked to a major or career area that interests you, and then search through the alphabetic database for articles about people who are noted in that area.

Find three biographical articles and read them. Answer the following:

- What values and goals seem most important to the success of the people you read about?
- Do you find your values and goals to be similar to or different from the values you've listed?
- Based on what you've read, has your interest in this area increased or decreased?

Building Will and Self-Awareness

Make Responsible Choices

Answer the following question on a separate piece of paper or in a journal.

Considering how your personal values relate to the majors and careers that interest you, answer the following:

- Name three of your most important personal values. What career areas or jobs can you think of that might be true to these values? Name at least one career area or job for each value.
- Now work backward. Identify three career areas or jobs that interest you right now. Do these choices line up with your most important values? If so, how? If not, what other values do they reflect?
- What would you do if your chosen career area or job asked you to do something that violated an important personal value? For example, you are an attorney asked to defend a case that goes against your beliefs, or your boss asks you to lie in order to protect a business deal. Explain the plan you would follow and why you would choose to act in this way.

Chapter Summary

As you use the summary on the following pages to review the concepts you learned in this chapter, focus also on its format—in this case a **think link,** in other chapters a formal outline, and in still others the Cornell system. As you become comfortable with the organization and style of these various formats, try using each of them to take class and reading notes, noting which approach works best for you in particular situations.

Endnotes

1. The following material is based on/adapted from Claire Ellen Weinstein and Laura M. Hume, *Study Strategies for Lifelong Learning.* Washington, DC: American Psychological Association, 1998, pp. 10–12.

2. Ibid.

3. *Keys to Lifelong Learning Telecourse.* Dir. Mary Jane Bradbury. Videocassette. Intrepid Films, 2000.

4. *A Report from the Center for Academic Integrity,* Center for Academic Integrity, Kenan Institute for Ethics, Duke University, October 1999. Available: www.academicintegrity.org (March 2001).

5. *Keys to Lifelong Learning Telecourse.*

6. Jane B. Burka, Ph.D. and Lenora M. Yuen, Ph.D., *Procrastination: Why You Do It and What to Do About It.* Reading, MA: Perseus Books, 1983, pp. 21–22.

7. Ibid.

8. The following articles were used as sources in this section: Glenn C. Altschuler, "Adapting to College Life in an Era of Heightened Stress," *The New York Times,* Education Life, Section 4A, August 6, 2000, p. 12; Carol Hymowitz and Rachel Emma Silverman, "Can Workplace Stress Get Worse?" *The Wall Street Journal,* January 16, 2001, p. B1; Robert M. Sapolsky, "Best Ways to Reduce Everyday Levels of Stress . . . Bad Ol' Stress," *Bottom Line Personal,* January 15, 2000, p. 13; Kate Slaboch, "Stress and the College Student: A Debate," www.jour.unr.edu/outpost/voices/voi.slaboch.stress.htm (April 4, 2001); University of South Florida, The Counseling Center for Human Development, "Coping with Stress in College," http://usfweb.usf.edu/counsel/self-hlp/stress.htm (April 4, 2001); Jodi Wilgoren, "Survey Shows High Stress Levels in College Freshmen," *The New York Times,* January 23, 2000, p. NA.

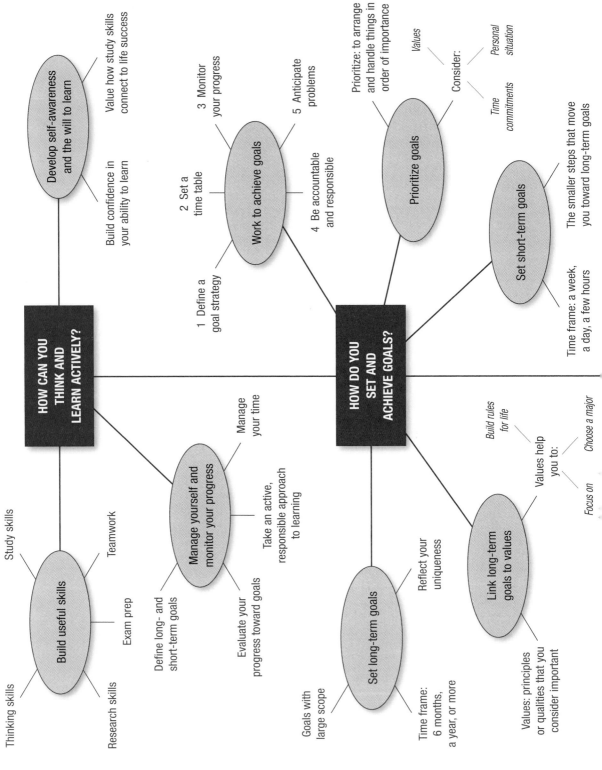

HOW CAN YOU THINK AND LEARN ACTIVELY?

Develop self-awareness and the will to learn
- Value how study skills connect to life success
- Build confidence in your ability to learn

Build useful skills
- Study skills
- Thinking skills
- Teamwork
- Exam prep
- Research skills

Manage yourself and monitor your progress
- Manage your time
- Take an active, responsible approach to learning
- Define long- and short-term goals
- Evaluate your progress toward goals

HOW DO YOU SET AND ACHIEVE GOALS?

Work to achieve goals
- 1 Define a goal strategy
- 2 Set a time table
- 3 Monitor your progress
- 4 Be accountable and responsible
- 5 Anticipate problems

Prioritize goals
- Prioritize: to arrange and handle things in order of importance
- Consider:
  - Values
  - Personal situation
  - Time commitments

Set short-term goals
- The smaller steps that move you toward long-term goals
- Time frame: a week, a day, a few hours

Set long-term goals
- Reflect your uniqueness
- Goals with large scope
- Time frame: 6 months, a year, or more

Link long-term goals to values
- Values help you to:
  - Build rules for life
  - Focus on
  - Choose a major
- Values: principles or qualities that you consider important

34

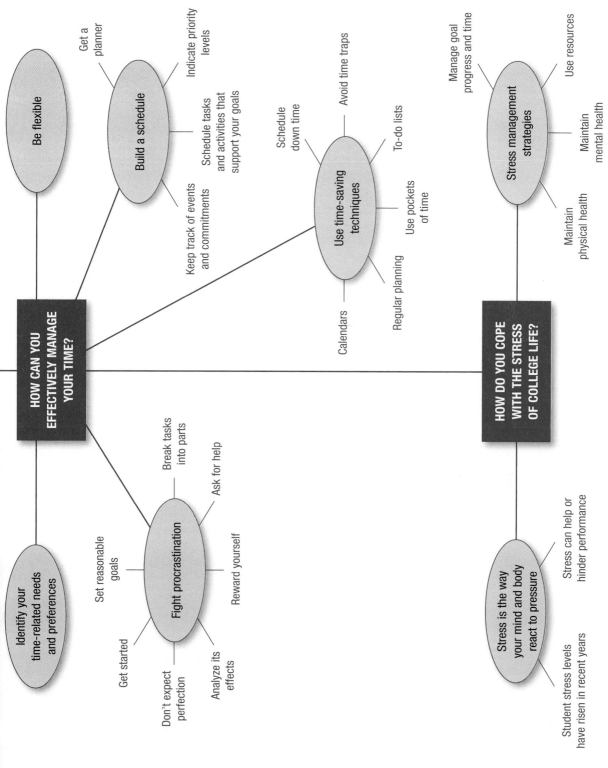

HOW CAN YOU EFFECTIVELY MANAGE YOUR TIME?

- Be flexible
- Identify your time-related needs and preferences
- Build a schedule
  - Get a planner
  - Indicate priority levels
  - Schedule tasks and activities that support your goals
  - Keep track of events and commitments
- Use time-saving techniques
  - Avoid time traps
  - Schedule down time
  - To-do lists
  - Use pockets of time
  - Regular planning
  - Calendars
- Fight procrastination
  - Break tasks into parts
  - Ask for help
  - Reward yourself
  - Analyze its effects
  - Don't expect perfection
  - Get started
  - Set reasonable goals

HOW DO YOU COPE WITH THE STRESS OF COLLEGE LIFE?

- Stress management strategies
  - Manage goal progress and time
  - Use resources
  - Maintain mental health
  - Maintain physical health
- Stress is the way your mind and body react to pressure
  - Stress can help or hinder performance
  - Student stress levels have risen in recent years

35

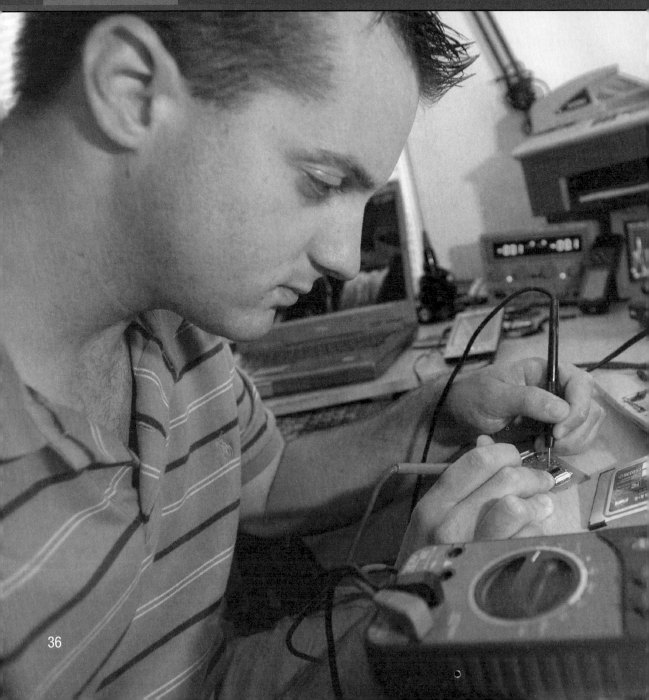

"To be what we are, and to become
what we are capable of becoming,
is the only end of life."

ROBERT LOUIS STEVENSON, SCOTTISH NOVELIST AND POET

Learning Styles, Majors, and Careers

KNOWING YOUR TALENTS AND FINDING YOUR DIRECTION

As a college student, you are investing valuable resources—time, effort, and money—in your education. Learning is the return on that investment. How well you learn, and therefore how good a return you receive, depends, in part, on knowing yourself in two ways: knowing *how* you learn, and knowing what you want to *do* with what you learn.

This chapter focuses first on helping you identify your learning styles, because when you understand how you learn, you can make more active and effective decisions about how to choose study strategies and pursue learning goals. Then you will read about majors and careers, because knowing where you want your education to take you will inspire you to work hard and stay motivated. Finally, the chapter includes important information about identifying and managing learning disabilities.

In this chapter you will explore answers to the following questions:

- How can you discover your learning styles?
- What are the benefits of knowing how you learn?
- How can you choose a major?
- How can you identify and manage learning disabilities?

HOW CAN YOU DISCOVER YOUR LEARNING STYLES?

Your *learning style*—your mind's particular way of taking in and processing information—is as unique as you are. Everyone has some things that they do well and other things that they find difficult. To learn successfully, you need to maximize your strengths and compensate for your weaknesses. The first step toward that goal is pinpointing what those strengths and weaknesses *are*—and that's what learning styles assessments will help you discover.

This chapter presents two assessments designed to help you figure out how you learn and interact. The first—*Multiple Pathways to Learning*—focuses on learning strengths and preferences and is based on Professor Howard Gardner's Multiple Intelligences Theory. The second—the *Personality Spectrum*—is based on the Myers–Briggs Type Inventory® (MBTI) and helps you evaluate how you react to people and situations.

Put Assessment Results in Perspective

First, remember that any assessment is simply a snapshot, a look at who you are at a given moment. Your answers can, and will, change as you and the circumstances around you change. These assessments help you look at the present—and plan for the future—by asking questions: Who am I right now? How does this compare to who I want to be?

Second, there are no "right" answers, no "best" set of scores. Think of your responses in the same way you would if you were trying on a new set of eyeglasses to correct blurred vision. The glasses will not create new paths and possibilities, but they will help you see more clearly the ones that already exist.

Following each assessment is information about the typical traits of, and appropriate study strategies for, each intelligence or personality spectrum dimension. As you will see from your scores, you have abilities in all areas, though some are more developed than others. Therefore, you will find useful suggestions under all the headings. As an active thinker, your job is to try different techniques and continue to use what works for you.

Assess Your Multiple Intelligences

In 1983, Howard Gardner, a Harvard University professor, changed the way people perceive intelligence and learning with his theory of Multiple Intelligences. As defined by Gardner, an *intelligence* is an ability to solve problems or fashion products that are useful in a particular cultural setting or community. Gardner believes that there are at least eight intelligences

Key 2.1	Each intelligence is linked to specific abilities.

INTELLIGENCE	DESCRIPTION
Verbal-Linguistic	Ability to communicate through language (listening, reading, writing, speaking)
Logical-Mathematical	Ability to understand logical reasoning and problem solving (math, science, patterns, sequences)
Bodily-Kinesthetic	Ability to use the physical body skillfully and to take in knowledge through bodily sensation (coordination, working with hands)
Visual-Spatial	Ability to understand spatial relationships and to perceive and create images (visual art, graphic design, charts and maps)
Interpersonal	Ability to relate to others, noticing their moods, motivations, and feelings (social activity, cooperative learning, teamwork)
Intrapersonal	Ability to understand one's own behavior and feelings (self-awareness, independence, time spent alone)
Musical	Ability to comprehend and create meaningful sound and recognize patterns (music, sensitivity to sound and patterns)
Naturalistic	Ability to understand features of the environment (interest in nature, environmental balance, ecosystem, stress relief brought by natural environments)

possessed by all people, and that every person has developed some intelligences more fully than others (see Key 2.1 for descriptions). According to this theory, when you find a task or subject easy, you are probably using a more fully developed intelligence. When you have trouble, you may be using a less developed intelligence.[1]

Gardner believes that the way you learn is a unique blend of intelligences, resulting from your distinctive abilities, challenges, experiences, and training. In addition, ability in the intelligences may develop or recede as your life changes. Gardner thinks that the traditional view of intelligence, based on mathematical, logical, and verbal measurements, doesn't reflect the entire spectrum of human ability:

I believe that we should . . . look . . . at more naturalistic sources of information about how peoples around the world develop skills important to their way of life. Think, for example, of sailors in the South Seas, who find their way around hundreds, or even thousands, of islands by looking at the constellations of stars in the sky, feeling the way a boat passes over the water, and noticing a few scattered landmarks. A word for intelligence in a society of these sailors would probably refer to that kind of navigational ability.[2]

The Multiple Pathways to Learning assessment helps you determine the levels to which your eight intelligences are developed. Key 2.2, immediately following the assessment, describes specific skills associated with the eight intelligences as well as study techniques that maximize each. Finally, the Multiple Intelligence Strategies grids in Chapters 4 through 11 will demonstrate how to apply your learning styles knowledge to key college success skills.

The more you know about your learning styles and intelligences, the more prepared you will be for school, for work, and for life.

MULTIPLE PATHWAYS TO LEARNING [3]

Each intelligence has a set of numbered statements. Consider each statement on its own. Then rate how closely it matches who you are right now by writing a number on the line next to the statement. Finally, total each set of six questions.

 RARELY　　 **SOMETIMES**　　 **USUALLY**　　 **ALWAYS**

1. _____ I enjoy physical activities.
2. _____ I am uncomfortable sitting still.
3. _____ I prefer to learn through doing.
4. _____ When sitting I move my legs or hands.
5. _____ I enjoy working with my hands.
6. _____ I like to pace when I'm thinking or studying.
_____ TOTAL for **BODILY–KINESTHETIC**

1. _____ I enjoy telling stories.
2. _____ I like to write.
3. _____ I like to read.
4. _____ I express myself clearly.
5. _____ I am good at negotiating.
6. _____ I like to discuss topics that interest me.
_____ TOTAL for **VERBAL–LINGUISTIC**

1. _____ I use maps easily.
2. _____ I draw pictures/diagrams when explaining ideas.
3. _____ I can assemble items easily from diagrams.
4. _____ I enjoy drawing or photography.
5. _____ I do not like to read long paragraphs.
6. _____ I prefer a drawn map over written directions.
_____ TOTAL for **VISUAL–SPATIAL**

1. _____ I like math in school.
2. _____ I like science.
3. _____ I problem-solve well.
4. _____ I question how things work.
5. _____ I enjoy planning or designing something new.
6. _____ I am able to fix things.
_____ TOTAL for **LOGICAL–MATHEMATICAL**

1. _____ I listen to music.
2. _____ I move my fingers or feet when I hear music.
3. _____ I have good rhythm.
4. _____ I like to sing along with music.
5. _____ People have said I have musical talent.
6. _____ I like to express my ideas through music.
_____ TOTAL for **MUSICAL**

1. _____ I need quiet time to think.
2. _____ I think about issues before I want to talk.
3. _____ I am interested in self-improvement.
4. _____ I understand my thoughts and feelings.
5. _____ I know what I want out of life.
6. _____ I prefer to work on projects alone.
_____ TOTAL for **INTRAPERSONAL**

1. _____ I like doing a project with other people.
2. _____ People come to me to help settle conflicts.
3. _____ I like to spend time with friends.
4. _____ I am good at understanding people.
5. _____ I am good at making people feel comfortable.
6. _____ I enjoy helping others.
_____ TOTAL for **INTERPERSONAL**

1. _____ I enjoy nature whenever possible.
2. _____ I think about having a career involving nature.
3. _____ I enjoy studying plants, animals, or oceans.
4. _____ I avoid being indoors except when I sleep.
5. _____ As a child I played with bugs and leaves.
6. _____ When I feel stressed I want to be out in nature.
_____ TOTAL for **NATURALISTIC**

Developed by Joyce Bishop, Ph.D., and based upon Howard Gardner's *Frames of Mind: The Theory of Multiple Intelligences.*

SCORING GRID FOR MULTIPLE PATHWAYS TO LEARNING

For each intelligence, shade the box in the row that corresponds with the range where your score falls. For example, if you scored 17 in Bodily-Kinesthetic intelligence, you would shade the middle box in that row; if you scored a 13 in Visual-Spatial, you would shade the last box in that row. When you have shaded one box for each row, you will see a "map" of your range of development at a glance.

A score of 20–24 indicates a high level of development in that particular type of intelligence, 14–19 a moderate level, and below 14 an underdeveloped intelligence.

	20-24 (HIGHLY DEVELOPED)	14-19 (MODERATELY DEVELOPED)	Below 14 (UNDERDEVELOPED)	
Bodily-Kinesthetic				
Visual-Spatial				
Verbal-Linguistic				
Logical-Mathematical				
Musical				
Interpersonal				
Intrapersonal				
Naturalistic				

Key 2.2 How to put your Multiple Intelligences to work for you.

ABILITIES AND SKILLS ASSOCIATED WITH EACH INTELLIGENCE

VERBAL/LINGUISTIC

- Analyzing own use of language
- Remembering terms easily
- Explaining, teaching, learning, using humor
- Understanding syntax and word meaning
- Convincing someone to do something

MUSICAL/RHYTHMIC

- Sensing tonal qualities
- Creating/enjoying melodies, rhythms
- Being sensitive to sounds and rhythms
- Using "schemas" to hear music
- Understanding the structure of music

LOGICAL/MATHEMATICAL

- Recognizing abstract patterns
- Reasoning inductively and deductively
- Discerning relationships and connections
- Performing complex calculations
- Reasoning scientifically

VISUAL/SPATIAL

- Perceiving and forming objects accurately
- Recognizing relationships between objects
- Representing something graphically
- Manipulating images
- Finding one's way in space

BODILY/KINESTHETIC

- Connecting mind and body
- Controlling movement
- Improving body functions
- Expanding body awareness to all senses
- Coordinating body movement

INTRAPERSONAL

- Evaluating own thinking
- Being aware of and expressing feelings
- Understanding self in relation to others
- Thinking and reasoning on higher levels

INTERPERSONAL

- Seeing things from others' perspectives
- Cooperating within a group
- Communicating verbally and nonverbally
- Creating and maintaining relationships

NATURALISTIC

- Deep understanding of nature
- Appreciation of the delicate balance in nature

Key 2.2   Continued.

STUDY TECHNIQUES TO MAXIMIZE EACH INTELLIGENCE

VERBAL/LINGUISTIC

- Read text; highlight no more than 10%
- Rewrite notes
- Outline chapters
- Teach someone else
- Recite information or write scripts/debates

MUSICAL/RHYTHMIC

- Create rhythms out of words
- Beat out rhythms with hand or stick
- Play instrumental music/write raps
- Put new material to songs you already know
- Take music breaks

LOGICAL/MATHEMATICAL

- Organize material logically
- Explain material sequentially to someone
- Develop systems and find patterns
- Write outlines and develop charts and graphs
- Analyze information

VISUAL/SPATIAL

- Develop graphic organizers for new material
- Draw mind maps
- Develop charts and graphs
- Use color in notes to organize
- Visualize material (method of loci)

BODILY/KINESTHETIC

- Move or rap while you learn; pace and recite
- Use "mental walk" memory strategy
- Move fingers under words while reading
- Create "living sculptures"
- Act out scripts of material, design games

INTRAPERSONAL

- Reflect on personal meaning of information
- Visualize information/keep a journal
- Study in quiet settings
- Imagine experiments

INTERPERSONAL

- Study in a group
- Discuss information
- Use flash cards with others
- Teach someone else

NATURALISTIC

- Connect with nature whenever possible
- Form study groups of people with like interests

Adapted from Lazear, *Seven Pathways of Learning*, 1994.

Assess Your Personality
with the Personality Spectrum

Personality assessments help you understand how you respond to the world around you—including information, thoughts, feelings, people, and events.

The assessment used in this chapter is based on one of the most widely used personality inventories in the world— the Myers–Briggs Type Inventory, developed by Katharine Briggs and her daughter, Isabel Briggs Myers. It also relies upon the work of David Keirsey and Marilyn Bates, who combined the 16 Myers–Briggs types into four temperaments and developed an assessment called the Keirsey Sorter based on those temperaments.

The Personality Spectrum assessment adapts and simplifies this material into four personality types—Thinker, Organizer, Giver, and Adventurer—and was developed by *Keys to College Studying* co-author Dr. Joyce Bishop. The Personality Spectrum helps you identify the kinds of interactions that are most, and least, comfort-

These students, listening to podcasts while studying pieces at the Museum of Modern Art in Manhattan, are engaging verbal-linguistic and visual-spatial learning skills with the help of technology.

able for you. Key 2.3 shows techniques that improve performance, learning strategies, and ways of relating to others for each personality type.

PERSONALITY SPECTRUM

STEP 1. Rank order all 4 responses to each question from most like you (4) to least like you (1) so that for each question you use the numbers 1, 2, 3, and 4 one time each. Place numbers in the boxes next to the responses.

4 MOST LIKE ME   **3** MORE LIKE ME   **2** LESS LIKE ME   **1** LEAST LIKE ME

1. I like instructors who
   - a. ☐ tell me exactly what is expected of me.
   - b. ☐ make learning active and exciting.
   - c. ☐ maintain a safe and supportive classroom.
   - d. ☐ challenge me to think at higher levels.

2. I learn best when the material is
   - a. ☐ well organized.
   - b. ☐ something I can do hands-on.
   - c. ☐ about understanding and improving the human condition.
   - d. ☐ intellectually challenging.

3. A high priority in my life is to
   - a. ☐ keep my commitments.
   - b. ☐ experience as much of life as possible.
   - c. ☐ make a difference in the lives of others.
   - d. ☐ understand how things work.

4. Other people think of me as
   - a. ☐ dependable and loyal.
   - b. ☐ dynamic and creative.
   - c. ☐ caring and honest.
   - d. ☐ intelligent and inventive.

5. When I experience stress I would most likely
   - a. ☐ do something to help me feel more in control of my life.
   - b. ☐ do something physical and daring.
   - c. ☐ talk with a friend.
   - d. ☐ go off by myself and think about my situation.

6. I would probably not be close friends with someone who is
   - a. ☐ irresponsible.
   - b. ☐ unwilling to try new things.
   - c. ☐ selfish and unkind to others.
   - d. ☐ an illogical thinker.

7. My vacations could be described as
   - a. ☐ traditional.
   - b. ☐ adventuresome.
   - c. ☐ pleasing to others.
   - d. ☐ a new learning experience.

8. One word that best describes me is
   - a. ☐ sensible.
   - b. ☐ spontaneous.
   - c. ☐ giving.
   - d. ☐ analytical.

STEP 2. Add up the total points for each letter.

TOTAL FOR   **a.** ☐ Organizer   **b.** ☐ Adventurer   **c.** ☐ Giver   **d.** ☐ Thinker

STEP 3. Plot these numbers on the brain diagram on page 47.

Write your scores from p. 46 in the four circles just outside the brain diagram—Thinker score at top left, Giver score at top right, Organizer score at bottom left, and Adventurer score at bottom right.

Each circle has a line of numbers that go from the circle to the center of the diagram. For each of your four scores, place a dot on the appropriate number in the line near that circle. For example, if you scored 15 in the Giver spectrum, you would place a dot between the 14 and 16 in the upper right-hand line of numbers. If you scored a 26 in the Organizer spectrum, you would place a dot on the 26 in the lower left-hand line of numbers.

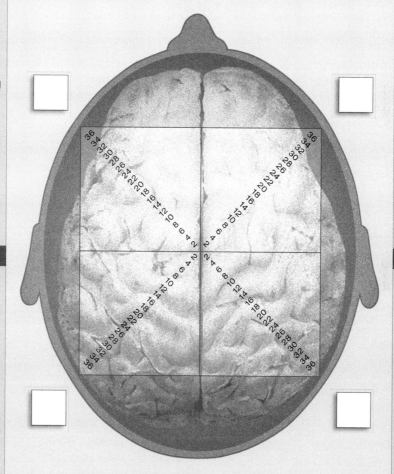

THINKER

Technical
Scientific
Mathematical
Dispassionate
Rational
Analytical
Logical
Problem Solving
Theoretical
Intellectual
Objective
Quantitative
Explicit
Realistic
Literal
Precise
Formal

ORGANIZER

Tactical
Planning
Detailed
Practical
Confident
Predictable
Controlled
Dependable
Systematic
Sequential
Structured
Administrative
Procedural
Organized
Conservative
Safekeeping
Disciplined

*Connect the four dots to make a four-sided shape.
If you like, shade the four sections inside the shape
using four different colors.*

GIVER

Interpersonal
Emotional
Caring
Sociable
Giving
Spiritual
Musical
Romantic
Feeling
Peacemaker
Trusting
Adaptable
Passionate
Harmonious
Idealistic
Talkative
Honest

ADVENTURER

Active
Visual
Risking
Original
Artistic
Spatial
Skillful
Impulsive
Metaphoric
Experimental
Divergent
Fast-paced
Simultaneous
Competitive
Imaginative
Open-minded
Adventuresome

*For the Personality Spectrum,
26–36 indicates a strong tendency in that dimension,
14–25 a moderate tendency,
and below 14 a minimal tendency.*

Source for brain diagram: *Understanding Psychology*, 3/e, by Morris, © 1996. Adapted by permission of Prentice-Hall, Inc., Upper Saddle River, NJ.

Key 2.3　How to put your Personality Spectrum to work for you.

CHARACTERISTICS OF EACH PERSONALITY TYPE	STUDY TECHNIQUES TO MAXIMIZE PERSONALITY TYPES
THINKER	**THINKER**
■ Solving problems ■ Developing models and systems ■ Analytical and abstract thinking ■ Exploring ideas and potentials ■ Ingenuity ■ Going beyond established boundaries ■ Global thinking—seeking universal truth	■ Find time to reflect independently on new information ■ Learn through problem solving ■ Design new ways of approaching issues ■ Convert material into logical charts ■ Try to minimize repetitive tasks ■ Look for opportunities to work independently
ORGANIZER	**ORGANIZER**
■ Responsibility, reliability ■ Operating successfully within social structures ■ Sense of history, culture, and dignity ■ Neatness and organization ■ Loyalty ■ Orientation to detail ■ Comprehensive follow-through on tasks ■ Efficiency	■ Try to have tasks defined in clear, concrete terms so that you know what is required ■ Look for a well-structured, stable environment ■ Request feedback ■ Use a planner to schedule tasks and dates ■ Organize material by rewriting and organizing class or text notes, making flash cards, or carefully highlighting
GIVER	**GIVER**
■ Honesty, authenticity ■ Successful, close relationships ■ Making a difference in the world ■ Cultivating potential of self and others ■ Negotiation; promoting peace ■ Openness; communicating with others ■ Helping others	■ Study with others ■ Teach material to others ■ Seek out tasks, groups, and subjects that involve helping people ■ Find ways to express thoughts and feelings clearly and honestly ■ Put energy into your most important relationships
ADVENTURER	**ADVENTURER**
■ High ability in a variety of fields ■ Courage and daring ■ Hands-on problem solving ■ Living in the present ■ Spontaneity and action ■ Ability to negotiate ■ Nontraditional style ■ Flexibility ■ Zest for life	■ Look for environments that encourage non-traditional approaches ■ Find hands-on ways to learn ■ Seek people whom you find stimulating ■ Use or develop games and puzzles to help memorize terms ■ Fight boredom by asking to do something extra or perform a task in a more active way

DEVELOP IDEAS ABOUT PERSONALITY TYPES

Divide into groups according to the four types of the Personality Spectrum—Thinker-dominant students in one group, Organizer-dominant students in another, Giver-dominant students in a third, and Adventurer-dominant students in the fourth. If you have scored the same in more than one of these types, join whatever group is smaller. With your group, brainstorm the following lists for your type:

1. the strengths of this type
2. the struggles it brings
3. the stressors (things that cause stress) for this type
4. career areas that tend to suit this type
5. career areas that are a challenge for this type
6. people this type has trouble relating to (often because they are strong in areas where this type needs to grow)

If there is time, each group can present this information to the entire class; this will boost understanding and acceptance of diverse ways of relating to information and people.

WHAT ARE THE BENEFITS OF KNOWING HOW YOU LEARN?

When you have a handle on your multiple intelligences and personality traits, you can choose strategies that will help you learn more, remember better, and use your knowledge more actively—in any academic or workplace situation. Knowing how you learn will also help you to set goals for positive change in areas that you find more difficult and use strategies that will most effectively move you toward those goals.

Study Benefits

Knowing how you learn helps you choose study techniques that capitalize on your strengths. Note taking is one example: "Students learn better when they know their learning style and adjust their note-taking style to it," says Andrea Worrell of the ITT Institute. "When a visual learner is presented with organizational sequences during a class lecture, he can graph the information instead

49

of using more conventional notes. Taking notes according to your learning style helps you process information—when you hear it for the first time and when you go back to study it later on."[4]

What you know about how you learn will also help you to:

- **Avoid strategies that don't work for you.** A visual learner who has always struggled to study by rewriting notes, for example, might find relief after switching to a strategy involving highlighting in different colors.
- **Build skill areas that don't come so easily.** An Adventurer who does *not* respond well to reading page after page of uninterrupted text, for example, has two choices when faced with a lengthy linear presentation. She can apply her strengths to the material—for example, she might create a hands-on approach—or she can strengthen the study skills she needs to handle the material.

When you study with others, understanding of diverse learning styles will help you assign tasks effectively, learn more comprehensively, communicate more successfully, and appreciate different perspectives. An interpersonal learner might take the lead in teaching material to others; an Organizer might be the schedule coordinator for the group. A musical learner might follow the creative example of Defined Mind (a company that uses New York club bands to record vocabulary-building songs for students preparing for standardized tests) or www.physicssongs.org (a website that catalogs well-known songs rewritten to help students understand and remember physics concepts). You can use the same approach by writing new lyrics, based on the material the group is studying, to a currently popular tune. You can then perform the song for group members and pass out copies of the words for reference.

Classroom Benefits

Your college instructors will most likely have a range of teaching styles (an instructor's teaching style often reflects his or her dominant learning style). Your particular learning style may work well with some instructors but be a mismatch with others. After several class meetings, you should be able to assess an instructor's teaching styles (see Key 2.4).

Although presentation styles vary, the standard lecture is still the norm in most classrooms. For this reason, the traditional college classroom is generally a happy home for the verbal or logical learner and the Thinker and Organizer. However, many students learn best when interacting more than a lecture allows. What actions can you take to compensate for styles that don't match up well with your own?

Key 2.4   Instructors often rely on one or more teaching styles.

TEACHING STYLE	WHAT TO EXPECT IN CLASS
Lecture—Verbal Focus	Instructor speaks to the class for the entire period, with little class interaction. Lesson is taught primarily through words, either spoken or written on the board, overhead projector, handouts, or text.
Group Discussion	Instructor presents material but encourages class discussion.
Small Groups	Instructor presents material and then breaks class into small groups for discussion or project work.
Visual Focus	Instructor uses visual elements such as diagrams, photographs, drawings, and transparencies.
Logical Presentation	Instructor organizes material in a logical sequence, such as by time or importance.
Random Presentation	Instructor tackles topics in no particular order, and may jump around a lot or digress.

Play to your strengths. For example, a logical-mathematical learner in a seminar class dominated by open discussion could rewrite notes in an outline format to bring structure to concepts and insert facts where they fit best. Likewise, a Giver taking a straight lecture course with no student-to-student contact might meet with a study group to go over the details and fill in factual gaps.

Work to build weaker areas. In other words, use study strategies that don't come naturally to you, in order to become better at them. As a visual learner reviews notes from a structured lecture course, for example, he could outline them (logical-mathematical), allot extra quiet study time to master the material (intrapersonal), and work with a study group (interpersonal). A Thinker, studying for a test from notes delivered by an Adventurer instructor, could find hands-on ways to review the material such as working in a science lab (bodily-kinesthetic, Adventurer).

Try the latest technology. Certain technological tools may help you use your strengths to review and remember lecture material. For example, at Duke University and Drexel University, some students are using iPods (portable MP3 players) as academic tools. One professor records lectures that students can download onto iPods and study by listening to them, for example; others are using iPods as recording devices for classes and interviews or using them to store data downloaded from college or course websites.[5]

Ask your instructor for additional help. If you are having trouble with coursework, communicate with your instructor through e-mail or face-to-face during office hours. This is especially important in large lectures where you are anonymous unless you speak up. The visual learner, for example, might ask the instructor to recommend graphs or figures that illustrate the lecture.

Instructors are unique. No instructor can give each of a diverse group of learners exactly what each one needs. The flexibility that you need to mesh your learning style with instructors' teaching styles is also a tool for career and life success. Just as you can't hand-pick your instructors, you will rarely, if ever, be able to choose your supervisors or their work styles.

Workplace Benefits

Knowing how you learn has tangible career benefits:

Better performance through self-awareness. Since your learning styles are essentially the same as your working styles, understanding how you learn will help you identify career and work environments that suit you. Knowing your strengths will help you use and highlight them on the job. When a task involves one of your weaker skills, you can either take special care to accomplish it or suggest someone else who is a better fit do it.

Better teamwork. The more attuned you are to abilities and personality traits, the better you will be at identifying the tasks you and others can best perform in team situations. For example, a Giver might enjoy helping new hires get used to the people and the environment. Or a supervisor directing an intrapersonal learner might offer the chance to take material home to think about before a meeting.

Better career planning. The more you know about how you learn and work, the more you will be able to focus on career paths that could work well for you. Use the following strategies to connect what you know about yourself with what's out there:

- Link your learning style profile to career areas. Think about what who you are as a learner says about where you would be happiest and most productive in the working world, and consult people in your school's career center for advice. A strength in one or more areas may lead you to a major, an internship, and even a lifelong career. Key 2.5 lists some possibilities for the eight intelligence types. This list represents only a fraction of the available opportunities. Use what you see here to inspire thought and investigation.

Key 2.5   Multiple Intelligences may open doors to majors, internships, and careers.

MULTIPLE INTELLIGENCE	CONSIDER MAJORING IN . . .	THINK ABOUT AN INTERNSHIP AT A(N) . . .	LOOK INTO A CAREER AS . . .
Bodily–Kinesthetic	Massage Therapy Physical Therapy Kinesiology Construction Engineering Chiropractics Sports Medicine Anatomy Dance Theater	Sports Physician's Office Athletic Club Physical Therapy Center Chiropractor's Office Construction Company Surveying Company Dance Studio Athletic Facility Drafting Firm Theater Company	Carpenter Draftsman Recreational Therapist Physical Therapist Mechanical Engineer Massage Therapist Dancer or Acrobat Exercise Physiologist Actor
Intrapersonal	Psychology Sociology English Finance Liberal Arts Biology Computer Science Economics	Research and Development Firm Accounting Firm Computer Company Publishing House Pharmaceutical Company Engineering Firm Biology Lab	Research Scientist Motivational Speaker Engineer Physicist Sociologist Computer Scientist Economist Author Psychologist
Interpersonal	Psychology Sociology Education Real Estate Public Relations Nursing Business Hotel/Restaurant Management Rhetoric/Communications	Hotel or Restaurant Travel Agency Real Estate Agency Public Relations Firm Human Resources Customer Service School Marketing/Sales Counseling Office Social Service Office	Social Worker PR Rep/Media Liaison Human Resources Travel Agent Sociologist Anthropologist Counselor Therapist Teacher Nurse
Naturalistic	Forestry Astronomy Geology Biology Zoology Atmospheric Sciences Oceanography Agriculture Animal Husbandry Environmental Law Physics	Museum National Park Oil Company Botanical Gardens Environmental Law Firm Outward Bound Adventure Travel Agency Zoo Camp Biological Research Firm	Forest Ranger Botanist or Herbalist Geologist Ecologist Marine Biologist Archaeologist Astronomer Adventure Travel Agent Wildlife Tour Guide Landscape Architect

Key 2.5   Continued.

MULTIPLE INTELLIGENCE	CONSIDER MAJORING IN . . .	THINK ABOUT AN INTERNSHIP AT A(N) . . .	LOOK INTO A CAREER AS . . .
Musical	Music	Performance Hall	Lyricist or Composer
	Musical History	Radio Station	Singer or Musician
	Musical Theory	Record Label	Voice Coach
	Performing Arts	Ballet or Theater Company	Music Teacher or Critic
	Composition	Recording Studio	Record Executive
	Voice	Children's Music Camp	Conductor
	Liberal Arts	Orchestra or Opera Company	Radio DJ
	Entertainment Law	Musical Talent Agency	Sound Engineer
		Entertainment Law Firm	Entertainment Lawyer
Logical– Mathematical	Math	Law Firm	Doctor, Dentist, or Veterinarian
	Accounting	Health Care Office	
	Physics	Real Estate Brokerage	Accountant
	Economics	Accounting Firm	Pharmacist
	Medicine	Animal Hospital	Chemist
	Banking/Finance	Science Lab	Physicist
	Astronomy	Consulting Firm	Systems Analyst
	Computer Science	Pharmaceutical Firm	Investment Banker
	Systems Theory	Bank	Financial Analyst
	Law		Computer Scientist
	Chemistry		
	Engineering		
Verbal–Linguistic	Communications	Newspaper/Magazine	Author
	Marketing	Network TV Affiliate	Playwright
	English/Literature	Publishing House	Journalist
	Journalism	Law Firm	TV/Radio Producer
	Foreign Languages	PR/Marketing Firm	Literature Teacher
	Linguistic Theory	Speech Therapist	Speech Pathologist
	Political Science	Ad Agency	Business Executive
	Advertising/PR	Training Company	Copywriter or Editor
		Human Resources Agency	
		Customer Service	
Visual–Spatial	Visual Arts	Art Gallery	Graphic Artist
	Architecture	Museum	Photographer
	Interior Design	Photography Studio	Architect
	Multimedia Design	Design Firm	Cinematographer
	Film Theory	Advertising Agency	Art Therapist
	Photography	Theater Shop	Designer
	Art History	Multimedia Firm	Cartoonist/Illustrator
		Architecture Firm	Art Museum Curator
		Film Studio	Art Teacher

■ **Test your self-knowledge through active hands-on exploration.** Try out extracurricular activities, volunteering opportunities, and internships that seem to involve your strengths and learning preferences. For example, a student interested in teaching may volunteer as a camp counselor or an after-school tutor or may complete a summer internship at a school. Check out opportunities at your school's career office or try internship websites such as www.erecruiting.com.

■ **Keep what you value in mind.** Ask yourself what careers support the principles that guide your life. How important to you are service to others, financial security, a broad-based education, and time for family? Consider talking to people whose career accomplishments mirror your own values.

■ **Follow your passion.** Find something you love doing more than anything else in the world, and then find a way to make money doing it. If you are sure of what you love to do but cannot pinpoint a career niche, ask instructors or career counselors for advice.

Go For It! BUILDING YOUR SKILLS

ACTIVE
THINKING

SKILL WILL SELF-MGMT.

DESIGN A SELF-PORTRAIT

Because self-knowledge helps you to make the best choices about your future, a self-portrait is an important step in your career exploration. Use this exercise to synthesize everything you have been exploring about yourself into one comprehensive "self-portrait." Design your portrait in "think link" style, using words and visual shapes to describe your dominant Multiple Intelligences and Personal Spectrum dimensions, values, abilities, career interests, and anything else that is an important part of who you are.

A think link, also called a "mind map" or "word web," is a visual construction of related ideas that represents your thought process. Ideas are written inside geometric shapes, often boxes or circles, and related ideas and facts are attached to those ideas by lines that connect the shapes. See Chapter 7 for more about think links.

Use the style shown in the example in Key 2.6 or create your own. For example, in this exercise you may want to create a "wheel" or "web" of ideas coming off your central shape, entitled "Me." Then, spreading out from each of those ideas (interests, learning style, etc.), draw lines connecting all of the thoughts that go along with that idea. Connected to "Interests," for example, might be "singing," "stock market," and "history."

You don't have to use the wheel image. You might want to design a treelike think link or a line of boxes with connecting thoughts written below the boxes, or anything else you like. Refer to pages 72–73 and 110–111 for other examples of think link styles. Let your design reflect who you are, just as the think link itself does.

Key 2.6   One example of a self-portrait.

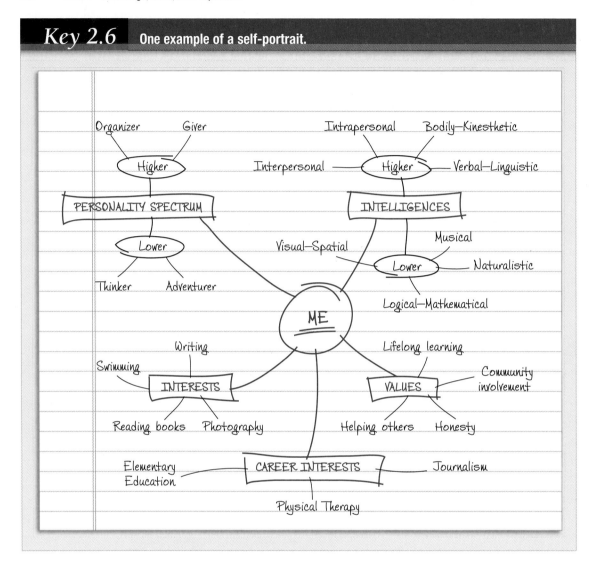

The bottom line is that, at school as well as in life, you can make the most of your skills and work through your challenges by actively thinking through and using different strategies. "I didn't have a good experience through many of my school years because of struggling in certain classes," says Joyce Bishop, professor of psychology at Golden State College. "School is based very strongly on verbal-linguistic learning, which is my weakest intelligence. Students who have strong verbal-linguistic and logical-mathematical intelligences are usually successful in school, while those of us who are strong in the other six intelligence areas have a harder time. What's important to learn is that there are tools that can help us work around our learning-style problems and that having another type of intelligence defines us as an individual in the most positive way."[6]

A better understanding of your learning strengths and preferences and personality traits will aid you in a particular educational challenge—choosing the right major.

HOW CAN YOU CHOOSE A MAJOR?

At some point after you complete your general education requirements, you will be asked to declare an academic *major*—an academic subject area chosen as a field of specialization and requiring a specific course of study. Declaring a major largely determines the courses you take, what you learn, and with whom you spend your school time. Your major may also have a significant influence on your future career.

Taking a practical approach to declaring a major can help you avoid feeling overwhelmed. Think of it as a long-term goal made up of multiple actions or steps (short-term goals) that begin with knowing your learning styles, interests, and talents; exploring academic options; and establishing your academic schedule. You will be wise to start the process now, even if you don't need to decide right away—and even if, as is true of many students, you don't yet know what you want to study.

Short-Term Goal #1: Use Learning Styles Assessments to Identify Interests and Talents

Considering what you like and what you do well can lead to a fulfilling area of study. When you identify your interests and talents and choose a major that focuses on them, you are likely to have a positive attitude and perform at your highest level, both at school and beyond. Whereas some people have sensed a direction since they were very young, others don't have any idea what feels right and often discover their majors—and their careers—by chance.

To pinpoint the areas that spark your interest, use the results of your Multiple Intelligence and Personality Spectrum assessments to answer the following questions:

- What courses have I enjoyed the most in college and high school? What do these courses have in common?
- What subjects am I drawn to in my personal reading?
- What activities do I look forward to most?

- In what skills or academic areas do I perform best? Am I a "natural" in any area?
- What do people say I do well?
- What are my dominant learning styles?

Short-Term Goal #2: Explore Academic Options

Next, find out about the academic choices available at your school. Plan to achieve the following mini-goals in order to reach this short-term goal:

Colleges offer many different areas of study and types of classes. These students at West Hills Community College are learning to plot farmland using a global positioning system.

Learn what's possible. Consult your college catalog for guidelines on declaring (and changing) your major. Find answers to these questions:

- When do I have to declare a major? (generally at the end of the second year for four-year programs; earlier for associate or certificate programs)
- What are my options in majoring? (double majors, minors, interdisciplinary majors)
- What majors are offered at my school?

If a major looks interesting, explore it further by answering these questions:

- What minimum grade point average, if any, does the department require before it will accept me as a major?
- What GPA must I maintain in the courses included in the major?
- What preparatory courses (prerequisites) are required?
- What courses will I be required to take and in what sequence? How many credits do I need to graduate in the major?

- Will I need to write a thesis to graduate in this major?
- If I plan to go to graduate school, is this major appropriate for the kind of graduate school in which I am interested?

Work closely with your advisor. Early on, begin discussing your major with your advisor; he or she can help you evaluate different options.

Visit the academic department. When considering a major, analyze your comfort with the academic department as well as with the material. Take a look around the department office during weekday hours, and ask the department secretary for pertinent information. Then sit in on several classes to get a feel for the instructors and the work. Consider asking an instructor for an appointment to discuss the major (you may be able to set up an appointment with an instructor through the secretary). Check out the department website if one exists, for other details.

Speak to people with experience in the major. Ask students who are a year or two ahead of you to describe their experiences with the courses, the workload, and the instructors.

Consider creative options for majoring. Think beyond the traditional majoring path, and investigate the possibilities at your school. One or more of the following may be open to you:

- **Double majors.** If, for example, you want to major in English and philosophy, ask your academic advisor if it is possible to meet the requirements for both departments.
- **Interdisciplinary majors.** If your preferred major isn't in the catalog, consult your advisor. Some schools allow students to design majors with guidance from advisors and instructors.
- **Minors.** A minor involves a concentration of departmental courses, but has fewer requirements than a major. Many students choose a minor that is suited for a career. For example, a sociology major who wants to work in an inner-city hospital may minor in Spanish.
- **Majors involving courses outside your school.** Some schools may have study abroad programs (students spend a semester or a year at an affiliated college in a different country) or opportunities to take courses at nearby schools. Such courses might apply to a major that interests you.

Short-Term Goal #3: Establish Your Academic Schedule

Effective time management will enable you to fulfill the requirements of your major and complete all additional credits:

Look at your time frame. Do you intend to finish your requirements in four years (or two years if you attend community college) or do you think it will take longer? Be honest with yourself about what you can reasonably expect to accomplish, considering all your responsibilities. If you're working 20 to 30 hours a week *and* attending school, it may be very difficult to graduate on schedule. Do you plan to attend graduate school? If so, do you plan to go there directly after graduation or take time off?

Set timing for short-term goals. Within your time frame, pinpoint when to accomplish the important short-term goals that lead to graduation. What are the deadlines for completing core requirements, declaring a major, or writing a thesis? Although you won't need to map out your entire college course load at one shot, drafting a tentative *curriculum*—the particular set of courses required for a degree, both within and outside your major—can help clarify where you are heading.

Identify dates connected to your goal fulfillment. Pay attention to academic dates (you will find an academic calendar in each year's college catalog and on the college website). Such dates include registration dates, final date to declare a major, final date to drop a course, and so forth. Plan ahead so you don't miss a deadline.

Be Flexible as You Come to a Decision

As with any serious challenge that involves defining your path, flexibility is essential. Many students change their minds as they consider majors; some declare a major and then change it one or more times before finding a good fit. Early in your college experience, you may think that you would enjoy majoring in a particular subject, even though you may know little or nothing about it. When you take a course in that subject, however, you might discover that you don't like something that is central to that subject—writing papers (in a history course), for example, or working in the lab (for a biology course). This is a significant clue that you should consider an alternative academic route.

If you decide that a change is right for you, act on it as soon as possible—once you have considered it carefully—by informing your advisor, completing any required paperwork, and redesigning your schedule to reflect your new choices. Keep in mind that if you change your major after taking a semester or a year of courses, your graduation may be affected since you have to fulfill the requirements in your new major. This is one reason why it is smart to fulfill all fundamental course requirements first, before focusing on the courses for your major.

Go For It!   BUILDING YOUR SKILLS

LINK YOUR INTERESTS TO INTRIGUING MAJORS

After looking at a list of the majors your school offers, write down three that you want to consider.

1. _____
2. _____
3. _____

Now look at the list again. Other than what you wrote above, what majors catch your eye? Write down three intriguing majors—*without* thinking about what you would do with them or whether they are practical choices.

1. _____
2. _____
3. _____

Choose one major from the second list and explore it. Talk to your advisor about the major. Read about it in your college catalog. Consider a minor in the subject. Speak to an instructor in the department about related careers. Take notes on everything you discover.

Finally, gather your findings and summarize them, including your thoughts on what you've learned, on a separate piece of paper or in a journal. You will have taken a casual interest and turned it into a viable academic option.

Although almost everyone faces challenges in college, people with diagnosed learning disabilities have unique challenges that may interfere with college success. Focused assistance can help learning-disabled students manage their conditions and excel in school.

HOW CAN YOU IDENTIFY AND MANAGE LEARNING DISABILITIES?

Some learning disabilities cause reading problems, some create difficulties in math, and still others make it difficult for students to process the language they hear. The following will help you understand learning disabilities and, should you be diagnosed with one, give you the tools to manage your disability successfully.

Identifying a Learning Disability

The National Center for Learning Disabilities (NCLD) defines learning disabilities in terms of what they are and what they are not:[7]

- They are neurological disorders that interfere with one's ability to store, process, and produce information.
- They do *not* include mental retardation, autism, behavioral disorders, impaired vision, hearing loss, or other physical disabilities.
- They do *not* include attention deficit disorder and attention deficit hyperactivity disorder (disorders involving consistent and problematic inattention, hyperactivity, and/or impulsivity), although these problems may accompany learning disabilities.[8]
- They often run in families and are lifelong, although learning-disabled people can use specific strategies to manage and even overcome areas of weakness.
- They must be diagnosed by professionals in order for the disabled person to receive federally funded aid.

How can you determine whether you should be evaluated for a learning disability? According to the NCLD, persistent problems in any of the following areas may indicate a learning disability:[9]

- reading or reading comprehension
- performing math calculations, understanding language and concepts
- social skills or interpreting social cues
- following a schedule, being on time, meeting deadlines
- reading or following maps
- balancing a checkbook

| Key 2.7 | Understand and know how to recognize different learning disabilities. |

DISABILITY/CONDITION	WHAT ARE THE SIGNS?
Dyslexia and related reading disorders	Problems with reading (including spelling, word sequencing, and comprehension) and processing (translating written language to thought or thought to written language)
Dyscalculia (developmental arithmetic disorders)	Difficulties in recognizing numbers and symbols, memorizing facts, aligning numbers, understanding abstract concepts like fractions, and applying math to life skills (time management, gauging distance, handling money, etc.)
Developmental writing disorders	Difficulties in composing complete sentences, organizing a writing assignment, or translating thoughts coherently to the page
Handwriting disorders (dysgraphia)	Disorder characterized by writing disabilities, including writing that is distorted or incorrect. Sufferers have poor handwriting that is difficult to read because of inappropriately sized and spaced letters. The use of wrong or misspelled words is also common
Speech and language disorders	Problems with producing speech sounds, using spoken language to communicate, and/or understanding what others say
LD-related social issues	Problems in recognizing facial or vocal cues from others, controlling verbal and physical impulsivity, and respecting others' personal space
LD-related organizational issues	Difficulties in scheduling and in organizing personal, academic, and work-related materials

Source: LD Online: Learning Disabilities Information and Resources, www.ldonline.org/accessed 3/17/04. © 2001 WETA.

- following directions, especially on multistep tasks
- writing, sentence structure, spelling, and organizing written work

Details on specific learning disabilities appear in Key 2.7. For an evaluation, contact your school's learning center or student health center for a referral to a licensed professional.

Managing a Learning Disability

If you are diagnosed with a learning disability, focused action will help you manage it and maximize your ability to learn and succeed:

Be informed about your disability. Search the library and the Internet—try NCLD at www.ncld.org or LD Online at www.ldonline.org. Or call NCLD at

1-888-575-7373. Make sure you understand your Individualized Education Program (IEP)—the document describing your disability and recommended strategies. Know about how many people suffer from your disability, how others cope, and what schools may have the most helpful programs for students with your disability.

Seek assistance from your school. Speak with your advisor about specific accommodations that will help you learn. Among the services mandated by law for learning-disabled students are:

- extended time on tests
- note-taking assistance (for example, having a fellow student take notes for you)
- assistive technology devices (tape recorders or laptop computers)
- modified assignments
- alternative assessments and test formats

Other services include tutoring, study skills assistance, and counseling.

Be a dedicated student. Be on time and attend class. Read assignments before class. Sit where you can avoid distractions. Review notes soon after class. Spend extra time on assignments. Ask for help.

Build a positive attitude. See your accomplishments in light of how far you have come. Rely on people who support you. Know that the help you receive will give you the best possible chance to learn and grow.

As you move through your college career, continue to build your understanding of yourself as a learner. Reflect on your reaction to your educational experiences—each course, each instructor, each project, each test. Every experience will give you another piece of information about how you take in and process information. Ultimately, your discoveries will help lead you to the academic focus and life choices that are right for you.

"Learning is not attained by chance, it must be sought for with ardor and attended to with diligence."

ABIGAIL ADAMS
second First Lady of the United States

Test Competence: Measure What You've Learned

MULTIPLE CHOICE. *Circle or highlight the answer that seems to fit best.*

1. A learning style is
   A. the best way to learn when attending classes.
   B. a particular way of being intelligent.
   C. an affinity for a particular job choice or career area.
   D. a way in which the mind receives and processes information.

2. "An ability to solve problems or fashion products that are useful in a particular setting or community," according to Howard Gardner, is
   A. bodily–kinesthetic intelligence.
   B. a learning style.
   C. an intelligence.
   D. a personality profile.

3. Intrapersonal intelligence is the ability to
   A. relate to others.
   B. understand one's own behavior and feelings.
   C. understand spatial relationships.
   D. use the physical body skillfully.

4. The ability to communicate through language refers to
   A. visual intelligence.
   B. visual–spatial intelligence.
   C. interpersonal intelligence.
   D. verbal–linguistic intelligence.

5. The Personality Spectrum personality types are
   A. Myers-Briggs, Keirsey, Gardner, and Bishop.
   B. Thinker, Organizer, Giver, and Adventurer.

    C. Visual, Verbal, Interpersonal, and Intrapersonal.

    D. Thinker, Visionary, Organizer, and Verbal.

6. Working in study groups and interacting with honesty bring out the best in

    A. a Giver.

    B. an Organizer.

    C. an Adventurer.

    D. a Thinker.

7. An adventurer's strengths include

    A. skillfulness and a hands-on approach to learning.

    B. loyalty and obligation.

    C. exploring ideas and solving problems.

    D. honesty and cultivating potential.

8. The best way to use learning-style assessments is to see them as

    A. a message that shows the paths you must take in order to be successful.

    B. a tool with which to see yourself more clearly.

    C. a way to find the group of learners with whom you work best.

    D. a definitive label for your working style.

9. You are thinking about declaring a major. After you use learning styles to assess your strengths and talents, your next short-term goal is to

    A. establish your academic schedule.

    B. make a decision.

    C. explore academic options.

    D. consider a double major.

10. Exploring your options for majoring includes all of the following except:

    A. majoring in an area where your closest contacts at school are also majoring.

    B. consulting your college catalog for the majors offered at your school.

    C. visiting the department of a major you are considering.

    D. discussing the process with your advisor.

TRUE/FALSE. *Place a T or an F beside each statement to indicate whether you think it is true or false.*

_____ 1. There is one best way to learn any academic subject.

_____ 2. Only logical–mathematical learners can succeed in math courses.

_____ 3. In an area of limitation, your best bet is to look at where you are and set goals that will help you reach where you want to be.

_____ 4. Time management plays an important role in choosing and fulfilling the requirements of a major.

_____ 5. Attention deficit disorder is classified as a learning disability.

Target and Achieve a Goal

Commit to one specific learning styles strategy from this chapter to improve your study skills.

Name the strategy here: _____

_____

Describe your goal—what you want to gain by using this strategy. _____

_____

_____

_____

Describe how you plan to use this strategy through the semester to achieve this goal.

_____

_____

_____

Building Your Skills

Brain Power: Build Vocabulary Fitness

Here is a selection from the current media. Read the material, paying special attention to the context of the vocabulary words shown in bold type. Then choose the correct definition for each word in the table that follows. Use a dictionary to check your answers. Finally, on a separate sheet, use each vocabulary word in a sentence of your own to solidify your understanding.

This excerpt from The New York Times *discusses the naming of species.*

The system by which new species are named has worked well since it was introduced by Carl Linnaeus in 1758. Just about any name will do as long as it follows the Linnaean style and other rules established and updated by several international **commissions** on **nomenclature.**

Keeping track of all those names, however, has become a real headache, particularly in **zoology,** with its 1.5 million animal species described so far. With the explosion of research in recent decades and the discovery of more new species (15,000 to 20,000 animal species are named every year, for example), it is difficult for biologists to keep up.

Descriptions and names for new species are published in hundreds of different journals.

Perhaps the Internet can bring order out of the chaos. A group of zoologists led by Andrew Polaszek, executive secretary of the International Commission on Zoological Nomenclature, is proposing the creation of a **universal** Web-based registry of animal names, to be called ZooBank.

Writing in *Nature*, the group suggests that it be made **mandatory** that all new species names be entered in the registry. Eventually, existing names would be entered as well. Access would be open to all, and scientists could sign up for e-mail alerts when a new species of interest to them is named.

Because the registration would be accomplished by filling in Web-based forms, the registry would also help **eliminate** names that do not conform to the rules, a **perennial** problem in biological nomenclature.

Source: Henry Fountain, "Too Many Names." *The New York Times,* September 27, 2005, p. F3.

Circle the word or phrase that best defines each term as it is used in the excerpt.

VOCABULARY WORDS	A	B	C
1. commissions (noun)	authorized groups	sets of guidelines	governments
2. nomenclature (noun)	science of names	system of naming	scientific law
3. zoology (noun)	animal captivity	biology	animal science
4. universal (adj.)	stellar	worldwide	cosmic
5. mandatory (adj.)	required	suggested	official
6. eliminate (verb)	consider	reject	change
7. perennial (adj.)	annual	recurrent	floral

Get to the Root

Every time you learn a Greek or Latin root, you increase your ability to recognize English vocabulary words that include that root and to figure out their meaning. Grow your vocabulary by studying this root and its related words, writing in two more words from the same root, and including definitions for both new words.

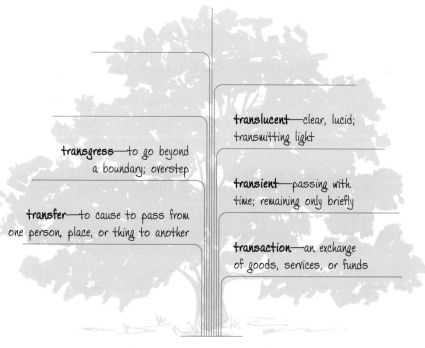

translucent—clear, lucid; transmitting light

transgress—to go beyond a boundary; overstep

transient—passing with time; remaining only briefly

transfer—to cause to pass from one person, place, or thing to another

transaction—an exchange of goods, services, or funds

trans—across, origin: Latin

Investigate Using Research Navigator

First, look at Key 2.5 and choose one of your strongest intelligences. Looking at the Career box for that intelligence, select two careers to explore. Next, access Research Navigator using the Internet address shown on page 32. Sign on to the service using your Login Name and Password. Scroll through the database titles listed for Content Select. Choose a database linked to one of the careers you selected, and then enter a keyword that is likely to call up articles with information about this career—for example, "career," "job," "workplace," or "job market." Read at least two articles and answer the following questions. Repeat the process for the second career.

- What do current job prospects look like for this career?
- What seem to be some of the most important qualities that someone in this career needs in order to succeed?
- How do these qualities match up with what you consider to be your strengths?
- After exploring the articles, do you feel that pursuing a career in this area is a possibility for you? Why or why not?

ACTIVE THINKING

SKILL   WILL   SELF-MGMT.

Building Will and Self-Awareness

Make Responsible Choices

Answer the following question on a separate piece of paper or in a journal.

Think about what the personal assessments in this chapter have taught you about yourself. Then, answer the following questions:

- What have you learned about your strengths? List your most significant strengths. For what you consider to be your greatest strength, discuss how you plan to use it to your advantage this semester.
- What have you learned about your weaknesses? Choose a weakness that has given you difficulty in school, and brainstorm ways to compensate for it and/or strengthen it this semester.
- Consider the possibility that a weakness of yours will put you in an unfavorable situation such as failing a test or a course, getting into a serious conflict with an instructor or a fellow student, being unable

to keep an academic scholarship due to a low GPA, or being unable to enter or stay in a particular degree program. How do you intend to handle a situation that taps into a weakness? How do you think your manner of dealing with problems like this in college will impact the way you deal with them later in life?

Chapter Summary

As you use the summary on the following pages to review the concepts you learned in this chapter, focus also on its format—in this case a **think link,** in other chapters a formal outline, and in still others the Cornell system. As you become comfortable with the organization and style of these various formats, try using each of them to take class and reading notes, noting which approach works best for you in particular situations.

Endnotes

1. Howard Gardner, *Multiple Intelligences: The Theory in Practice.* New York: HarperCollins, 1993, pp. 5–49.

2. Ibid., p. 7.

3. Developed by Joyce Bishop, Ph.D., Psychology faculty, Golden West College, Huntington Beach, CA. Based on Howard Gardner, *Frames of Mind: The Theory of Multiple Intelligences.* New York: HarperCollins, 1993.

4. *Keys to Lifelong Learning Telecourse.* Dir. Mary Jane Bradbury. Videocassette. Intrepid Films, 2000.

5. Brock Read, "Seriously, iPods Are Educational," March 18, 2005. *The Chronicle of Higher Education,* volume 51, Information Technology Section, Issue 28, p. A30.

6. *Keys to Lifelong Learning Telecourse.*

7. National Center for Learning Disabilities. "LD at a Glance" [online]. Available: www.ncld.org/LDInfo Zone/InfoZone_FactSheet_LD.cfm (May 2003).

8. National Center for Learning Disabilities. "Adult Learning Disabilities: A Learning Disability Isn't Something You Outgrow. It's Something You Learn to Master" (pamphlet). New York: National Center for Learning Disabilities.

9. National Center for Learning Disabilities. "LD Advocates Guide" [online]. Available: www.ld.org/Advocacy/tutorial_talking_about.cfm (May 2003).

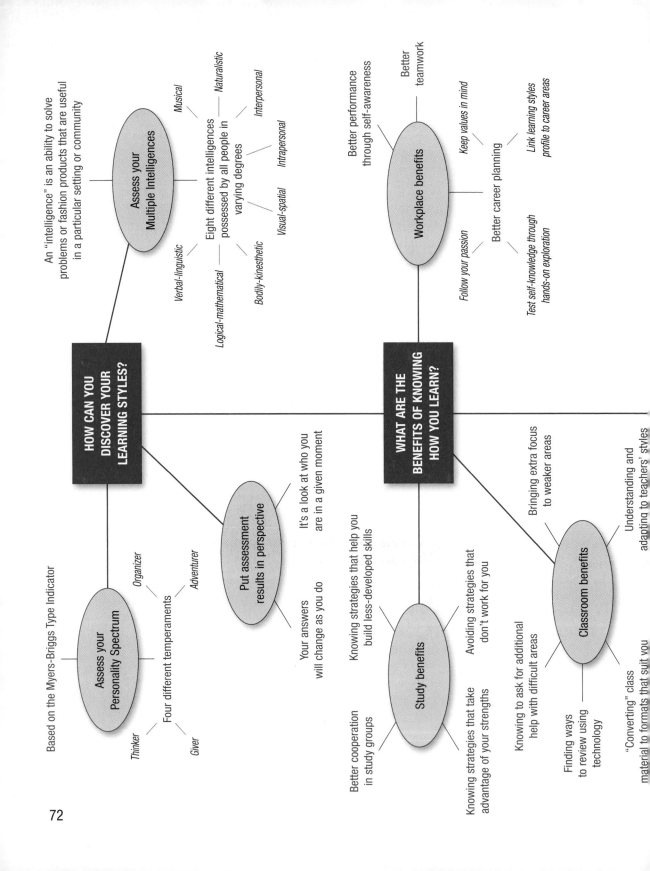

HOW CAN YOU DISCOVER YOUR LEARNING STYLES?

Assess your Multiple Intelligences

An "intelligence" is an ability to solve problems or fashion products that are useful in a particular setting or community

Eight different intelligences possessed by all people in varying degrees

Musical
Naturalistic
Interpersonal
Intrapersonal
Visual-spatial
Bodily-kinesthetic
Logical-mathematical
Verbal-linguistic

Assess your Personality Spectrum

Based on the Myers-Briggs Type Indicator

Four different temperaments

Organizer
Adventurer
Thinker
Giver

Put assessment results in perspective

It's a look at who you are in a given moment

Your answers will change as you do

WHAT ARE THE BENEFITS OF KNOWING HOW YOU LEARN?

Workplace benefits

Better performance through self-awareness

Better teamwork

Keep values in mind

Link learning styles profile to career areas

Better career planning

Follow your passion

Test self-knowledge through hands-on exploration

Study benefits

Knowing strategies that help you build less-developed skills

Avoiding strategies that don't work for you

Knowing to ask for additional help with difficult areas

Knowing strategies that take advantage of your strengths

Better cooperation in study groups

Classroom benefits

Bringing extra focus to weaker areas

Understanding and adapting to teachers' styles

Finding ways to review using technology

"Converting" class material to formats that suit you

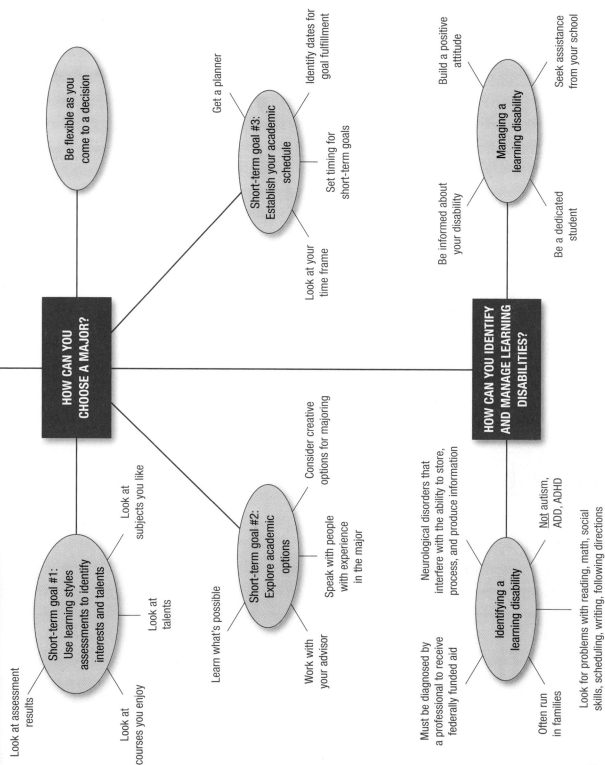

HOW CAN YOU CHOOSE A MAJOR?

Be flexible as you come to a decision

Short-term goal #1: Use learning styles assessments to identify interests and talents
- Look at assessment results
- Look at courses you enjoy
- Look at talents
- Look at subjects you like

Short-term goal #2: Explore academic options
- Learn what's possible
- Work with your advisor
- Speak with people with experience in the major
- Consider creative options for majoring

Short-term goal #3: Establish your academic schedule
- Look at your time frame
- Get a planner
- Set timing for short-term goals
- Identify dates for goal fulfillment

HOW CAN YOU IDENTIFY AND MANAGE LEARNING DISABILITIES?

Identifying a learning disability
- Must be diagnosed by a professional to receive federally funded aid
- Often run in families
- Look for problems with reading, math, social skills, scheduling, writing, following directions
- Neurological disorders that interfere with the ability to store, process, and produce information
- Not autism, ADD, ADHD

Managing a learning disability
- Be informed about your disability
- Be a dedicated student
- Build a positive attitude
- Seek assistance from your school

"As jogging is to the body, thinking is to the brain.
The more we do it, the better we become."

NOB YOSHIGAHARA, JAPANESE MATHEMATICIAN AND PUZZLE MASTER

Critical and Creative Thinking

SOLVING PROBLEMS AND MAKING DECISIONS

College teaches you facts and figures—everything from the rules of English grammar to the structure and function of the human pancreas to the impact of the U.S. Census on social policy. To serve you successfully, though, your education must do more than fill your head with information—it must also give you the tools to be a critical and creative thinker. Your success in school, career, and life depends on your willingness and ability to actively think through problems, make informed decisions, and overcome obstacles.

Critical and creative thinking skills can be developed and improved with practice. This chapter will help you understand how to analyze information, come up with creative ideas, and implement problem-solving and decision-making plans. With these skills you will be better able to learn and to reach the goals that mean the most to you.

In this chapter you will explore answers to the following questions:

- What is important to know about thinking?
- How can you improve your critical thinking skills?
- How can you improve your creative thinking skills?
- How can you use your thinking skills to solve problems and make decisions?

WHAT IS IMPORTANT TO KNOW ABOUT THINKING?

As a college student, you are required to think in greater depth and complexity than ever before. Memorizing information right before a test is no longer enough. On the contrary, college success involves first and foremost a combination of *critical* and *creative* thinking, which includes and goes beyond the ability to memorize and retain what you learn.

Thinking Means Asking and Answering Questions

What is thinking? According to experts, it is what happens when you ask questions and move toward the answers.[1] Questioning propels the action of thinking. "To think through or rethink anything," says Dr. Richard Paul, director of research at the Center for Critical Thinking and Moral Critique, "one must ask questions that stimulate our thought. Questions define tasks, express problems, and delineate issues . . . only students who have questions are really thinking and learning."[2]

As you answer questions, you transform raw data into information that you can use to achieve goals large and small. A *Wall Street Journal* article entitled "The Best Innovations Are Those That Come from Smart Questions" relays the story of a cell biology student, William Hunter, whose professor told him that "the difference between good science and great science is the quality of the questions posed." Later, as a doctor and the president and CEO of a pharmaceutical company, Dr. Hunter asked questions about new ways to use drugs. His questions led to the development of a revolutionary product—a drug-coated coronary stent (a slender catheter made to fit into a blood vessel) that prevents scar tissue from forming. Through seeking answers to probing questions, Dr. Hunter reached a significant goal.[3]

You use questions in order to think both critically ("What test grades do I need in biology this semester?") and creatively ("How can I earn those grades?"). Later in the chapter, you will find examples of the kinds of questions that drive each skill. Like any aspect of thinking, questioning is not often a straightforward process. Sometimes the answer doesn't come right away. Often the answer leads to further, and more specific, questions. Don't be discouraged if the answers don't come right away; patience is key in following what can be a long process of exploration to an important end result.

In order to ask useful questions, you need to know *why* you are questioning. In other words, you need to define your purpose. Not knowing your purpose may lead you to ask questions that take you in irrelevant directions and waste your time. For example, if an assignment asks you to analyze the effectiveness of John F. Kennedy's foreign policy during his presidency, asking questions about his personal life is likely to lead you off track.

A general question can be your starting point for defining your purpose: "What am I trying to accomplish, and why?" As you continue your thought process, you will find more specific purposes, or short-term goals, that help you generate questions along the way.

Critical and Creative Thinking Depend on Each Other

Some tasks require only one thinking skill, or ability, at a time. You might use critical thinking to complete a multiple-choice quiz, or creative thinking to come up with an idea for an essay. However, with all but the most straightforward situations, and especially when you need to solve a problem or make a decision, you use critical and creative thinking skills together to move forward.

You need to think creatively to come up with ideas and solutions; likewise, you need to think critically to evaluate the quality and usefulness of your creative ideas. Here is an example from inventor and entrepreneur Wayne Kuna: "To me as a toy inventor, critical thinking is an absolute necessity. It gives us the tools to find not just the next step, but also the step after the next step. By looking at all the things around us—the fads, the movies, the Internet—and mixing it together with what we know about how kids play and . . . where they live, we begin to develop new and better ideas that no one ever thought of before."[4]

Thinking Power Is Yours to Build

You ask and answer critical and creative thinking questions every day, whether or not you realize it. For example, in deciding to pursue a college degree—a major life decision—you asked these kinds of questions as you thought through the consequences of the choice. "If I attend class full-time, what will that do to my schedule at work and at home?" "If I don't go to school, how will that affect my ability to earn a living in the short and long term?"

Other examples of students using critical and creative thinking are:

- choosing the best term paper topic by looking at the list of topics, thinking about the available library and Internet sources, and taking your personal interest and the instructor's approval into consideration
- deciding between two different courses by reading course descriptions and talking to your advisor
- after listening to one point of view in a class discussion, offering a solidly supported opposing opinion
- citing examples that back up the central idea of a paper you are writing

You can improve, now and over a lifetime, your ability to think. Studies have shown that your brain will continue to develop throughout your life if you stay active in your quest to learn new things.[5] As you increase your thinking skill, you increase your value both in school and on the job. Critical and creative thinkers are in demand because of their ability to apply what they know, think comprehensively through a situation, innovate, and solve problems and make decisions effectively.

The *Go For It!* exercises within this chapter will give you an idea of how you perceive yourself as a critical and creative thinker and encourage the development of those skills. All the other chapter sets of *Go For It!* exercises, along with the *Make Responsible Choices* exercises at the end of each chapter, help you to build your thinking skills and apply them to chapter topics. In short, your work throughout the book is geared toward building your thinking power.

Begin by exploring the skills that every active thinker uses on a daily basis.

HOW CAN YOU IMPROVE YOUR CRITICAL THINKING SKILLS?

Critical thinking is the process of gathering information, analyzing it in different ways, and evaluating it for the purposes of gaining understanding, solving a problem, or making a decision. It is as essential for real-life problems and decisions as it is for thinking through the hypothetical questions on your chemistry homework.

Before you get into the analytical process, you need to define your purpose. What do you want to analyze, and why? Perhaps you need to analyze the plot of a novel in order to determine its structure; maybe you want to analyze your schedule in order to figure out whether you are arranging your time and responsibilities effectively.

Once you define your purpose, the process involves gathering the necessary information, analyzing and clarifying the ideas, and evaluating what you've found. Remember that, throughout the process, you will formulate new questions that may take you in new directions or even change your purpose. Stay flexible and open to where your thinking can lead you.

Gather Information

Information is the raw material for thinking. Choosing what to gather requires a careful analysis of how much information you need, how much time to spend gathering it, and whether the information is relevant. Say, for instance, that your assignment is to choose a style of American jazz music and discuss its influence on a particular culture. If you gathered every available resource on the topic, the course would be over long before you got to the writing stage.

Here's how you might use analysis to effectively gather information for that paper:

- Reviewing the assignment, you learn that the paper should be 10 pages and cover at least three influential musicians.

- At the library and online, you find lots of what appears to be relevant information.

- You choose a jazz movement, find five or six comprehensive pieces on it, and then select three in-depth sources on each of three musicians.

These students, working with their instructor to produce a literary journal, demonstrate that successful critical thinking often requires teamwork.

In this way you achieve a subgoal—a selection of useful materials—on the way to your larger goal of writing a well-crafted paper.

Analyze and Clarify Information

Once you've gathered the information, the next step is to analyze it to determine whether the information is reliable and useful in helping you answer your questions.

Break Information into Parts

When analyzing information, you break information into parts and examine the parts so that you can see how they relate to each other and to information you already know. The following strategies help you break information down into pieces and set aside what is unclear, unrelated, or unimportant, resulting in a deeper and more reliable understanding.

Separate the ideas. If you are reading about the rise of the Bebop movement, you might name events that influenced it, key musicians, facts about the sound, and ideas behind it.

Compare and contrast. Look at how things are similar to, or different from, each other. You might explore how three Bebop musicians are similar in style. You might look at how they differ in what each musician intends to communicate with the music.

Examine cause and effect. Look at the possible reasons why something happened (possible causes) and its consequences (effects, both positive and negative). You might examine the causes that led up to the Bebop sound as well as its effects on other nonjazz musical styles.

An important caution: Analyze carefully to seek out *true causes*—some apparent causes may not be actual causes (often called "false causes"). For example, events in the musical world and general society took place when the first musicians were developing the Bebop style. Some may have led directly to the new style; others may simply have occurred at the same time.

Look for themes, patterns, and categories. Note connections that form as you look at how bits of information relate to one another. A theme of freedom vs. structure, for example, might emerge out of an examination of Bebop vs. swing jazz. A pattern of behavior might develop as you look at how different musicians broke off from the swing movement. Musicians with different styles might fall into the Bebop category based on their artistic goals.

Once the ideas are broken down, you will need to examine whether examples support ideas, separate fact from opinion, consider perspective, and investigate hidden assumptions.

Examine Whether Examples Support Ideas

When you encounter an idea or claim, examine how it is supported with examples or evidence (facts, expert opinion, research findings, personal experience, and so on). How useful an idea is to your work may depend on whether, or how well, it is backed up with solid evidence or made concrete with examples. Be critical of the information you gather; don't take it at face value.

For example, an advertisement for a weight-loss pill, claiming that it allows users to drop a pound a day, quotes "Anne," who says that she lost 30 pounds in 30 days. The word of one person, who may or may not be telling the truth, is not adequate support. On the other hand, a peer-reviewed medical study, involving 10,000 participants and published in the world-renowned *New England Journal of Medicine,* that points to the effectiveness of a combination calorie reduction and exercise regimen to lose weight may be more reliable.

The Research Investigator materials—both online and in your booklet—go into more detail about the importance of evaluating the credibility of sources. Finding credible, reliable information with which to answer questions and come up with ideas enables you to separate fact from opinion.

Distinguish Fact from Opinion

A *statement of fact* is information presented as objectively real and verifiable ("It's raining outside right now"). In contrast, a *statement of opinion* is a belief, conclusion, or judgment that is inherently difficult, and sometimes impossible, to verify ("This is the most miserable rainstorm ever"). Key 3.1 defines important characteristics of fact and opinion.

Key 3.1 Examine how fact and opinion differ.	
OPINIONS INCLUDE STATEMENTS THAT . . .	**FACTS INCLUDE STATEMENTS THAT . . .**
. . . show evaluation. Any statement of value indicates an opinion. Words such as *bad, good, pointless,* and *beneficial* indicate value judgments. Example: "Jimmy Carter is the most successful peace negotiator to sit in the White House."	*. . . deal with actual people, places, objects, or events.* Example: "In 1978, Jimmy Carter's 13-day summit meeting with Egyptian president Anwar Sadat and Israeli prime minister Menachem Begin led to a treaty between the two countries."
. . . use abstract words. Words that are complicated to define, like *misery* or *success,* usually indicate a personal opinion. Example: "The charity event was a smashing success."	*. . . use concrete words or measurable statistics.* Example: "The charity event raised $5,862."
. . . predict future events. Statements that examine future occurrences are often opinions. Example: "Mr. Barrett's course is going to set a new enrollment record this year."	*. . . describe current events in exact terms.* Example: "Mr. Barrett's course has 378 students enrolled this semester."
. . . use emotional words. Emotions are by nature unverifiable. Chances are that statements using such words as *delightful* or *miserable* express an opinion. Example: "That class is a miserable experience."	*. . . avoid emotional words and focus on the verifiable.* Example: "Citing dissatisfaction with the instruction, 7 out of the 25 students in that class withdrew in September."
. . . use absolutes. Absolute qualifiers, such as *all, none, never,* and *always,* often point to an opinion. Example: "To pay tuition, all college students require financial aid support."	*. . . avoid absolutes, using words like "may," "possibly," and "perhaps."* Example: "To pay tuition, some college students require financial aid support." Or "College students may require financial support to pay tuition."

Source: Adapted from Ben E. Johnson, *Stirring Up Thinking.* New York: Houghton Mifflin, 1998, pp. 268–270.

Even though facts may seem more solid, you can also make use of opinions if you determine that they are backed up with facts. However, it is important to examine opinions for their underlying perspectives and assumptions.

Examine Perspectives and Assumptions

Perspective is a characteristic way of thinking about people, situations, events, and ideas. Perspectives can be broad, such as a generally optimistic or pessimistic view of life. Or they can be more focused, such as an attitude about whether students should commute or live on campus.

Perspectives are associated with *assumptions*—judgments, generalizations, or biases influenced by experience and values. For example, the perspective that there are many different successful ways to raise a family leads to assumptions such as "Single-parent homes can provide nurturing environments" and "Same-sex couples can rear well-adjusted children." Having a particular experience with single-parent homes or same-sex couples can build or reinforce a perspective.

Assumptions often hide within questions and statements, blocking you from considering information in different ways. Take this classic puzzler as an example: "Which came first, the chicken or the egg?" Thinking about this question, most people assume that the egg is a chicken egg. If you think past that assumption and come up with a new idea—such as, the egg is a dinosaur egg—then the obvious answer is that the egg came first!

Examining perspectives and assumptions is important for two reasons. First, they often affect your perception of the validity of materials you read and research. Second, your own perspectives and assumptions can cloud your interpretation of the information you encounter.

Perspective and assumptions in information. Being able to determine the perspectives that underlie materials will help you separate biased from unbiased information. For example, the conclusions in two articles on federal versus state government control of education may differ radically if one appears in a politically conservative publication and one appears in a liberal publication. Comparing those articles will require that you understand and take into account the conservative and liberal perspectives on government's role in education. You may even want to acknowledge, depending on the situation, the possibility of skewed information coming from a source because of a biased perspective.

Assumptions often affect the validity of materials you read and research. A historical Revolutionary War document that originated in the colonies, for example, may assume that the rebellion against the British was entirely justified and leave out information to the contrary. Clearly understanding such a document means separating the assumptions from the facts.

Personal perspectives and assumptions. Your own preferences, values, and prejudices—which influence your perspective—can affect how accurately you view information. A student who thinks that the death penalty is wrong, for example, may have a hard time analyzing the facts and arguments in an article that supports it. Or, in a research situation, he might use only materials that agree with his perspective.

Consider the perspectives and assumptions that might follow from your values. Then, when you have to analyze information, try to set them aside. "Anticipate your reactions and prejudices and then consciously resist their influence," says Colby Glass, professor of information research and philosophy at Palo Alto College.[6]

In addition to helping you analyze accurately, opening yourself to new perspectives will help you build knowledge. The more you know, the more information you have to work with as you move through life and encounter new problems and decisions. Come to school ready to hear, read, and discuss new ideas; think about their merits; and make informed decisions about what you believe. If you open up your mind to new information, you may be surprised to find yourself agreeing with ideas you would not have imagined accepting before.

Evaluate Information

You've gathered and analyzed your information. You have examined its components, its evidence, its validity, its perspective, and any underlying assumptions. Now, based on an examination of evidence and careful analysis, you *evaluate* whether an idea or a piece of information is important or unimportant, applicable or trivial, strong or weak, and why. You then set aside what is not useful and use the rest to form an opinion, a possible solution, or a decision.

For example, you're working on a presentation on the effects of television on young children. You've gathered information that relates to your topic, come up with an idea, and analyzed whether the information supports this idea. Now you evaluate all of the evidence, presenting what's useful in an organized, persuasive way. Another example: In creating a resume, you decide which information to include that will generate the most interest in potential employers and present you in the best light possible.

See Key 3.2 for some questions you can ask to build and use critical-thinking skills.

Key 3.2   Ask questions like these in order to think critically.

To gather information, ask:	▪ What requirements does my goal have?
	▪ What kinds of information do I need to meet my goal?
	▪ What information is available?
	▪ Where and when is it available? Where and when can I get to it?
	▪ Of the sources I found, which ones will best help me achieve my goal?
To analyze, ask:	▪ What are the parts of this information?
	▪ What is similar to this information? What is different?
	▪ What are the reasons for this? Why did this happen?
	▪ What ideas or themes emerge from this material?
	▪ How would you categorize this information?
	▪ What conclusions can you make about this information?
To see if examples support an idea, ask:	▪ What examples, or evidence, support the idea?
	▪ Does the evidence make sense?
	▪ Does the evidence support the idea/claim?
	▪ Is this evidence key information that I need to answer my question?
	▪ Are there examples that might disprove the idea/claim?
To distinguish fact from opinion, ask:	▪ Do the words in this information signal fact or opinion? (See Key 3.1)
	▪ What is the source of this information? Is the source reliable?
	▪ How does this information compare to other facts or opinions?
	▪ If this is an opinion, is it supported by facts?
	▪ How can I use this fact or opinion?
To examine perspectives and assumptions, ask:	▪ Who is the author? What perspectives might this person have?
	▪ What might be emphasized or left out as a result of the perspective?
	▪ How could I consider this information from a different perspective?
	▪ What assumptions might lie behind this statement or material?
	▪ How could I prove, or disprove, an assumption?
	▪ What contradictory assumptions might be equally valid?
	▪ How might a personal perspective or assumption affect the way I see this material?
To evaluate, ask:	▪ Do I agree with this information?
	▪ Does this information fit what I'm trying to prove or accomplish?
	▪ Is this information strong or weak, and why?
	▪ How important, or applicable, is this information?
	▪ Which ideas or pieces of information would I choose to focus on?

Adapted from www-ed.fnal.gov/trc/tutorial/taxonomy.html (Richard Paul, *Critical Thinking: How to Prepare Students for a Rapidly Changing World,* 1993) and from www.kcmetro.edu/longview/ctac/blooms.htm, Barbara Fowler, Longview Community College, "Bloom's Taxonomy and Critical Thinking."

ASSESS AND BUILD YOUR CRITICAL THINKING SKILLS

This is a two-part exercise: Part I provides insight into your ability as a critical thinker, and Part II helps you build your skill.

Part I: Assess yourself. How do you perceive yourself as a critical thinker? For each statement, circle the number that feels right to you, from 1 for "least like me" to 5 for "most like me."

1. I tend to perform well on objective tests.   ① ② ③ ④ ⑤

2. People say I'm a "thinker," "brainy," "studious."   ① ② ③ ④ ⑤

3. I am not comfortable with gray areas—I prefer information to be laid out in black and white.   ① ② ③ ④ ⑤

4. In a group setting, I like to tackle the details of a problem.   ① ② ③ ④ ⑤

5. I sometimes overthink things and miss my moment of opportunity.   ① ② ③ ④ ⑤

Total your answers here: _____

If your total ranges from *5 to 12,* you consider your critical thinking skills to be *weak.*

If your total ranges from *13 to 19,* you consider your critical thinking skills to be *average.*

If your total ranges from *20 to 25,* you consider your critical thinking skills to be *strong.*

Part II: Use critical-thinking skills to analyze a statement. Thinking about this statement, answer the questions that follow.
"The Internet is the best place to find information about any topic."

Is this statement fact or opinion? Why? _____

_____

_____

What examples can you think of that support, or negate, this statement? _____

_____

_____

What perspective(s) are guiding this statement? _____

_____

_____

What assumption(s) underlie the statement? What effects might result from accepting these assumptions and therefore agreeing with the statement?

_____

_____

_____

As a result of your critical thinking, what is your evaluation of this statement?

_____

_____

_____

As important as critical thinking is, it can't stand alone. Pursuing your goals, in school and in the workplace, requires not just analyzing information but also thinking creatively about how to use what you've concluded from your analysis.

HOW CAN YOU IMPROVE YOUR CREATIVE THINKING SKILLS?

Some researchers define creativity as combining existing elements in an innovative way to create a new purpose or result. For example, in 1970 Spencer Silver, a researcher for the paper company 3M, created a weak adhesive; four years later, another 3M scientist, Arthur Fry, used it to mark pages in a book. Post-it Notes are now an office staple. Others see creativity as the art of generating ideas from taking a fresh look at how things are related (noting what ladybugs eat inspired organic farmers to bring them in to consume crop-destroying aphids).[7] Still others define it as the ability to make unusual connections—to view information in quirky ways that bring about unique results.[8]

To think creatively is to actively generate new ideas that often go against conventional wisdom and may bring change. Consider how, in the 1940s, mathematician Grace Murray Hopper pioneered the effort to create computer languages that non-mathematicians could understand; her efforts opened the world of computers to a wide audience.

Creativity is not limited to inventions. For example, Smith College junior Meghan E. Taugher used her creative mind in two ways. First, she and her study group, as part of their class on electrical circuits, devised a solar-powered battery for a laptop computer. Second, her positive experience of putting learning to work in real life led her to generate an idea of a new major and career plan—engineering.[9]

Where does creativity come from? Some people, through luck or natural inclination, seem to come up with inspired ideas more often than others. However, creative thinking, like critical thinking, is a skill that can be developed. Creativity expert Roger von Oech says that mental flexibility is essential. "Like race-car drivers who shift in and out of different gears depending on where they are on the course," he says, you can enhance your creativity by learning to "shift in and out of different types of thinking depending on the needs of the situation at hand."[10]

The following actions will help you make those shifts and build your ability to think creatively. Note that, because creative ideas often pop up at random, writing them down as they arise will help you remember them. Keep a pen and paper by your bed, your PDA in your pocket, a notepad in your car, or a small tape recorder in your backpack so that you can grab ideas before they fade from your mind.

In the writing room at CollegeHumor.com, these writers experience how creative thinking can come from people brainstorming together.

Brainstorm

Brainstorming—letting your mind free-associate to come up with different ideas or answers—is also referred to as *divergent thinking*: You start with a question and then let your mind diverge—go in many different directions—in search of solutions. Think of brainstorming as *deliberate* creative thinking— you go into it fully aware that you are attempting to create new ideas. When you brainstorm, generate ideas without immediately considering how useful they are; evaluate their quality later. Brainstorming works well in groups because group members can become inspired by, and make creative use of, one another's ideas.[11]

One way to inspire ideas when brainstorming is to think of similar situations—in other words, to make *analogies*. For example, the discovery of Velcro is a product of analogy: When imagining how two pieces of fabric could stick to each other, the inventor thought of the similar situation of a bur sticking to clothing.

When you are brainstorming ideas, don't get hooked on finding the one right answer. Questions may have many "right answers"—or many answers that have degrees of usefulness. The more possibilities you generate, the better your chance of finding the best one. Make sure to write down all ideas so that you don't forget them. Also, don't stop the process when you think you have the best answer—keep going until you are out of steam. You never know what may come up in those last gasps of creative energy.[12]

Take a New and Different Look

Just because everyone believes something doesn't make it so; just because something "has always been that way" doesn't make it good or right. If no one ever questioned established opinion, people would still think the earth was flat. Changing how you look at a situation or problem can inspire creative ideas. Here are some ways to do it:

Challenge assumptions. In the late 1960s, conventional wisdom said that school provided education and television provided entertainment. Jim Henson, a pioneer in children's television, asked, "Why can't we use TV to educate young children?" From that question, the characters of Sesame Street, and eventually a host of other educational programs, were born.

Shift your perspective. Try on new perspectives by asking others for their views, reading about new ways to approach situations, or deliberately going with the opposite of your first instinct.[13] Then use those perspectives to inspire creativity. For your English lit course, analyze a novel from the point of view of one of the main characters. For political science, craft a position paper for a presidential or senatorial candidate. Perception puzzles are a fun way to experience how looking at something in a new way can bring a totally different idea (see Key 3.3).

Ask "what if" questions. Set up hypothetical environments in which new ideas can grow: "What if I knew I couldn't fail?" "What if I had unlimited money or time?" Ideas will emerge from your "what if" questions. For example, the founders of Seeds of Peace, faced with generations of conflict in the Middle East, asked: What if Israeli and Palestinian teens met at a summer camp in Maine so that the next generation has greater understanding and respect than the last? And what if follow-up programs and reunions are set up to cement friendships so that relationships change the politics of the Middle East? Based on the ideas that came up, they created an organization to prepare teenagers from the Middle East with the leadership skills needed to coexist peacefully.

Key 3.3 Use perception puzzles to experience a shift in perspective.

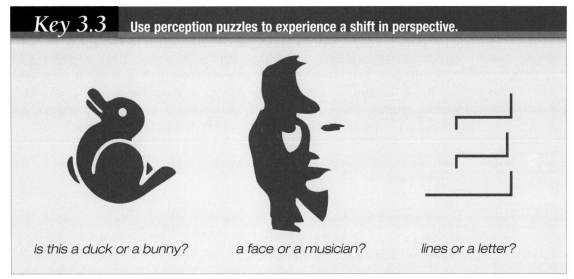

is this a duck or a bunny?   a face or a musician?   lines or a letter?

Source for face puzzle: "Sara Nader" illustration from *Mind Sights* by Roger Shepard. Copyright 1990 by Roger Shepard. Reprinted by permission of Henry Holt & Company, LLC.

Set the Stage for Creativity

Use these strategies to give yourself the best possible chance at generating creative ideas.

Choose, or create, environments that free your mind. Find places that energize you. Play music that moves you. Paint your study walls your favorite color. Seek out people who inspire you.[14]

Be curious. Try something you consider new and different: Take a course that has nothing to do with your major, try a new sport or game, listen to a new genre of music, read a magazine or book that you've never seen before, get to know someone outside of your circle of friends. Try something you don't think you would like, in order to see if you had misjudged your reaction. Seeking out new experiences and ideas will broaden your knowledge, giving you more raw materials with which to build creative ideas.[15]

Give yourself time to "sit" with a question. American society values speed, so much so that to say someone is "quick" is to consider that person intelligent.[16] Equating speed with intelligence can stifle creativity, because many creative ideas come when you allow time for thoughts to percolate. Take breaks when figuring out a problem. Take the pressure off by getting some exercise, napping, talking with a friend, working on something else, doing something fun. Creative ideas often come when you give your brain permission to "leave the job" for a while.[17]

Believe in yourself as a creative thinker. While it is normal to want critical approval and success for your creative efforts, you may not get it right away, especially if your ideas break new ground. When Gustav Mahler's Symphony No. 2—the Resurrection Symphony—was performed in 1910, critics walked out of the concert hall because of its innovative sound. Today, the Resurrection Symphony is considered one of the formative compositions of its era. Like Mahler, you must believe in your creative expression, no matter what others say. Critics, after all, can be wrong or simply a step or two behind.

Take Risks

Creative breakthroughs can come from sensible risk taking.

Fly in the face of convention. Entrepreneur Michael Dell turned tradition on its ear when he took a "tell me what you want and I will build it for you"

Key 3.4	Ask questions like these in order to jump-start creative thinking.
To brainstorm, ask:	■ What do I want to accomplish? ■ What are the craziest ideas I can think of? ■ What are 10 ways that I can reach my goal? ■ What ideas or strategies have worked before and how can I apply them? ■ How else can this be done?
To shift your perspective, ask:	■ How has this always been done—and what would be a different way? ■ What is another way to look at this situation? ■ How can I approach this task from a completely new angle? ■ How would someone else do this? How would they view this? ■ What if . . . ?
To set the stage for creativity, ask:	■ Where, and with whom, do I feel relaxed and inspired? ■ What music helps me think out of the box? ■ When in the day or night am I most likely to experience a flow of creative ideas? ■ What do I think would be new and interesting to try, to see, to read? ■ What is the most outrageous outcome of a situation that I can imagine?
To take risks, ask:	■ What is the conventional way of doing this? What would be a totally different way? ■ What would be a risky approach to this problem or question? ■ What choice would people caution me about and why? ■ What is the worst that can happen if I take this risk? What is the best? ■ What have I learned from this mistake?

approach to computer marketing instead of a "build it and they will buy it" approach. The possibility of failure did not stop him from risking money, time, energy, and reputation to achieve a truly unique and creative goal.

Let mistakes be okay. Open yourself to the learning that comes from not being afraid to mess up. When Dr. Hunter—successful inventor of the drug-coated coronary stent—and his company failed to develop a particular treatment for multiple sclerosis, he said, "You have to celebrate the failures. If you send the message that the only road to career success is experiments that work, people won't ask risky questions, or get any dramatically new answers."[18]

As with critical thinking, asking questions powers creative thinking. See Key 3.4 for examples of the kinds of questions you can ask to get your creative juices flowing.

Go For It! BUILDING YOUR SKILLS

ACTIVE THINKING

SKILL | WILL | SELF-MGMT.

ASSESS AND BUILD YOUR CREATIVE THINKING SKILLS

This is a two-part exercise: Part I provides insight into your ability as a critical thinker, and Part II helps you build your skill.

Part I: Assess yourself. How do you perceive yourself as a creative thinker? For each statement, circle the number that feels right to you, from 1 for "least like me" to 5 for "most like me."

1. I tend to resist rules and regulations.   ① ② ③ ④ ⑤
2. People say I'm "expressive," "full of ideas," "innovative."   ① ② ③ ④ ⑤
3. I break out of my routine and find new experiences.   ① ② ③ ④ ⑤
4. In a group setting, I like to toss ideas into the ring.   ① ② ③ ④ ⑤
5. If you say something is too risky, I'm all for it.   ① ② ③ ④ ⑤

Total your answers here: _____

If your total ranges from *5 to 12,* you consider your creative thinking skills to be *weak.*

If your total ranges from *13 to 19,* you consider your creative thinking skills to be *average.*

If your total ranges from *20 to 25,* you consider your creative thinking skills to be *strong.*

Part II: Gather evidence of your creativity. Think about the past month; then, make a list of five creative acts you performed—small, earth-shattering, or anything in between.

1. _____
2. _____
3. _____
4. _____
5. _____

Now think of a situation for which you are currently trying to come up with an idea. It could be an essay that's due, a plan for studying for a test, a sticky situation with an instructor, etc. Briefly jot down two new ideas for how to deal with your situation.

1. _____
2. _____

Keep these in mind. You may want to use one soon!

When you have a problem to solve or decision to make, creative thinking allows you to generate possible solutions and choices, and critical thinking enables you to evaluate them. However, choices aren't enough and potential solutions must be tried out. You need an action plan in order to make the best solution or choice happen.

HOW CAN YOU USE YOUR THINKING SKILLS TO SOLVE PROBLEMS AND MAKE DECISIONS?

Since many on-paper academic problems—math problem sets, answering essay questions—can be solved with a fairly straightforward critical-thinking approach, it's easy to think that critical thinking alone is your ticket to success. However, real-world problems and decisions usually aren't so clear-cut, and the stakes are often higher. Your success in a sociology class, for example, may depend as much if not more on finding a way to get along with your instructor than it does on answering multiple-choice questions correctly.

Furthermore, academic knowledge on its own isn't enough to bring you success in the workplace. You need to be able to actively apply what you know to problems and decisions that come up periodically in your work. For example, while elementary education students may successfully quote child development facts on an exam, it won't mean much to their career success unless they can evaluate and address real children's needs in the classroom.

Now that you have an understanding of what it means to think critically and creatively, explore how to put your skills into action to solve problems and make decisions successfully. Problem solving and decision making follow similar paths. Both require you to identify and analyze a situation, generate possible solutions, choose one, follow through on it, and evaluate its success. Key 3.5 gives an overview of the paths, indicating how you think at each step.

Key 3.5	Solve problems and make decisions using a plan of action.	
PROBLEM SOLVING	**THINKING SKILL**	**DECISION MAKING**
Define the problem—recognize that something needs to change, identify what's happening, look for true causes.	**Step 1** **Analyze**	Define the decision—identify your goal (your need) and then construct a decision that will help you get it.
Analyze the problem—gather information, break it down into pieces, verify facts, look at perspectives and assumptions, evaluate information.	**Step 2** **Analyze**	Examine needs and motives—considering the layers of needs carefully, and be honest about what you really want.
Generate possible solutions—use creative strategies to think of ways you could address the causes of this problem.	**Step 3** **Create**	Name and/or generate different options—use creative questions to come up with choices that would fulfill your needs.
Evaluate solutions—look carefully at potential pros and cons of each, and choose what seems best.	**Step 4** **Evaluate**	Evaluate options—look carefully at potential pros and cons of each, and choose what seems best.
Put the solution to work—persevere, focus on results, and believe in yourself as you go for your goal.	**Step 5** **Choose and Act**	Act on your decision—go down the path and stay on target.
Evaluate how well the solution worked—look at the effects of what you did.	**Step 6** **Re-evaluate**	Evaluate the success of your decision—look at whether it accomplished what you had hoped.
In the future, apply what you've learned—use this solution, or a better one, when a similar situation comes up again.	**Step 7** **Apply Results**	In the future, apply what you've learned—make this choice, or a better one, when a similar decision comes up again.

Key 3.6	How problems and decisions may differ.	
SITUATION	**YOU HAVE A PROBLEM IF . . .**	**YOU NEED TO MAKE A DECISION IF . . .**
Planning summer activities	Your low GPA means you need to attend summer school—and you've already accepted a summer job.	You've been accepted into two summer abroad internship programs.
Declaring a major	It's time to declare but you don't have all the prerequisites for the major you want.	There are three majors that appeal to you and you qualify for them all.
Relationships with instructors	You are having trouble following the lecture style of a particular instructor.	The Intro to Psychology course you want to take has seven sections taught by different instructors; you have to choose one.

How do you choose which path to follow? Understanding the differences between problem solving and decision making will help:

- Problem solving generally requires more focus on coming up with possible solutions. In contrast, when you face a decision, your choices are often determined.
- Problem solving aims to remove or counteract negative effects. In contrast, decision making aims to fulfill a need.

See Key 3.6 for some examples. Remember, too, that whereas all problem solving requires you to make a decision—when you decide on a solution—only some decision making requires you to solve a problem.

Solving a Problem

A problem exists when a situation has negative effects. Recognizing that there is a problem—being aware of those effects—is essential before you can begin to solve it. In other words, your first move is to go from the effects—"I'm unhappy/uneasy/angry"—to determining why: "My schedule is overwhelming me." "I'm over my head in this course." "My credit card debt is out of control." Then you begin the problem-solving process in earnest.

What happens if you don't solve a problem effectively? Take for example a student having an issue with an instructor. He may get into an argument with the instructor during class time. He may stop showing up to class. He may not make an effort with assignments. All of these choices have negative consequences for him.

Now look at how this student might work through this problem using his critical and creative thinking skills. Key 3.7 shows how his effort can pay off.

As you go through the problem-solving process, keep these tips in mind.

Use probing questions to define problems. Focus on causes. If you are not happy in a class, for example, you could ask questions like these:

- What do I think about when I feel unhappy?
- Do my feelings involve my instructor? My classmates?
- Is the subject matter difficult? The volume of work too much?
- Is my attitude toward just this one class in particular, or toward school in general?

Chances are that how you answer one or more of these questions may lead to a clear definition—and ultimately to the right solution.

Analyze carefully. Gather all the information you can, so that you can consider the situation comprehensively. Consider what you can learn from how the problem is similar to, or different from, other problems. Clarify facts. Note your own perspective, and ask others for theirs. Make sure you are not looking at the problem through the lens of an assumption.

Generate possible solutions based on causes, **not effects**. Addressing a cause provides a lasting solution, whereas "fixing" an effect cannot. Say, for example, that your shoulder hurts when you use your computer. Getting a friend to massage it is a nice but temporary solution, because the pain returns whenever you go back to work. Changing the height of your keyboard and mouse is a better idea, because it eliminates the cause of your pain. As you consider possible solutions, ask questions:

- What do I know that might apply to this situation?
- What have I seen or heard about what others have done that might help here?
- How does this situation compare to past situations I've been involved in? What has worked, or not worked, before?

Be comprehensive with your final evaluation and let it lead you to future action. It's easy to skip the evaluation step when something is over and done with—but don't be tempted. From looking at how things went, you

Key 3.7 | Examine a problem-solving process in action.

DEFINE PROBLEM HERE	ANALYZE THE PROBLEM
I don't like my Freshman Composition instructor	We have different views and personality types— I don't feel respected or heard. I'm not interested in being there and my grades are suffering from my lack of motivation.

Use boxes below to list possible solutions:

POTENTIAL POSITIVE EFFECTS	SOLUTION #1	POTENTIAL NEGATIVE EFFECTS
List for each solution: Don't have to deal with that instructor Less stress	Drop the course	*List for each solution:* Grade gets entered on my transcript I'll have to take the course eventually; it's required for my major

	SOLUTION #2	
Getting credit for the course Feeling like I've honored a commitment	Put up with it until the end of the semester	Stress every time I'm there Lowered motivation Probably not such a good final grade

	SOLUTION #3	
A chance to express myself Could get good advice An opportunity to ask direct questions of the instructor	Schedule meetings with advisor and instructor	Have to face instructor one-on-one Might just make things worse

Now choose the solution you think is best . . .   . . . circle it and make it happen.

ACTUAL POSITIVE EFFECTS	ACTION TAKEN	ACTUAL NEGATIVE EFFECTS
List for each solution: Got some helpful advice from advisor Talking in person with the instructor actually promoted a fairly honest discussion I won't have to take the course again	I scheduled and attended meetings with both advisor and instructor, and opted to stick with the course.	*List for each solution:* The discussion was difficult and sometimes tense I still don't know how much learning I'll retain from this course

RE-EVALUATE: Was it a good or bad solution?
The solution has improved things. I'll finish the course, and even though the instructor and I aren't the best of friends, we have a mutual understanding now. I feel more respected and more willing to put my time into the course.

can learn valuable information that will help you repeat effective actions and avoid ineffective ones in the future. Ask questions like these:

- What worked well, or not so well, about my choice?
- What do I know I would do again? Why?
- What would I change if I had to do it all over again? Why?
- What effect did my actions have on others?

Making a Decision

Psychologists who have studied decision making have learned that many random factors influence the choices people make. For example, you may choose a major, not because you love the subject, but because you think your parents will approve of it. The goal is to make well-considered decisions despite factors that may derail your thinking.

What happens when you make important decisions too quickly? Consider a student trying to decide whether to transfer schools. If she makes her decision based on a reason that ultimately is not important enough to her, she may regret her choice later—most likely because she didn't consider cause and effect carefully when deciding.

Now look at how this student might make a well-considered decision. Key 3.8 shows how she worked through the parts of the process.

As you use the steps in Key 3.8 to make a decision, remember these hints.

Look at the given options—then try to think of more. Some decisions have a given set of options. For example, your school may allow you to major, double major, or major and minor. When you are making your decision, however, you may be able to brainstorm with an advisor to come up with more options—such as an interdisciplinary major you create on your own. As with problem solving, consider similar situations you've been in or heard about, what decisions were made, and what resulted from those decisions.

Think about how your decision affects others. For example, the student thinking about a transfer considers the impact on friends and family. What she concludes about that impact may play a role in her decision about when she transfers and even the school she chooses.

Gather perspectives. Talk with others who have made similar decisions. There are more ways of doing things than one brain can possibly imagine on its own.

Look at the long-term effects. As with problem solving, the final evaluation is a crucial part of the process. For important decisions, do a short-term

Key 3.8   Examine a decision-making process in action.

DEFINE THE DECISION	EXAMINE NEEDS AND MOTIVES
Whether or not to transfer schools	I attend a small private college. My father has changed jobs and can no longer afford my tuition. My goal is to become a physical therapist, so I need a school with a full physical therapy program. My family needs to cut costs. I need to transfer credits.

Use boxes below to list possible solutions:

POTENTIAL POSITIVE EFFECTS	CHOICE #1	POTENTIAL NEGATIVE EFFECTS
List for each solution: No need to adjust to a new place or new people Ability to continue course work as planned	Continue at the current college	List for each solution: Need to finance most of my tuition and costs on my own Difficult to find time for a job Might not qualify for aid
Opportunity to connect with some high school friends Cheaper tuition and room costs Credits will transfer	CHOICE #2 Transfer to a state college	Need to earn some money or get financial aid Physical therapy program is small and not very strong
Many physical therapy courses available School is close so I could live at home and save room costs Reasonable tuition; credits will transfer	CHOICE #3 Transfer to the community college	No personal contacts there that I know of Less independence if I live at home No bachelor's degree available

Now choose the solution you think is best . . .   . . . circle it and make it happen.

ACTUAL POSITIVE EFFECTS	ACTION TAKEN	ACTUAL NEGATIVE EFFECTS
List for each solution: Money saved Opportunity to spend time on studies rather than on working to earn tuition money Availability of classes I need	Go to community college for two years; then transfer to a four-year school to get a B.A. and complete physical therapy course work.	List for each solution: Loss of some independence Less contact with friends

RE-EVALUATE: Was it a good or bad solution?

I'm satisfied with the decision. It can be hard being at home at times, but my parents are adjusting to my independence and I'm trying to respect their concerns. With fewer social distractions, I'm really getting my work done. Plus the financial aspect of the decision is ideal.

evaluation and another evaluation after a period of time. Examine whether your decision has sent you down a path that has continued to bring positive effects.

Work Together   **BUILDING YOUR SKILLS**

ACTIVE
THINKING

SKILL   WILL   SELF-MGMT.

SOLVE A PROBLEM

On a 3-by-5 card or a plain sheet of paper, each student in the class writes an academic problem—this could be a fear, a challenge, or a roadblock. Students hand these in without names. The instructor writes the list up on the board.

Divide into groups of two to four. Each group chooses one problem to work on (try not to have two groups working on the same problem). Use the empty problem-solving flowchart (Key 3.9) to fill in your work.

1. **Define the problem.** As a group, look at the negative effects and state your problem specifically. Then, explore and write down the causes.
2. **Examine the problem.** Pick it apart to see what's happening. Gather information from all group members, verify facts, go beyond assumptions.
3. **Generate possible solutions.** From the most likely causes of the problem, derive possible solutions. Record all the ideas that group members offer. After 10 minutes or so, each group member should choose one possible solution to evaluate independently.
4. **Evaluate each solution.** In thinking independently through the assigned solution, each group member should (a) weigh the positive and negative effects, (b) consider similar problems, and (c) describe how the solution affects the causes of the problem. Evaluate your assigned solution. Is it a good one? Will it work?
5. **Choose a solution.** Group members then come together, share observations and recommendations, and take a vote: Which solution is the best? You may have a tie or may want to combine two different solutions. Try to find the solution that works for most of the group. Then, together come up with a plan for how you would put your solution to work.
6. **Evaluate your solution.** As a group, share and discuss what you had individually imagined the positive and negative effects of this solution would be. Try to come to agreement on how you think the solution would work out.

Key 3.9   Work through a problem using this flowchart.

DEFINE PROBLEM HERE

ANALYZE THE PROBLEM

Use boxes below to list possible solutions:

POTENTIAL POSITIVE EFFECTS

SOLUTION #1

POTENTIAL NEGATIVE EFFECTS

List for each solution:

List for each solution:

SOLUTION #2

SOLUTION #3

Now choose the solution you think is best . . .   *. . . circle it and make it happen.*

ACTUAL POSITIVE EFFECTS

ACTION TAKEN

ACTUAL NEGATIVE EFFECTS

List for each solution:

List for each solution:

RE-EVALUATE: Was it a good or bad solution?

As you engage your thinking skills on the road to success, keep these final tips in mind.

- **Stay motivated.** Work to persevere when you face a problem. Get started on achieving results instead of dwelling on exactly how to start. Translate thoughts into concrete actions.

- **Make the most of your personal strengths.** What you've learned in Chapter 2 will help you see what you do best. Apply those strengths when you encounter problems and decisions.

- **Manage time and tasks effectively.** Use what you know from Chapter 1 to plan your time in a way that promotes goal accomplishment. Avoid the pitfalls of procrastination. Accurately gauge what you can handle—don't take on too many projects, or too few.

- **Learn from your missteps.** Examine what happened when things go wrong. Learn from the experience and continue to apply what you have learned so that you don't repeat a mistake.

- **Focus on the goal.** Keep your eye on the big picture and complete what you've planned, rather than getting lost in the details or side-tracked by distractions.

- **Believe in yourself.** Have faith in your ability to achieve what you set out to do.

Let the obstacles come, as they will for everyone, in all aspects of life. You can face and overcome them with the power of your critical and creative thinking.

"No problem can stand the assault of sustained thinking."

VOLTAIRE (FRANÇOIS-MARIE AROUET)
French writer and philosopher

Building Skill, Will, and Self-Management

Monitoring Your Progress

Test Competence: Measure What You've Learned

MULTIPLE CHOICE. *Circle or highlight the answer that seems to fit best.*

1. The questioning process is central to critical thinking because
   A. it requires that you reword new information in question form.
   B. it shows others your willingness to ask questions.
   C. it helps you transform raw data into information you can use.
   D. none of the above.

2. Statements of opinion include all of the following except:
   A. value judgments.
   B. abstract words that are hard to define.
   C. concrete words or measurable statistics.
   D. absolute qualifiers.

3. Statements of fact include all of the following except:
   A. actual people, places, objects, or events.
   B. description of current events in exact terms.
   C. non-emotional words.
   D. abstract words that are complicated to define.

4. Assumptions are
   A. your direct observations of how people relate to one another.
   B. value-based evaluations or generalizations.
   C. value-free evaluations that are linked to observations of cause and effect.
   D. attitudes that only prejudiced people hold.

5. An example of an absolute qualifier would be

   A. all.

   B. some.

   C. may.

   D. sometimes.

6. _____ means deciding whether an idea or a piece of information is important or unimportant, strong or weak, and why.

   A. Logic

   B. Evaluation

   C. Bias

   D. Clarification

7. A person who can devise clever new uses for an everyday item has developed _____ thinking skills.

   A. creative

   B. analytical

   C. critical

   D. ethical

8. Advertising agencies often employ what creative thinking strategy to come up with catchy jingles and effective ad campaigns?

   A. analogy

   B. hypothesis

   C. brainstorming

   D. assessment

9. _____ generally requires a focus on coming up with possible solutions and aims to remove or counteract negative effects.

   A. Decision making

   B. Problem solving

   C. Brainstorming

   D. Hypothesizing

10. In _____, the choices are often determined and you are trying to fulfill a need.

   A. problem solving

   B. brainstorming

   C. hypothesizing

   D. decision making

TRUE/FALSE. *Place a T or an F beside each statement to indicate whether you think it is true or false.*

_____ 1. Defining your purpose is the first step when preparing to analyze information or a situation.

_____ 2. *Perspective* is a characteristic way of thinking about people, situations, events, and ideas.

_____ 3. Every question has one right answer.

_____ 4. Accepting and exploring mistakes is part of successful creative thinking.

_____ 5. The problem-solving process is complete when you choose a solution and put it to work.

Target and Achieve a Goal

Commit to one specific thinking strategy from this chapter to improve your study skills.

Name the strategy here: _____

_____

Describe your goal—what you want to gain by using this strategy. _____

_____

_____

_____

Describe how you plan to use this strategy through the semester to achieve this goal.

_____

_____

_____

Building Your Skills

Brain Power: Build Vocabulary Fitness

Here is a selection from the current media. Read the material, paying special attention to the context of the vocabulary words shown in bold type. Then choose the correct definition for each word in the table on the next page. Use a dictionary to check your answers. Finally, on a separate sheet, use each vocabulary word in a sentence of your own to solidify your understanding.

Attorney Louise Phipps Senft, an expert mediator, offers an approach to mediation that focuses on each party understanding the other's point of view.

It may be true that to err is human and to forgive divine. But to sit down and resolve a conflict between two parties doesn't always require an act of divine intervention—sometimes it just takes a **neutral** third party. Or so the work of Louise Phipps Senft (Psychology '83) seems to prove.

Voted Baltimore's Best Mediator by *Baltimore Magazine,* Senft, an attorney, founded the Baltimore Mediation Center in 1993. Since then, she has provided both **mediation** services and training to thousands of individuals in family, employment, business, board, church, university, and government settings.

Her approach to mediation and conflict resolution is far from traditional. Senft believes the key to resolving conflicts, whether between individuals or corporate **entities,** is for those involved to have the opportunity to understand the other party's point of view. This others-consciousness, which she calls a "relational worldview," is at the heart of the **transformative** framework approach to mediation that she and other scholars have developed.

Where traditional mediation aims **chiefly** to solve problems and settle disputes, the transformative framework approach focuses on the quality of the **dialogue.** The process involves building the strength of the participants and giving them the chance to see the situation as a whole rather than from one perspective. The conflict usually resolves as a natural by-product. Merely "fixing" the problem is never the mediator's goal.

Source: Heather Ferngren Morton, "We Can Work It Out," *Arts & Sciences,* vol. 23, no. 1, January 2005, The College and Graduate School of Arts & Sciences at the University of Virginia.

Circle the word or phrase that best defines each term as it is used in the excerpt.

VOCABULARY WORDS	A	B	C
1. neutral (adj.)	unallied	genderless	negative
2. mediation (noun)	talk	intervention	trance
3. entities (noun)	companies	units	ideas
4. transformative (adj.)	electric	involving cooperation	involving change
5. chiefly (adv.)	carefully	first	especially
6. dialogue (noun)	conversation	scene	argument

Get to the Root

Every time you learn a Greek or Latin root, you increase your ability to recognize English vocabulary words that include that root and to figure out their meaning. Grow your vocabulary by studying this root and its related words, writing in two more words from the same root, and including definitions for both new words.

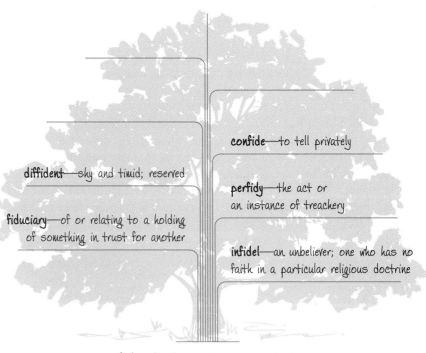

confide—to tell privately

diffident—shy and timid; reserved

perfidy—the act or
an instance of treachery

fiduciary—of or relating to a holding
of something in trust for another

infidel—an unbeliever; one who has no
faith in a particular religious doctrine

fid—faith, trust, origin: Latin

Investigate Using Research Navigator

Access Research Navigator using the Internet address shown on page 32. Then sign on to the service using your Login Name and Password. Look at the *Link Library* area. Scrolling down the list of topics, choose one career area or field that interests you and hit "go." You will come to a collection of links grouped according to the initial letter of each link topic. Use what's available through the letter links to find informational articles on at least two people who are or have been prominent in this area/field. After reading these articles, answer the following:

- What makes each of these individuals a critical thinker? Give one or more examples.
- What makes each of these individuals a creative thinker? What idea or product did each create?
- What inspires you personally about the thinking abilities and achievements of one or more of these people? Do you have any further interest in this area/field as a result of reading their stories?

Building Will and Self-Awareness

ACTIVE
THINKING

SKILL   WILL   SELF-MGMT.

Make Responsible Choices

Answer the following question on a separate piece of paper or in a journal.

Think about a decision you made at school or at work that, looking back, you wish you had handled differently.

- Describe what the decision was and what option you chose. What did not feel right about this decision? What happened as a result?
- Describe what you would do if you could make the decision again. How could stronger critical and/or creative thinking have helped you reach a more successful outcome?
- What did you learn from your experience that you can apply to other decisions?

Chapter Summary

As you use the summary on pages 110–111 to review the concepts you learned in this chapter, focus also on its format—in this case a **think link**, in other chapters a formal outline, and in still others the Cornell system. As you become comfortable with the organization and style of these various formats, try using each of them to take class and reading notes, noting which approach works best for you in particular situations.

Endnotes

1. Vincent Ruggiero, *The Art of Thinking*, 2001, quoted in "Critical Thinking," Oregon State University [online]. Available: http://success.oregonstate.edu/study/learning.cfm (April 2004).

2. Richard Paul, "The Role of Questions in Thinking, Teaching, and Learning," The Center for Thinking and Learning, 1995 [online]. Available: www.critical thinking.org/University/univclass/roleofquest.html (April 2004).

3. "The Best Innovations Are Those That Come from Smart Questions," *The Wall Street Journal*, April 12, 2004, B1.

4. *Keys to Lifelong Learning Telecourse.* Dir. Mary Jane Bradbury. Videocassette. Intrepid Films, 2000.

5. Lawrence F. Lowery, "The Biological Basis of Thinking and Learning," 1998, Full Option Science System at the University of California at Berkeley [online]. Available: http://lhsfoss.org/newsletters/archive/pdfs/FOSS_BBTL.pdf (April 2004).

6. Colby Glass, "Strategies for Critical Thinking," March 1999 [online]. Available: www.accd.edu/pac/philosop/phil1301/ctstrategies.htm) (April 2004).

7. Charles Cave (August 1999). "Definitions of Creativity" [online]. Available: http://members.ozemail.com.au/~caveman/Creative/Basics/definitions.htm (April 2003).

8. Robert J. Sternberg, *Successful Intelligence*. New York: Plume, 1997, p. 189.

9. Elizabeth F. Farrell, "Engineering a Warmer Welcome for Female Students: The Discipline Tries to Stress Its Social Relevance, an Important Factor for Many Women," *The Chronicle of Higher Education*, February 22, 2002 [online]. Available: http://chronicle.com/weekly/v48/i24/24a03101.htm (March 2004).

10. Roger von Oech, *A Kick in the Seat of the Pants*. New York: Harper & Row, 1986, pp. 5–21.

11. Dennis Coon, *Introduction to Psychology: Exploration and Application*, 6th ed. St. Paul: West Publishing Company, 1992, p. 295.

12. Roger von Oech, *A Whack on the Side of the Head*. New York: Warner Books, 1990, pp. 11–168.

13. J. R. Hayes, *Cognitive Psychology: Thinking and Creating*. Homewood, IL: Dorsey, 1978.

14. Sternberg, p. 219.

15. Adapted from T. Z. Tardif and R. J. Sternberg, "What Do We Know About Creativity?" in *The Nature of Creativity,* ed. R. J. Sternberg, 1988. London: Cambridge University Press.

16. Sternberg, p. 212.

17. Hayes.

18. "The Best Innovations Are Those That Come from Smart Questions," *The Wall Street Journal,* April 12, 2004, B1.

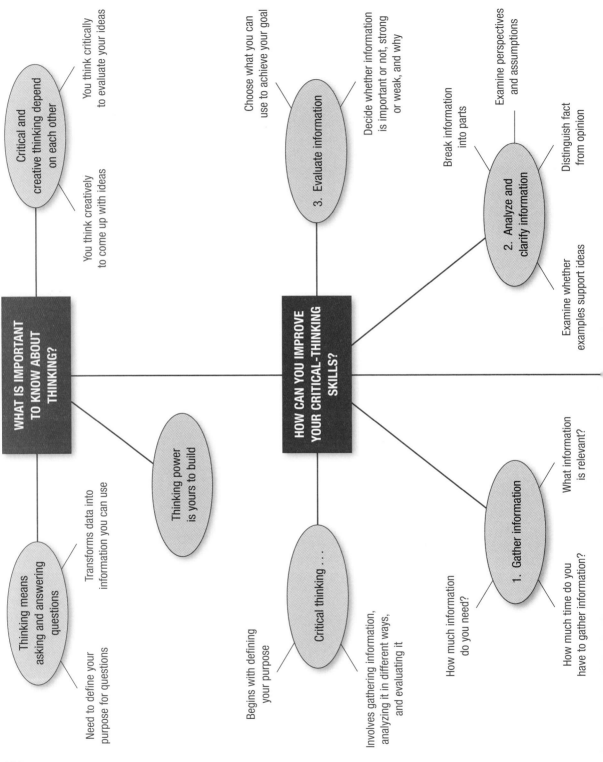

WHAT IS IMPORTANT TO KNOW ABOUT THINKING?

Critical and creative thinking depend on each other
- You think critically to evaluate your ideas
- You think creatively to come up with ideas

Thinking means asking and answering questions
- Transforms data into information you can use
- Need to define your purpose for questions

Thinking power is yours to build

HOW CAN YOU IMPROVE YOUR CRITICAL-THINKING SKILLS?

3. Evaluate information
- Choose what you can use to achieve your goal
- Decide whether information is important or not, strong or weak, and why

2. Analyze and clarify information
- Break information into parts
- Examine perspectives and assumptions
- Distinguish fact from opinion
- Examine whether examples support ideas

1. Gather information
- What information is relevant?
- How much information do you need?
- How much time do you have to gather information?

Critical thinking . . .
- Begins with defining your purpose
- Involves gathering information, analyzing it in different ways, and evaluating it

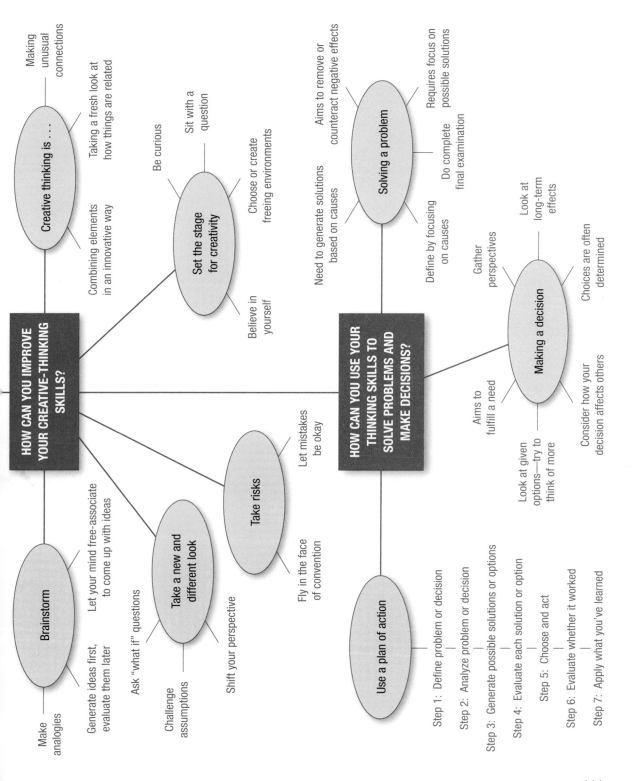

HOW CAN YOU IMPROVE YOUR CREATIVE-THINKING SKILLS?

Creative thinking is . . .
- Making unusual connections
- Taking a fresh look at how things are related
- Combining elements in an innovative way

Set the stage for creativity
- Be curious
- Sit with a question
- Choose or create freeing environments
- Believe in yourself

Brainstorm
- Make analogies
- Generate ideas first, evaluate them later
- Let your mind free-associate to come up with ideas
- Ask "what if" questions

Take a new and different look
- Challenge assumptions
- Shift your perspective

Take risks
- Let mistakes be okay
- Fly in the face of convention

HOW CAN YOU USE YOUR THINKING SKILLS TO SOLVE PROBLEMS AND MAKE DECISIONS?

Solving a problem
- Aims to remove or counteract negative effects
- Requires focus on possible solutions
- Do complete final examination
- Define by focusing on causes
- Need to generate solutions based on causes

Making a decision
- Gather perspectives
- Look at long-term effects
- Choices are often determined
- Consider how your decision affects others
- Look at given options—try to think of more
- Aims to fulfill a need

Use a plan of action
- Step 1: Define problem or decision
- Step 2: Analyze problem or decision
- Step 3: Generate possible solutions or options
- Step 4: Evaluate each solution or option
- Step 5: Choose and act
- Step 6: Evaluate whether it worked
- Step 7: Apply what you've learned

Active Thinking

MONITORING YOUR PROGRESS

Find Connections Among Ideas

The following multiple-choice, true/false, fill-in-the-blank, matching, and essay questions reinforce the concepts you learned in the three chapters that make up Part I, *Knowledge, Skills, and Preparation: Where the Future Begins*. These questions differ from the end-of-chapter objective quizzes in an important way. Instead of focusing on concepts in individual chapters, they encourage you to compare and integrate material from *different* chapters as you find ways to connect ideas. Recognizing relationships among ideas is essential to active learning because it builds critical thinking skills, adds meaning to information, and makes it more likely that you will retain what you learn.

MULTIPLE CHOICE. *Circle or highlight the answer that seems to fit best.*

1. Being aware of your learning style is important for all of the following reasons except:
   A. it will prepare you to be part of a rapidly changing working world that demands lifelong learning.
   B. it will help you choose a major.
   C. it will give you a reliable, unchanging identity as a learner.
   D. it will help you try out and select the study strategies that work best for you.

2. One important part of using critical thinking skills to choose your best study strategies is:
   A. evaluating whether a given strategy produces positive or negative results for you.
   B. making a list of strategies that are available to you.
   C. brainstorming ideas about new study strategies.
   D. seeing what strategies match your dominant learning styles.

3. As a time manager, a thinker-dominant, logical-mathematical learner might be:

A. consistently late to class.

B. always prompt, or perhaps even early, to appointments.

C. loose with scheduling; sometimes late, sometimes early.

D. usually on time but not conscientious about calling when late.

4. If you were to use the creative strategy "choose or create new environments" in order to reduce academic stress, you might:

A. brainstorm ideas about ways to get exercise during study break time.

B. decorate your primary study area with colors and pictures that inspire you.

C. try study strategies you've never used before.

D. challenge your assumptions about what causes you stress.

5. Knowing how to manage goals, time, and stress forms the basis for academic success because

A. studying is a process that forces you to examine your personal style.

B. effective studying demands that you stay in control of your time.

C. studying is often done in groups, and this knowledge will help you adapt to the styles of other group members.

D. you are responsible for your work and your progress in the college environment.

TRUE/FALSE *Place a T or an F beside each statement to indicate whether you think it is true or false.*

_____ 1. The questioning process that is at the heart of critical thinking is incompatible with effective time management.

_____ 2. Academic integrity is essential for retaining what you learn and being able to use that knowledge in your work and personal life.

_____ 3. Study skills are the most important factor in being a strategic learner.

_____ 4. Once you understand the steps of the problem-solving process, you may be less likely to procrastinate.

_____ 5. Self-awareness implies a self-centered approach that will most likely interfere with teamwork.

FILL-IN-THE-BLANK. *Complete the following sentences with the appropriate word(s) or phrase(s) that best reflect what you learned in Part I. Choose from the items that follow each sentence.*

1. Being responsible for your work is part of the _____ aspect of strategic learning. (skill building, will and self-awareness, self-management)

2. You will be more motivated to achieve a long-term goal if you base it on your _____. (short-term goals, values, talents)

3. Self-esteem, a crucial part of the will to learn, has two components: _____ and taking action. (working through roadblocks, thinking positively, teamwork)

4. Howard Gardner's theory of multiple intelligences recognizes _____ distinctive forms of intelligence. (8, 6, 2)

5. The more _____ the members of a team are, the more likely new ideas and options are to surface. (diverse, similar, focused)

6. It is important to set short-term goals that lead you step by step toward your _____ (personal mission, learning style, long-term goals).

7. Keeping your personal schedule written down will help you effectively manage your _____. (career options, time, money)

8. Through the process of _____, critical thinking enables you to transform raw data into information you can use (problem solving, memorization, questioning)

9. Various _____ may make up the structure of one person's _____. (evaluations/opinions, assumptions/perspective, perspectives/inventions)

10. _____ is often referred to as "divergent thinking." (Brainstorming, Taking risks, Questioning)

MATCHING. *Match each item in the left-hand column to an item in the right-hand column by writing the letter from the right that corresponds best to the number on the left.*

_____ 1. opinion

_____ 2. dyslexia

_____ 3. lecture

_____ 4. bodily-kinesthetic learners

_____ 5. naturalistic intelligence

_____ 6. priorities

_____ 7. procrastination

_____ 8. analogy

_____ 9. cause and effect

_____ 10. stress

A. people who have the ability to learn through bodily sensations

B. postponing a task until later

C. a comparison between two similar things or situations

D. a belief or judgment

E. ability to understand environmental features

F. the dominant method of classroom instruction

G. reasons and consequences

H. the way in which your mind and body react to pressure

I. personal decisions and actions that define what is important to you and how you will spend your time

J. a reading-related learning disability

ESSAY QUESTION. *Carefully read the following excerpt from* Psychology, *3rd ed., by Saul Kassin, a college textbook published by Prentice Hall, and then answer the essay question that follows. This exercise will help you focus on the meaning of the selection, apply your personal knowledge and experiences to the reading, organize your ideas, and communicate your thoughts effectively in writing.*

Before you begin writing your essay, it is a good idea to spend a few minutes planning. Try brainstorming possible approaches, writing a thesis statement, and jotting down your main thoughts in the form of an outline or think link. Because most essay tests are timed, limit the time you take to write your response to no more than one-half hour. This will force you to write quickly and effectively as it prepares you for actual test conditions.

WHAT PEOPLE DREAM ABOUT

In *Our Dreaming Mind*, Robert Van de Castle (1994) notes that dreams have always fascinated people. More than eight thousand years ago, the Assyrians believed that dreams were messages sent from evil spirits. Later, Egyptians believed they were messages sent by the gods. The Inuits of Hudson Bay and the Pantani of Malaysia believe that one's soul leaves the body during sleep and enters another world. Among the Kurds and Zulus, dreaming of an adulterous affair is considered an offense, and if you dream of receiving a gift, you must compensate the gift giver in waking life. In Western cultures, people assume that dreams, if properly analyzed, tell us something about the dreamer's past, present, or future. To some extent, then, dreams reflect a culture's beliefs, values, and concerns (Shulman & Stroumsa, 1999).

Over the years, psychologists and anthropologists have looked for common themes in what people from different cultures tend to dream about. Summarizing this research, G. William Domhoff (1996) notes that certain aspects of the dreams found in Western cultures are found elsewhere as well. For example, it appears that people everywhere dream more about acts of aggression than about friendship and kindness, and in these dreams, we are more likely to dream of being victims of aggression than the perpetrators. Certain gender differences in dream content also seem to be universal. For example, men dream more about aggression, while women dream more about acquaintances, friends, and family members.

Although there are cultural similarities in dream reports, Domhoff (1996) notes that there are also some striking differences that uniquely reflect each culture's beliefs, values, and social structures. In India, devout Hindus who live gender-segregated lives report having precious few sex characters in their dreams. In Japan, a "collective" society that places family and group interests ahead of those of the individual, people's dreams contain more human characters than are found in American dreams—and these characters are more likely to be familiar. Among the Yir Yomont hunters of Australia, men dream often of killing animals—and of sharing meat with familiar female characters and others. Clearly, what we dream about is shaped by our waking lives, which, in turn, is shaped by the invisible hand of culture.

Source: Excerpted from Saul Kassin, *Psychology,* 3rd ed., Upper Saddle River, NJ: Prentice Hall, 2001, p. 149. Reprinted with permission.

YOUR QUESTION. Describe a recent dream you remember or a dream you have had many times in the past. Discuss how your dream is consistent with or different from the ethnic or religious culture in your family and how it is consistent with or divergent from the general American culture. Based on your response, explain why you agree or disagree with the author's statement that "dreams reflect a culture's beliefs, values, and concerns."

Be Accountable for Your Goals from Part I

ACTIVE THINKING

SKILL • WILL • SELF-MGMT.

Look back at the goals you set in the *Target and Achieve a Goal* exercises at the ends of Chapters 1, 2, and 3. In the space provided below, write a short journal entry in which you assess your progress (use or continue on a separate piece of paper if you need more room). In your discussion, consider questions such as the following:

- Have you used the strategies you intended to use?
- What effect have these strategies had on your work?
- Have you achieved the goals you set? Why or why not?
- What is your plan going forward for these strategies and goals?

READING, UNDERSTANDING, AND REMEMBERING

MASTERING ESSENTIAL LEARNING SKILLS

Reading Comprehension, Vocabulary, and Speed

READING FASTER AND UNDERSTANDING MORE

Studying Textbooks and Course Materials

MASTERING CONTENT

Listening and Memory

TAKING IN AND REMEMBERING INFORMATION

4

Reading Comprehension, Vocabulary, and Speed

READING FASTER AND UNDERSTANDING MORE

While the reading and studying skills you've developed over time may have worked well enough to get you into college, they may not prepare you for the kind of complex, lengthy assignments you will face in the years ahead. To keep up with the sheer volume of material and to grasp what it all means, you need skills that improve your comprehension and pace. The material in this chapter will present active learning techniques to increase comprehension and build vocabulary while boosting speed. You may even experience an unexpected, pleasurable benefit—enjoying what you read.

In this chapter you will explore answers to the following questions:

- What will improve your reading comprehension?
- How can you set the stage for reading?
- How do you build a better vocabulary?
- How can you increase your reading speed?

WHAT WILL IMPROVE YOUR READING COMPREHENSION?

Reading is a process that requires you, the reader, to *make meaning* from written words—that is, to master concepts in a personal way. Your familiarity with a subject, your background and life experiences, and even your personal interpretation of words and phrases affect understanding.

Because these factors are different for everyone, reading experiences are unique. If, for example, your family owns a hardware store where you worked during summers, you will read a retailing chapter in a business text in the context of your background. While you are comparing text concepts to your family's business practices, most of your classmates are reading for basic vocabulary and concepts.

The goal of reading comprehension is complete understanding. This is a crucial skill in college, where you are asked to master material on your own and use what you learn as a foundation in upper-level courses. When you struggle through and master concepts that you considered impossible the first time you read them, you'll be proud of your ability to overcome obstacles and not give up. This pride will motivate you every time you read.

Following are attitudes and strategies that may help you tackle assignments.

Don't expect to master material on the first pass. Instead, create a multistep plan: On your first reading, your goal is to gain an overview of key concepts and interrelationships. On subsequent readings, you grasp ideas and relate them to what you already know. By your last reading, you master concepts and details and can apply the material to problems. (Chapter 5 will introduce the SQ3R reading technique, a multistep reading plan.)

Think positively. Instead of telling yourself that you cannot understand, think positively. Tell yourself: *I can learn this material. I am a good reader.*

Think critically. Ask yourself questions: Do I understand the sentence, paragraph, or chapter I just read? Are ideas and supporting evidence clear? Am I able to explain the material to someone else? Chapter 5 presents strategies for critical reading.

Build vocabulary. Lifelong learners never stop learning new words. The larger your vocabulary, the greater your understanding and the faster your reading speed.

Look for order and meaning in seemingly chaotic reading materials. Use SQ3R and critical reading strategies to discover patterns and connections.

Build knowledge through reading and studying. More than any other factor, what you already know before you read provides a context for new material.

HOW CAN YOU SET THE STAGE FOR READING?

On any given day, you may be faced with reading assignments like these:

- a textbook chapter on the history of South African apartheid (world history)
- an original research study on the relationship between sleep deprivation and the development of memory problems (psychology)
- the first 100 pages in John Steinbeck's classic novel, *The Grapes of Wrath* (American literature)
- a technical manual on the design of computer antivirus programs (computer science—software design)

This material is rigorous by anyone's standards. In fact, many students are surprised at how much reading there is in college, and that they are often expected to learn concepts that are never covered in class. Fortunately, strategies like the following will help you set the stage for reading success.

If you have a reading disability, if English is not your primary language, or if you have limited reading skills, seek out the support programs your college offers at reading and tutoring centers (see Chapter 2 for more on learning disabilities and support services). Your ability to succeed is linked to your ability to ask for help.

Take an Active Approach to Difficult Texts

Because college texts are generally written to challenge the intellect, even well-written texts may be tough going. Generally, the further you advance in your education and your career, the more complex required reading is likely to be. You may encounter concepts and terms that are foreign to you. This is often the case when assignments are from *primary sources*—original documents, including academic journal articles and scientific studies, rather than another writer's interpretation of these documents.

Some academic writing has earned the reputation of being difficult for the sake of difficulty—an observation that motivated George Orwell, the author of *1984* and *Animal Farm,* to write a parody of how a passage from the Old Testament would read if it were translated into academic prose (see Key 4.1).

Your challenge is to approach difficult material actively and positively. The following strategies will help:

Have an open mind. Be careful not to prejudge assignments as impossible or boring or a waste of time and energy before you begin.

Key 4.1   George Orwell demonstrates academic writing at its worst.

ECCLESIASTES 9:11

"I returned, and saw under the sun,

that the race is not to the swift,

nor the battle to the strong,

neither yet bread to the wise,

nor yet riches to men of understanding,

nor yet favor to men of skill;

but time and chance happeneth to them all."

GEORGE ORWELL'S PARODY OF ECCLESIASTES

"Objective consideration of contemporary phenomena compels the conclusion that success or failure in competitive activities exhibits no tendency to be commensurate with innate capacity, but that a considerable element of the unpredictable must invariably be taken into account."

Expect to go through difficult chapters more than once before you finally get it. One reading is almost never enough—especially when the material is complicated. You do not have to read and review the material all in one sitting. Breaks help things sink in.

Know that some texts require extra work and concentration. You may have to look back at last semester's text to refresh your memory. If the material still doesn't click, scan background material for information that will help you understand. Set a goal to make your way through the material, whatever it takes. If you want to learn, you will.

Define unclear concepts. Consult resources—instructors, study-group partners, reference materials—for help. Build a library of texts in your major and minor areas of study and refer to them when needed. "If you find yourself going to the library to look up the same reference again and again, consider purchasing that book," advises library expert Sherwood Harris.[1]

Ask yourself questions. University of Michigan psychology professor and textbook author Charles G. Morris recommends that you engage in an internal question-and-answer session before reading a chapter. Look at the chapter outline or chapter headings and then think about what the material means and why it is being presented in this way. Write down your thoughts. Then read the chapter summary to see if your questions are answered.[2]

(As you will see in Chapter 5, questioning is at the heart of SQ3R.)

Choose the Right Setting

Finding a place and time that minimize distractions will help you focus on your reading:

Select the right company (or no company at all). If you prefer to read alone, establish a relatively interruption-proof place and time, such as an out-of-the-way spot at the library or an hour in an empty classroom. Even if you don't mind activity nearby, try to minimize distractions.

Select the right location. Many students study at a library desk. Others prefer an easy chair at the library, in their dorm, or at home. Still others prefer spreading papers out on the floor. Avoid studying in bed, since you are likely to fall asleep. After choosing a spot, adjust the temperature and light to do your best work.

Select a time when you are alert and focused. Eventually, you will associate certain times with focused reading. Pay attention to your natural body rhythms and study when your energy is high. Whereas night owls are productive when everyone else is sleeping, for example, morning people have a hard time working during late-night sessions.

As they stock up on the texts their instructors assign, college students often find themselves with an overwhelming array of reading materials.

Students with young children have an additional factor to consider when they are thinking about when, where, and how to read. Key 4.2 explores some ways that parents or others caring for children can maximize their study efforts. (You can also use these techniques after college if you work from home.)

Learn to Concentrate

When you focus your attention on one thing and one thing only, you are engaged in the act of *concentration*. Without concentration, you are likely to remember little as your mind wanders. Following are active-learning methods for remaining focused as you study:

Be intensely involved. Tell yourself that what you are doing is important and needs your full attention—no matter what is going on around you.

Key 4.2   Use these techniques to manage children while studying.

KEEP THEM UP TO DATE ON YOUR SCHEDULE

Let them know when you have a big test or project due and when you are under less pressure, and what they can expect of you in each case.

EXPLAIN WHAT YOUR EDUCATION ENTAILS

Tell them how it will improve your life and theirs. This applies, of course, to older children who can understand the situation and compare it with their own schooling.

FIND HELP

Ask a relative or friend to watch your children or arrange for a child to visit a friend. Consider trading baby-sitting hours with another parent, hiring a sitter to come to your home, or using a day-care center.

KEEP THEM ACTIVE WHILE YOU STUDY

Give them games, books, or toys. If there are special activities that you like to limit, such as watching videos or TV, save them for your study time.

STUDY ON THE PHONE

You might be able to have a study session with a fellow student over the phone while your child is sleeping or playing quietly.

OFFSET STUDY TIME WITH FAMILY TIME AND REWARDS

Children may let you get your work done if they have something to look forward to, such as a movie night or a trip for ice cream.

SPECIAL NOTES FOR INFANTS

Study at night if your baby goes to sleep early, or in the morning if your baby sleeps late.

Study during nap times if you aren't too tired yourself.

Lay your notes out and recite information to the baby. The baby will appreciate the attention, and you will get work done.

Put baby in a safe and fun place while you study, such as a playpen, motorized swing, or jumping seat.

It might help to place a purpose statement at the top of your desk. For example, "I'm concentrating on the U. S. Constitution because it is the basis for our laws and because it will be on Friday's American government exam."

Banish extraneous thoughts onto paper. Don't let unrelated thoughts block your efforts. When such thoughts come up, write them down on a separate piece of paper and deal with them later. Keeping a monthly calendar of classes, appointments, and events will help you organize your life and be less distracted.

Deal with internal distractions. Internal distractions—for example, personal worries or even hunger—can get in the way of work. Even if it means time away from your books, taking a break to deal with what's bothering you will make you more efficient. Physical exercise may relax and focus you, studying while listening to music may relieve stress, and a snack break will reduce your hunger.

Compartmentalize your life. Social invitations may be easier to resist if you have a policy of separating study time from playtime. No one will think less of you if you refuse an invitation so that you can concentrate on work. You may even influence others to study. Plus, when you have a successful study session, you are likely to enjoy your downtime more.

Analyze your environment to see if it helps or hurts concentration. Think about your last study session. How long did you *try to* concentrate and how long did you *actually* concentrate? If you spent more than 10 percent of your time blocking out distractions (people, things going on, noises, etc.), try another location with fewer distractions.

Don't let technology distract you. If you are reading near a computer, force yourself to place Web surfing, e-mail, and instant messaging off limits. In addition, turn your cell phone off, and check your voice mail only after you finish your work.

Structure your study session so you know the time you will spend and the material you will study. No one can concentrate for unlimited periods, so set realistic goals and a specific plan for dividing your time.

Plan a reward. After concentrating for hours, go to the movies; have dinner with friends; jog around campus; do anything that gives you a break. Plan your reward in advance so you have something to look forward to, because you deserve it!

The strongest motivation to concentrate comes from within—not from the fear of failing a test, or disappointing a teacher. When you see the connection between what you study and your short- and long-term goals, you will be better able to focus on your readings, to remember, to learn, and to apply.

Familiarize Yourself with What's Ahead

Successful readers try to familiarize themselves with material before reading it in depth because they know that material they have seen before is easier to grasp than material they know nothing about. Here are two ways to do this:

- Using the surveying techniques of SQ3R, scan the table of contents of your texts for an overview of content, organization, and theme; pre-read chapter headings, objectives, and summaries; and skim paragraphs for main ideas.
- When you begin to study an unfamiliar topic, read a basic primer for an understanding of general concepts and interrelationships. For example, before opening a college astronomy text, review basic concepts in an astronomy book for general readers, on a general information website, or in a lower-level text.

Become Emotionally Involved

Successful readers also understand that they are more likely to remember material that evokes an emotional response than material that does not affect them. Student success expert Eric Jensen explains: "When your emotions are engaged, the brain codes the content you're reading by triggering the release of chemicals that single out and mark the experience as important and meaningful. . . . The stronger you feel about something you read the more likely you are to remember it and make sense out of it. The good thing about this is that it works both ways; hating something or disagreeing with something works just as well as liking something or strongly agreeing with it."[3]

How do you surround normally "dry" text material with emotions? These suggestions might help:

- Stop and think about your reaction to ideas, to the author's point of view and writing style, to chapter features and text design, and even to the chapter order.
- Discuss specific points with classmates and don't hold back your comments when you disagree. This will also help you understand the material.
- Think through the implications of a concept when it is applied in the real world.

TRIGGER YOUR EMOTIONS

This exercise will show you how to spark your emotions to make the following text paragraph on the history of hypnosis important and memorable:

> In mid-eighteenth-century Europe, Anton Mesmer, a Viennese physician, fascinated audiences by putting patients into trances to cure their illnesses. Hence the term *mesmerism* was first used to describe the phenomenon now known as hypnosis (*Hypnos* was the Greek god of sleep). Mesmerism was initially discredited by a French commission chaired by Benjamin Franklin; but in the nineteenth century some respectable physicians revived interest in hypnosis when they discovered it could be used to treat certain forms of mental illness. Even today, disagreement persists about how to define hypnosis and even whether it is a valid altered state of consciousness.[4]

Activate your emotional response by . . .

- . . . investigating these questions: Do I believe in the power of hypnosis to unlock my subconscious mind? Have I ever been hypnotized? What do I know about Benjamin Franklin's role in the French commission mentioned in the paragraph? What Greek myth involved Hypnos and what role did he play in the myth?

- . . . asking friends what they think of hypnosis and if they've ever been placed in a hypnotic trance.

- . . . thinking about how hypnosis is used in the real world—for example, its use in helping people to stop smoking and to deal with chronic pain.

Finally, evaluate how well this strategy worked for you, how you might change it, and whether you will use it again. Write your thoughts below:

_____

_____

Define Your Reading Purpose

When you define your purpose, you ask yourself *why* you are reading particular material. One way to do this is by completing this sentence: "In reading this material, I intend to define/learn/answer/achieve . . ." *Write your goal down before you begin and look at it whenever you lose focus or get bogged down in details.* With a clear purpose you can decide how much time and effort to expend on various assignments. Nearly 375 years ago,

Francis Bacon, the great English philosopher, recognized, "Some books are to be tasted, others to be swallowed, and some few to be chewed and digested; that is, some books are to be read only in parts, others to be read but not curiously; and some few to be read wholly, and with diligence and attention." Bacon's philosophy is particularly true in college, where you may be overwhelmed by assignments unless you prioritize. In Chapter 5, you will find suggestions for evaluating and prioritizing the readings on your plate.

Achieving your reading purpose requires adapting to different materials. Being a flexible reader—adjusting your strategies and pace—will help you get what you want from each assignment. You are in control.

Purpose Determines Reading Strategy

Following are four reading purposes, examined briefly. You may have one or more for any "reading event."

Purpose 1: Read for understanding. Studying involves reading to comprehend concepts and details. These components depend on each other. Details help explain or support general concepts, and concepts provide a framework for remembering details.

Purpose 2: Read to evaluate critically. Critical evaluation involves understanding. It means approaching material with an open mind, examining causes and effects, evaluating ideas, and asking questions that test the writer's argument and assumptions. Critical reading brings a level of understanding that goes beyond basic information recall.

Purpose 3: Read for practical application. A third purpose for reading is to gather usable information that you can apply toward a specific goal. When you read a textbook preface or an instruction booklet for a new software package, your goal is to learn how to do or use something. Reading and action usually go hand in hand.

Purpose 4: Read for pleasure. Some materials you read for entertainment, such as *Sports Illustrated* magazine, the latest page-turner by *DaVinci Code* author Dan Brown, or even novels by Charles Dickens and Jane Austen. As Yale professor Harold Bloom points out, reading for pleasure gives you the opportunity to enlarge your life and to enter into "alternate realities." "Why read?" Bloom asks. "Because you can know, intimately, only a very few people, and perhaps you never know them at all. After reading [the Thomas Mann masterpiece] *The Magic Mountain* you know Hans Castorp thoroughly, and he is greatly worth knowing."[5]

Use your class syllabus to help you define your purpose for each assignment. If, for example, you know that the topic of inflation will be discussed in your next economics class, read the assigned chapter, targeting what your instructor will expect you to know and do with the material. For example, she may expect you to master definitions, economic models, causes and consequences, government intervention strategies, and historical examples and to be able to apply what you know to economic problems. In this case, depending on what your instructor expects, you have three reading purposes—understanding, critical evaluation, and practical application. If you are confused about your purpose, e-mail your instructor for clarification.

Purpose Determines Pace

"Good readers are flexible readers," says George M. Usova, a Johns Hopkins University education specialist. "They read at a variety of rates and adapt them to the reading purpose at hand, the difficulty of the

Key 4.3 Link your reading pace to your reading purpose.		
TYPE OF MATERIAL	**READING PURPOSE**	**PACE**
Academic readings ▪ Textbooks ▪ Original sources ▪ Articles from scholarly journals ▪ On-line publications for academic readers ▪ Lab reports ▪ Required fiction	▪ Critical analysis ▪ Overall mastery ▪ Preparation for tests	Slow, especially if the material is unfamiliar
Manuals ▪ Instructions ▪ Recipes	Practical application	Slow to medium
Journalism and nonfiction for the general reader ▪ Nonfiction books ▪ Newspapers ▪ Magazines ▪ On-line publications for the general public	Understanding of general ideas, key concepts, and specific facts for personal understanding and/or practical application	Medium to fast
Nonrequired fiction	Understanding of general ideas, key concepts, and specific facts for enjoyment	Variable, but tending toward faster speeds

Source: Adapted from Nicholas Reid Schaffzin, *The Princeton Review Reading Smart.* New York: Random House, 1996, p. 15.

material, and their familiarity with the subject."[6] For example, you may need to read complex, unfamiliar text assignments more slowly than newspapers, magazine, and online publications. As Key 4.3 shows, good readers link the pace of reading to their reading purpose.

Spend Enough Time

You'll need more than good intentions to finish assignments on schedule. You'll have to put in many hours of work. One formula for success is this: For every hour you spend in the classroom each week, spend at least two hours preparing for the class. For example, a course load of 15 credit hours means that you should spend 30 hours per week studying and doing homework outside of class.

Students who fall far short of this goal are likely to have a hard time keeping up. According to a recent National Survey of Student Engagement, most students study far less than they should. As Key 4.4 indicates, in 2002 only about 23 percent of both freshmen and seniors studied 21 or more hours a week, and nearly the same percentages (19 percent of freshmen and 20 percent of seniors) studied 1 to 5 hours a week.

Key 4.4 Many college freshmen and seniors don't study enough.		
NUMBER OF HOURS PER WEEK SPENT PREPARING FOR CLASS,* 2002		
	PROPORTION OF FIRST-YEAR STUDENTS	**PROPORTION OF SENIORS**
5 or fewer	19.0%	20.0%
6 to 10	23.9%	24.5%
11 to 15	19.0%	17.7%
16 to 20	15.6%	14.9%
21 to 25	10.4%	9.6%
26 to 30	6.8%	6.4%
More than 30	5.3%	7.0%

* Defined in the survey as studying, reading, writing, rehearsing, and other activities related to academic programs.

Source: "The American Freshman: National Norms for Fall 2001," published by American Council on Education and University of California at Los Angeles Higher Education Research Institute; National Survey of Student Engagement, Indiana University. Cited in Jeffrey R. Young, "Homework? What Homework? Students Seem to Be Spending Less Time Studying Than They Used To," *The Chronicle of Higher Education,* December 6, 2002.

CONSIDER SIGNING AN ACADEMIC RESPONSIBILITY "CONTRACT"

University of Hawaii-Manoa classics professor Robert J. Ball has an unusual method for encouraging students to complete their reading and homework assignments, as explained in his quote below. In your study group, evaluate this unorthodox approach and discuss whether it would work for you by answering the questions that follow.

> At the first class I distribute a detailed syllabus to all . . . students. The syllabus spells out everything relevant to the execution of the course: the goal, the books to be used, instructions on preparing homework, procedures to be followed in class, and the determination of the final grade. The syllabus specifies every date on which the students must submit homework and take examinations, as well as the penalties incurred unless they present a . . . medical note or other acceptable document. At the end of the first class, the students sign, detach, and return to [me] a form on the syllabus that reads: "I have read the . . . syllabus and understand the requirements of the course." The teacher and the students have thus entered into a contract, a written agreement based on the syllabus . . . Although a few [students] may drop the course once they see how rigorously the teacher sticks to the syllabus, most will work hard to meet their deadlines.[7]

- What does your study group think of Professor Ball's method for increasing academic responsibility? Discuss the pros and cons of his approach.

- Discuss whether signing a "contract" in each of your courses would motivate you to complete your assignments on schedule and to prepare for class.

- Each group member should then read his or her own course syllabi to make sure reading assignment, homework submission, and examination dates are clear. If they are not, work with group members to transform each syllabus into a working document that will guide your semester's work.

- Finally, make a group pact to complete all the academic responsibilities that are defined in the syllabi. Write out the pact in your own "contract" and pass it around to sign.

A strong vocabulary increases reading speed and comprehension. The next section will help you learn strategies to expand your vocabulary.

HOW DO YOU BUILD A BETTER VOCABULARY?

As your reading materials become more complex, how much you comprehend—and how readily you do it—is influenced by your vocabulary. Is your word power minimal, general, and static? Or is it large, specialized, and ever-expanding? Use the following techniques to learn unfamiliar words as you encounter them.

Analyze Word Parts

If you understand part of a word, oftentimes you can figure out what the entire word means. This is true because many English words combine Greek and Latin prefixes, roots, and suffixes. *Prefixes* are word parts that are added to the beginning of a root. The *root* is the central part or basis of a word around which prefixes and/or suffixes are added to produce different words. *Suffixes* are added to the end of the root.

Key 4.5 contains just a few of the prefixes, roots, and suffixes you will encounter as you read. There are literally thousands more, including the roots you will learn in the end-of-chapter *Get to the Root* exercises. Taking the time to memorize these verbal building blocks will help you grow your vocabulary, since you will encounter them in many different words. (Keep in mind that although prefixes, roots, and suffixes are reliable language tools, they do not always apply to words with complex etymologies.)

Use a Dictionary

When reading a textbook, the first "dictionary" to search is the glossary. Textbooks often include an end-of-book glossary that explains technical words and concepts. The definitions there are usually limited to the meaning of the term as it is used in the text.

Standard dictionaries provide broader information such as word origin, pronunciation, part of speech, synonyms, antonyms, and multiple meanings. Buy a standard dictionary, keep it nearby, and consult it for help in understanding unfamiliar words. You may even want to invest in an electronic handheld dictionary, which you can take wherever you go. If you prefer an online version, websites like dictionary.com provide information similar to that found in dictionaries in book form.

The following suggestions will help you make the most of your dictionary.

Key 4.5 Build your vocabulary with common prefixes, roots, and suffixes.

PREFIX	PRIMARY MEANING	EXAMPLE
a, ab	from	abstain, avert
ad, af, at	to	adhere, affix, attain
con, cor, com	with, together	convene, correlate, compare
di	apart	divert, divorce
il	not	illegal, illegible
ir	not	irresponsible
post	after	postpone, postpartum
pro	before	prologue
sub, sup	under	subordinate, suppose

ROOT	PRIMARY MEANING	EXAMPLE
-logue	to speak	dialogue
-com	fill	incomplete
-strict	bind	restriction
-cept	take	receptacle
-chron	time	synchronize
-ann	year	biannual
-sper	hope	desperate
-clam	cry out	proclamation
-voc	speak, talk	convocation

SUFFIX	PRIMARY MEANING	EXAMPLE
-able	able	recyclable
-arium	place for	aquarium, solarium
-cule	very small	molecule
-ist	one who	pianist
-meter	measure	thermometer
-ness	state of	carelessness
-sis	condition of	hypnosis
-y	inclined to	sleepy

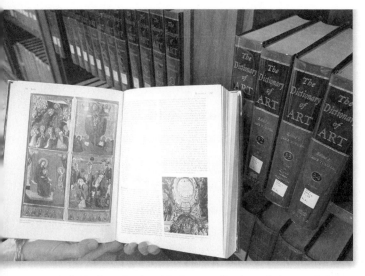

Individual academic subject areas often have their own dictionaries. Pictured is one page of the 34-volume Grove Dictionary of Art.

Read every meaning, not just the first. Think critically about which meaning suits the context of the word in question, and choose the one that makes the most sense to you.

Say the word out loud—then write it down to make sure you can spell it. Check your pronunciation against the dictionary symbols as you say each word. Speaking and writing new words will boost recall.

Use your chosen definition. Imagine, for example, that you encounter the following sentence and do not know what the word *indoctrinated* means:

The cult indoctrinated its members to reject society's values.

In the dictionary, you find several definitions, including *brainwashed* and *instructed*. You decide that the one closest to the correct meaning is *brainwashed*. With this term, the sentence reads as follows:

The cult brainwashed its members to reject society's values.

Restate the definition in your own words. When you can do this with ease, you know that you understand the meaning and are not merely parroting a dictionary definition.

Try to use the word in conversation in the next 24 hours. Not only does this demonstrate that you know how the word is used, but it also aids memorization.

Learn Specialized Vocabulary

As you learn a subject, you will encounter specialized vocabulary (see Key 4.6 for examples from four college texts). Most of these words, phrases, and acronyms may be unfamiliar unless you have studied the topics before. Even if you feel like you are diving into a foreign language, know that continual exposure will create mastery as the semester progresses.

Apply a basic vocabulary-building approach to learn these terms. Understand words in the context of the chapter; then turn to the glossary

MULTIPLE INTELLIGENCE STRATEGIES FOR BUILDING VOCABULARY. Tap into these Multiple Intelligence strategies to build your vocabulary.

INTELLIGENCE	SUGGESTED STRATEGIES	WHAT WORKS FOR YOU? WRITE NEW IDEAS HERE
Verbal-Linguistic	■ For each new vocabulary word, make an entry in your journal that explains the context in which you learned the word. ■ Write two sentences using the word.	
Logical-Mathematical	■ Learn new words by analyzing word roots, prefixes, and suffixes. ■ Learn new word in the order in which you encountered them in your text or class.	
Bodily-Kinesthetic	■ Record words and definitions into a tape recorder and learn the material as you walk between classes or while exercising. ■ Learn five new words from the same textbook, and then, while taking a walk, think about how the words relate to one another.	
Visual-Spatial	■ Create vocabulary flash cards with cartoon images that help you remember the words. ■ Create word-root diagrams that link Greek and Latin roots to related vocabulary.	
Interpersonal	■ Ask a study partner to test your knowledge of vocabulary terms. ■ Use ten new vocabulary words correctly while speaking with a study partner.	
Intrapersonal	■ Look at all the dictionary definitions of a word and recall whether you have ever used them. ■ Take your flashcards to a quiet spot and start memorizing.	
Musical	■ Listen to music while you learn new words. ■ Create a mnemonic in the form of a musical rhyme to help you memorize.	
Naturalistic	■ Study your flashcards while sitting outdoors.	

Key 4.6   Every text includes specialized vocabulary.

BIOLOGY TEXT	CRIMINAL JUSTICE TEXT	PSYCHOLOGY TEXT	BUSINESS TEXT
actin	biometrics	experimental method	double-entry accounting
chaparral	detainee	great person theory	leverage
exoskeleton	habitual offender	homeostasis	relationship marketing
gravitropism	RICO statute	trichromats	strategic alliance
prophase	writ of habeas corpus	vestibular senses	Uniform Commercial Code (UCC)

for a review, record definitions in your notes, create vocabulary flash cards, use terms in your own sentences, and more. Don't rush through unfamiliar words. Rather, look them up, ask other students about them, and relate them to concepts you already know.

Your instructors will test you on your ability to define and use course-specific vocabulary, so make sure you understand terms well enough to define them correctly on short-answer tests and to use them on essay exams.

Go For It!   BUILDING YOUR SKILLS

START NOW TO BUILD YOUR VOCABULARY

List and define five words that you learn today in your classes or in your assigned readings. Use each word in a sentence to be sure you know its meaning.

New Vocabulary Word #1:

Describe the context in which you encountered this word:

_____

Definition: _____

Use the word in a sentence: _____

_____

New Vocabulary Word #2: _____

Describe the context in which you encountered this word:

_____

Definition: _____

Use the word in a sentence: _____

_____

New Vocabulary Word #3: _____

Describe the context in which you encountered this word:

_____

Definition: _____

Use the word in a sentence: _____

_____

New Vocabulary Word #4: _____

Describe the context in which you encountered this word:

_____

Definition: _____

Use the word in a sentence: _____

_____

New Vocabulary Word #5: _____

Describe the context in which you encountered this word:

_____

Definition: _____

Use the word in a sentence: _____

_____

Use Memory Aids to Ensure Recall

Most students find that their most important vocabulary-building tool is the flash card. Your efforts will pay off if you study several cards a day and push yourself to use your new words in conversation and writing. You may also want to work together with another student to review each other's cards. A buddy system may motivate you to master your new vocabulary as it exposes you to your study partner's words. Memorization tools, including mnemonic devices and flash cards, are discussed in Chapter 6.

HOW CAN YOU INCREASE YOUR READING SPEED?

Most students lead busy lives, carrying heavy academic loads while perhaps working or even caring for a family. With so much to do in so little time, it is often difficult to finish reading assignments on schedule. The workplace has similar pressures. For example, accountants must keep abreast of changing tax regulations and physical therapists read journals in search of research findings. Whether you are in school or at work, increasing your reading speed makes it possible to keep up—and it may free up some time to relax.

Rapid reading won't do you any good if you can't remember the material or answer questions about it. However, reading too slowly can eat up valuable time and give your mind the opportunity to wander. Your goal is to read for maximum speed *and* comprehension. Because greater comprehension is the primary goal and actually promotes faster reading, make comprehension a priority over speed.

Use the following formula to calculate how quickly you read:

- Note the time it takes you in minutes to read a passage—a half a text page, for example. Use decimals for fractions of a minute. That is, if it takes you 1 minute and 45 seconds, then write 1.75 minutes.
- Divide the number of words in the passage by your reading time.
- The number you come up with is your reading speed in words per minute.

TEST YOUR SPEED AND COMPREHENSION

Time how rapidly you read the following 500-word text selection from start to finish without stopping. Using the formula above, if you spend 1.75 minutes reading this 500-word selection, you would divide 500 by 1.75 to come up with a reading speed of approximately 286 words per minute:

Although today's college campuses are filled with 18- to 22-year-olds, they are also filled with older, nontraditional students who are returning to school. Nearly 1.5 million women and more than 700,000 men over the age of 35 are attending college—as 4-year students, in 2-year degree programs, and as graduate students. While there has been a dramatic increase in this segment of the college population, the percentage of typical college students—men and women between the ages of 18 and 22—has actually declined since 1980.

This dramatic demographic shift coincides with the recognition that humans are lifelong learners with cognitive abilities that adapt to life demands. Despite societal stereotypes that the primary period for learning is over after adolescence, we now know that it is during middle age that adults acquire the information and skills they need to meet the changing demands of their jobs. This is as true for bankers as it is for computer scientists, both of whom work in fields that have changed radically in recent years as a result of an explosion in technology.

In large part, middle-aged students are returning to school because they have to. Many are unemployed—the victims of corporate downsizing. Others are moving into the job market after spending time at home as full-time parents. A financial planner who stopped working for 5 years to raise her daughter may need recertification before any firm will hire her. Even adults who worked part-time during their child-rearing years may have to return to school to acquire the knowledge they need to qualify for a full-time job. This is especially true in fields with a high degree of professional obsolescence.

Whatever the reason for their return, studies show that the majority of middle-aged students are conscientious about their work. They attend classes regularly and get better grades, on average, than other segments of the student population.

The decision to return to school involves personal introspection and assessment of one's skills and abilities. The student role is generally different from the other roles middle-aged adults assume, and it requires considerable adaptation. A student is in a subordinate position as a learner. Also, mature adults may find themselves among a large number of students who are considerably younger than they are, and the faculty may also be younger. Initially, the age difference may be a source of discomfort.

Family members must often take on new responsibilities when a middle-aged member assumes the role of college student. A husband may have to do more household chores, while a wife may have to return to work to supplement the family income. In addition, the student may need emotional support. Sometimes this involves awkward role reversals and the disruption of familiar interaction patterns.

With the realization that middle-aged students are here to stay, community colleges and universities are making substantial adjustments to meet their needs. In addition many students receive the training they need at work. Many large corporations run training departments designed to maintain a competent workforce.

Source: Human Development, 7/E by Craig, © 1996. Adapted by permission of Prentice-Hall, Inc., Upper Saddle River, NJ.

Now answer the following questions without looking back at the text. You'll find the correct answers upside down at the end:

1. How many men and women over the age of 35 are now enrolled in various college programs?

    A. approximately 1.5 million women and 700,000 men

    B. 5 million men and women

    C. approximately 1.5 million men and 700,000 women

2. How has the enrollment of 18- to 22-year-old college students changed since 1980 in relationship to the total college population?

    A. The percentage of students in this age group has increased.

    B. The percentage of students in this age group has remained the same.

    C. The percentage of students in this age group has decreased.

3. According to the passage, which one of the following reasons does not describe why older adults return to school?

    A. Unemployed adults return to school to acquire new work-related skills.

    B. After spending time at home raising children, many adults are moving on to another stage of life, which involves returning to work.

    C. Adults with discretionary income are choosing to invest money in themselves.

4. According to the text, why is the student role different from the other roles middle-aged adults assume?
   A. As learners, students are in a subordinate position, which can be uncomfortable for mature adults.
   B. Adults are not used to studying.
   C. Middle-aged adults often find it difficult to talk to young adults.

In general, your comprehension percentage, as judged by the number of questions like these that you answer correctly, should be above 70 percent, so you should have answered three out of the four questions correctly. Lower scores mean that you are missing or forgetting important information.

Problems and Solutions for Slower Readers

The average American adult reads between 150 and 350 words per minute. Slow readers fall below this range while faster readers are capable of speeds of 500 to 1,000 words per minute and sometimes faster.[8] Researchers point to a number of specific causes for slow reading. Identifying these problems, such as those in the list that follows, is your first step to correcting them. You are then ready to apply proven solutions.[9]

Word-by-word reading. When you first learned to read, your teachers may have told you to read one word at a time as you moved systematically from one line to the next. This technique limits your reading speed. As a speed reader, you must train your eyes to "capture" and read groups of words at a time. Try swinging your eyes from side to side as you read a passage instead of stopping at various points to read individual words. When reading narrow columns, focus your eyes in the middle of the column and read down the page. With practice, you'll be able to read the entire column width.

Lack of concentration. Word by word reading leads to poor concentration. That is, you may be reading too slowly to keep your mind occupied, and soon your thoughts begin to wander. Reading groups of words, instead of single words, will help counteract this effect as you provide your mind with the stimulation it needs to remain engaged.

Vocalization and subvocalization. *Vocalizers* tend to speak words as they read them or move their lips while reading. In contrast, *subvocalizers* pronounce inwardly every word they read. Both habits will slow your reading speed. Your first step to changing this behavior is awareness. Monitor your reading; if you notice either habit, make a conscious effort to stop what you're doing. Attaching a self-adhesive note to the page with the reminder *Don't vocalize* may help your efforts in the early stages.

Limited vocabulary and knowledge gaps. If your vocabulary is small, you may be puzzled by the meanings of different words. Trying to figure out meaning from context or consulting a dictionary will slow you down. The suggestions from the vocabulary-building section earlier in the chapter will help you build your vocabulary.

Similarly, if you failed to master material that is the foundation for what you are currently reading, you will struggle with concepts. The solution: Make sure you are comfortable with the subject and have the basics under your belt.

Unconscious regression. This involves rereading words that you've already read because your eyes stay on the same line instead of moving ahead. If you find yourself doing this, use your index finger or a six-inch ruler as a visual guide. Reading expert Steve Moidel explains the technique:

> When you finish a line, bring your index finger to the beginning of the next line with a motion as fast and smooth as you can make it. It is important that the return be fluid. If you jerk your finger back, it may become a distraction and ultimately hurt your comprehension. Pretend that your finger is gliding, skiing, or ice skating back to the beginning of the next line: fast yet smooth.[10]

As they learn new material, even the best readers move their eyes back and forth as they return to material of which they're not quite sure. But these eye movements are purposeful. Instead of randomly jumping back to different parts of difficult material, good readers look back at the start of sentences that are giving them trouble, then move their eyes smoothly through the material they want to reread.

Slow recovery time. The time it takes your eye to move from the end of one line to the beginning of the next is known as *recovery time*. Slow readers spend far too long searching for the next line. Using your finger as a guide will also help speed recovery time.

Treating all reading assignments the same. Slow readers may fail to prioritize their reading assignments, ignoring the advice from Sir Francis Bacon quoted earlier in this chapter. Learning to skim and scan less important material is critical to your success and to having time to read important materials in depth.

The key to building reading speed is practice and more practice. To achieve your goal of reading between 500 and 1,000 words per minute, Moidel suggests that you start practicing at three times the rate you want to achieve, a rate that is much faster than you can comprehend. For example, if your goal is 500 words per minute, speed up to 1,500 words per minute. Reading at such an accelerated rate will push your eyes and mind to adjust to the faster pace. When you slow down to 500 words per minute—the pace at which you can read and comprehend—the rate will feel comfortable even though it is much faster than your original speed.

"I find television very educational. Every time someone turns it on, I go in the other room and read a book."

GROUCHO MARX
legendary comedian

Building Skill, Will, and Self-Management

Monitoring Your Progress

Test Competence: Measure What You've Learned

MULTIPLE CHOICE. *Circle or highlight the answer that seems to fit best.*

1. Making meaning from written words is a personal process because
   A. you may not want to read the material.
   B. you connect to the concepts on the page.
   C. reading comprehension is always objective.
   D. it is unrelated to your reading purpose.

2. Taking an active approach to a difficult text includes all of the following strategies *except:*
   A. having an open mind.
   B. being willing to study the material more than once.
   C. continually asking questions.
   D. refusing to challenge yourself.

3. The *most important* goals in choosing a particular setting for reading are to
   A. minimize distractions and maximize focus and discipline.
   B. find the best people with whom to read and work with them.
   C. learn how to concentrate in a library and study there regularly.
   D. learn how to read with children around and decide how to distract them.

4. A reading purpose can be described as
   A. the list of required texts you receive from your instructors.
   B. what you intend to learn or gain from your reading material.
   C. how quickly you intend to complete an assigned work.
   D. not related to any specific goals.

5. You can improve your concentration with all but *which* of the following?

   A. Being very clear why you are studying the material.

   B. Working with a friend and taking regular breaks.

   C. Carving out study time.

   D. Writing down unrelated thoughts and getting back to them when you are finished studying.

6. To become emotionally involved with what you are reading, you should try all but *which* of the following?

   A. Try to find material in the text that will make you cry.

   B. Think about your reactions to the material.

   C. Discuss the material with your classmates.

   D. Think about real-world applications.

7. You can build a better vocabulary by focusing on all but *which* of the following elements?

   A. prefixes

   B. word roots

   C. sentence structure

   D. suffixes

8. For maximum comprehension when you use a dictionary, you should

   A. read only the first meaning of a word.

   B. memorize the exact wording of the dictionary definition.

   C. list all the new words you learn in a journal, without including their definitions.

   D. restate the definition in your own words and use it in a sentence.

9. Slow readers tend to do all but *which* of the following?

   A. Believe that slow reading is better reading.

   B. Read words one at a time.

   C. Vocalize and subvocalize.

   D. Lose their place as they read and read the same line more than once.

10. At work your vocabulary is likely to do all but *which* of the following?

   A. Grow as you are exposed to specialized words, phrases, and initials linked to your field.

   B. Remain static since your vocabulary-building years are now behind you.

C. Give your coworkers information about your educational background.

D. Affect your career advancement.

TRUE/FALSE. *Place a T or an F beside each statement to indicate whether you think it is true or false.*

_____ 1. For every hour you spend in the classroom, you should spend at least two hours studying.

_____ 2. The specialized vocabulary you learn in an introductory-level course will have little value to you after the course is over.

_____ 3. Reading comprehension is influenced by the knowledge you have gained through previous reading and studying.

_____ 4. Academic writing is no more difficult than any other writing.

_____ 5. While regression and slow recovery time can slow your reading speed, one solution is to use your index finger as a visual guide on the page.

Target and Achieve a Goal

Commit to one specific reading comprehension, vocabulary building, or reading speed enhancement strategy from this chapter to improve your study skills.

Name the strategy here: _____

_____

Describe your goal—what you want to gain by using this strategy. _____

_____

_____

Describe how you plan to use this strategy through the semester to achieve this goal.

_____

_____

_____

Building Your Skills

Brain Power: Build Vocabulary Fitness

Here is a selection from the current media. Read the material, paying special attention to the context of the vocabulary words shown in bold type. Then choose the correct definition for each word in the table that follows. Use a dictionary to check your answers. Finally, on a separate sheet, use each vocabulary word in a sentence of your own to solidify your understanding.

In the following excerpt, New York Times *columnist David Brooks reflects on a reality that you might be discovering yourself—namely, that being successful in high school does not necessarily prepare you for college or life success. Brooks also focuses on the importance of choosing a college that is right for you and that allows you to soar.*

Once you reach adulthood, the key to success will not be demonstrating . . . competence across fields; it will be finding a few things you love and then committing yourself passionately to them.

The traits you used [in high school] getting good grades might actually hold you back [in college]. To get . . . high marks . . . you were encouraged to develop a **prudential** attitude toward learning. You had to calculate which reading was essential and which was not. You could not allow yourself to be obsessed by one subject because if you did, your marks in . . . other subjects would suffer. . . .

You learned to study subjects that are **intrinsically** boring to you. . . . You just knew that each class was a hoop you must jump through. . . . You learned to thrive in adult-supervised settings.

If you have done all these things and you are still an interesting person, congratulations, because the system has been trying to **whittle** you down into a bland, **complaisant** achievement machine.

But in adulthood, you'll find that a talent for **regurgitating** what superiors want to hear will take you only halfway up the ladder, and then you'll stop there. The people who succeed most spectacularly . . . **venture out** and thrive where there is no supervision, where there are no preset requirements.

As for the quality of education [you'll find in college], that's a matter of your actually wanting to learn and being fortunate enough to meet a professor who **electrifies** your interest. . . .

There are a lot of smart . . . people in this country, and you will find them at whatever school you go to. . . . Your [challenge is to find a college] with the personality and character that **complements** your own.

Source: David Brooks, "Stressed for Success?" *The New York Times,* March 30, 2004, p. A21.

Circle the word or phrase that best defines each term as it is used in this excerpt.

VOCABULARY WORDS	A	B	C
1. **prudential** (adj.)	casual	stingy	cautious
2. **intrinsically** (adv.)	superficially	by their very nature	apparently
3. **whittle** (verb)	reduce	mold	broaden
4. **complaisant** (adj.)	passionate	narrow	amiable
5. **regurgitating** (verb)	parroting	reframing	analyzing
6. **venture out** (verb)	remain secluded	take a risk	hold on to the status quo
7. **electrifies** (verb)	gives an electric shock	molds	excites intensely
8. **complements** (verb)	differs from	expresses respect for	fills up; completes

Get to the Root

Every time you learn a Greek or Latin root, you increase your ability to recognize English vocabulary words that include that root and to figure out their meaning. Grow your vocabulary by studying the root word on page 151 and its related words, writing in two more words from the same root, and including definitions for both new words.

Investigate Using Research Navigator

Access Research Navigator using the Internet address shown on page 32. Then sign on to the service using your Login Name and Password. Scroll through the subject titles listed for *The New York Times* on the Web. Choose a subject linked to a major that interests you and select a related keyword. For example, if you are thinking of majoring in Health Administration, you could choose the Health Administration database and enter "hospitals" as a keyword.

When the database generates a list of articles, choose one that seems interesting and open its full text. Read the article using the strategies you have examined in this chapter. Then evaluate your comprehension, vocabulary, and speed in writing.

- Which area—comprehension, vocabulary, or speed—do you feel is your strong point?
- Which is toughest for you?
- What can you do to improve your area of challenge?

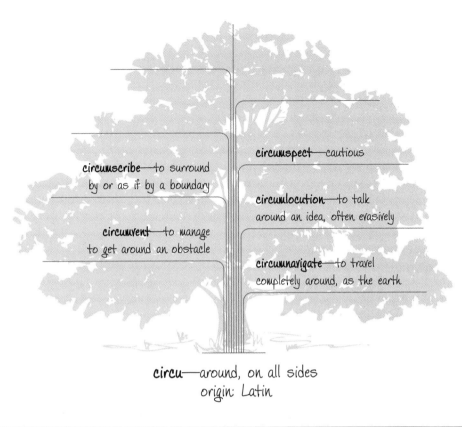

circumscribe—to surround
by or as if by a boundary

circumvent—to manage
to get around an obstacle

circumspect—cautious

circumlocution—to talk
around an idea, often evasively

circumnavigate—to travel
completely around, as the earth

circu—around, on all sides
origin: Latin

Building Will and Self-Awareness

ACTIVE
THINKING

SKILL   WILL   SELF-MGMT.

Make Responsible Choices

Answer the following question on a separate piece of paper or in a journal.

In most jobs you are constantly faced with material you need to read and understand. With this in mind:

- Think about, and describe, your greatest challenge in reading. How might this problem affect your performance when you begin working? If you have chosen a career—or are thinking about one—try to answer in terms of the kind of reading you are likely to do for work.

- Describe your plan for addressing this challenge, using any of the strategies in this chapter that you think will help you improve.

- From an ethical perspective, think about and discuss whether it's all right to shortcut important job-related readings—for example, to skim material instead of reading it in depth or to ask coworkers for a quick summary.

Are these shortcuts acceptable if they do not affect job performance? Are they acceptable if they lessen your performance? How do you think time pressure will affect your reading? With too much to read and too little time, are you likely to cut corners or are you likely to work longer hours?

Chapter Summary

As you use the summary below to review the concepts you learned in this chapter, focus also on its format—in this case a **formal outline,** in other chapters a think link or the Cornell system. As you become comfortable with the organization and style of these formats, try using each of them to take notes, seeing which approach works best for you in particular situations.

CHAPTER 4

I. Measures to improve reading comprehension

A. Understanding material requires time, persistence, critical thinking, and an active approach.

B. It also requires a positive attitude and the use of studying (SQ3R) and vocabulary-building tools.

II. Setting the stage for reading success

A. When college texts are difficult, strategies are needed to master content.

1. Start with a positive attitude, an open mind, and a willingness to wade through difficult material several times. Take a critical-thinking approach to the material and define unclear concepts as you become actively involved with them.

2. Choose the right time and spot for studying to maximize concentration.

3. Learn to concentrate by choosing a location without distractions, dealing with internal problems, making to-do lists of things that are on your mind, studying for a period and then taking a break, and rewarding yourself for your accomplishments.

4. Familiarize yourself with what's ahead before you start studying.

   a. Use SQ3R.

   b. Read a primer on the topic.

5. Become emotionally involved with the material.

6. Define your reading purpose to determine how you read and your reading pace.

   a. Purpose 1: read for understanding

   b. Purpose 2: read to evaluate critically

      c. Purpose 3: read for practical application

      d. Purpose 4: read for pleasure

    7. Spend enough time studying: a course load of 15 credit hours means that you should spend 30 hours per week studying and doing homework outside of class.

III. Building a strong vocabulary improves reading comprehension and speed.

    A. Analyze word parts including roots, prefixes, and suffixes.

    B. Use a dictionary or text glossary to look up unfamiliar words.

    C. Learn the specialized vocabulary of academic fields.

    D. Use various memory aids to cement recall.

IV. Increasing your reading speed will enable you to handle large reading loads.

    A. Among the problems slow readers face are word-by-word reading, lack of concentration, vocalization and subvocalization, a limited vocabulary and knowledge base, unconscious regression, slow recovery time, and treating all assignments the same.

      1. Studying and mastering strategies for each of these problems will help you read faster and understand more.

Endnotes

1. Sherwood Harris, *The New York Public Library Book of How and Where to Look It Up*. Englewood Cliffs, NJ: Prentice Hall, 1991, p. 13.

2. *Keys to Lifelong Learning Telecourse*. Dir. Mary Jane Bradbury. Videocassette. Intrepid Films, 2000.

3. Eric Jensen, *Student Success Secrets*, 5th ed. New York: Barron's Educational Series, 2003, p. 88.

4. Charles G. Morris and Albert A. Maisto, *Psychology: An Introduction*, 12th ed. Upper Saddle River, NJ: Pearson Prentice Hall, 2005, p. 179.

5. See Harold Bloom, *How to Read and Why*. New York: Scribner, 2000.

6. George M. Usova, *Efficient Study Strategies: Skills for Successful Learning*. Pacific Grove, CA: Brooks/Cole Publishing, 1989, p. 45.

7. Robert J. Ball, "Letter to the Editor: Making Students Toe the Mark," *The Chronicle of Higher Education*, March 19, 2004, p. B18.

8. Steven Moidel, *Speed Reading*. Hauppauge, NY: Barron's Educational Series, 1994, p. 18.

9. Ibid., pp. 18–25.

10. Ibid., p. 32.

"The man who does not read good books
has no advantage over the man
who can't read them."

MARK TWAIN, AMERICAN HUMORIST

Studying Textbooks and Course Materials

MASTERING CONTENT

T
he key to understanding and retaining what you read is to become an active reader. As you will see in this chapter, the SQ3R study technique transforms reading from a passive into an active activity as it helps you grasp ideas quickly, remember more, and review effectively for tests.

The process of asking and answering questions nurtures involvement as you decide what is important enough to include in your notes, to highlight in your text, and to commit to memory. At its heart, SQ3R is a *reading strategy* that is also a *learning strategy* for mastering and thinking critically. In the years ahead, it will help you master job-related readings. In addition, its core of critical questioning will give you tools to interpret the meaning of visual aids.

In this chapter you will explore answers to the following questions:

- How can SQ3R help you own what you read?
- How do you customize your text with highlighting and notes?
- How can you respond critically to what you read?
- How do you read visual aids?
- How will good reading skills help you in your career?

HOW CAN SQ3R HELP YOU OWN
WHAT YOU READ?

SQ3R stands for *Survey, Question, Read, Recite,* and *Review.* Developed about 60 years ago by Francis Robinson, the technique is still used today because it works.[1]

As you move through the stages of SQ3R, you will skim and scan your text. *Skimming* involves the rapid reading of such chapter elements as section introductions and conclusions, boldfaced or italicized terms, pictures and charts, and chapter summaries. The goal of skimming is a quick construction of the main ideas. In contrast, *scanning* involves the careful search for specific facts and examples. You might use scanning during the review phase of SQ3R to locate particular information (such as a chemistry formula).

Approach SQ3R as a flexible framework on which to build your study method. When you bring your personal learning styles and study preferences to the system, it will work better than if you follow it rigidly. For example, you and another classmate may focus on elements in a different order when you survey, write different types of questions, or favor different sets of review strategies. Explore the strategies, evaluate what works, and then make the system your own. Note that although SQ3R will help you as you study almost every subject, it is not appropriate for literature.

Survey

Surveying, the first stage in SQ3R, is the process of previewing, or prereading, a book before you study it. Compare it to looking at a map before starting a road trip; determining the route and stops along the way in advance will save time and trouble while you travel.

Most textbooks include elements that provide a big-picture overview of the main ideas and themes. You need the big picture to make sense of the thousands of information nuggets contained in the text and to learn the order of topics and the amount of space allotted to each. You'll gain an overview by surveying the following text elements.

Front Matter

Skim the *table of contents* for the chapter titles, the main topics in each chapter, and the order in which they will be covered, as well as special features. Then skim the *preface,* which is a personal note from the author that tells you what the book will cover and its point of view. For example, the preface for the American history text *Out of Many* states that it highlights "the experiences of diverse communities of Americans in the unfolding story of our country."[2] This tells you that cultural diversity is a central theme.

Chapter Elements

Generally, every chapter includes devices that structure the material and highlight important content. Among these are:

- chapter title, which establishes the topic and often the author's perspective
- chapter introduction, outline, list of objectives, or list of key topics
- first-, second-, and third-level headings, including those in question form
- information in the margins including definitions, quotations, thought questions, and exercises
- tables, charts, photographs, and captions that express important concepts
- side-bar boxed features that are connected to textwide themes
- particular styles or arrangements of type (**boldface,** *italics,* <u>underlining,</u> larger fonts, bullet points, boxed text) that call attention to vocabulary or concepts
- an end-of-chapter summary that reviews chapter content
- review questions and exercises that help you master concepts and think critically about what you have read

In Key 5.1, a typical page from the college textbook *Psychology: An Introduction*[3] by Charles G. Morris and Albert A. Maisto, how many elements do you recognize? How do these elements help you grasp the subject even before reading it?

Back Matter

Some texts include a *glossary* that defines text terms. You may also find an *index* to help you locate topics and a *bibliography* that lists additional readings.

Key 5.1   **Various survey elements are included on this text page.**

 186   **Chapter 5** • Learning

Classical (or Pavlovian) conditioning The type of learning in which a response naturally elicited by one stimulus comes to be elicited by a different, formerly neutral stimulus.

Unconditioned stimulus (US) A stimulus that invariably causes an organism to respond in a specific way.

Unconditioned response (UR) A response that takes place in an organism whenever an unconditioned stimulus occurs.

Conditioned stimulus (CS) An originally neutral stimulus that is paired with an unconditioned stimulus and eventually produces the desired response in an organism when presented alone.

Conditioned response (CR) After conditioning, the response an organism produces when only a conditioned stimulus is presented.

you are experiencing insight. When you imitate the steps of professional dancers you saw last night on television, you are demonstrating observational learning. Like conditioning, cognitive learning is one of our survival strategies. Through cognitive processes, we learn which events are safe and which are dangerous without having to experience those events directly. Cognitive learning also gives us access to the wisdom of people who lived hundreds of years ago, and it will give people living hundreds of years from now some insight into our experiences and way of life.

Our discussion begins with *classical conditioning*. This simple kind of learning serves as a convenient starting point for examining what learning is and how it can be observed.

Classical Conditioning

How did Pavlov's discovery of classical conditioning help to shed light on learning?

Ivan Pavlov (1849–1936), a Russian physiologist who was studying digestive processes, discovered classical conditioning almost by accident. Because animals salivate when food is placed in their mouths, Pavlov inserted tubes into the salivary glands of dogs to measure how much saliva they produced when they were given food. He noticed, however, that the dogs salivated before the food was in their mouths: The mere sight of food made them drool. In fact, they even drooled at the sound of the experimenter's footsteps. This aroused Pavlov's curiosity. What was making the dogs salivate even before they had the food in their mouths? How had they learned to salivate in response to the sound of the experimenter's approach?

To answer these questions, Pavlov set out to teach the dogs to salivate when food was not present. He devised an experiment in which he sounded a bell just before the food was brought into the room. A ringing bell does not usually make a dog's mouth water but, after hearing the bell many times just before getting fed, Pavlov's dogs began to salivate as soon as the bell rang. It was as if they had learned that the bell signaled the appearance of food, and their mouths watered on cue even if no food followed. The dogs had been conditioned to salivate in response to a new stimulus—the bell—that would not normally have prompted that response (Pavlov, 1927). Figure 5–1, shows one of Pavlov's procedures in which the bell has been replaced by a touch to the dog's leg just before food is given.

Elements of Classical Conditioning

Generally speaking, **classical (or Pavlovian) conditioning** involves pairing an *involuntary* response (for example, salivation) that is usually evoked by one stimulus with a different, formerly neutral stimulus (such as a bell or a touch on the leg). Pavlov's experiment illustrates the four basic elements of classical conditioning. The first is an **unconditioned stimulus (US)**, such as food, which invariably prompts a certain reaction—salivation, in this case. That reaction—the **unconditioned response (UR)**—is the second element and always results from the unconditioned stimulus: Whenever the dog is given food (US), its mouth waters (UR). The third element is the neutral stimulus—the ringing bell—which is called the **conditioned stimulus (CS)**. At first, the conditioned stimulus is said to be "neutral" with respect to the desired response (salivation), because dogs do not salivate at the sound of a bell unless they have been conditioned to react in this way by repeatedly presenting the CS and US together. Frequent pairing of the CS and US produces the fourth element in the classical conditioning process: the **conditioned response (CR)**. The conditioned response is the behavior that the animal has learned in response to the conditioned stimulus. Usually, the unconditioned response and the conditioned

SURVEY A TEXT

Practice will improve your surveying skills. So start now with this text or another you are currently using:

- Skim the front matter, including the table of contents and preface. What does this material tell you about the theme? About the book's approach and point of view?

  _____

  _____

  _____

- Are there unexpected topics listed in the table of contents? Are there topics you expected to see but are missing?

  _____

  _____

- Now look at a typical text chapter. List the devices that organize the structure and content of the material.

  _____

  _____

- After skimming the chapter, what do you know about the material? What elements helped you skim quickly?

  _____

  _____

- Finally, skim the back matter. What back-matter elements can you identify?

  _____

  _____

- How do you plan to use each of these elements when you begin studying?

  _____

  _____

Key 5.2   Use surveying devices to preview your text.

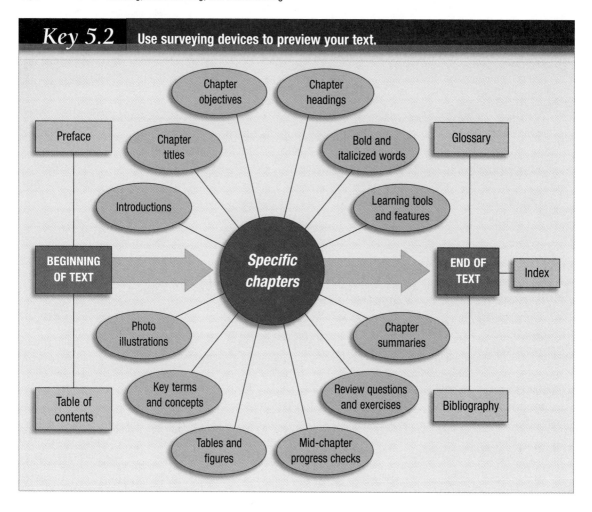

Key 5.2 shows the variety of survey elements. Start now to apply these techniques to your current texts by writing down what you learn from the front matter, chapter elements, and back matter.

Question

Now that you have surveyed your text, your next step is to *ask questions* about your assignment. The process of asking questions leads you to discover knowledge on your own, which is the essence of critical thinking (see Chapter 3). As you pose questions and discover the answers in your text, you teach yourself the material.

Step 1: Ask Yourself What You Know About the Topic

Before you begin reading, take a few minutes to summarize in writing what you already know about the topic, if anything. This exercise forces you to delve into your knowledge base as you set the context for adding more information or correcting misconceptions.

Thinking about your current knowledge is especially important in your major, where the concepts you learn in one course prepare you for those you will learn in subsequent courses. For example, while your first business course may introduce the broad concept of marketing research, an upper-level marketing course may explore, in depth, how marketing research analyzes consumer behavior according to age, education, income and economic status, and attitudes. Learning this advanced material depends on understanding the basics.

Step 2: Write Questions Linked to Chapter Headings

Next, examine the chapter headings and, on a separate page or in the text margins, write *questions* linked to them. When you encounter an assignment without headings, divide the material into logical sections, and then develop questions based on what you think is the main idea of each section.

Key 5.3 shows how this works. The left column contains primary- and secondary-level headings from a section of *Out of Many*. The right column rephrases these headings in question form.

Key 5.3	Creating questions from headings.
THE MEANING OF FREEDOM	**WHAT DID FREEDOM MEAN FOR BOTH SLAVES AND CITIZENS IN THE UNITED STATES?**
Moving About	Where did African Americans go after they were freed from slavery?
The African American Family	How did freedom change the structure of the African American family?
African American Churches and Schools	What effect did freedom have on the formation of African American churches and schools?
Land and Labor after Slavery	How was land farmed and maintained after slaves were freed?
The Origins of African American Politics	How did the end of slavery bring about the beginning of African American political life?

There is no "correct" set of questions. Given the same headings, you could create different questions. Your goal is to engage the material as you begin to think critically about it.

Read

Your text survey and questions give you a starting point for *reading*, the first R in SQ3R. Retaining what you read requires an active approach:

Focus on the key points of your survey. Pay special attention to points raised in headings, in boldface type, in chapter objectives and summary, and so forth.

ACTIVE THINKING

Go For It!　　BUILDING YOUR SKILLS

TURN CHAPTER HEADINGS INTO QUESTIONS

Put pencil to paper with the one primary-level heading and eight secondary-level headings from the "Groups and Organization" chapter of the 10th edition of *Sociology* by John J. Macionis. Create questions that will make you think about the subject—even if you know nothing about it right now.

HEADINGS IN MACIONIS'S "GROUPS AND ORGANIZATION" CHAPTER	WRITE QUESTIONS THAT WILL HELP YOU THINK CRITICALLY ABOUT THE MATERIAL
Social Groups	
Primary and Secondary Groups	
Group Leadership	
Group Conformity	
Reference Groups	
In-Groups and Out-Groups	
Group Size	
Social Diversity: Race, Class, and Gender	
Networks	

Source: John J. Macionis, *Sociology,* 10th edition. Upper Saddle River, NJ: Pearson Prentice Hall, 2005, pp. 162–170.

Focus on your Q-stage questions. Read the material with the purpose of answering each question. Write down or highlight ideas and examples that relate to your questions.

Mark up your text and take text notes. You may want to write notes in the margins or on separate paper, circle key ideas, or highlight key points to remind you of what's important. These cues will help you study for exams. Text-marking and note-taking techniques will be examined later in the chapter.

Create text tabs. Place plastic index tabs or adhesive notes at the start of different chapters to help you flip back and forth with ease. Locating pages can be frustrating, so you want to do everything you can to make it stress-free.

Find the Main Idea

Understanding what you read depends on your ability to recognize *main ideas* and link other ideas to them. You are likely to find these core ideas

- in a topic sentence at the beginning of the paragraph, stating the topic of the paragraph and what about that topic the author wants to communicate, followed by sentences adding support.
- at the end of the paragraph, following supporting details that lead up to it.
- buried in the middle of the paragraph, sandwiched between supporting details.
- in a compilation of ideas from various sentences, each of which contains a critical element. Sometimes, it is up to you to piece these elements together to find the author's main idea.
- never explicitly stated, but implied in the passage.

When the main idea of a passage is not clear, how do you decide what it is? Ophelia H. Hancock, a specialist in improving reading skills for college students, suggests a three-step approach:[4]

1. **Search for the topic of the paragraph.** The topic of the paragraph is not the same as the main idea. Rather, it is the broad subject being discussed—for example, former president John F. Kennedy, hate crimes on campus, or the Internet.

2. **Identify the aspect of the topic that is the paragraph's focus.** If the general topic is former president John F. Kennedy, the author may focus on any of thousands of aspects of that topic, such as his health problems, his civil rights policies, or his effectiveness as a public speaker.

3. **Find what the author wants you to know about that specific aspect; this is the main idea.** The main idea of a paragraph dealing with President Kennedy as a public speaker may be this: *President Kennedy was a gifted, charismatic speaker who used his humor, charm, and intelligence to make the presidency accessible to all Americans during regularly televised presidential news conferences.*

Go For It!   BUILDING YOUR SKILLS

FIND THE MAIN IDEA OF A PARAGRAPH

Use the three-step approach described on pp. 163–164 to find the main idea of the following paragraph from the seventh edition of *Biology: Life on Earth* by Teresa and Gerald Audesirk and Bruce E. Byers.[5]

> Organisms reproduce, giving rise to offspring of the same type and creating *continuity of life*. The processes by which this occurs vary, but the result—the perpetuation of the parents' genetic material—is the same. The *diversity of life* occurs in part because offspring, though arising from the genetic material provided by their parents, are usually somewhat different from their parents. . . . The specific mechanisms by which traits are passed from one generation to the next, using genetic information that is recombined in various ways, produce these variable offspring.

- What is the topic of this paragraph?

  _____

- What aspect of this topic is being discussed?

  _____

- What main idea is being communicated?

  _____

- Now choose a meaty paragraph from one of your current texts and use the same questions to find the paragraph's main idea. How do these questions help you focus on the paragraph's important points?

  _____

  _____

Prioritize Your Reading Assignments

Ask yourself what information is important and what you have to remember. According to Adam Robinson, cofounder of the *Princeton Review* and author of *What Smart Students Know,* successful students are able to tell the difference between important information worthy of study, information they should know about in a general way, and information they should ignore. Says Robinson, "The only way you can effectively absorb the relevant information is to ignore the irrelevant information. . . . Trying to digest and understand all the information in a textbook is . . . an excellent way to become quickly and hopelessly confused."[6]

The following questions will help you determine if text material is important enough to study in depth:

- Is the material stressed in headings, charts, tables, captions, key terms, and definitions? In midchapter and end-of-chapter exercises? In the chapter introduction and summary? (Surveying before reading will enable you to answer these questions.)
- Is the material a definition, a crucial concept, an example, an explanation of a variety or type, a critical relationship or comparison?
- Does it spark questions and reactions as you read?
- Does it surprise or confuse you?
- Did your instructor stress the material in class? Does your assignment ask you to focus on something specific?

When trying to figure out what to study and what to skim, ask yourself whether your instructor would expect you to know the material. (The more experience you have with your instructor, the easier it will be to make these judgments.) If you are unsure and if the topic is not on your syllabus, e-mail your instructor and ask for clarification.

Many dorms and libraries have nooks designed to facilitate either individual reading sessions or group study.

Recite

Once you finish reading a topic, stop and answer the questions you raised in the Q stage of SQ3R. *Even if you have already done this during the reading phase, do it again now—with the purpose of learning and committing the material to memory.*

You may decide to *recite* each answer aloud, silently speak the answers to yourself, "teach" the answers to another person, or write your ideas and answers in note form. Whatever recitation method you choose, make sure you know how ideas connect to one another and to the general concept being discussed.

Writing is the most effective way to learn new material. Using your own words to explain new concepts gives you immediate feedback: When you can do it effectively, you know the material. When you can't, you still need to work with the text or with a study partner. Whatever you do, don't get discouraged. Just go back and search for what you missed.

Writing comprehensive responses at this stage can save time later. As you record responses to your Q-stage questions, you can compare what you have written to your text and make adjustments, a process that will help you digest the material. Your responses then become a study tool for review.

Keep your learning styles in mind when you explore different strategies (see Chapter 2). For example, an intrapersonal learner may prefer writing, while an interpersonal learner may choose to recite answers aloud to a classmate. A logical-mathematical learner may benefit from organizing material into detailed outlines or charts, whereas a musical learner might want to chant information aloud to a rhythm.

When do you stop to recite? Waiting for the end of a chapter is too late; stopping at the end of a paragraph is too soon. The best plan is to recite at the end of each distinct text section, right before a new text heading. Repeat the question-read-recite cycle until you complete the entire chapter.

University of Michigan professor and textbook author Charles G. Morris suggests that "chunking" will help you learn as you read and recite. "I tell students to read a chunk and then stop and ask themselves, what have I learned? How does that relate to my life? Can I think of examples? You need active involvement before going on."[7] For instance, relating a president's isolationist foreign policy to the way your grandmother avoids her neighbors will help you recall the president's stance.

If you find yourself fumbling for thoughts, you may not yet own the ideas. Reread the section that's giving you trouble until you master its contents.

Review

Review soon after you finish a chapter. Reviewing, both immediately and periodically in the days and weeks after you read, will help you learn and memorize material as it prepares you for exams. If you close the book after reading it once, chances are that you will forget almost everything, which is why students who read material for the first time right before a test often do poorly. Reviewing is your key to learning.

Reviewing the same material over time will also help you identify knowledge gaps. It's natural to forget material between study sessions, especially if it's confusing or complex. When you come back after a break, you can focus on your deficits.

Here are some reviewing techniques. Try them all, and use what work best:

- Reread your notes. Then summarize them from memory.
- Review and summarize in writing the text sections you highlighted or bracketed. Try to condense the material so that you can focus on key ideas.
- Answer the end-of-chapter review, discussion, and application questions.
- Reread the preface, headings, tables, and summary.
- Recite important concepts to yourself, or record them and play them back on a tape player.
- Make flash cards with a word or concept on one side and a definition, examples, or other related information on the other. Test yourself.
- Quiz yourself, using the questions you raised in the Q-stage. If you can't answer a question, scan the text for the answer.
- Discuss the concepts with a classmate or in a study group. Boost learning by using one another's Q-stage questions.
- Finally, ask your instructor for help with difficult material. Define exactly what you want to discuss, and then schedule a meeting during office hours or e-mail your questions.

All this effort takes time, but the potential payoff is huge if you're motivated to work hard. Although, at times, it may be tempting to photocopy a classmate's text notes instead of reading and taking your own notes, you will learn only if you do the work yourself.

Refreshing your knowledge is easier and faster than learning it the first time. Make a review schedule—for example, once a week—and stick to it until you're sure of your knowledge. Use different reviewing techniques as you work toward mastering the material.

Key 5.4 summarizes how SQ3R turns you into an active reader.

Transforming your textbook into a valuable work tool through highlighting and notes will help you make the most of study time as you set the stage for review.

HOW DO YOU CUSTOMIZE YOUR TEXT WITH HIGHLIGHTING AND NOTES?

Today's textbooks are designed and written with students in mind, but they are not customized to meet your unique reading and studying needs. It is up to you to do that for yourself through text highlighting

Key 5.4   Use SQ3R to become an active reader and learn new concepts.

STAGE OF SQ3R	DESCRIPTION
Survey	Pre-reading a book before studying it—involves skimming and scanning as you examine the front matter, chapter elements, and back matter for clues about text content and organization.
Question	Developing questions linked to chapter headings and to what you already know about the topic. Questioning engages your critical thinking skills.
Read	Reading the material to answer the questions formulated in the Q stage and find main ideas. You can take notes as you read or highlight key ideas and information in your text.
Recite	Recitation involves answering—perhaps for a second time—your Q-stage questions. You may decide to recite the answers aloud or silently to yourself, teach them to a study partner, or record them in writing.
Review	Using various techniques to learn the material before an exam. Become actively involved with the material through summarizing notes, answering study questions, writing outlines or think links, reciting concepts, using flash cards, thinking critically, and so on.

and notes. Your goal is to transform your texts into invaluable—and very personal—study tools.

How to Highlight a Text

Highlighting involves the use of special highlighting markers or regular pens or pencils to flag important passages. When used correctly, highlighting is an essential study technique. Here are some techniques that will help you transform highlighting into a learning tool:

- Develop a **highlighting system and stick to it.** For example, decide in advance if you will use different-colored markers for different elements, brackets for long passages, or pencil underlining. Make a key that identifies each notation.
- **Consider using a regular pencil or pen instead of a highlighter pen.** The copy will be cleaner and some students prefer less color in their textbooks.

- **Read an entire paragraph before you begin to highlight, and don't start until you have a sense of what is important.** Only then put pencil or highlighter to paper as you pick out key terms, phrases, and ideas.

- **Highlight key terms and concepts.** Mark examples that explain and support important ideas.

- **Avoid overmarking.** A phrase or two in any paragraph is usually enough. Enclose long passages with brackets rather than marking every line. Avoid underlining entire sentences, when possible. The less color the better.

Although these techniques will help you highlight effectively, they won't help you learn the material and, ironically, they may actually obstruct learning as you diligently add color to the page. Experts agree that you will not learn what you highlight unless you *interact* with the material through surveying, questioning, reciting, and review. Without this interaction, all you are doing is marking your book.

Convinced that interactions are essential, Lia Mandaglio, a student at Lafayette College, explains how she combines highlighter and pen to mark and learn: "I highlight important material and then use a pen to circle words I don't understand and to write definitions in the margins and short notes connecting the material to what I already know or previously read. When I'm confused, I put a question mark in pen next to the passage so that I remember to ask my instructor. This method really works for me because I've assigned the highlighter and pen different jobs."

Work Together **BUILDING YOUR SKILLS**

SHARPEN YOUR HIGHLIGHTING SKILLS

Join with your study partners to sharpen your highlighting skills. This technique will help group members help each other:[8]

- Photocopy a three- to four-page section from an introductory text, and ask everyone to highlight the important material. Then compare versions, asking group members to explain why they highlighted certain words, phrases, and sentences and not others. Your goal is to learn from each other and to get in the habit of using critical thinking as you highlight.

How to Take Text Notes

When you combine highlighting with marginal notes or text flags, you remind yourself what a particular passage is about and why you consider it important. This combination customizes your text, which helps you study for exams. Going a step further by taking a full set of text notes is an excellent way to commit material to memory.

As you will also see in Chapter 7, note taking on texts and in class is critical since material is cumulative—that is, what you learn today builds on what you learned yesterday and the day before since the beginning of the semester. Notes will help you master what you need to know and review effectively for midterms and finals.

Taking Marginal Notes

Here are some tips for taking marginal notes right on the pages of your text:

- Use pencil so you can easily erase comments or questions that are answered as you read.
- Write your Q questions from SQ3R in the margins right next to text headings.
- Mark critical sections with marginal notations such as "Def." for definition, "E.g." for helpful example, "Concept" for an important concept, "Dates" for an important chronology, etc.
- Write notes at the bottom of the page connecting the text to what you learned in class or in research. If you don't have enough room, attach adhesive notes with your comments.

Key 5.5 illustrates how to highlight effectively and take marginal notes. It shows an introduction to business textbook page that introduces the concept of target marketing and market segmentation.

Go For It!   BUILDING YOUR SKILLS

MARK UP A PAGE TO LEARN A PAGE

On page 172, the text material in Key 5.5 continues and is shown unmarked. Put your own pencil to paper as you highlight concepts and take marginal notes. Compare your efforts to those of your classmates to see how each of you approached the task and what you can learn from different methods.

Key 5.5   Underlining and taking marginal notes help you master content.[9]

Chapter 10: Understanding Marketing Processes and Consumer Behavior   **297**

How does target marketing and market segmentation help companies sell product?

▉ TARGET MARKETING AND MARKET SEGMENTATION

Definitions ↙

Marketers have long known that products cannot be all things to all people. Buyers have different tastes, goals, lifestyles, and so on. The emergence of the marketing concept and the recognition of consumer needs and wants led marketers to think in terms of **target markets**—groups of people with similar wants and needs. <u>Selecting target markets is usually the first step in the marketing strategy.</u>

target market
Group of people that has similar wants and needs and that can be expected to show interest in the same products

Target marketing requires **market segmentation**—dividing a market into categories of customer types or "segments." <u>Once they have identified segments, companies may adopt a variety of strategies.</u> Some <u>firms market products to more</u> than one ← *GM eg* <u>segment. General Motors</u> *(www.gm.com)*, for example, offers compact cars, vans, trucks, luxury cars, and sports cars with various features and at various price levels. GM's strategy is to provide an automobile for nearly every segment of the market.

market segmentation
Process of dividing a market into categories of customer types

GM makes cars for diff. market segments

In contrast, <u>some businesses offer a narrower range of products</u>, each aimed toward a specific segment. Note that segmentation is a strategy for analyzing consumers, not products. The process of fixing, adapting, and communicating the nature of the product itself is called *product positioning*.

How do companies identify market segments?

Identifying Market Segments

By definition, <u>members of a market segment</u> must <u>share some common traits that affect</u> their <u>purchasing decisions</u>. In identifying segments, researchers look at several different influences on consumer behavior. Three of the most important are *geographic, demographic,* and *psychographic variables.*

What effect does geography have on segmentation strategies?

Geographic Variables Many buying decisions are affected by the places people call home. The heavy rainfall in Washington State, for instance, means that people there buy more umbrellas than people in the Sun Belt. Urban residents don't need agricultural equipment, and sailboats sell better along the coasts than on the Great Plains. **Geographic variables** are the geographical units, from countries to neighborhoods, that may be considered in a segmentation strategy.

Buying decisions influenced by where people live

geographic variables
Geographical units that may be considered in developing a segmentation strategy

<u>These patterns affect decisions about marketing mixes for a huge range of products.</u> For example, consider a plan to market down-filled parkas in rural Minnesota. Demand will be high and price competition intense. Local newspaper ads may be

— good eg —
selling parkas in Minnesota

Thought
Geographical variables change with the seasons

Source: Business Essentials, 5th ed. by Ebert/Griffin, © 2005. Reprinted by permission of Pearson/Prentice Hall, Upper Saddle River, NJ.

Key 5.5   Continued

effective, and the best retail location may be one that is easily reached from several small towns.

Although the marketability of some products is geographically sensitive, others enjoy nearly universal acceptance. Coke, for example, gets more than 70 percent of its sales from international markets. It is the market leader in Great Britain, China, Germany, Japan, Brazil, and Spain. Pepsi's international sales are about 15 percent of Coke's. In fact, Coke's chief competitor in most countries is some local soft drink, not Pepsi, which earns 78 percent of its income at home.

demographic variables
Characteristics of populations that may be considered in developing a segmentation strategy

Demographic Variables Demographic variables describe populations by identifying such traits as age, income, gender, ethnic background, marital status, race, religion, and social class. For example, several general consumption characteristics can be attributed to certain age groups (18–25, 26–35, 36–45, and so on). A marketer can, thus, divide markets into age groups. Table 10.1 lists some possible demographic breakdowns. Depending on the marketer's purpose, a segment can be a single classification (*aged* 20–34) or a combination of categories (*aged* 20–34, *married with children, earning* $25,000–$34,999). Foreign competitors, for example, are gaining market share in U.S. auto sales by appealing to young buyers (under age 30) with limited incomes (under $30,000). Whereas companies such as Hyundai *(www.hyundai.net)*, Kia *(www.kia.com)*, and Daewoo *(www.daewoous.com)* are winning entry-level customers with high quality and generous warranties, Volkswagen *(www.vw.com)* targets under-35 buyers with its entertainment-styled VW Jetta.[4]

psychographic variables
Consumer characteristics, such as lifestyles, opinions, interests, and attitudes, that may be considered in developing a segmentation strategy

Psychographic Variables Markets can also be segmented according to such **psychographic variables** as lifestyles, interests, and attitudes. Take, for example, Burberry *(www.burberry.com)*, whose raincoats have been a symbol of British tradition since 1856. Burberry has repositioned itself as a global luxury brand, like Gucci *(www.gucci.com)* and Louis Vuitton *(www.vuitton.com)*. The strategy, which recently resulted in a 31-percent sales increase, calls for attracting a different type of customer—the top-of-the-line, fashion-conscious individual—who shops at such stores as Neiman Marcus and Bergdorf Goodman.[5]

Psychographics are particularly important to marketers because, unlike demographics and geographics, they can be changed by marketing efforts. For example, Polish companies have overcome consumer resistance by promoting the safety and desirability of using credit rather than depending solely on cash. One product of changing attitudes is a booming economy and the emergence of a robust middle class.

TABLE 10.1

Demographic Variables

Age	Under 5, 5–11, 12–19, 20–34, 35–49, 50–64, 65+
Education	Grade school or less, some high school, graduated high school, some college, college degree, advanced degree
Family life cycle	Young single, young married without children, young married with children, older married with children under 18, older married without children under 18, older single, other
Family size	1, 2–3, 4–5, 6+
Income	Under $9,000, $9,000–$14,999, $15,000–$24,999, $25,000–$34,999, $35,000–$45,000, over $45,000
Nationality	African, American, Asian, British, Eastern European, French, German, Irish, Italian, Latin American, Middle Eastern, Scandinavian
Race	Native American, Asian, Black, White
Religion	Buddhist, Catholic, Hindu, Jewish, Muslim, Protestant
Sex	Male, female

Your customized text will be uniquely yours; no one else will highlight or take text notes as you do because no one else has your knowledge, learning style, or study techniques. Because text customization is so important to mastering course material, you may encounter a problem if you buy used texts that are heavily highlighted or filled with marginal notations. Even if the previous owner was a good student, he or she is not you—and that fact alone may make a huge difference in your ability to master content.

Taking Full-Text Notes

Taking a full set of notes on assigned readings helps you learn as you summarize main ideas in your own words. Taking notes makes you an active participant as you think about how material fits into what you already know and how to capture key points.

To construct a *summary,* focus on the main ideas and the examples that support them. Don't include any of your own ideas or evaluations at this point. Your summary should simply condense the material, making it easier to focus on concepts and how they relate to one another when you review.

Here are suggestions for creating effective full-text summaries:

- Try to use your own words, since repeating the author's words may mean parroting concepts you do not understand. If you're in the habit of transcribing verbatim what you've highlighted, you're probably learning very little and may find yourself thinking of other things or even dozing as you write. When studying a technical subject with precise definitions, you may have little choice but to use text wording.

- Try to make your notes, simple, clear, and brief. Include what you need to understand the topic, while eliminating less important details.

- Consider outlining the text so you can see at a glance the interrelationship among ideas.

- Before you write, identify the main idea of a passage.

- Once that idea ends and another begins, begin taking notes from memory, using your own words. Go back into the text, as needed, to cull information that you didn't get on the first reading.

- Take notes on tables, charts, photographs, and captions; these visual presentations may contain information presented no where else in the text. You may want to make sketches to remind you what these visuals look like.

- Use shorthand symbols to write quickly (see Chapter 7).

- Use visual formats:
    - Construct your own charts, tables, and diagrams that visually express the concepts in the written text.

MULTIPLE INTELLIGENCE STRATEGIES FOR READING. Use selected reading techniques in Multiple Intelligence areas to strengthen your ability to read for meaning and retention.

INTELLIGENCE	SUGGESTED STRATEGIES	WHAT WORKS FOR YOU? WRITE NEW IDEAS HERE
Verbal-Linguistic	■ Mark up your text with marginal notes while you read. ■ When tackling a chapter, use every stage of SQ3R, taking advantage of each writing opportunity (writing Q stage questions, writing summaries, and so on).	
Logical-Mathematical	■ Read material in sequence. ■ Think about the logical connections between what you are reading and the world at large; consider similarities, differences, and cause-and-effect relationships.	
Bodily-Kinesthetic	■ Take physical breaks during reading sessions—walk, stretch, exercise. ■ Pace while reciting important ideas.	
Visual-Spatial	■ As you read, take particular note of photos, tables, figures, and other visual aids. ■ Make charts, diagrams, or think links illustrating difficult concepts you encounter in your reading.	
Interpersonal	■ With a friend, have a joint reading session. One should read a section silently and then summarize aloud the important concepts for the other. Reverse the order of summarizer and listener for each section. ■ Discuss reading material and clarify important concepts in a study group.	
Intrapersonal	■ Read in a solitary setting and allow time for reflection. ■ Think about how a particular reading assignment makes you feel, and evaluate your reaction by considering the material in light of what you already know.	
Musical	■ Play music while you read. ■ Recite important concepts in your reading to rhythms or write a song to depict those concepts.	
Naturalistic	■ Read and study in a natural environment. ■ Before reading indoors, imagine your favorite place in nature in order to create a relaxed frame of mind.	

- Devise a color-coding system to indicate level of importance of different ideas, and then mark up your notes with these colors.
- Devise symbols and numbers and use them consistently to indicate the level of importance of different ideas. Write these in different-colored pens.

HOW CAN YOU RESPOND CRITICALLY TO WHAT YOU READ?

Think of critical reading as an extension of the Q stage of SQ3R. When you read critically, you develop probing questions that explore whether ideas are true and accurate, that compare and evaluate information sources, that enable you to judge whether information meets your academic purpose, that investigate whether the author's thesis holds up against scrutiny, and more.

Instead of simply accepting what you read, seek understanding by questioning the material as you move from idea to idea. The best critical readers question every argument for accuracy, relevance, and logic.

Use Knowledge of Fact and Opinion to Evaluate Arguments

Critical readers evaluate arguments to determine if they are accurate and logical. In this context, *argument* refers to a persuasive case—a set of connected ideas supported by examples—that a writer makes to prove or disprove a point.

It's easy—and common—to accept or reject an argument outright, according to whether it fits your point of view. Through questioning, however, you try to understand the argument in greater depth as you judge the quality of the evidence, whether the support fits the concept, and whether connections are logical. When quality evidence combines with appropriate support and tight logic, the argument is solid.

What Is the Quality of the Evidence?

Ask the following questions to evaluate the evidence:

- What is the source?
- Is the source reliable and free of bias?
- Who wrote this and with what intent?
- What assumptions underlie this material?
- Is the argument based on opinion?
- How does the evidence compare to evidence from other sources?

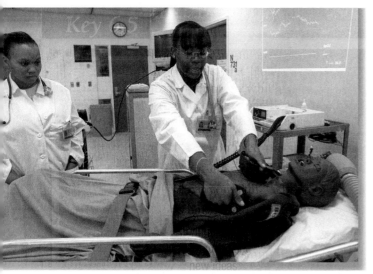

What you learn in your textbook is often enhanced and solidified by hands-on experience. These respiratory therapy students put their knowledge to work on a medical mannequin.

How Well Does the Evidence Support the Idea?

Ask these questions to determine whether the evidence fits the concept:

- Is there enough evidence to support the central idea?
- Do examples and ideas logically connect to one another?
- Is the evidence convincing? Do the examples build a strong case?
- What different and perhaps opposing arguments seem just as valid?

As you assess evidence, keep in mind that the *amount* of evidence is less important than the *strength* of the evidence. A good way to determine quality is to identify all the evidence you have and then analyze which is flawed and which is strong, applicable, and significant. Approach every argument with both an open mind and healthy skepticism. Use critical thinking to make an informed evaluation.

Remember that critical reading takes focus. Give yourself a chance to be successful by finding a time, place, and purpose for your reading. Then, says California State University English professor Kim Flachmann, "challenge assumptions, question ideas, and reject ideas. There is nothing passive in this process."[10] Also, cross-fertilize your ideas with those of your classmates by working in groups whenever you can.

HOW DO YOU READ VISUAL AIDS?

Visual aids present data in tables, charts, illustrations, maps, and photographs. Their purpose is to present, clarify, or summarize information in a form that shows comparisons and that is easy to read and understand. Visual aids save space and speed up reading. A table or chart can present information more concisely than if the information were presented in paragraph form, so don't skip over them.

Visual aids are in nearly every college text and are a staple of business documents, including e-mail. Their popularity has spread because PowerPoint and other software products make them so easy to create.

Reading Tables

Tables arrange data and/or words systematically in rows and columns in order to provide information and facilitate comparisons. Key 5.6 shows a model of a typical table, including the individual parts and their arrangements on the page. Keep in mind that some tables have all these elements while others include only a few.

- *Table number* identifies the table and is usually referred to in the text.
- *Table title* helps readers focus on the table's message.
- *Captions,* also known as column titles, identify the material that falls below.
- *Subcaptions* divide the columns into smaller sections.
- *Stubs* refer to the captions running along the horizontal rows. The nature of the stubs is identified by the stub head.
- *Footnotes* are used to explain specific details found in the table.
- The *source* acknowledges where the information comes from.

Reading Charts

Charts, also known as graphs, show statistical comparisons in visual form. They present *variables,* which are numbers that can change, often along

Key 5.6	**The parts and arrangements of a table.**				

TABLE NUMBER	TITLE OF TABLE				
	CAPTION		CAPTION		
STUB HEAD	Subcaption	Subcaption	Subcaption	Subcaption
Stub	XXXX	XXXX	XXXX	XXXX
Stub	XXXX	XXXX[a]	XXXX	XXXX
Stub	XXXX	XXXX	XXXX	XXXX
Stub	XXXX	XXXX	XXXX	XXXX
Stub	XXXX	XXXX	XXXX	XXXX
Total	XXXX	XXXX	XXXX[b]	XXXX

[a]Footnote
[b]Footnote

Source: "The Parts and Arrangements of a Table" from *Business Writing,* 2/e by J. Harold Jainis and Howard R. Dresner. Copyright © 1956, HarperCollins Publishers, Inc.

vertical—top to bottom—and *horizontal*—side to side—axes. Common comparisons include:

- *trends over time* (for example, the number of computers with Internet connections per household in 2006 as compared to the number in 2001)
- *relative rankings* (for example, the size of the advertising budgets of four major consumer-products companies)
- *distributions* (for example, student performance on standardized tests by geographic area)
- *cycles* (for example, the regular upward and downward movement of the nation's economy as defined by periods of prosperity and recession)

These comparisons are presented in different forms including pie charts, bar charts, and line charts.

Understanding Pie Charts

The *pie chart* presents data as wedge-shaped sections of a circle in order to show the relative size of each item as a percentage of the whole. If you look at a pie chart as representing 100 percent of a whole, each wedge is a portion of the whole, with the combined wedges equaling the entirety. Key 5.7

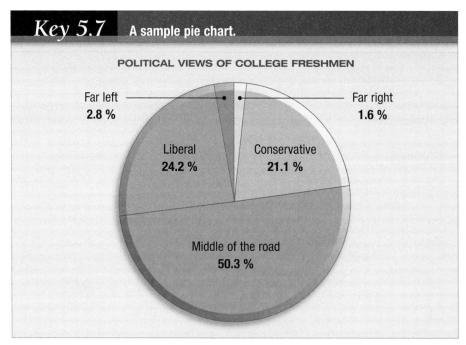

Key 5.7   A sample pie chart.

POLITICAL VIEWS OF COLLEGE FRESHMEN

Far left — 2.8 %

Far right — 1.6 %

Liberal 24.2 %

Conservative 21.1 %

Middle of the road 50.3 %

Source: Sax, L. J., Lindholm, J. A., Astin, A. W., Korn, W. S., Mahoney, K. M. (2001). *The American Freshman: National Norms for Fall 2001.* Los Angeles: Higher Education Research Institute, UCLA. Used with permission.

is an example of a pie chart that shows the political views of freshmen at four-year colleges.

Understanding Bar and Column Charts

Bar charts, also known as bar graphs, consist of horizontal bars of varying length, with each bar symbolizing a different item. Unlike pie charts, which compare the components of a single whole, bar charts compare different items. To be effective and meaningful, a bar chart must always compare items in the same category.

The bar chart in Key 5.8 compares the probable majors chosen by college freshmen in a recent survey. With the length of the bars arranged in descending order from most to least popular, readers can quickly get the information they need.

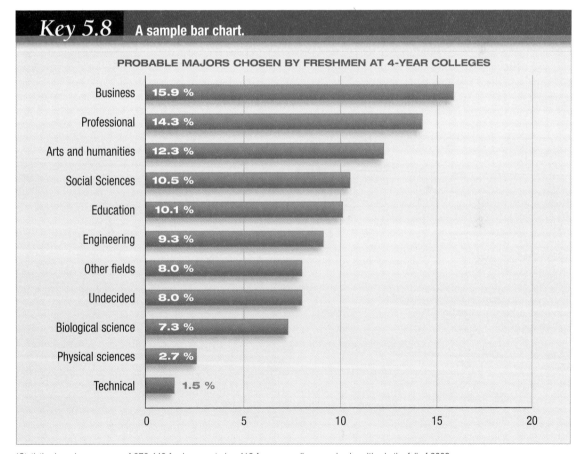

Key 5.8   A sample bar chart.

PROBABLE MAJORS CHOSEN BY FRESHMEN AT 4-YEAR COLLEGES

Major	Percentage
Business	15.9 %
Professional	14.3 %
Arts and humanities	12.3 %
Social Sciences	10.5 %
Education	10.1 %
Engineering	9.3 %
Other fields	8.0 %
Undecided	8.0 %
Biological science	7.3 %
Physical sciences	2.7 %
Technical	1.5 %

*Statistics based on a survey of 276,449 freshmen entering 413 four-year colleges and universities in the fall of 2003.

Source: Data from American Council on Education and University of California at Los Angeles, Higher Education Research Institute, "The American Freshman: National Norms for Fall 2003." Reprinted in *The Chronicle of Higher Education: Almanac* Issue 2004–5, August 27, 2004, p. 19.

Understanding Line Charts

Finally, *line charts* show continuous trends over time. The horizontal axis shows a span of time, while the vertical axis represents a specific measurement such as dollars or units of various kinds. The line chart in Key 5.9 shows immigration to the United States by decade.

Use Critical Thinking to Evaluate Visual Aids

Although most charts accurately show important relationships and comparisons, it is important to look at every chart with a critical mind.[11] This careful analysis is important because charts, especially line charts, may actually distort the facts they are trying to show. This often happens when the person or group presenting the data wants to convince you to accept his or her point of view.

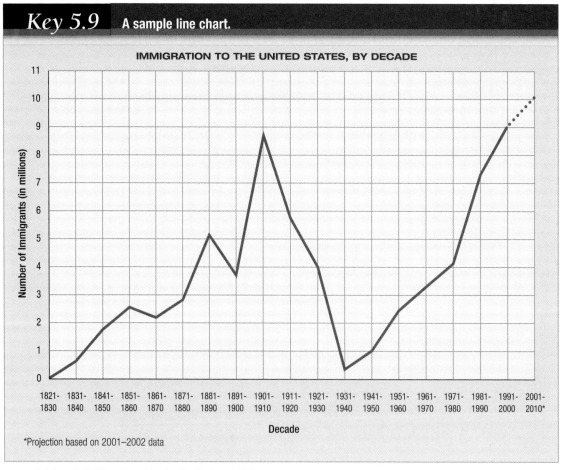

Key 5.9   **A sample line chart.**

IMMIGRATION TO THE UNITED STATES, BY DECADE

*Projection based on 2001–2002 data

Source: Data from U. S. Citizenship and Immigration Services (2003).

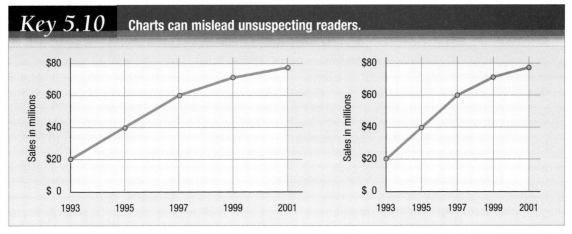

Key 5.10   Charts can mislead unsuspecting readers.

Source: Adapted From *How to Lie with Statistics,* by Darrell Huff and illustrated by Irving Geis. © 1954, 1982 by Huff and Geis. Used by permission of W.W. Norton & Company, Inc.

For example, if it is improperly drawn, a line chart can indicate more growth or fewer problems than actually occurred. Look at the charts in Key 5.10 to see how this distortion can occur. Although the charts are based on the same statistical data, the sales trend line in the chart on the left indicates a slower growth than the line in the chart on the right. This occurs because the horizontal scale on the right is shortened in comparison to the scale on the left. As a result, if you were shown just the chart on the right, you might be more impressed with the sales increase than if you were shown the chart on the left. See Key 5.11 for some critical thinking questions that will help you avoid statistical manipulations.

Key 5.11   Ask these questions to avoid being fooled by visual aids.

- Do the charts include all relevant data?

- Are the charts complete or has an important variable been omitted?

- Have the proportions between the vertical and horizontal axes been changed to produce a desired effect?

- Have the axes been extended or shortened to change the trend line?

- Does the author have an agenda that would give him or her reason to manipulate the data or to draw the chart in a way that unfairly supports a specific point of view?

Charts that distort information are generally not found in textbooks. Textbook authors try their best to present accurate data without distortion. You are more likely to find misleading charts in business where it is in a company's best interest to present products, services, and its financial picture in a favorable light.

Government regulations help protect the public against statistical manipulation of business data. For example, public companies are required to present their financial data according to Security and Exchange Commission guidelines, to submit their financial statements to independent auditors, and to use generally accepted accounting practices. Even with these safeguards, it makes good sense to use critical thinking to analyze the accuracy of charts so you are not misled.

When you begin your career, you will quickly realize the need to keep up with the latest trends and information in your field. Workplace success demands that you avoid the tendency to "coast," thinking that you learned everything you need to know in college. This attitude will leave you far behind. The final section of this chapter links the reading skills you acquire in college to career success.

HOW WILL GOOD READING SKILLS HELP YOU IN YOUR CAREER?

In our era of advanced technology, much of your on-the-job reading will be as demanding—or even more demanding—than your college texts. However, you will have an important advantage with this material, since this knowledge focuses on a field in which you have interest, knowledge, and ability. You learned the concepts and the vocabulary that were "state of the art" during your college years. Now you need to build on this foundation to remain personally competitive in an ever-changing job market.

Reading expert Norma B. Kahn advises that you keep reading and learning throughout your career. "Keeping up with current knowledge . . . is a professional responsibility that not only makes you better at what you do, but also makes you more interested in it and enthusiastic about it."[12] In many career fields, you can stay abreast by reading industry publications, visiting websites, and attending seminars and conferences—all requiring focused, effective reading skills.

Strategies for Effective Reading at Work

Here are suggestions for applying the reading/study skills you learned in Chapter 4 as well as this chapter to the reading challenges you will face at work. Based on what you have learned in these chapters, think of additional strategies that will work for you.

Define your purpose for reading each document. Then decide how you will read it. Will you skim for an overview, scan for specific details, or read it closely? Your decision will depend, in part, on how relevant the material is to your job. Say, for example, you are a corporate employee-relations manager in charge of making sure your company complies with federal employment standards. Every time the Federal Equal Employment Opportunity Commission issues new guidelines, you have to learn them well enough to apply key concepts.

Apply speed-reading techniques. These skills will be invaluable in handling the hundreds of work-related documents that many employees must deal with on a regular basis.

Continually build career-related vocabulary. Use flash cards to memorize new terms, and bring a stack wherever you go, since you never know when you have time for review. Make new words part of your work-related writing—in documents and e-mails—and use them in conversation. Take note when your colleagues use them as well.

Use SQ3R to study and learn important documents. This technique will help you identify and learn important job-related concepts in ways that will maximize recall and critical thinking.

Read critically, asking questions. The best employees analyze and evaluate new information so they can apply it effectively to their work.

Manage distractions. Encourage coworkers to respect the privacy of your space, especially if you work in a cubicle. You may want to save important reading material for quiet times or for your commute if using public transportation.

Finding Sources of Work-Related Information

Unlike college, where professors assign material for study, you will have to locate many of your career-related readings on your own. This is not difficult if you develop a strategy to uncover current sources:

Exchange information with coworkers. Observe the publications, websites, and articles others are reading.

Join professional organizations. If you are an accountant, for example, become a member of the American Institute of Certified Public Accountants. If you are a travel agent, join the American Society of Travel Agents. Attend meetings, listen to lectures, make regular visits to the organization's website and linked pages, and study suggested readings that apply to what you do. Scan monthly newsletters for sources related to your field.

Do research. Browse through libraries and bookstores for books, magazines, and journals with the latest information. Set up a filing system to organize work-related newspaper, magazine, and journal articles.

Visit websites that focus on your career interests. Think of them as information sources and leads to additional sites. Print the material you want to study in depth. Bookmark career-related websites so you can make easy return visits.

Most important, consider all your efforts as a commitment to personal improvement. You are on the road to lifelong learning. The journey is yours.

"Books were my pass to personal freedom. I learned to read at age three, and soon discovered there was a whole world to conquer that went beyond our farm."

OPRAH WINFREY
media star

Building Skill, Will, and Self-Management

Monitoring Your Progress

5

ACTIVE THINKING

SKILL WILL SELF-MGMT.

Test Competence: Measure What You've Learned

MULTIPLE CHOICE. *Circle or highlight the answer that seems to fit best.*

1. All of the following are true about SQ3R *except:*
   A. It is a multistage study process that helps you understand ideas and remember them for tests.
   B. It must be followed exactly as described in the chapter.
   C. It requires critical thinking.
   D. It can be used to study materials in your career.

2. Scanning involves
   A. a careful search for specific facts and examples.
   B. rapid reading of chapter elements.
   C. a quick construction of the main ideas.
   D. coming up with questions.

3. Selective highlighting *does not* include
   A. marking the text after reading it once through.
   B. highlighting key terms and concepts.
   C. marking important paragraphs in their entirety.
   D. using highlighter and pencil for different purposes.

4. The reciting phase of SQ3R requires that you
   A. recite the verses of your favorite poem as you study your text.
   B. always speak the answers to your Q-stage questions out loud.
   C. recite answers to Q-stage questions out loud, silently speak the answers to yourself, or write your answers down.
   D. wait until you are finished reading an entire assignment before reciting.

5. Which of the following statements is *not* true about highlighting?
   A. You should develop a highlighting system and try to use it consistently.
   B. You should consider combining highlighting with marginal or full-text notes to personalize your text.
   C. You should use SQ3R as you highlight.
   D. You can learn as much from someone else's highlighting and text notes as you can from your own.

6. When you combine highlighting with marginal notes you should
   A. write as much in the text margin as you can fit.
   B. have a goal of transforming your text into a valuable study tool.
   C. create the only study aid you will need.
   D. close the book and never look at the material again.

7. When you evaluate the quality of evidence in a text, you should look at all but *which* of the following?
   A. the source of the material
   B. overt or hidden bias
   C. opinions that are presented as fact
   D. the number of sources because the more sources the better

8. Which of the following is *not* a reason why visual aids are used extensively in college textbooks?
   A. They summarize key relationships in a way that is easy to see and understand.
   B. They prepare you to handle similar visual presentations at work.
   C. They are entertaining.
   D. They clarify complex comparisons.

9. It is important to critically evaluate visual aids because
   A. line charts, in particular, can be improperly drawn.
   B. they can be used to distort information.
   C. chart designers may have an agenda that leads them to manipulate the visual.
   D. all of the above.

10. The most important workplace goal that your reading skills will help you achieve is
    A. staying on top of the latest technology advancements.
    B. attending seminars and workshops at a professional conference.

C. meeting with more advanced workers in your field.

D. keeping current on the latest knowledge in your career area.

TRUE/FALSE. *Place a T or an F beside each statement to indicate whether you think it is true or false.*

_____ 1. SQ3R refers to Survey, Query, Read, Reread, Review.

_____ 2. Reciting means reading an entire section of text aloud to another person.

_____ 3. All reading assignments have the same importance and should be studied in depth.

_____ 4. The topic of a paragraph is always the same as the main idea of a paragraph.

_____ 5. Computers have reduced the amount of reading material you will have to master in your career.

Target and Achieve a Goal

Commit to one specific study/reading strategy from this chapter to improve your study skills.

Name the strategy here: _____

_____

Describe your goal—what you want to gain by using this strategy. _____

_____

_____

_____

Describe how you plan to use this strategy through the semester to achieve this goal.

_____

_____

_____

Building Your Skills

Brain Power: Build Vocabulary Fitness

Here is a selection from the current media. Read the material, paying special attention to the context of the vocabulary words shown in bold type. Then choose the correct definition for each word in the table that follows. Use a dictionary to check your answers. Finally, on a separate sheet, use each vocabulary word in a sentence of your own to solidify your understanding.

The science you study in the classroom is connected to scientific exploration of all sorts—explorations into space, into healing the body through biochemical-based pharmaceutical research, into creating new products. The following Scientific American *article about a space probe that crashed in the Utah desert will help you see that understanding science depends on a strong vocabulary.*

After traveling 1.5 million kilometers beyond Earth to obtain bits of the solar wind, NASA's first **automated** sample-return mission, Genesis, ended in a crash. . . . Researchers do not know just why the parafoil failed to **deploy,** but they . . . feel confident that they can still accomplish the major goals of the mission despite the damaged capsule. . . . Conclusions stemming from the mission, however, may remain **dubious** because of the . . . possibility of contamination.

Genesis had onboard an estimated 20 micrograms of solar-wind particles collected over three years in space. These particles came from the sun's visible surface, called the photosphere.

The original retrieval plan had called for a helicopter to snag Genesis's parachute in midair. . . . But because the parafoil failed to open, Genesis slammed into the desert. . . . On impact, sand, dust, and other **contaminants** entered the capsule. . . . An . . . inspection . . . revealed a 7.6-centimeter-wide hole in the sample container. Peering inside revealed that many of the **hexagonal** wafers, which collected the solar-wind samples, were broken. . . .

[Despite the contamination, the mission] investigator remains optimistic: "I am sure that some, if not most, of the science will be . . . recovered from the samples."

Gilbert V. Levin, a former astrobiologist on two NASA Mars missions, thinks the Genesis team is mistaken. "It is unlikely that any such sample recovery will be without controversy," he said. He points to the Martian meteorite ALH84001 as an example. In 1996 some scientists concluded that **fossilized** forms of unusual bacteria were inside; however, other researchers **attributed** the forms to early contamination. The Martian debate is a "**harbinger** of the same issue arising with . . . Genesis," Levin says.

Source: Barry DiGregorio, "Flawed revelations? Contamination may undermine Genesis data," *Scientific American,* November 2004, pp. 24–26. Reprinted with permission.

Circle the word or phrase that best defines each term as it is used in this excerpt.

VOCABULARY WORDS	A	B	C
1. automated (adj.)	independently operated, with no humans on board	round-trip	run by automotive engineering
2. deploy (verb)	enter the earth's atmosphere	to arrange itself in an appropriate position	float
3. dubious (adv.)	doubtful	certain	costly
4. contaminants (noun)	particles	dust	impurities
5. hexagonal (adj.)	having seven angles and seven sides	having six angles and six sides	flat
6. fossilized (adj.)	old-fashioned	unusual	changed into a fossil
7. attributed (verb)	ascribed	blamed	endorsed
8. harbinger (noun)	exact copy	forerunner	clue

Get to the Root

Every time you learn a Greek or Latin root, you increase your ability to recognize English vocabulary words that include that root and to figure out their

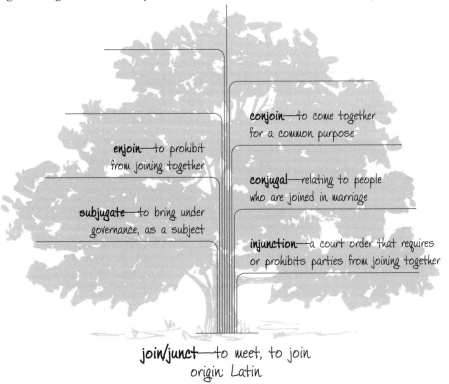

conjoin—to come together for a common purpose

enjoin—to prohibit from joining together

conjugal—relating to people who are joined in marriage

subjugate—to bring under governance, as a subject

injunction—a court order that requires or prohibits parties from joining together

join/junct—to meet, to join
origin: Latin

meaning. Grow your vocabulary by studying this root and its related words, writing in two more words from the same root, and including definitions for both new words.

Investigate Using Research Navigator

Access Research Navigator using the Internet address shown on page 32. Then sign on to the service using your Login Name and Password. Scroll through the database titles listed for Content Select. Choose a database linked to a course you are taking this semester, and then enter a career-related keyword. For example, if you are taking a psychology course, you could choose the Psychology database and enter "social work" as a keyword.

- When the database generates a list of articles, choose one that seems interesting or is related to a topic you are covering in class and open its full text. You may be reading an academic journal article, the kind of reading often required on the job in many career areas.
- Read the article using SQ3R. Then evaluate your experience in writing.

  - How did SQ3R help you navigate this article?
  - What was the most useful aspect of this reading strategy?
  - Do you feel that you came away with a solid understanding of what you read?
  - Did your critical reading skills lead you to disagree with any part of the article?

ACTIVE THINKING

SKILL   WILL   SELF-MGMT.

Building Will and Self-Awareness

Make Responsible Choices

Answer the following question on a separate piece of paper or in a journal.

The reading and studying techniques in this chapter will help you in college. Use these questions to consider how they will also help you in your career.

- Do you see yourself using SQ3R in your career? Describe specifically how it might help you master different types of reading materials. Then describe ideas for customizing it so it helps you even more.
- Imagine that while reading about the career you want to pursue after graduation, you learn something that makes you doubt whether you are making the right choice. Explain how this information will affect

you. Are you likely to change career direction? Would you answer differently if you were just beginning to explore the field than you would if you've taken a year or more of course work?

Chapter Summary

As you use this summary to review the concepts you learned in this chapter, focus also on its format—in this case a **formal outline,** in other chapters a think link, and in still others the Cornell system. As you become comfortable with the organization and style of these various formats, try using each of them to take class and reading notes, noting which approach works best for you in particular situations.

CHAPTER 5

I. SQ3R—survey, question, read, recite, review—is a reading/studying system that helps you learn concepts.

  A. Surveying involves previewing a text before studying it.

    1. Among the elements you can survey are the front matter (table of contents, preface), a variety of chapter elements (for example, headings, features and exercises, tables, charts and captions, and fonts that emphasize key terms), and back matter (glossary and bibliography).

  B. Questioning requires that you think about and question what you read.

    1. Step 1: Ask yourself what you know about the topic.

    2. Step 2: Write questions linked to chapter headings.

  C. Reading—the first R in SQ3R—requires an active approach.

    1. Take steps to find the main idea of the material.

    2. Learn to prioritize your assignments so that you can handle your reading load and study in depth what is important.

  D. Reciting—the second R in SQ3R—requires that you take an active approach to answering the questions you raised in the Q stage.

    1. You can recite answers aloud, speak them silently to yourself, write them down, or teach the material to another person.

    2. Recite regularly as you study after you complete distinct text sections.

  E. Reviewing—the third R in SQ3R—should be done soon after you finish a chapter and on a regular basis during the semester.

II. Customizing your text with highlighting and notes will personalize your text as you learn.

  A. Highlighting involves careful marking of the text to highlight key terms and concepts.

    1. Hold off highlighting until you have read the material at least once and have an overview.

    2. It is important to avoid overmarking, to use a consistent marking system, and to use a pencil and a highlighter.

  B. Taking marginal notes will personalize your text even more.

    1. Use shorthand to note important terms and definitions.

    2. Write Q-questions in the margins.

  C. Taking full-text notes involves summarizing the assignment's main ideas.

III. Responding critically to what you read aids understanding and learning.

  A. An important part of critical reading is using your knowledge of fact and opinion to evaluate arguments. You must ask questions.

    1. What is the quality of the evidence?

    2. How well does the evidence support the idea?

IV. Visual aids—including tables, charts, illustrations, maps, and photographs—present concepts as they clarify relationships and summarize information.

  A. Tables present words and data.

  B. Three types of charts show various statistical comparisons in visual form including trends over time, relative rankings, distributions, and cycles.

    1. Pie charts

    2. Bar charts

    3. Line charts

  C. Critically evaluate all visual aids because they can distort data and lead to incorrect conclusions.

V. The reading skills you acquire in college will help you succeed at work.

  A. The same strategies will help you understand more and read faster.

  B. To find career-related readings, talk to coworkers, visit career-related websites, join professional organizations, and do research.

Endnotes

1. Francis P. Robinson, *Effective Behavior.* New York: Harper & Row, 1941.

2. John Mack Faragher, et al., *Out of Many,* 3rd ed. Upper Saddle River, NJ: Prentice Hall, p. xxxvii.

3. Charles G. Morris and Albert A. Maisto, *Psychology: An Introduction,* 12th ed. Upper Saddle River, NJ: Pearson Prentice Hall, 2005, p. 186.

4. Ophelia H. Hancock, *Reading Skills for College Students,* 5th ed. Upper Saddle River, NJ: Prentice Hall, 2001, pp. 54–59.

5. Teresa Audesirk, Gerald Audesirk, and Bruce E. Byers, *Biology: Life on Earth.* Upper Saddle River, NJ: Pearson Prentice Hall, 2005, p. 6.

6. Adam Robinson, *What Smart Students Know.* New York: Three Rivers Press, 1993, p. 82.

7. *Keys to Lifelong Learning Telecourse.* Dir. Mary Jane Bradbury. Videocassette. Intrepid Films, 2000.

8. Technique suggested by Mel Levine, *A Mind at a Time.* New York: Simon & Schuster, 2002, pp. 67–68.

9. Source: Ronald J. Ebert and Ricky W. Griffin, *Business Essentials,* 5th ed., 2005, p. 297. Reprinted by permission of Pearson Education, Inc. Upper Saddle River, NJ.

10. *Keys to Lifelong Learning Telecourse.*

11. Information for this section from Darrell Huff, *How to Lie with Statistics.* New York: W. W. Norton, 1954, pp. 165–166, 278.

12. Norma B. Kahn, *More Learning in Less Time: A Guide for Student, Professionals, Career Changers, and Lifelong Learners,* 5th ed. Gwynedd Valley, PA: Ways-to Books, 1998, p. 22.

6

"No one is as deaf as the person
who will not listen."

Listening and Memory

TAKING IN AND REMEMBERING INFORMATION

A key to learning is skilled, active listening. As a student, you are challenged to remember much of what you hear during lectures, labs, and class discussions, not only because you may be tested on the material, but because it may be important to your future studies and career. If you are a nursing student, getting an A on an infectious diseases exam is useful only if you can remember how the symptoms of the common cold differ from those of the flu when you are treating patients.

This chapter will help you take an active-learning approach to listening and remembering so that you can learn new material and hang on to it for the long term.

In this chapter you will explore answers to the following questions:

- How can you become a better listener?

- How does memory work?

- What memory strategies can improve recall?

- How can you use mnemonic devices to boost memory power?

HOW CAN YOU BECOME A BETTER LISTENER?

The act of hearing isn't the same as the act of listening. Hearing refers to sensing spoken messages from their source. *Listening* involves a complex process of communication. Successful listening occurs when the listener understands the speaker's intended message. In school and at work, poor listening may cause communication breakdowns and mistakes. Skilled listening, however, promotes progress and success. The good news is that listening is a teachable—and learnable—skill, says psychologist Beatrice Harris. "People can be trained to listen to content and tone. But learning [to listen] takes persistence and motivation."[1]

To see how complex listening can be, look at Key 6.1. The left-hand column contains an excerpt from a typical classroom lecture on peer-group influence during adolescence, and the right-hand column records what an 18- or 19-year-old student might be thinking while the instructor is speaking. The column on the right reveals the complexity of listening as well as some of the barriers that block communication.

As Key 6.1 shows, this student doesn't focus consistently on the information presented. Instead, she reacts to specific parts of the message and gets caught up in evaluating and judging what she hears. Understanding the listening process and why people may have trouble listening well can help you overcome barriers.

Know the Stages of Listening

Listening is made up of four stages that build on one another: sensing, interpreting, evaluating, and reacting. These stages take the message from the speaker to the listener and back to the speaker (see Key 6.2).

- During the *sensation* stage (also known as hearing) your ears pick up sound waves and transmit them to the brain. For example, you are sitting in class and hear your instructor say, "The only opportunity to make up last week's test is Tuesday at 5:00 P.M."

- In the *interpretation* stage, listeners attach meaning to a message. This involves understanding what is being said and relating it to what you already know. You relate this message to your knowledge of the test, whether you need to make it up, and what you are doing on Tuesday at 5:00.

- In the *evaluation* stage of listening, you decide how you feel about the message, whether, for example, you like it or agree with it. This involves evaluating the message as it relates to your needs and values. If the message goes against your values or does not fulfill your needs,

Key 6.1   Barriers may interfere with listening at every stage.

A peer group is a social group made up of members with a lot in common. During adolescence, common interests often center on dating, popular music, clothing, and sports.

"Peer groups!" I've heard that term before. I'd better take notes; it'll probably be on the test.

The appeal of the group often comes from the fact that adults would not approve of what group members are doing. As a result, illicit activities—such as car racing, alcohol abuse, and drugs—are often the most popular.

What's this guy saying? That my friends and I do things just because our parents would object? Yeah, I guess I want to be different, but gimme a break! I don't drink and drive. I don't do drugs. I don't ignore my school work. Anyway, I'd better remember the connection between peer group popularity and adult disapproval. What were his exact words? I wish I remembered . . . on second thought maybe he has a point. I know kids who do things just to get a rise out of their parents.

Peer groups exert such a strong influence during adolescence because they give students the opportunity to form social relationships that are separate and apart from the one they have with their families. This is a time of rebellion and breaking away: a rough time for both adolescents and their parents.

Is it lunchtime yet? I'm really hungry! Stop thinking of food and start listening . . . back to work! Yeah, he's right, social relationships that have nothing to do with my family are important to me. I'd better write this down.

The good news for parents is that peer group pressure is generally strongest during adolescence. Teens achieve a greater balance between the influence of family and friends as the years pass. This doesn't make it any easier for parents trying to persuade their sons and daughters not to dye their hair green or pierce their eyebrows, but at least it tells them that the rebellion is temporary.

Why is he talking down to us? Why is he reassuring parents instead of focusing on how hard it is for teens to deal with life? He must be a parent himself . . . I wish those guys behind me would stop talking! I can't hear the lecture . . . there's a generation gap coming from the front of the room that's the size of the Grand Canyon! What's wrong with green hair and pierced eyebrows? He sounds like he knows all the answers and that we'll eventually see the light. I'm going to ask him how teens are supposed to act when they believe that their parents' values are wrong. Now, how should I word my question . . .

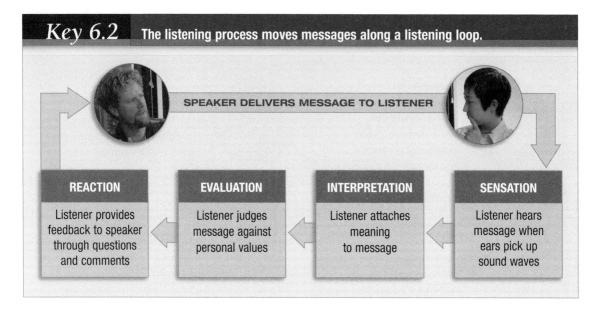

Key 6.2   The listening process moves messages along a listening loop.

SPEAKER DELIVERS MESSAGE TO LISTENER

REACTION
Listener provides feedback to speaker through questions and comments

EVALUATION
Listener judges message against personal values

INTERPRETATION
Listener attaches meaning to message

SENSATION
Listener hears message when ears pick up sound waves

you may reject it, stop listening, or argue in your mind with the speaker. In this example, if you need to make up the test but have to work Tuesday at 5:00, you may evaluate the message as less than satisfactory. As Key 6.1 showed, what happens during the evaluation phase can interfere with listening.

- The final stage of listening is a *reaction* to the message in the form of direct feedback. In a classroom, direct feedback often comes in the form of questions and comments. Your reaction, in this case, may be to ask the instructor if she can schedule another test time. If the student in Key 6.1 actually asks a question, she will give the instructor the opportunity to clarify the lecture, or perhaps to add information.

Improving your listening skills involves two primary actions involving self-awareness and skill building: managing listening challenges (maximizing the sensation stage) and becoming an active listener (maximizing the interpretation and evaluation stages). Although becoming a better listener will help in every class, it is especially important in subjects that challenge you. For example, if your natural strength is in English, your ability to listen in physics class may affect how much you learn and whether you pass the course. Similarly, a copywriter for an ad agency may have trouble listening to a budget presentation, but that does not lessen his responsibility to understand and apply the budget to his work projects.

Manage Listening Challenges

Classic studies have shown that immediately after listening, students are likely to recall only half of what was said. This low retention rate is partly due to such listening challenges as divided attention and distractions, the tendency to shut out the message, the inclination to rush to judgment, and partial hearing loss or learning disabilities.[2]

Divided Attention and Distractions

Imagine yourself at a noisy end-of-year party, talking with a friend about plans for the summer, when you hear your name mentioned across the room. Your name was not shouted, and you weren't consciously listening to anything outside your own conversation. However, once you hear your name, you strain to hear more as you now listen with only half an ear to what your friend is saying. Chances are you hear neither person very well.

Situations like this happen all the time at school and on the job, and they demonstrate the consequences of divided attention. Although you are capable of listening to more than one message at the same time, you may not completely hear or understand any of them. Learning to focus your attention—even as it is being pulled in different directions—is one of your most important listening challenges.

Internal and external distractions often divide your attention. *Internal distractions* include anything from hunger to headache to personal worries. Something the speaker says may also trigger a recollection that may cause your mind to drift. In contrast, *external distractions* include noises (whispering, sirens) and excessive heat or cold. Your goal is to reduce all distractions so that you can concentrate on what you're hearing.

You'll listen better if you are relaxed, comfortable, and awake. Get enough sleep to stay alert, eat enough to avoid hunger pangs, and dress comfortably. In addition, save worrying about personal problems for time outside of class, advises communications consultant Kathy York. "Research suggests that a poor attitude can undermine the listening process," she explains. "So if you wake up late one morning and get a speeding ticket on your way to the lecture hall, you'll certainly be in a bad mood when you get there. You have to be able to put that aside, improve your attitude, and concentrate on getting the key points from the lecture."[3]

Work to eliminate external distractions during class by sitting near the front of the room, where you can clearly see and hear, and moving away from others who are chatting. If there's a chance that the classroom will be over- or under-heated, bring an extra layer of clothing that you can put on or take off.

Shutting Out the Message

Although instructors are responsible for communicating information, they cannot force you to listen. As an active learner, the responsibility to listen consistently is in your hands. If students perceive that a subject is difficult or uninteresting, they may tune out and miss information that forms the foundation for what comes next. Many students also fall into the trap of focusing on specific points and shutting out the rest of the message. It's tough to refocus after these kinds of listening lapses.

One way to avoid this is to remind yourself that what your instructors say in class is valuable even if it is not obvious or in the textbook. Instructors often present non–text material in class and include that material on tests. If you work to take in the whole message in class, you will be able to read over your notes later, combine your class and text notes, and think critically about what is important. If you experience a listening lapse, refocus your concentration quickly instead of worrying about what you missed. After class, ask to see a classmate's notes to fill in the gaps.

The Rush to Judgment

As Key 6.1 illustrates, people may stop listening when they hear something they don't like. Their focus turns to their personal reactions and away from the content of the message. Students who disagree during a lecture often spend valuable class time figuring out how to word a question or comment in response.

Judgments also involve reactions to the speakers themselves. If you do not like your instructors or if you have preconceived notions about their ideas or cultural background, you may decide that their words have little value or that you don't understand them. Anyone whose words have ever been ignored because of race, ethnic background, gender, sexual preference, or disability understands how prejudice can interfere with listening.

When students react negatively to foreign-born teaching assistants, they may be demonstrating prejudice rather than a genuine inability to comprehend their speech. In a recent experiment, University of Georgia professor Donald L. Rubin played the same taped lecture to two groups of undergraduate students. The lecturer, who spoke in a clear male voice, sounded like he came from middle America. As the students listened, an image of the speaker was projected at the front of the classroom. For half of the students, the projected image showed an American named "John Smith from Portland." For the other half, the image showed an Asian named "Li Wenshu from Beijing." Both men dressed in similar professional clothing. Students were then asked to fill in missing words from a transcript of the lecture. They made 20 percent more mistakes when looking at the image of Li Wenshu than when looking at John Smith.

To Professor Rubin, these results demonstrate the impact of unconscious prejudice. "Students who expect that non-native instructors will be poor instructors and unintelligible speakers can listen to what we know to be the most standard English speech and the most well-formed lecture, and yet experience some difficulties in comprehension. All the pronunciation improvements in the world will not by itself halt the problem of students' dropping classes or complaining about their instructors' language."[4]

Although it is human nature to stop listening, at times, in reaction to a speaker or message, this tendency can get in the way of your education. Before you give in to your inclination to tune out, think about this:

Listening demands sustained focus and concentration. These students demonstrate this focus during a lecture.

- An important part of your education involves using critical thinking to evaluate other points of view—even those radically different from your own. Be open to the possibility that your instructor may say something to change your mind.

- You are under no obligation to like every instructor. However, academic integrity requires that you listen respectfully. It benefits you to listen with an open mind.

Being aware of what you tend to judge will help you avoid putting up barriers against messages that clash with your opinions. Consider education as a continuing search for evidence, regardless of whether that evidence supports or negates your point of view.

Partial Hearing Loss and Learning Disabilities

If you have some level of hearing loss, seek out special services, including tutoring and equipment, that can help you listen in class. For example, listening to a tape of a lecture at a higher-than-normal volume can help you hear things you missed. Meeting with your instructor outside of class to clarify your notes may help, as will sitting near the front of the room.

Disabilities involving difficulty with processing spoken language, or other issues such as attention deficit disorder can add to listening challenges. People with these problems may have trouble paying attention or understanding what they hear. While some find ways to compensate for their listening problems, others continue to struggle. If you have a disability that creates a listening challenge, seek help through your counseling or student health center, an advisor, or an instructor.

Become an Active Listener

On the surface, listening seems like a passive activity: You sit back and listen as someone else speaks. Effective listening, however, is really an active process that involves being a presence in class, setting a listening purpose, focusing on understanding, asking questions, paying attention to verbal signposts, and knowing what helps and hinders listening.

Ironically, passive listeners may think they are actually learning material when all they are doing is taking it in on a superficial level. They have not challenged themselves to understand, organize, or digest the material on their own, but simply rely on their instructor's rendering. Many of these students experience a rude awakening when they have trouble with exams or assignments that test their active, analytical knowledge. You can avoid this scenario by using the following strategies.

Be There

Being an active listener requires that you show up on time—preferably a few minutes before class is scheduled to begin. Why? Because instructors often make important announcements during the first few minutes of class and may also summarize the last lecture. You goal is to be settled in your seat with your notebook open so that you can take in information as soon as the instructor starts speaking.

Set Purposes for Listening

In any situation, establish what you want to achieve through listening, such as understanding the material better or mastering a specific task. Many instructors state their purpose at the start of the class. A political science instructor might say, for example, "Today, we're going to talk about campaign financing." Listening carefully to the purpose and writing it down will help you focus on the message.

Accomplishing your purpose requires that you read assignments before class (your syllabus will tell you when reading assignments are due) and review your notes from the previous class. This preparation will allow you to follow the lecture successfully, helping you to differentiate between material to take notes on and material that is less important. Without it, you may find yourself scrambling to take down every word your instructor says—which also gets in the way of listening (see Chapter 7 for an in-depth discussion of note taking).

Making your purpose for listening personal will motivate you to listen closely. As you prepare for class, ask yourself how the material relates to your academic goals and interests and to other material you need to know. When you come to class with the mind-set that what you hear will help *you,* you will be better able to block out internal and external distractions.

An implicit purpose of listening is to learn what your instructor considers important about a topic. Often, instructors ask students to provide information and analysis that supplements their own presentation, so don't stop listening when a classmate starts talking. In fact, in many classrooms, you can learn as much from classmates as you can from instructors.

Focus on Understanding

Listening without understanding has no value, so make sure you understand what you hear. Rather than taking notes on everything your instructor says, record information when you can say to yourself, "I get it!" If you miss important material, leave space in your notes and return later. Your instructor may repeat the point you missed, or something else he says may give you clues to piece it together.

Ask Questions

A willingness to ask questions shows a desire to learn and is the mark of an active listener, says education professor Paul Eggen of the University of North Florida: "Successful students are constantly looking for links between what they are learning and other information. Less successful students tend to learn information in isolation through cramming. In most cases, this information will stay with them for a short time because it isn't linked to anything else. When you listen to a lecture, ask yourself questions: What is this part of? What's the bigger idea? How is it similar to the topic we dealt with in the last class? How is it different? By identifying similarities and differences, you're associating the ideas you are trying to learn with other memories and making it more likely that you will remember."[5]

Although questions and comments turn you into an active participant, they may sometimes divert your attention from the speaker. One way to avoid this is to jot down your questions quickly and come back to them during a discussion period. When you know that your question is on paper, you can relax and listen to everything that is said.

Pay Attention to Verbal Signposts

Your instructors' choice of words may tell you a lot about the information they consider important and help you predict test questions. For example, an idea described as "new and exciting" or "classic" is more likely to be on a test than one described as "interesting." *Verbal signposts*—words or phrases that call your attention to what you will hear next—help organize information, connect ideas, and indicate what is important and what is not. Let phrases like those in Key 6.3 direct your attention to the material that follows.

Over time, you will also learn your instructor's nonverbal speaking style. For example, after a few classes, you may realize that when she looks at her notes before speaking, she is probably telling you something important. You may also learn that when he asks questions about the same topic he is repeating for emphasis, or when she gets excited about a question she is flagging both the question and answer as crucial.

Know What Helps and Hinders Listening

Ralph G. Nichols, a pioneer in listening research, defined the characteristics of successful and unsuccessful listeners by studying 200 freshmen at the University of Minnesota over a nine-month period. His findings, summarized

---

Key 6.3   Pay attention to verbal signposts.

SIGNALS POINTING TO KEY CONCEPTS	SIGNALS OF SUPPORT
A key point to remember . . .	A perfect example, . . .
Point 1, point 2, etc. . . .	Specifically, . . .
The impact of this was . . .	For instance, . . .
The critical stages in the process are . . .	Similarly, . . .
SIGNALS POINTING TO DIFFERENCES	**SIGNALS THAT SUMMARIZE**
On the contrary, . . .	From this you have learned, . . .
On the other hand, . . .	In conclusion, . . .
In contrast, . . .	As a result, . . .
However, . . .	Finally, . . .

Key 6.4   Effective listening is linked to attitude and skill.

LISTENING IS HELPED BY . . .	LISTENING IS HINDERED BY . . .
. . . making a conscious decision to work at listening; viewing difficult material as a listening challenge.	. . . caring little about the listening process; tuning out difficult material.
. . . fighting distractions through concentration.	. . . refusing to listen at the first distraction.
. . . continuing to listen when a subject is difficult or dry, in the hope that one might learn something interesting.	. . . giving up as soon as one loses interest.
. . . withholding judgment until hearing everything.	. . . becoming preoccupied with a response as soon as a speaker makes a controversial statement.
. . . focusing on the speaker's theme by recognizing organizational patterns, transitional language, and summary statements.	. . . getting sidetracked by unimportant details.
. . . adapting a note-taking style to the unique style and organization of the speaker.	. . . always taking notes in outline form, even when a speaker is poorly organized, leading to frustration.
. . . pushing past negative emotional responses and forcing oneself to continue to listen.	. . . letting an initial emotional response disrupt listening.
. . . using excess thinking time to evaluate, summarize, and question what one just heard and anticipate what will come next.	. . . thinking about other things and, as a result, missing much of the message.

in Key 6.4, demonstrate that effective listening depends as much on a positive attitude as on specific skills.[6]

Engage Professor Nichols's strategies to turn on and tune up your listening when you take a class that doesn't interest you. With a positive attitude, you may learn something important and even grow to like the material.

CHANGE YOUR LISTENING HABITS

Think about your personal listening habits in the classroom. Then complete the following:

Look again at Key 6.4. Which habits, helpful or not so helpful, are part of your listening pattern?

_____

_____

How do you react when you strongly disagree with something your instructor says—when you are convinced that you are "right" and your instructor is "wrong"?

_____

_____

If one of the purposes of a college education is to open you to new ideas and opinions, how do feelings of being "right" affect your education?

_____

_____

List two changes you could make in your listening to improve your performance in college.

1. _____

2. _____

Through effective listening, you acquire knowledge, but acquisition is not enough. You must also retain what you learn, whether you learn it in the classroom, through reading, or via direct experience. As you will see next, a good memory improves with practice and the use of memory-improving strategies.

HOW DOES MEMORY WORK?

Your accounting instructor is giving a test tomorrow on key concepts in preparing federal tax returns. You feel confident because you spent hours last week memorizing your class and text notes. Unfortunately, as you start the test, you realize that you have forgotten almost everything you learned. This is not surprising, since most forgetting occurs within minutes after memorization.

In a classic study conducted in 1885, researcher Herman Ebbinghaus memorized a list of meaningless three-letter words such as CEF and LAZ.

He then examined how quickly he forgot them. Within one hour he had forgotten more than 50 percent of what he had learned; after two days, he knew fewer than 30 percent of the memorized words. Although Ebbinghaus's recall of the nonsense syllables remained fairly stable after that, his experiment shows how fragile memory can be—even when you take the time and expend the energy to memorize information.[7]

If forgetting is so common, why do some people have better memories than others? Some may have an inborn talent for remembering. More often, though, they succeed because they take an active approach and have mastered techniques for improving recall.

How Your Brain Remembers: Short-Term and Long-Term Memory

Learning is a physical process—your brain undergoes physical changes when you hear, interpret, and work to remember information. Understanding how your brain commits information to memory will motivate actions that strengthen your ability to remember.

Memories are stored in three different "storage banks" in your brain. The first, called *sensory memory,* is an exact copy of what you see and hear and lasts for a second or less. Certain information is then selected from sensory memory and moved into *short-term memory,* a temporary information storehouse that lasts no more than 10 to 20 seconds. You are consciously aware of material in short-term memory. Unimportant information is quickly dumped. Important information is transferred to *long-term memory*—the mind's more permanent information storehouse.

Although all three stages of memory are important, targeting long-term memory will solidify learning the most. "Short-term—or working—memory is useful when we want to remember a phone number until we can dial or an e-mail address until we can type it in to the computer," says biologist James Zull. "We use short-term memory for these momentary challenges, all the time, every day, but it is limited in capacity, tenacity, and time."[8] Zull explains that short-term memory can only hold small amounts of information for brief periods of time. In addition, it is unstable—a distraction can easily bump out information.

Retaining information in long-term memory engages your brain in a four-stage learning process. Key 6.5 illustrates how this works.

1. **Experiencing** the material (*concrete experience*). Your brain takes in the information through one or more of your senses.
2. **Relating** the material to what you already know (*reflexive observation*). You reflect on the new information and connect it to previous knowledge.

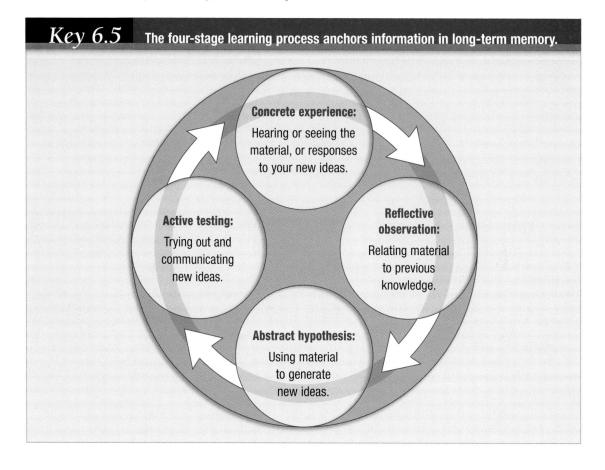

Key 6.5   The four-stage learning process anchors information in long-term memory.

3. **Forming** new ideas (*abstract hypothesis*). You come up with new insights from the combination of what you knew before and what you are learning now.

4. **Trying out and communicating** new ideas (*active testing*). You explore your ideas to see if they make sense and work.

Here's an example to illustrate the process.

1. In your introduction to business course, you hear the following information during the lecture: "During the economic bubble of the 1990s, ethical lapses were frequent at the highest levels of business. Among the major corporations involved in ethical abuses were Enron, WorldCom, Citibank, and Tyco. Executives at these companies bent the rules and ignored the law to maximize personal gain."

2. You think about the material in relation to what you know. First, you remember reading about the unethical practices of the millionaires of the 1930s, including J.P. Morgan and Andrew Carnegie, who built

corporate empires—and amassed personal fortunes—through unethical business practices. Second, you think about ethical and unethical behavior you have seen in people you know personally.

3. You form a new idea: Government regulations are necessary to curb the all-too-human tendency to bend rules for personal gain.

4. You try out your idea by talking to various students and thinking further about your own ideas.

Result: Information about business ethics is solidly anchored in long-term memory.

Go For It! BUILDING YOUR SKILLS

ANALYZE THE LINK BETWEEN MEMORIZATION AND CRITICAL THINKING

Identify the course you are most interested in this semester and the role memorization and critical thinking are likely to play in your efforts to do well. Then complete the following:

- Describe some material you will have to memorize.

_____

_____

_____

- Describe the specific ways in which you will use critical thinking to help you learn and retain the material.

_____

_____

_____

- Evaluate whether or not the material you have to remember for this course will be important to your working and/or personal life after college.

_____

_____

As you learn new material, your goal is to anchor information in long-term memory. Memory strategies will help you succeed.

WHAT MEMORY STRATEGIES CAN IMPROVE RECALL?

The following strategies will help improve your ability to remember what you learn.

Have Purpose and Intention

Why can you remember the lyrics to dozens of popular songs but not the functions of the pancreas? Perhaps this is because you want to remember the lyrics or you have an emotional tie to them. To achieve the same results at school, try to create in yourself the purpose and will to remember. This is often linked to your emotional involvement with the material.

For example, as a student in a city-planning course, it may be easier for you to remember the complex rules surrounding federal, state, and local housing subsidies if you think about the families, including children and the elderly, who benefit from these programs. If someone you know lives in a city housing project, the personal connection will probably make it easier to remember these rules.

Genuine interest and passion for a subject are invaluable memory tools. When you care about something, your brain responds differently, and learning is easier (see Chapter 4).

Understand What You Memorize

Something that has meaning is easier to recall than something that makes little sense. This basic principle applies to everything you study—from biology and astronomy to history and literature. Determine the logical connections in the information, and use these connections to help you learn. For example, in a plant biology course, memorize plant families; in a history course, memorize events by linking them in a cause-and-effect chain.

The best way to guarantee that concepts become part of your long-term memory is to understand them inside and out. With a depth of learning comes the framework on which to place related concepts. Thus, if you are having trouble remembering something new, think about how the new idea fits into what you already know.

A simple example: If you continually forget the definition of a new vocabulary word, try to identify the word's root, prefix, or suffix. Knowing that the root *bellum* means "war" and the prefix *ante* means "before" will help you recognize and remember that *antebellum* means "before the war." The *Get to the Root* exercise at the end of every chapter encourages you to link new vocabulary to what you already know.

Finally, use organizational tools, such as an outline or a think link (see Chapter 7 for more on these note-taking techniques), to record the material you want to recall and the logical connections among the elements. These tools will expose gaps in your understanding as they help you study and learn.

Use critical thinking. Critical thinking encourages you to associate new information with what you already know. During the "abstract hypothesis" stage of learning, you reference and rearrange knowledge to form new relationships and ideas.

Imagine that you have to remember information about a specific historical event—for example, the signing of the Treaty of Versailles, the agreement that ended World War II. You might use critical thinking in the following ways:

- Recall everything that you know about the topic.
- Think about how this event is similar to other events in history.
- Consider what is different and unique about this treaty in comparison to other treaties.
- Explore the causes that led up to this event, and look at the event's effects.
- From the general idea of treaties that ended wars, explore other examples of such treaties.
- Think about examples of what happened during the treaty signing, and from those examples come up with ideas about the tone of the event.
- Looking at the facts of the event, evaluate how successful you think the treaty was.

By critically exploring the Treaty of Versailles in this fashion, you are more likely to remember the specific facts and overarching concepts assocated with it.

Limit and organize the items you are processing. This involves two key activities during the observation stage of learning:

- **Separate main points from unimportant details.** Ask yourself: What is the most important information? Highlight only the key points in your texts, and write notes in the margins about central ideas. See the example in Key 5.5 on pages 171–172.
- **Divide material into manageable sections.** Generally, when material is short and easy to understand, studying it from start to finish improves recall. With longer material, however, you may benefit from dividing it into logical sections, mastering each section, putting all the sections together, and then testing your memory of all the material. Actors take this approach when learning the lines of a play, and it can work just as well for students trying to learn new concepts.

Recite, Rehearse, and Write

When you *recite* material, you repeat key concepts aloud, in your own words, to help you memorize them. You also summarize these concepts. *Rehearsing* is similar to reciting but is done silently. *Writing* is reciting on paper. All three processes actively involve you in learning and memorizing material.

You will get the greatest benefit if you separate your learning into the following steps:

- Focus as you read on the key points you want to remember. These are usually found in the topic sentences of paragraphs. Then recite, rehearse, or write the ideas down.

- Convert each main idea into a keyword, phrase, or visual image—something that is easy to recall and that will set off a chain of memories that will bring you back to the original information. Write each keyword or phrase on an index card.

- One by one, look at the keywords on your cards and recite, rehearse, or write all the associated information you can recall. Check your recall against your original material.

These steps are part of the process for consolidating and summarizing your lecture and text notes as you study (see Chapter 7).

Reciting, rehearsing, and writing involve much more than simply rereading material and parroting words out loud, in your head, or on paper. Because rereading does not necessarily require any involvement, you can reread without thinking or learning. However, you cannot help but think and learn as you convert text concepts into key points, rewrite key points as keywords and phrases, and judge your learning by assessing what you know and what you still need to learn.

Study During Short, Frequent Sessions

Research has shown that you can improve your chances of remembering material if you learn it more than once. Spread your study sessions over time: For example, a pattern of short sessions, say three 30-minute study sessions followed by brief periods of rest is more effective than continual studying with little or no rest. With this in mind, try studying during breaks in your schedule, and even consider using these time slots to study with classmates. Although studying between classes isn't for everyone, you may find that it can help you remember more information.

Sleep can actually aid memory because it reduces interference from new information. Since you can't always go to sleep immediately after studying for an exam, try postponing the study of other subjects until your exam is over. When studying for several tests at once, avoid studying two similar subjects back to back. Your memory is likely to be more accurate when you study history right after biology rather than, for example, chemistry after biology.

Practice the Middle

When you are trying to learn something, you usually study some material first, attack other material in the middle of the session, and approach still other topics at the end. The weak link in your recall is likely to be the material you study midway. It pays to give this material special attention in the form of extra practice.

Create Groupings

When items do not have to be remembered in any particular order, the act of *grouping*—forming digestible information segments that are easy to remember—can help you recall them better. Say, for example, that you have to memorize these five 10-digit numbers:

9806875087 9876535703 7636983561 6724472879 3122895312

It may look impossible. If you group the numbers to look like telephone numbers, however, the job may become more manageable:

(980) 687–5087 (987) 653–5703 (763) 698–3561 (672) 447–2879
(312) 289–5312

In general, try to limit groups to around 10 items or fewer. It's hard to memorize more at one time. According to Edward Tenner, a technology expert and author of *Why Things Bit Back: Technology and the Revenge of Unintended Consequences*, the human memory is best suited for memorizing no more than nine digits—and adding even a single additional digit adds discomfort that makes recall harder.[9]

Use Flash Cards

Flash cards are a great visual memory tool. They give you short, repeated review sessions that provide immediate feedback, and they are portable, which gives you the flexibility to use them wherever you go. Use the front of a 3-by-5-inch index card to write a word, idea, or phrase you want to remember. Use the back for a definition, an explanation, and other key facts. Key 6.6 shows two flash cards used to study for a pychology exam.

Here are some suggestions for making the most of your flash cards:

- Use the cards as a self-test. As you go through them, divide them into two piles—the material you know and the material you are learning.

Key 6.6   Flash cards help you memorize important facts.

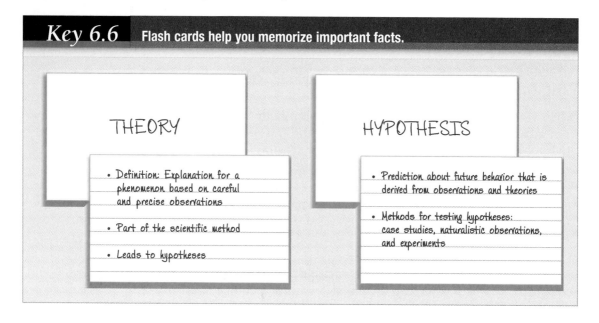

THEORY

- Definition: Explanation for a phenomenon based on careful and precise observations
- Part of the scientific method
- Leads to hypotheses

HYPOTHESIS

- Prediction about future behavior that is derived from observations and theories
- Methods for testing hypotheses: case studies, naturalistic observations, and experiments

- **Carry the cards with you and review them frequently.** You'll learn the most if you start using cards early in the course, well ahead of exam time.
- **Shuffle the cards and learn the information in various orders.** This will help you avoid putting too much focus on some information and not enough on the other.
- **Test yourself in both directions.** First, look at the terms and provide the definitions or explanations. Then turn the cards over and reverse the process.
- **Reduce the stack as you learn.** You can eliminate cards as you are certain of your knowledge. (Ask a classmate to test you to be sure that you *really* know the material.) Watching the pile get smaller is a reward that reinforces your motivation. As test time approaches, put all the cards together again for a final review.

Use Tape-Recorded Material

Questions on tape can work like audio flash cards. One method is to record short-answer study questions, leaving 10 to 15 seconds between questions for you to answer out loud. Recording the correct answer after the pause will give you immediate feedback. For example, part of a recording for a writing class might say, "The three elements of effective writing are . . . [10–15 seconds] . . . topic, audience, and purpose."

Use the Information

In the days and weeks after you learn something new, try to use the information in every way you can. Think about other contexts in which it applies and link it to new problems. Then test your knowledge to make sure the material is in long-term memory. "Don't confuse recognizing information with being able to recall it," says learning expert Adam Robinson. "Be sure you can recall the information without looking at your notes for clues. And don't move on until you have created some sort of sense-memory hook for calling it back up when you need it."[10]

Memory is often aided by repeated listening. This professor of music at Northeastern University has students solidify their knowledge of Mozart and Beethoven by listening to recordings.

Choose the strategies that are likely to help you the most in different memory challenges. In general, the more information and ideas you can associate with the new item you're trying to remember, the more successful you will be. As you will see next, mnemonic devices help you form sense-memory hooks that tend to stay with you.

HOW CAN YOU USE MNEMONIC DEVICES TO BOOST MEMORY POWER?

Certain performers entertain audiences by remembering the names of 100 strangers or flawlessly repeating 30 ten-digit numbers. Although these performers probably have superior memories, they also rely on memory techniques, known as *mnemonic devices* (pronounced neh-MAHN-ick), for assistance.

Mnemonic devices depend on vivid associations (relating new information to other information) that engage your emotions. Instead of learning new facts by rote (repetitive practice), associations give you a "hook" on which to hang these facts and retrieve them later. Mnemonic devices make information familiar and meaningful through unusual, unforgettable mental associations and visual pictures.

There are different kinds of mnemonic devices, including visual images and associations and acronyms. Study how these devices work, then apply them to your own memory challenges. As you will see, these devices take time and effort to create, and you'll have to be motivated to remember them. Because of this, it is smart to use mnemonic devices only when you really need them—for instance, to distinguish confusing concepts that consistently trip you up or to recall items in order.

Create Visual Images and Associations

Turning information into mental pictures helps improve memory, especially for visual learners. To remember that the Spanish artist Picasso painted *The Three Women,* you might imagine the women in a circle dancing to a Spanish song with a pig and a donkey (pig-asso). The more outlandish the image the better, since such images are the most memorable. The best mental images involve bright colors, three dimensions, action scenes, inanimate objects with human traits, and humor.

Here is another example: Say you are trying to learn some basic Spanish vocabulary, including the words *carta, río,* and *dinero.* Instead of trying to learn these words by rote, you might come up with mental images such as those in Key 6.7.

Use Visual Images to Remember Items in a List

Two mental imagery techniques will help you remember items in a list: taking a mental walk in a familiar place and using the number/shape mnemonic.

Using the *mental walk* strategy, you imagine that you store new ideas in familiar locations. Say, for example, that for your biology course you have to remember the major endocrine glands, starting in the brain and working

Key 6.7	Visual images aid recall.	
SPANISH WORD	**DEFINITION**	**MENTAL IMAGE**
carta	letter	A person pushing a shopping cart filled with letters into a post office.
río	river	A school of sharks rioting in the river. One of the sharks is pulling a banner inscribed with the word *riot.* A killer shark bites off the *t* in riot as he takes charge of the group. "I'm the king of this river," he says.
dinero	money	A man is eating lasagna at a diner. The lasagna is made of layers of money.

downward through the body. To do this, think of your route to the library. You pass the college theater, the science center, the bookstore, the cafeteria, the athletic center, and the social science building before reaching your destination. At each spot along the way, you "place" the concept you want to learn. You then link the concept with a similar-sounding word that brings to mind a vivid image (see Key 6.8).

- At the campus theater, you imagine bumping into the actor Brad **Pitt,** who is holding **two** cell phones and has a **terri**ble cold (pituitary gland).
- At the science center, you visualize Mr. Universe with bulging **thighs.** When you are introduced, you learn that his name is **Roy** (thyroid gland).
- At the campus bookstore, you envision a second Mr. Universe with his **thighs** covered in **mus**tard (thymus gland).
- In the cafeteria, you see an **ad** for **Dean Al** for president (adrenal gland).
- At the athletic center, you visualize a student throwing a ball into a **pan** and **creatures** applauding from the bleachers (pancreas).
- At the social science building, you imagine receiving a standing **ova**tion (ovaries).
- And at the library, you visualize sitting at a table taking a **test** that is **easy** (testes).

The *number/shape mnemonic* will help you remember items in a specific order by linking each to a vivid image that is associated with the number. Start by creating images in the forms of shapes for the numbers—in this case 1 through 10—like those in Key 6.9. (These images can be used over and over again for different lists you need to remember.) Then link the shape you have associated with each number with the information you want to remember (see the right column in Key 6.9). In this case, the student is trying to remember the moons of the planet Uranus in order of their distance from the planet.

Create a Vocabulary Cartoon

Visual cartoons use the DAP method—definition, association, and picture—to harness the power of humor to help you remember challenging vocabulary. The recall is accomplished through the following steps:

Step 1. Write down the new vocabulary word followed by its pronunciation and *definition.* For example:

word: histrionic
pronunciation: (his tree AHN ik)
definition: overly dramatic, theatrical

Key 6.8   A mental walk mnemonic helps you remember items in a list.

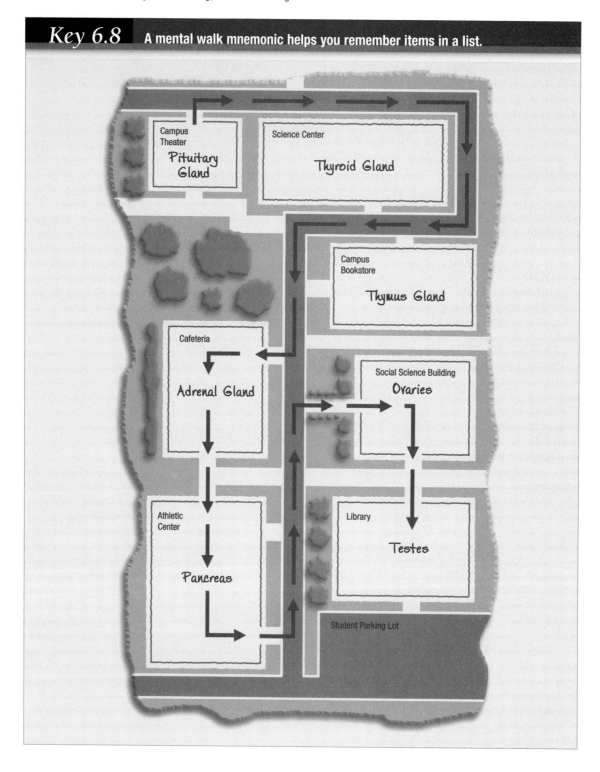

Key 6.9		**Use a number/shape mnemonic to recall a sequenced list.**

NUMBER	YOUR IMAGE FOR THE NUMBER	ASSOCIATED IMAGES FOR THE MOONS OF URANUS IN THE ORDER OF THEIR DISTANCE FROM THE PLANET
1	A stick, pole, or arrow	A **cord** attached to a pole with a banner reading "I have a **deal** for **ya**" (closest moon is Cordelia)
2	A flexible goose-necked lamp twisted in the shape of a swan	An **oaf** sitting under a goose-necked lamp saying, "I **feel ya** pain." (second moon is Ophelia)
3	A pitcher's target with two spots—one for high pitches, the other for low pitches	A **bee** stings the pitcher's **ankle** (third moon is Bianca)
4	A sail on a sailboat	A water**cress** sandwich eaten by a sailor named **Ida** (fourth moon is Cressida)
5	Captain Hook's hook	Captain Hook chasing a man named **Desie** who **moans** after the hook claws his back (fifth moon is Desdemona)
6	A ball on the ground with a string loosely tied to it	A ball with a string covered with **jewel**s and a man nearby warning, "Don't touch **it yet**." (sixth moon is Juliet)
7	A ski jump	A **Porsche** sports car racing over a ski jump (seventh moon is Portia)
8	An egg timer	A **rose** covered with **lint** against the backdrop of an egg timer (eighth moon is Rosalind)
9	The moon with a loose string attached to its side	The string attached to the moon is attached at the other end to a **bell** clanging in the **wind** (ninth moon is Belinda)
10	A shovel next to a hole	The shovel hitting a hockey **puck** into the hole (tenth moon is Puck)

Step 2. Think of a link word—an *association*—that rhymes with your word or sounds like it:

association: history

Step 3. Create a *picture* or simple cartoon with the main and link word to serve as a visual mnemonic. Then write a caption that connects the word you are trying to learn with the link word in a way that defines its meaning in the context of the picture:

"Professor Bradley liked his History on the Histrionic side—with a lot of theatrics."

Step 4. Use the word in sentences of your own:

The histrionic child threw herself on her bed when she didn't get her way.
The histrionic actor's portrayal of the sedate professor did not ring true.

HISTRIONIC
(his tree AHN ik)
overly dramatic, theatrical
Link: HISTORY

Sam Burchers, *Vocabulary Cartoons: Building an Educated Vocabulary with Visual Mnemonics.* Punta Gorda, FL: New Monic
Books, 1997, p. 40. Reprinted with permission.

Go For It!   BUILDING YOUR SKILLS

CREATE YOUR OWN MNEMONIC

Identify specific content you have to memorize for a course. Then complete the following:

- Create a mnemonic to help you memorize all the details. (If you need more space, use a separate sheet of paper.)

_____

_____

- Describe the types of visual images you used in the mnemonic. Were they humorous, ridiculous, or colorful?

_____

_____

_____

_____

- Why do you think these types of images help you retain information?

_____

_____

_____

_____

Create Acronyms

Another helpful association method involves the use of the *acronym,* a word formed from the first letters of a series of words created in order to help you remember the series. In history class, you can remember the Allies during World War II—Britain, America, and Russia—with the acronym BAR. This is an example of a *word acronym,* because the first letters of the items you want to remember spell a word. The word (or words) spelled don't necessarily have to be real words; see Key 6.10 for an acronym—the name Roy G. Biv—that will help you remember the colors of the spectrum.

Other acronyms take the form of an entire sentence in which the first letter of each word in each sentence stands for the first letter of the memorized term. This is called a *list order acronym.* For example, when astronomy students want to remember the list of planets in order of their distance from the sun (Mercury, Venus, Earth, Mars, Jupiter, Saturn, Uranus, Neptune, and Pluto), they learn the sentence:

My very elegant mother just served us nine pickles.

Here's another example, from music. Use this phrase to remember the notes that correspond to the lines on the treble clef (E, G, B, D, and F).

Every Good Boy Does Fine.

Key 6.10   **This acronym helps you remember the colors of the spectrum.**

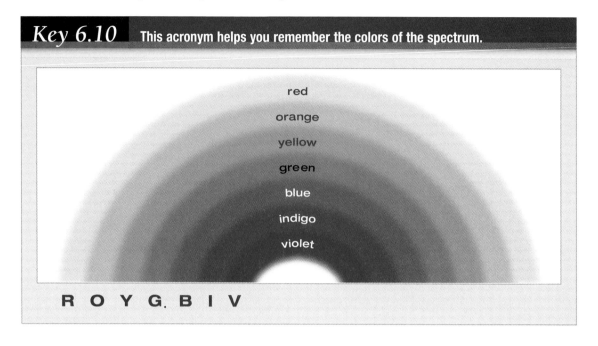

red

orange

yellow

green

blue

indigo

violet

R O Y G. B I V

You can create your own acronyms. Suppose you want to remember the names of the first six U. S. presidents. You notice that the first letters of their last names—Washington, Adams, Jefferson, Madison, Monroe, and Adams—together read W A J M M A. To remember them, first you might insert an e after the J and create a short nonsense word: wajemma. Then, to make sure you don't forget the nonsense word, you might picture the six presidents sitting in a row and wearing pajamas.

ACTIVE
THINKING

Work Together   **BUILDING YOUR SKILLS**

SKILL   WILL   SELF-MGMT.

ASSESS YOUR MEMORY AND THEN BOOST ITS POWER

Gather as a class if there are fewer than 20 people, or divide into two groups if it is larger. Then do the following:

- Each person in your group should contribute at least one item to lay on a table (try to avoid repeats). When all the items are laid out, allow one minute to look at them (use a watch or clock to time yourselves).
- Then cover the items, and, allowing five minutes, have each person list on paper as many as possible.
- Compare lists to the actual items to see how you did.

- Talk as a group about the results, what you didn't remember and why, and what helped you remember. List your observations here and on a separate sheet, if necessary.

_____

_____

_____

_____

- Now repeat the exercise using a mnemonic device. For example, create a new group of items, and then allow five minutes to look at them and to develop an acronym or idea chain in that time. Then cover the items and make lists again. Finally, talk about whether this helped you remember more items. Write your findings here:

_____

_____

_____

Use Songs or Rhymes

Some of the classic mnemonic devices are rhyming poems that tend to stick in your mind effectively. One you may have heard is the rule about the order of "i" and "e" in spelling:

I before E, except after C, or when sounded like "A" as in "neighbor" and "weigh."
Four exceptions if you please: either, neither, seizure, seize.

Make up your own poems or songs, linking tunes or rhymes that are familiar with information you want to remember. Thinking back to the "wajemma" example from the previous section, imagine that you want to remember the presidents' first names as well. You might set those first names—George, John, Thomas, James, James, and John—to the tune of "Happy Birthday." Or, to extend the history theme, you might use the first musical phrase of the National Anthem.

Haverford College physics professor Walter Smith hosts a website— www.physicssongs.org—dedicated to helping students enjoy physics and learn essential concepts by putting them to music. Here, for example, is

MULTIPLE INTELLIGENCE STRATEGIES FOR MNEMONIC DEVICES. Tap into these Multiple Intelligence strategies to develop more effective mnemonics.

INTELLIGENCE	SUGGESTED STRATEGIES	WHAT WORKS FOR YOU? WRITE NEW IDEAS HERE
Verbal-Linguistic	■ Develop a story line for the mnemonic first, then work on the visual images. ■ Choose language-based mnemonics such as word- or list-order acronyms.	
Logical-Mathematical	■ Think of a mnemonic device that flows logically from the material. ■ Develop three or four mnemonic device structures and use them repeatedly with different content.	
Bodily-Kinesthetic	■ Create a storyboard for your mnemonic on large pieces of paper. Tape them up on your walls as you memorize the material. ■ Record the mnemonic onto a tape and learn it as you walk between classes.	
Visual-Spatial	■ Focus on visual mnemonics such as mental walks and idea chains. ■ Use markers to add color to the images.	
Interpersonal	■ Work with a study partner to develop helpful mnemonics for the course. ■ Use the mnemonic to test each other on specific content.	
Intrapersonal	■ Take time alone to brainstorm ideas for the mnemonic. ■ After you develop the mnemonic, find a quiet spot to memorize the material.	
Musical	■ Play music while you are brainstorming ideas. ■ Create a mnemonic in the form of a musical rhyme.	
Naturalistic	■ Include images from nature in your mnemonic. ■ Learn the mnemonic while sitting outdoors.	

"The Gauss's Law Song," written by Professor Smith and Marian McKenzie and sung to the tune of "East Side, West Side":

> Inside, outside, count the lines to tell—
>
> If the charge is inside, there will be net flux as well.
>
> If the charge is outside, be careful and you'll see
>
> The goings in and goings out are equal perfectly.
>
> If you wish to know the field precise,
>
> And the charge is symmetric,
>
> you will find this law is nice—
>
> Q upon a constant—eps'lon naught they say—
>
> Equals closed surface integral of E dot n dA.
>
> © 2001 Walter Fox Smith. Reprinted with permission.[11]

Professor Smith's students credit musical mnemonics for helping them retain complex equations. Student Katie Baratz went one step further and started writing her own songs. For her final project in Professor Smith's class she paired lyrics entitled "In My Mind, I've Got Physics Equations" with the James Taylor tune "Carolina in My Mind." When friends asked her why she was spending so much time on the physicssongs.org website, she explained that she was having fun.[12]

Improving your memory requires energy, time, work—the active-learning components of will, skill, and self-management. It also helps to master SQ3R, the textbook study technique that was introduced in Chapter 5. By going through the steps in SQ3R and using the specific memory techniques described in this chapter, you can learn more in less time—and remember what you learn long after exams are over. These techniques will prove equally valuable when you start a career.

"We retain 10 percent of what we read, 20 percent of what we hear, 30 percent of what we see, 50 percent of what we hear and see, 70 percent of what we say, 90 percent of what we say and do."

UNKNOWN SOURCE

Building Skill, Will, and Self-Management

Monitoring Your Progress

ACTIVE THINKING

SKILL · WILL · SELF-MGMT.

Test Competence: Measure What You've Learned

MULTIPLE CHOICE. *Circle the answer that seems to fit best.*

1. When listening, you decide how you feel about a message in the
   A. interpretation stage.
   B. sensation stage.
   C. evaluation stage.
   D. reaction stage.

2. Listening challenges do *not* include
   A. rushing to judgment.
   B. divided attention and distractions.
   C. learning disabilities.
   D. slow recovery time.

3. Verbal signposts
   A. indicate what is important.
   B. involve unique speech patterns.
   C. help separate fact from opinion.
   D. all of the above.

4. You can increase your active listening skills by
   A. getting to class on time.
   B. asking questions that aid understanding.
   C. having a clear listening purpose.
   D. all of the above.

5. Short-term memory is a memory storage bank that
   A. lasts no more than 10 to 20 seconds.
   B. is an exact copy of what you see and hear.

   C. stores information you are not aware of.

   D. stores information for a set period of time.

6. You can improve your memory of particular material by

   A. spreading your study sessions over time.

   B. studying for an hour or two without a break.

   C. studying during class.

   D. studying in the evenings.

7. Strategies for using flash cards to help memory *do not* include

   A. testing yourself on one side of the cards only.

   B. using the cards as a self-test.

   C. shuffling the cards and learning the information in various orders.

   D. carrying cards with you and reviewing them frequently.

8. Association means

   A. considering how information is updated.

   B. finding the differences between two sets of information.

   C. considering new information on its own terms.

   D. considering new information in relation to information you already know.

9. A mental walk refers to

   A. a mnemonic device that uses visual images.

   B. ways to build pathways through the brain.

   C. memory strategies that use aural sensation.

   D. storage banks for memory.

10. A word formed from the first letters of a series of words, created in order to help you remember the series, is

   A. an acronym.

   B. a mnemonic device.

   C. a signpost.

   D. a visual image.

TRUE/FALSE. *Place a T or an F beside each statement to indicate whether you think it is true or false.*

_____ 1. Fatigue is an external distraction.

_____ 2. The four stages of the learning process are concrete experience, reflexive observation, abstract hypothesis, and passive testing.

_____ 3. The brain can readily remember up to 20 items at a time.

_____ 4. To get the most out of your study sessions, minimize study breaks.

_____ 5. Material you study midway through a study session tends to be a weak link in your recall.

Target and Achieve a Goal

Commit to one specific listening or memory strategy from this chapter to improve your study skills.

Name the strategy here: _____

_____

Describe your goal—what you want to gain by using this strategy. _____

_____

_____

Describe how you plan to use this strategy through the semester to achieve this goal.

_____

_____

Building Your Skills

Brain Power: Build Vocabulary Fitness

Here is a selection from the current media. Read the material, paying special attention to the context of the vocabulary words shown in bold type. Then choose the correct definition for each word in the table that follows. Use a dictionary to check your answers. Finally, on a separate sheet, use each vocabulary word in a sentence of your own to solidify your understanding.

While many active techniques improve memory—including those you learned about in this chapter—a passive technique also works wonders: getting a good night's sleep. Anahad O'Connor reported on a study of sleep's effectiveness in cementing memories in a recent New York Times *article.*

> History suggests that a burst of creative inspiration, or even a solution to a **baffling** problem, can work from the unconscious work of slumber. [For example,] Friedrich August Kekule **discerned** the ring shape of benzene in a **somnolent** vision of a snake biting its tail. While [this] might seem like an exceptional case, research confirms that a good night's sleep can open the door to insight.

In a [recent] study . . . researchers trained several groups of students to perform a memory task. Each student learned two rules for converting a string of eight numbers into a new string. A third, hidden rule would have reduced the steps in the calculation, allowing the students to solve the problem immediately. The groups were tested once after training and then again eight hours later.

Sixty percent of the students allowed to sleep in the **interval** figured out the hidden rule. Only 22 percent of those who stayed awake . . . discovered it.

Another group that slept for eight hours without being trained beforehand never figured the rule out, indicating that sleep helped only if the subjects formed memories of the tasks first. The control conditions also helped [eliminate] the possibility that . . . **circadian** rhythm accounted for the findings.

New memories, the findings suggest, are manipulated during sleep in a way that stimulates insight, which then seeps into consciousness. How this happens, or which brain regions are involved, is not clear. . . . **Anecdotal** evidence suggests that insight is **gleaned** from dreams, which occur in the rapid eye movement . . . stage of sleep.

Whatever the mechanisms behind creative slumber, if a crucial exam is **imminent**, . . . it is probably a good idea to sleep on it.

Source: Anahad O'Connor, "Really? The Claim: Sleep inspires creative thinking," *The New York Times,* November 9, 2004, p. F6. Copyright © 2004 by The New York Times Company. Reprinted with permission.

Circle the word or phrase that best defines each term as it is used in this excerpt.

VOCABULARY WORDS	A	B	C
1. baffling (adj.)	difficult	puzzling	complex
2. discerned (verb)	ignored	invented	showed insight
3. somnolent (adj.)	alert	sleepy	sorrowful
4. interval (noun)	time between events	daytime	period
5. circadian (adj.)	monthly	yearly	daily
6. anecdotal (adj.)	comprehensive	based on reports of observations	amusing
7. gleaned (verb)	gathered in a discriminating way	forgotten from	combined with
8. imminent (adj.)	about to occur	postponed	pressing

Get to the Root

Every time you learn a Greek or Latin root, you increase your ability to recognize English vocabulary words that include that root and to figure out their meaning. Grow your vocabulary by studying this root and its related words, writing in two more words from the same root, and including definitions for both new words.

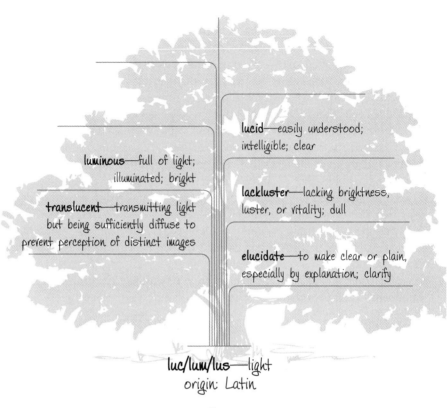

lucid—easily understood; intelligible; clear

luminous—full of light; illuminated; bright

lackluster—lacking brightness, luster, or vitality; dull

translucent—transmitting light but being sufficiently diffuse to prevent perception of distinct images

elucidate—to make clear or plain, especially by explanation; clarify

luc/lum/lus—light
origin: Latin

Investigate Using Research Navigator

Access Research Navigator using the Internet address shown on page 32. Then sign on to the service using your Login Name and Password. Scroll through the database titles listed for Content Select. Choose a database linked to a course you are taking this semester, and then enter a career-related keyword. For example, if you are taking an engineering course, you could choose the Engineering database and enter "civil engineering" as a keyword.

- When the database generates a list of articles, choose one that seems interesting or is related to a topic you are covering in class and open its full text. You may be reading an academic journal article, the kind of reading often required on the job in many career areas.

- Read the article and use one or more of the devices discussed in this chapter to commit the material to memory. Then evaluate your experience in writing.

  - Which memory strategies did you choose? How did they help you remember important details?

  - When did you use these strategies—after you read and understood the article or while you were reading the material the first time? Evaluate whether you think your timing was effective.

- Do you think you will use these strategies again at school? When you begin working?

- Why is retaining information just as important at work as it is at school?

Building Will and Self-Awareness

ACTIVE
THINKING
SKILL WILL SELF-MGMT.

Make Responsible Choices

Answer the following question on a separate piece of paper or in a journal.

Every student has memory and listening challenges. Be determined to improve your skills by thinking about . . .

■ *your biggest memory challenge and the technique you learned in this chapter that will help you overcome it.* Briefly describe what you plan to do to increase your recall after studying. Be specific about how you will use specific memory-improvement techniques to get better grades this semester.

■ *your obligation to continue listening even when you disagree with what your instructor says.* If you decide to tune in, is your motivation wanting to do well in the course or being open to different perspectives? Does your motivation make a difference, as long as you continue to listen? Explain.

Chapter Summary

As you use this summary to review the concepts you learned in this chapter, focus also on its format—in this case a **formal outline**, in other chapters a think link, and in still others the Cornell system. As you become comfortable with the organization and style of these various formats, try using each of them to take class and reading notes, noting which approach works best for you in particular situations.

CHAPTER 6

I. Listening skills can be improved with knowledge and strategy.

   A. Listening process has four stages: sensation, interpretation, evaluation, and reaction.

   B. Listening challenges may occur at each stage.

      1. Internal distractions include such things as personal worry and hunger. Examples of external distractions are noise and excess heat.

2. Shutting out all or part of the message may lead to listening lapses.

3. Personal reactions to instructors may lead you to devalue what they say.

4. Partial hearing loss or a learning disability may make it difficult to listen.

C. The best listeners are active listeners. Take steps to get yourself actively involved:

1. Show up on time and be ready to concentrate.

2. Be clear on your listening purpose: What do you expect to learn?

3. Listen to understand. Real learning requires understanding.

4. Question what you hear. Write down your inquiries so they don't interfere with listening.

5. Pay attention to instructor's signals that tell you what is important.

II. Memory strategies help you remember what you hear and read.

A. Three memory storage banks: sensory memory, short-term memory, and long-term memory (the mind's permanent information storehouse).

B. According to biologist James Zull, retaining information in long-term memory engages a four-stage learning process: concrete experience, reflexive observation, abstract hypothesis, and active testing.

III. Memory strategies help improve recall.

A. When you are interested and passionate about a subject, you remember more.

B. Understanding aids recall, so use critical thinking to associate new material with what you already know.

C. Reciting, rehearsing, and writing actively involve you in learning and aid recall.

D. Other strategies include studying material more than once, practicing the middle, creating groupings, and using flash cards and tape-recorded material.

E. Using the material often and linking it to what you know and to new facts and problems is the best way to transfer information to long-term memory.

IV. Mnemonic devices create vivid associations that engage your emotions as they aid recall.

A. Visual images and associations are easiest to remember.

B. Two mental imagery techniques will help you remember items in a list: taking a mental walk in a familiar place and using the number/shape mnemonic.

C. Vocabulary cartoons that link funny cartoons and captions to new vocabulary create unforgettable visual images.

D. Acronyms take two forms.

1. Words are formed from the first letters of a series of words.

2. List order acronyms are entire sentences in which the first letter of each word in each sentence stands for the first letter of the memorized term.

E. Mnemonic devices that are in song or rhyme form are often memorable.

Endnotes

1. In Louis E. Boone, David L. Kurtz, and Judy R. Block, *Contemporary Business Communication*. Upper Saddle River, NJ: Prentice Hall, 1994, p. 39.

2. Ralph G. Nichols, "Do We Know How to Listen? Practical Helps in a Modern Age," *Speech Teacher* (March 1961), pp. 118–124.

3. *Keys to Lifelong Learning Telecourse*. Dir. Mary Jane Bradbury. Videocassette. Intrepid Films, 2000.

4. John Gravois, "Teach Impediment: When the Student Can't Understand the Instructor, Who Is to Blame?" *The Chronicle of Higher Education*, April 8, 2005, pp. A10–A12.

5. *Keys to Lifelong Learning Telecourse*.

6. Ralph G. Nichols, "Do We Know How to Listen?"

7. Herman Ebbinghaus, *Memory: A Contribution to Experimental Psychology*, trans. H. A. Ruger and C. E. Bussenius. New York: Teachers College, Columbia University, 1885.

8. James Zull, *The Art of Changing the Brain: Enriching Teaching by Exploring the Biology of Learning*. Sterling, VA: Stylus Publishing, 2002.

9. Rachel Metz, "Think of a Number . . . Come on, Think!" *The New York Times*, March 18, 2005, p. G1.

10. Adam Robinson, *What Smart Students Know: Maximum Grades. Optimum Learning. Minimum Time*. New York: Three Rivers Press, 1993, p. 118.

11. Physics Songs.Org (www.physicssongs.org). Information taken from website on March 28, 2005 (www.haverford.edu/physics-astro/songs/Gauss).

12. Christopher Conkey, "It's All Relative: Songs to Make Physics Easier," *The Wall Street Journal*, March 17, 2005, p. B1.

Active Thinking

Find Connections Among Ideas

The following multiple-choice, true/false, fill-in-the-blank, matching, and essay questions reinforce the concepts you learned in the three chapters that make up Part II, *Reading, Understanding, and Remembering: Mastering Essential Learning Skills*. These questions differ from the end-of-chapter objective quizzes in an important way: Instead of focusing on concepts in individual chapters, they encourage you to compare and integrate material from *different* chapters as you find ways to connect ideas. Recognizing relationships among ideas is essential to active learning because it builds critical thinking skills, adds meaning to information, and makes it more likely that you will retain what you learn.

MULTIPLE CHOICE. *Circle or highlight the answer that seems to fit best.*

1. Improving comprehension is important for text reading for all of the following reasons *except:*
   A. You are likely to be tested on what you read in the textbooks and handouts you receive in class.
   B. Understanding what you read early in the semester gives you a foundation for understanding more complex information later in the semester.
   C. Comprehension is needed for critical thinking.
   D. If your comprehension is good, you will be able to resell your text immediately after the course is over.

2. Being able to recognize the meaning of prefixes, roots, and suffixes will help you
   A. do well when you study a foreign language.
   B. figure out the meaning of many new vocabulary words and remember information.

C. create visual aids.

D. identify your purpose for reading.

3. SQ3R is a textbook study method that depends, in part, on

   A. goal setting.

   B. time management.

   C. critical thinking.

   D. listening.

4. Becoming emotionally involved with what you learn is important because

   A. your instructor will be impressed that you care so much about the material.

   B. when you are emotionally involved, the brain codes the material as important and meaningful.

   C. your emotional response is more important than your intellectual response.

   D. you learn the most only when you laugh or cry.

5. It is important to improve your comprehension of tables and charts for all of the following reasons *except*:

   A. Learning to read and understand visual aids will help you study more effectively.

   B. Information is often more readily recalled when it is presented in visual form.

   C. Visual aids are more interesting than straight text.

   D. Textbooks often present critical information in visual form.

TRUE/FALSE. *Place a T or an F beside each statement to indicate whether you think it is true or false.*

_____ 1. When you highlight your text, it is important to start marking the first time you read the page.

_____ 2. During class, ideas worth learning come only from your instructor.

_____ 3. Listening is an intellectual skill as well as an interpersonal skill.

_____ 4. As you use SQ3R to question text concepts, it is important to add questions that occurred to you during class lectures.

_____ 5. Listening is a four-stage process whose order is: sensation, evaluation, interpretation, and reaction.

FILL-IN-THE-BLANK. *Complete the following sentences with the appropriate word(s) or phrase(s) that best reflect what you learned in Part II. Choose from the items that follow each sentence.*

1. As you set your study schedule, you should define your purpose for reading because purpose determines _____. (pace, interest, motivation)

2. Vocabulary building depends on memory aids including _____ and _____. (rote memorization/ motivation, effective listening/time management, mnemonic devices/flash cards)

3. A vocabulary cartoon links a word you want to learn with a _____ and a _____. (another new vocabulary word/humorous visual image, text concept/humorous visual image, rhyming link word/humorous visual image

4. _____ and _____ tend to be slow readers who have difficulty keeping up with their reading assignments and managing their time. (Procrastinators/critical thinkers, Vocalizers/subvocalizers, Flexible learners/foreign-born students)

5. SQ3R will encourage you to read _____. (critically, quickly, slowly)

6. The Q-stage of SQ3R is a two-step process in which you _____ and _____. (write questions as they occur to you/question your instructor about what the material means, ask yourself what you know about a topic/write questions linked to chapter headings, write questions linked to underlined words and bolded type in the text/write questions linked to chapter headings)

7. Personalizing your text with _____ and _____ will help you become an active learner. (highlighting/marginal notes, highlighting/full-text notes, highlighting/lecture notes)

8. Listening problems may be associated with _____ and _____. (vision problems/back problems, handwriting problems/poor time management, partial hearing loss/learning disabilities)

9. Active listeners pay attention to the instructor's _____ to identify important information before it is presented. (verbal signposts, body language, tone of voice)

10. Mnemonic devices include visual images, associations, and _____. (word prefixes, acronyms, word roots)

MATCHING. *Match each item in the left-hand column to an item in the right-hand column by writing the letter from the right that corresponds best to the number on the left.*

_____ 1. word root

A. graphs that show statistical comparisons in visual form

_____ 2. specialized work vocabulary

B. a problem, associated with rereading words, that slows down reading speed

_____ 3. SQ3R

C. words or phrases used by your instructor to call attention to what comes next

_____ 4. unconscious regression

D. central part of a word around which prefixes and suffixes are added

_____ 5. front matter

E. survey, question, read, recite, review

_____ 6. marginal text notes

F. a memory strategy that helps you learn new vocabulary by associating definitions with pictures

_____ 7. verbal signposts

G. words, phrases, and initials that convey meaning to people doing similar jobs

_____ 8. charts

H. a memory strategy in which you imagine that you store new ideas in familiar locations

_____ 9. vocabulary cartoon

I. the table of contents and preface that provide a text overview

_____ 10. mental walk

J. personal text notes that flag important ideas

ESSAY QUESTION. *Carefully read the following excerpt from* Business Essentials, *3rd ed., by Ronald J. Ebert and Ricky W. Griffin, a college textbook published by Prentice Hall, and then answer the essay question that follows. This exercise will help you focus on the meaning of the selection, apply your personal knowledge and experiences to the reading, organize your ideas, and communicate your thoughts effectively in writing.*

Before you begin writing your essay, it is a good idea to spend a few minutes planning. Try brainstorming possible approaches, writing a thesis statement, and jotting down your main thoughts in the form of an outline or think link. Because most essay tests are timed, limit the time you take to write your response to no more than one-half hour. This will force you to write quickly and effectively as it prepares you for actual test conditions.

MANAGERIAL STYLES

Early theories of leadership tried to identify specific traits associated with strong leaders. For example, physical appearance, intelligence, and public-speaking skills were once thought to be "leadership traits." Indeed, it was once believed that taller people made better leaders than shorter people. The trait approach, however, proved to be a poor predictor of leadership potential. Ultimately, attention shifted from managers' traits to their behaviors, or **managerial styles**—patterns of behavior that a manager exhibits in dealing with subordinates. Managerial styles run the gamut from autocratic to democratic to free rein. Naturally, most managers do not conform to any one style, but these three major types of styles involve very different kinds of responses to human relations problems. Under different circumstances, any given style or combination of styles may prove appropriate.

- Managers who adopt an **autocratic style** generally issue orders and expect them to be obeyed without question. The military commander prefers and usually needs the autocratic style on the battlefield. Because no one else is consulted, the autocratic style allows for rapid decision making. It may, therefore, be useful in situations testing a firm's effectiveness as a time-based competitor.

- Managers who adopt a **democratic style** generally ask for input from subordinates before making decisions but retain final decision-making power. For example, the manager of a technical group may ask other group members to interview and offer opinions about job applicants. The manager, however, will ultimately make the hiring decision.

- Managers who adopt a **free-rein style** typically serve as advisors to subordinates who are allowed to make decisions. The chairperson of a volunteer committee to raise funds for a new library may find a free-rein style most effective.

According to many observers, the free-rein style of leadership is currently giving rise to an approach that emphasizes broad-based employee input into decision making and the fostering of workplace environments in which employees increasingly determine what needs to be done and how.

Regardless of theories about the ways in which leaders ought to lead, the relative effectiveness of any leadership style depends largely on the desire of subordinates to share input or to exercise creativity. Whereas some people, for example, are frustrated, others prefer autocratic managers because they do not want a voice in making decisions. The democratic approach, meanwhile, can be disconcerting both to people who want decision-making responsibility and to those who do not. A free-rein style lends itself to employee creativity, and thus to creative solutions to pressing problems. This style also appeals to employees who like to plan their own work. Not all subordinates, however, have the necessary background or skills to make creative decisions. Others are not sufficiently self-motivated to work without supervision.

Source: Excerpted from Ronald J. Ebert and Ricky W. Griffin, *Business Essentials,* 3rd ed., Upper Saddle River, NJ: Prentice Hall, 2000, pp. 197–198.

YOUR QUESTION. If you are currently working or have worked for different employers in permanent, short-term, or part-time jobs, categorize your supervisors' managerial style. Provide specific examples that show why your supervisors fit into the categories you chose. Then, describe how you responded to each style: Did it motivate you to work harder or to slack off? Based on this analysis, evaluate which managerial style you would be likely to use if you were a department head.

Be Accountable for Your Goals from Part II

ACTIVE THINKING

SKILL WILL SELF-MGMT.

Look back at the goals you set in the *Target and Achieve a Goal* exercises at the ends of Chapters 4, 5, and 6. In the space provided, write a short journal entry in which you assess your progress (use or continue on a separate piece of paper if you need more room). In your discussion, consider questions such as the following:

- Have you used the strategies you intended to use?
- What effect have these strategies had on your work?
- Have you achieved the goals you set? Why or why not?
- What is your plan going forward for these strategies and goals?

NOTES, WRITING, AND MATH

BUILDING ACTIVE STUDY SKILLS

"Taking notes forces you to think about concepts as you select and transcribe the instructor's thoughts. Like a high-performance automobile, you're running on all eight cylinders instead of just two."

STEPHEN REID, PROFESSOR OF ENGLISH, COLORADO STATE UNIVERSITY

242

Taking Lecture Notes

RECORDING CONCEPTS AND INFORMATION

n class, your skills as an active listener affect what you learn from instructors and classmates. Your success in reviewing and retaining that information depends, in large part, on how well you take notes and how usable these notes are as study tools. This chapter will help you master the note-taking attitudes and skills needed for college success.

In this chapter you will explore answers to the following questions:

- How will taking notes help you succeed in college?

- What note-taking system should you use?

- How can you make the most of class notes?

- How do you combine class and text notes to create a master set?

- What can you do to take notes faster?

HOW WILL TAKING NOTES HELP YOU SUCCEED IN COLLEGE?

Note taking can be a challenge, especially when it gets in the way of listening to your instructor or studying what is written on the board. It's even more of a challenge when you're having trouble with difficult concepts or when, no matter how fast you write, you can't keep up with the instructor's pace.

These problems may leave you wondering whether notes are that important after all, especially since you have your text and other assigned materials to study. Don't be fooled: *The truth is that the act of note taking involves you in the learning process in ways you cannot do without.* Taking notes makes you an active class participant—even when you don't say a word—and provides you with study materials for tests. What's on the line, in many classes, is nothing short of your academic success (see Key 7.1).

Class notes have two primary purposes: to serve as a record of what happened in class and to use for studying, alone and in combination with your text notes. Because it is virtually impossible to take notes on everything you hear, note taking encourages you to think critically and evaluate what is worth remembering.

Asking yourself questions like the following will help you judge what is important enough to write down.

- Is this information important to the academic discipline I am studying, for my success in the course, and for my broad education and career success?

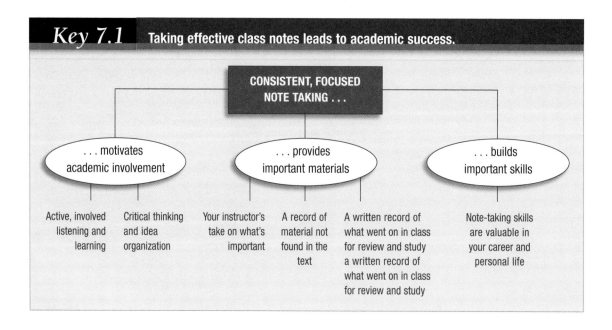

Key 7.1   Taking effective class notes leads to academic success.

CONSISTENT, FOCUSED NOTE TAKING . . .

. . . motivates academic involvement

. . . provides important materials

. . . builds important skills

Active, involved listening and learning

Critical thinking and idea organization

Your instructor's take on what's important

A record of material not found in the text

A written record of what went on in class for review and study a written record of what went on in class for review and study

Note-taking skills are valuable in your career and personal life

- Do I recognize its connections to what I already know?
- Do I want to learn it for myself?

Choosing the right note-taking system is an essential first step in becoming a better note taker.

WHAT NOTE-TAKING SYSTEM SHOULD YOU USE?

You will benefit most from a note-taking system that is comfortable and makes the most sense for the course content. The most common note-taking systems are outlines, the Cornell system, and think links. The summaries at the end of each *Keys to College Studying* chapter demonstrates one of these note-taking formats. The more familiar you are with each, the more likely you are to try it in your own work.

Take Notes in Outline Form

When a lecture seems well organized, you may choose to take notes in outline form. Outlining allows you to show the interrelationships and levels of importance among general concepts and supporting details.

Formal Versus Informal Outlines

Formal outlines indicate concepts and examples with Roman numerals, uppercase and lowercase letters, and numbers. In contrast, *informal outlines* show the same associations but replace the formality with a system of consistent indentations and dashes. Key 7.2 shows the difference between the two outline forms. Many students prefer using informal outlines to take class notes. Key 7.3 demonstrates how an informal outline is used to record notes on civil rights legislation.

Outlines are difficult to use with disorganized instructors, and you may have to abandon their structure when the presentation becomes chaotic. Focus instead on taking down whatever information you can as you try to connect key topics. After class, do your best to restructure your notes and, if possible, rewrite them in outline form. If you are unclear about how ideas link, review the concept in your text or ask a classmate or your instructor for help.

Guided Notes

From time to time, an instructor may give you a guide, usually in the form of an outline, to help you take notes. This outline may be on the board, on an overhead projector, on a handout, or as part of online materials.

Key 7.2   Outlines show levels of importance as they link details to main ideas.

FORMAL OUTLINE	INFORMAL OUTLINE
TOPIC	TOPIC

FORMAL OUTLINE

TOPIC

I. First Main Idea

   A. Major supporting fact

   B. Major supporting fact

      1. First reason or example

      2. Second reason or example

         a. First supporting fact

         b. Second supporting fact

II. Second Main Idea

   A. Major supporting fact

      1. First reason or example

      2. Second reason or example

   B. Major supporting fact

INFORMAL OUTLINE

TOPIC

First Main Idea

   —Major supporting fact

   —Major supporting fact

      —First reason or example

      —Second reason or example

         —First supporting fact

         —Second supporting fact

Second Main Idea

   —Major supporting fact

      —First reason or example

      —Second reason or example

   —Major supporting fact

Although *guided notes* help you follow the lecture and organize your thoughts, they do not replace your own notes. Because they are usually no more than a basic topic outline, they require that you fill in the details. If your mind wanders because you think that the guided notes are all you need, you may miss important information.

When you receive guided notes on paper, write directly on the paper if there is room. If not, use a separate sheet and write on it the outline categories that structure the guided notes. If the guided notes are on the board or overhead, copy them down but leave plenty of space for the information that comes up during the presentation. When you receive these notes online, be sure to take a printed copy to class.

Use the Cornell Note-Taking System

The *Cornell note-taking system*, also known as the T-note system, was developed by Walter Pauk at Cornell University and is now used throughout the world.[1] The system consists of three sections on ordinary notepaper.

Key 7.3 An informal outline is excellent for taking class notes.

Civil Rights Legislation: <u>1860–1968</u>

—Post-Civil War Era
  —Fourteenth Amendment, 1868: equal protection of the law for all citizens
  —Fifteenth Amendment, 1870: constitutional rights of citizens regardless
      of race, color, or previous servitude
—Civil Rights Movement of the 1960s
  —National Association for the Advancement of Colored People (NAACP)
      —Established in 1910 by W.E.B. DuBois and others
      —Legal Defense and Education fund fought school segregation
  —Martin Luther King Jr., champion of nonviolent civil rights action
      —Led bus boycott: 1955–1956
      —Marched on Washington, D.C.: 1963
      —Awarded NOBEL PEACE PRIZE: 1964
      —Led voter registration drive in Selma, Alabama: 1965
  —Civil Rights Act of 1964: prohibited discrimination in voting, education,
      employment, and public facilities
  —Voting Rights Act of 1965: gave the government power to enforce desegregation
  —Civil Rights Act of 1968: prohibited discrimination in the sale or rental of
      housing

- *Section 1*, the largest section, is on the right. Record your notes here in whatever form is most comfortable for you. Skip lines between topics so you can clearly see where a section begins and ends.
- *Section 2*, to the left of your notes, is the cue column. Leave it blank while you read or listen, and then fill it in later as you review. You might insert keywords or comments that highlight main ideas, clarify meaning, suggest examples, or link ideas and examples. You can even draw diagrams. Many students use this column to raise questions, which they answer when they study.

- *Section 3*, at the bottom of the page, is known as the summary area. Here you reduce your notes to only the most critical points. Restating your instructor's points in your own words will help you learn. Use this section to provide an overview of what the notes say.

Create this note-taking structure before class begins. Picture an upside-down letter T as you follow these directions:

- Start with a sheet of standard loose-leaf paper. Label it with the date and title of the lecture.
- To create the cue column, draw a vertical line about $2^1/_2$ inches from the left side of the paper. End the line about 2 inches from the bottom of the sheet.
- To create the summary area, start at the point where the vertical line ends (about 2 inches from the bottom of the page) and draw a horizontal line that spans the entire paper.

Key 7.4 shows how the Cornell system is used in a business course.

Create a Think Link

A *think link,* also known as a mind map or word web, is a visual form of note taking. When you draw a think link, you diagram ideas by using shapes and lines that link ideas and supporting details and examples. The visual design makes the connections easy to see, and shapes and pictures extend the material beyond just words. Because visual images are easier to recall than words alone, think links can be important tools as you study for exams.

To create a think link, start by circling or boxing your topic in the middle of a sheet of paper. Next, draw a line from the topic and write the name of one major idea at the end of the line. Circle that idea also. Then, jot down specific facts related to the idea, linking them to the idea with lines. Continue the process, connecting thoughts to one another by using circles, lines, and words. Key 7.5, a think link on the sociological concept called stratification, follows this particular structure.

Examples of think link designs include stair steps showing connected ideas that build toward a conclusion and a tree with trunk and roots as central concepts and branches as examples. (The end-of-chapter *Get to the Root* exercises use this design.) Look back at Key 7.1 for yet another type of think link called a "jellyfish."

A think link may be difficult to construct in class, especially if your instructor talks quickly. In this case, transform your notes later when you review.

Key 7.4   The Cornell system has space for notes, comments, and a summary.

October 3, 200x, p. 1

UNDERSTANDING EMPLOYEE MOTIVATION

Why do some workers have a better attitude toward their work than others?	Purpose of motivational theories —To explain role of human relations in motivating employee performance —Theories translate into how managers actually treat workers

Some managers view workers as lazy; others view them as motivated and productive.	2 specific theories
	—Human resources model, developed by Douglas McGregor, shows that managers have radically different beliefs about motivation.
	  —Theory X holds that people are naturally irresponsible and uncooperative
	  —Theory Y holds that people are naturally responsible and self-motivated

Maslow's Hierarchy
 	
self-actualization needs (challenging job)
esteem needs (job title)
social needs (friends at work)
security needs (health plan)
physiological needs (pay)
	—Maslow's Hierarchy of Needs says that people have needs in 5 different areas, which they attempt to satisfy in their work.
	  —Physiological need: need for survival, including food and shelter
	  —Security need: need for stability and protection
	  —Social need: need for friendship and companionship
	  —Esteem need: need for status and recognition
	  —Self-actualization need: need for self-fulfillment
	Needs at lower levels must be met before a person tries to satisfy needs at higher levels.
	—Developed by psychologist Abraham Maslow

Two motivational theories try to explain worker motivation. The human resources model includes Theory X and Theory Y. Maslow's Hierarchy of Needs suggests that people have needs in 5 different areas: physiological, security, social, esteem, and self-actualization.

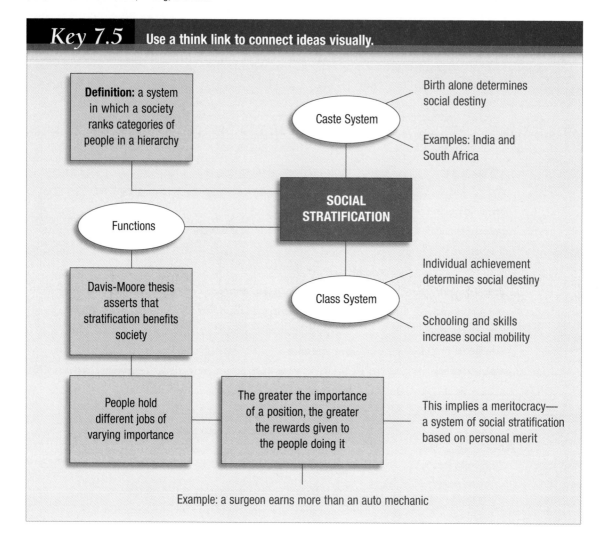

Key 7.5   Use a think link to connect ideas visually.

Definition: a system in which a society ranks categories of people in a hierarchy

Caste System

Birth alone determines social destiny

Examples: India and South Africa

SOCIAL STRATIFICATION

Functions

Davis-Moore thesis asserts that stratification benefits society

Class System

Individual achievement determines social destiny

Schooling and skills increase social mobility

People hold different jobs of varying importance

The greater the importance of a position, the greater the rewards given to the people doing it

This implies a meritocracy— a system of social stratification based on personal merit

Example: a surgeon earns more than an auto mechanic

Use Other Visual Note-Taking Strategies

Several other note-taking strategies will help you organize information and are especially useful to visual learners. These strategies may be too involved to complete quickly during class, so you may want to use them when taking text notes or combining class and text notes for review.

Timelines. Use a timeline to organize information into chronological order. Draw a vertical or horizontal line on the page and connect each item to the line, in order, noting the dates and basic event descriptions.

Tables. Use the columns and rows of a table to organize information as you condense and summarize your class and text notes. Use the basic elements of table design presented in Chapter 5. Many tables are included in *Keys to College Studying*, including the Multiple Pathways to Learning presentation in many chapters.

Hierarchy charts. Charts showing an information hierarchy can help you visualize how pieces fit together. You can use a hierarchy chart to show levels within a government bureaucracy or levels of scientific classification of animals and plants.

Go For It!   BUILDING YOUR SKILLS

ACTIVE THINKING

SKILL · WILL · SELF-MGMT.

CHOOSE THE BEST NOTE-TAKING STRATEGY FOR EVERY COURSE

The following questions will encourage you to think about the note-taking strategies that are best for you and most effective in each of your classes.

- What note-taking strategies fit most comfortably with your learning style? (Consult the Multiple Intelligence Strategies for Note Taking on page 254)

_____

_____

- List the courses you are taking this semester and briefly describe the content of each:

Course 1: _____

_____

Course 2: _____

_____

Course 3: _____

_____

Course 4: _____

_____

(continued)

- Briefly explain the instructor's teaching style for each course:

  Course 1: _____

  _____

  Course 2: _____

  _____

  Course 3: _____

  _____

  Course 4: _____

  _____

- With these factors in mind, name the best note-taking system for each course:

  Course 1: _____

  Course 2: _____

  Course 3: _____

  Course 4: _____

As you will see next, you can improve your skill as a note taker and the value of your notes as a study tool by defining note taking as a three-stage process to master material.

HOW CAN YOU MAKE THE MOST OF CLASS NOTES?

Like learning to ride a bicycle, taking good class notes improves with practice—practice preparing, practice doing, and practice reviewing.

Prepare for Note Taking

Showing up for class on time and having a pad and pen ready is important preparation, but it's only the beginning.

Preview your reading material. *More than anything else you can do, reading the text and other assigned materials before class will give you the background to take effective notes.* Check your class syllabi daily to determine when assignments are due, and plan your reading time with these deadlines in mind.

Try to get a sense of how each lecture relates to your reading assignment by comparing the lecture topic listed on the syllabus with the topic in the text. If the lecture material is not found in the text, you know you have a different kind of listening and note taking challenge than if the material is in the text. Why? Because hearing material for the first time is more difficult than hearing what is familiar.

Writing down important information helps to keep you involved. As they take notes, these community college students are staying connected to what's happening in class.

Coming to class fully prepared also gives you note-taking flexibility. Say, for example, your instructor defines a word on the chalkboard—a sure sign of its importance—but before you are through writing the definition, she presents an example that requires your full attention. If you read the text before class and know that you will find the definition there, you can listen carefully to the example.

Review what you know. Taking 15 minutes before each class to review your notes from the previous class and your reading assignment notes for that day will give you the context to follow the lecture from the start. Without this preparation, you may find yourself flipping back in your notebook instead of listening to new information.

Before your instructor begins, write down one or two questions about the material to put yourself in an active-listening frame of mind. If you know nothing about the topic, think about why learning it is important. If your preparatory questions are not answered during the lecture, *ask them.* Not only will this help you be an attentive listener, but it will tell your instructor that you are prepared for class and willing to participate.

Gather your supplies. Use a separate notebook for each course, and start a new page for each class. (Always put your name, phone number, and e-mail address in every notebook in case of loss.) If you use a three-ring binder,

MULTIPLE INTELLIGENCE STRATEGIES FOR NOTE TAKING. Note taking is a critical learning tool. The tips below will help you retain information for both the short and long term.

INTELLIGENCE	SUGGESTED STRATEGIES	WHAT WORKS FOR YOU? WRITE NEW IDEAS HERE
Verbal-Linguistic	▪ Rewrite important ideas and concepts in class notes from memory. ▪ Write summaries of your notes in your own words.	
Logical-Mathematical	▪ Organize the main points of a lecture or reading using outline form. ▪ Make charts and diagrams to clarify ideas and examples.	
Bodily-Kinesthetic	▪ Make note taking as physical as possible—use large pieces of paper and different colored pens. ▪ When in class, choose a comfortable spot where you have room to spread out your materials and shift body position when you need to.	
Visual-Spatial	▪ Take notes using colored markers. ▪ Rewrite lecture notes in think link format, focusing on the most important and difficult points from the lecture.	
Interpersonal	▪ Whenever possible, schedule a study group right after a lecture to discuss class notes. ▪ Review class notes with a study buddy. See what you wrote that he or she missed and vice versa.	
Intrapersonal	▪ Schedule some quiet time as soon as possible after a lecture to reread and think about your notes. If no class is meeting in the same room after yours and you have free time, stay in the room and review there.	
Musical	▪ Play music while you read your notes. ▪ Write a song that incorporates material from one class period's notes or one particular topic. Use the refrain to emphasize the most important concepts.	
Naturalistic	▪ Read or rewrite your notes outside. ▪ Review notes while listening to a nature CD—running water, rain, forest sounds.	

punch holes in handouts and insert them immediately after your notes for that day. If you take notes on a laptop, open the file containing your class notes right away.

If you are in the habit of placing handouts in the side pocket of your notebook, plan at the start of the semester what you will do when the pocket is packed and there is no place for the latest papers. Consider putting them, in order, in a folder for each class. Then when you study for midterms or finals, you'll find everything you need.

Location, location, location. Find a comfortable seat in a spot that helps you focus. Sit apart from friends if you will be distracted. Be ready to write as soon as the instructor begins speaking.

Choose the best note-taking system. Select a system, from those discussed earlier in this chapter, that will work best in each class. Take the following factors into account when making your choices:

- **The instructor's teaching style.** The instructor's style will be clear after a few classes. In the same semester, you may have an instructor who is organized and speaks slowly, another who jumps from topic to topic and talks rapidly, and a third who goes off on tangents in response to questions. Your challenge is to be flexible enough to adapt your note taking to each situation.

- **The course material.** You may decide that an informal outline works best for a highly structured lecture, but that a think link is right when the presentation is looser. Try a note-taking system for two or three classes, then make adjustments if necessary.

- **Your learning style.** Choose strategies that make the most of your strong points and help compensate for weaknesses. A visual–spatial learner might prefer think links or the Cornell system; a thinker type might be comfortable with outlines; an interpersonal learner might use the Cornell system and fill in the cue column in a study group (see Chapter 2 for a discussion of learning styles). You might even find that one system is best in class and another in review sessions.

Gather support. For each class, set up a support system with two students so that you can look at one or more sets of notes when you're absent. Although you can also look at classmates' notes when you are in class and have questions about material, it's important to limit your reliance, even if you think the other notes are better than yours. Writing down information yourself will help you learn.

PREPARE TO TAKE NOTES IN YOUR MOST CHALLENGING CLASS

In the spaces below, record the specific steps you will take to prepare to take notes in what you consider your most challenging course.

- Course name and date of next class:

  _____

- Consult your course syllabus, and then list all the readings you must complete before the next class (include pages from text and supplemental sources):

  _____

  _____

- List three strategies you intend to use to focus your attention and minimize distractions during the class:

  1. _____

  2. _____

  3. _____

- Which note-taking system is best suited for the class? Why?

  _____

  _____

- Write the names and e-mail addresses of two classmates whose notes you can borrow if you miss a class or if you are confused about material:

  1. _____

  2. _____

Record Information Effectively During Class

The following suggestions will help you record what is important in a format that you can review later:

- Date and identify each page. When you take several pages of notes, add an identifying letter or number to the date on each page: 11/27A,

256

11/27B, 11/27C, for example, or 11/27—1 of 3, 11/27—2 of 3, 11/27—3 of 3. This will help you keep track of page order.

- Add the specific topic of the lecture at the top of the page—for example: 11/27A—U. S. Immigration Policy After World War II—so that it's easy to gather and organize all your notes when it's time to study.
- If your instructor jumps from topic to topic during a single class, it may help to start a new page for each new topic.
- Record whatever your instructor emphasizes by paying attention to verbal and nonverbal cues (see Key 7.6).
- Write down all key terms and definitions.
- Try to capture explanations of difficult concepts by noting relevant examples, applications, and links to other material.
- Write down every question your instructor raises, since these questions may be on a test.

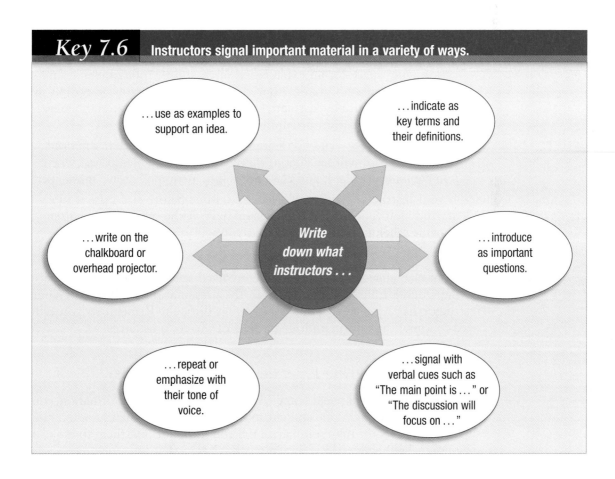

Key 7.6   Instructors signal important material in a variety of ways.

... use as examples to support an idea.

... indicate as key terms and their definitions.

... write on the chalkboard or overhead projector.

Write down what instructors ...

... introduce as important questions.

... repeat or emphasize with their tone of voice.

... signal with verbal cues such as "The main point is ..." or "The discussion will focus on ..."

- Be organized, but not fussy. Remember that you can always improve your notes later as long as you understand what you've written.

- Write quickly but legibly, perhaps using a personal shorthand (shorthand suggestions are presented later in this chapter). In addition, use short phrases instead of full sentences. For example, "Abraham Lincoln was elected president in the year 1860" becomes "Lincoln—elec. Pres. 1860."

- Leave one or more blank spaces between points so that when you review you can easily see where one topic ends and another begins. (This suggestion does not apply if you are using a think link.)

- Draw pictures and diagrams to illustrate ideas.

- Indicate material that is especially important with a star or by underlining. Don't try to highlight, since it takes too much time. Rather, use your highlighter pen as a tool to focus on the important parts of your notes during review sessions.

- Consistency is important. Use the same system for indicating importance—such as indenting, spacing, or underlining—on each page. This will help you perceive key information with a minimum of effort.

- If you have trouble understanding a concept, record as much as you can, leaving space for an explanation later, and then flag the margin with a large question mark. After class, try to clarify your questions in the text; work with a classmate who understands the material better; or ask your instructor for help.

- Consider that your class notes are part, but not all, of what you need to learn. As you will see later in this chapter, you will learn best when you combine your text and class notes into a comprehensive master set.

- If your instructor hands out a lecture outline before class, use it as a starting point, not as a complete summary. Although handouts often provide a helpful overview of what you will learn, they frequently omit the details.

Your challenge is to keep mentally involved and active—even if you are having trouble following the material, the presentation is boring, or your instructor has a voice that makes listening difficult. Remember, you will need to know the information, regardless of the circumstances.

Taking Notes During Extended Class Discussions

Classroom discussions yield some of the most important information you will learn all semester. One student may say something, then another, and finally the instructor may summarize the comments or link them to make a new point. Frequently, class discussions have tremendous value, but just as frequently information is presented in a disorganized, sometimes chaotic way. Here are suggestions for getting the most from these discussions:

- Listen carefully to everyone, since noting what other students say may give you a new perspective.
- Listen for idea threads that weave through the comments. These threads may signal an important point.
- Listen for ideas the instructor reinforces and emphasizes and for encouraging comments, such as "You make a great point," "I like your idea," and so on.
- Take notes when the instructor rephrases and clarifies a student's point. The intensity and articulation of his or her voice often indicates the significance of a discussion point.
- Try using a think link as your note-taking system, since discussions often take the form of brainstorming sessions. A think link will help you connect ideas that come from different perspectives and in different voices.
- Take careful notes during discussion sessions with teaching assistants, since it is the purpose of these sessions to clarify difficult material.

Review and Revise Your Notes

By their very nature, class notes are imperfect and require revision. They may be incomplete in some places, confusing in others, and illegible in still others. That is why it is critical that you review and revise your notes as soon as possible after class. This will enable you to fill in gaps with information that you still remember, to clarify sloppy handwriting, or to raise questions about confusing material. (This process reemphasizes the importance of leaving space between major points or ideas.)

Work Together   **BUILDING YOUR SKILLS**

TURN NEW NOTE-TAKING TECHNIQUES INTO HABITS

In this course or another, come together with two or three study group partners to review the quality and style of each others' class notes. Your goal is to strengthen your techniques by assessing the strengths and weaknesses of other notes.

- Start by passing around the class notes you took on a specific day. Try to choose a day when a lot of new material was covered and when student comments were important. Allow as much time as needed to review each other's work. (Make sure you reread your own notes as part of this step.)

- Then make a list of the strengths and weaknesses of each set of notes. As you assess the material, think back to what you considered important in the class and how you included that material in your own notes.

- Next, discuss each other's evaluations. Your goal is to pinpoint techniques that work well and to think about ways to incorporate them into your own note taking. Among the techniques you might consider are choice of note-taking system, effectiveness of shorthand, comprehensiveness of notes (material included and material omitted), and usefulness of the notes as a study tool.

- Finally, each person should choose what he or she considers the three best techniques and start using them right away. In a week, assess your progess in turning these techniques into note-taking habits.

Reviewing and revising your class notes prepares you for the vital step of combining class and text notes.

HOW DO YOU COMBINE CLASS AND TEXT NOTES TO CREATE A MASTER SET?

Studying from a single, comprehensive set of notes is much easier and efficient than flipping back and forth between multiple sets. So take the time to combine your class and text notes into a master set that reflects everything you've learned.

As was mentioned earlier, studying from either text or class notes alone is not enough since your instructor may use class time to present material that is not in your text. He may also gloss over particular topics that the text covers comprehensively. In either case, if you omit the step of combining your notes, you may study the wrong material or have significant knowledge gaps.

The process of combining class and text notes engages you in active studying rather than mere busy work. As you combine material, you may see patterns and relationships among ideas, find examples that explain difficult concepts, identify key conceptual differences, and much more.

Be Creative

Your goal is to create notes that help you learn and remember. You can boost recall with a creative visual approach, as college learning specialist Eric Jensen explains: "Your brain stores information as pictures, sounds, and feelings very well. That means put as much sensory information as possible into your notes and they'll work better for you."[2]

Your material will influence your choice of format. Though an outline may work for philosophy, a timeline may be better for history, diagrams for biology, and a think link for sociology. Whatever format you choose, your goal is to organize your master notes in a way that will help you remember. Feel free to find different relationships within the material and format your notes based on these relationships. For instance, instead of following the structure of the text or lecture on the topic of hate crimes, you might choose an alternate organizational structure and divide your notes into different categories, such as statistics, opinions, events, and definitions.

Take a Step-by-Step Approach

Follow these steps to combine your class and text notes:

Step 1: Act Quickly

Try to combine your class and reading notes into a logical, comprehensive presentation while the material is fresh in your mind. Practice by completing the exercise below.

Go For It! BUILDING YOUR SKILLS

ACTIVE THINKING

SKILL WILL SELF-MGMT.

COMBINE CLASS AND TEXT NOTES

Following are two presentations on the same topic: The first contains an excerpt on hate crimes from a sociology textbook and the second are class notes based on a lecture on the same topic. As you read, think about how you would combine the material into a master set.

EXCERPT ON HATE CRIMES FROM *SOCIOLOGY*, 10TH EDITION, BY JOHN J. MACIONIS

> The term **hate crime** refers to *a criminal act against a person or a person's property by an offender motivated by racial or other bias.* A hate crime may express hostility toward someone's race, religion, ancestry, sexual orientation, or physical disability. The federal government records about 10,000 incidents of hate crimes each year.
>
> Most people were stunned by the brutal killing in 1998 of Matthew Shepard, a gay student at the University of Wyoming, by two men filled with hate toward homosexuals. The National Gay and Lesbian Task Force reports that one in five lesbians and gay men is physically assaulted and that more than 90 percent are verbally abused because of sexual orientation (cited in Berrill, 1992:19–20). Victims of hate-motivated violence are especially likely to be people who contend with multiple stigmas, such as gay men of color. Yet hate crimes can victimize anyone: A recent

study found that about 25 percent of the hate crimes based on race targeted white people (Jenness & Grattet, 2001).

By 2002, forty-five states and the federal government had enacted legislation that increased penalties for crimes motivated by hatred. Supporters are gratified, but opponents charge that such laws punish "politically incorrect" thoughts.[3]

NOTES FROM SOCIOLOGY CLASS ON HATE CRIMES

What are hate crimes?
— also called bias crimes
— defined in a 1990 federal law as an offense "in which the defendant's conduct was motivated by hatred, bias, or prejudice, based on the actual or perceived race, color, religion, national origin, ethnicity, gender, or sexual orientation of another individual or group of individuals."
— Congress passed 2ⁿᵈ law in 1994 that focused on "crimes of violence motivated by gender." These crimes are committed because of the victim's gender and are punished as felonies.
— The same law declared as hate crimes offenses motivated by bias against people with disabilities
— Recent examples: Matthew Shepard was murdered in 1998 because he was gay; James Byrd Jr, was murdered in 1999 because of his race

Controversy over whether hate crimes should be punished more severely than crimes not motivated by bias?
— One side says they should:
— offender's motives have always been considered in weighing criminal responsibility
— hate crimes inflame the public more than nonhate crimes and punishment should be given with that in mind
— hate crime victims often have greater injury than victims of other crimes
— Critics disagree
— it is difficult to separate hard-core racism from impulsive acts, especially if the offender is a young person
— hate-crime laws are a potential threat to 1ˢᵗ Amendment guarantees of free speech in that hate-crime laws may lead to courts convicting people because of their attitudes and words, not their actions.

- List three key facts found in the class notes, but not in the text:

  1. _____

  2. _____

  3. _____

- What does this tell you about the importance of studying from a combination of class and text notes?

  _____

- On a separate piece of paper, combine these class and text notes into a comprehensive presentation on hate crimes. Be creative as you consider using one of the note-taking systems presented later in this chapter.

Step 2: Focus on What's Important by Condensing to the Essence

Now, reduce your combined notes so they contain only key terms and concepts. (You are likely to find repetition in your class and reading notes, which will make it easy to reduce the material.) Tightening and summarizing forces you to critically evaluate which ideas and examples are most important and to rewrite your notes with only this material. As you begin to study, move back and forth between the full set and the reduced set. Key 7.7 shows a comprehensive outline and a reduced key-term outline of the same material.[4]

Step 3: Recite What You Know

As you approach exam time, use the terms in your bare-bones notes as cues for reciting everything you know about a topic. Many students assume that they know concepts simply because they understand what they read. What they are actually demonstrating is a passive understanding that doesn't necessarily mean that they know the material well enough to recreate it in their own words on an exam or apply it to problems. Make the process more active by reciting out loud during study sessions, writing your responses on paper, making flash cards, or working with a study partner.

Key 7.7   Reducing a full set of notes into key-term notes will help you master content.

MASTER SET OF CLASS AND TEXT NOTES

Different Views of Freedom and Equality in the American Democracy

I. U.S. democracy based on 5 core values: freedom and equality, order and stability, majority rule, protection of minitory rights, and participation.

A. U.S. would be a "perfect democracy" if it always upheld these values.

B. U.S. is less than perfect; so it is called an "approaching democracy."

II. Freedom and Equality

A. Historian Isaiah Berlin defines freedom as either positive or negative.

1. Positive freedoms allow us to exercise rights under the Constitution, including right to vote.

2. Negative freedoms safeguard us from government actions that restrict certain rights, such as the right to assemble. The 1st Amendment restricts government action by declaring that "Congress shall make no law . . ."

B. The value of equality suggests that all people be treated equally, regardless of circumstance. Different views on what equality means and the implications for society.

1. Equality of opportunity implies that everyone has the same chance to develop inborn talents.

a. But life's circumstances—affected by factors like race and income—differ. This means that people start at different points and have different results. E.g., a poor, inner-city student will be less prepared for college than an affluent, suburban student.

b. It is impossible to equalize opportunity for all Americans.

2. Equality of result seeks to eliminate all forms of inequality, including economic differences, through wealth redistribution.

C. Freedom and equality are in conflict, say text authors Berman and Murphy: "If your view of freedom is freedom from government intervention, then equality of any kind will be difficult to achieve. If government stays out of all citizen affairs, some people will become extremely wealthy, others will fall through the cracks, and economic inequality will multiply. On the other hand, if you wish to promote equality of result, then you will have to restrict some people's freedoms—the freedom to earn and retain an unlimited amount of money, for example."[4]

Key 7.7   Continued

KEY-TERM OUTLINE OF THE SAME MATERIAL

Different Views of Freedom and Equality in the American Democracy

I. America's 5 core values: freedom and equality, order and stability, majority rule, protection of minitory rights, and participation.

   a. "Perfect democracy"

   b. "Approaching democracy"

II. Value #1—Freedom and equality

   a. Positive Freedoms and Negative Freedoms

   b. Different views of equality: equality of opportunity versus equality of result

   c. Conflict between freedom and equality centers on differing views of government's role

Step 4: Use Critical Thinking

Now toss around ideas in your mind as you reflect on your combined notes—both the comprehensive and reduced sets. Working with material in the following ways will help you learn it fully:

- Brainstorm and write down examples from other sources that illustrate central ideas. Write down new ideas or questions that come up as you review.
- Think of ideas, from your readings or from something your instructor said, that support or clarify your notes.
- Consider what in your class notes differed from your reading notes and why.
- Apply concepts to problems at the end of text chapters, to problems posed in class, or to real-world situations.

Step 5: Review and Review Again

To ensure learning and to prepare for exams, expound on your keyword summary and critical thinking questions until you demonstrate a solid knowledge of every topic. "Few of us are gifted with the kind of memory that allows us

Reviewing notes with your classmates is an excellent way to solidify what you've learned. These students combine lunch outdoors with a study session.

to reproduce something new and difficult after one exposure," explain study skills experts James and Ellin K. Deese.[5]

Try to vary your review methods—focusing on active involvement. Recite the material to yourself, have a Q-and-A session with a study partner, take a practice test. Another helpful technique is to summarize your notes in writing from memory after you review them. This is a good indication that you'll be able to recall the same information on a test. You may even want to summarize as you read, then summarize from memory, and compare the two summaries.

Step up your efforts before a test. Schedule longer review sessions, call a study group meeting, and review more frequently. Shorter sessions of intense review interspersed with breaks may prove more effective than long hours of continuous studying.

A word of warning about comparing notes with study-group partners: Don't be surprised if each of you has a radically different take on what went on in class, especially if the material was difficult or the presentation confusing. When this happens, work together to reconstruct critical information and, if necessary, bring in other perspectives.

Your success as a note taker depends, in part, on how quickly you can take down information. Personal shorthand will help you write fast enough to keep up with fast-talking instructors.

WHAT CAN YOU DO TO TAKE NOTES FASTER?

Using personal shorthand can help you push your pen faster. Because you are the only intended reader, you can spell and abbreviate words in ways that only you understand.

A danger of using shorthand is that you might forget what your writing means. To avoid this problem, review your notes while your abbreviations and symbols are fresh in your mind. If you are confused, spell out words as you review.

Another danger is forgetting to remove shorthand from work you hand in. This can happen when you use the same system for class notes as you do when you are talking to your friends online. For example, when students take notes in Instant Messenger "language," they may be so accustomed to omitting apostrophes and commas, using acronyms, and replacing long words with incorrect contractions that they may forget to correct their final work. Therefore, in order to avoid being penalized, take care not to hand in a paper with *2* instead of *too* or *thru* instead of *through*.

Here are some suggestions that will help you master personal shorthand. Many of these techniques will be familiar and, in fact, you may already use them to speed up your e-mail and instant messaging.

1. Use standard abbreviations in place of complete words.

w/	with		cf	compare, in comparison to
w/o	without		ff	following
→	means; resulting in		Q	question
←	as a result of		p.	page
↑	increasing		*	most importantly
↓	decreasing		<	less than
∴	therefore		>	more than
∴ or b/c	because		=	equals
≈	approximately		%	percent
+ or &	and		Δ	change
−	minus; negative		2	to; two; too
No. or #	number		vs	versus; against
i.e.	that is,		e.g.	for example
etc.	and so forth		c/o	care of
ng	no good		lb	pound

2. Shorten words by removing vowels from the middle of words.

prps	=	purpose
lwyr	=	lawyer
cmptr	=	computer

3. Substitute word beginnings for entire words.

assoc	=	associate; association
info	=	information
subj	=	subject

4. Form plurals by adding s to shortened words.

prblms	=	problems
drctrys	=	directories
prntrs	=	printers

5. Make up your own symbols and use them consistently.

b/4	=	before
4tn	=	fortune
2thake	=	toothache

6. Use standard or informal abbreviations for proper nouns such as places, people, companies, scientific substances, events, and so on.

DC	=	Washington, D.C.
H_2O	=	water
Moz.	=	Wolfgang Amadeus Mozart

7. If you know that a particular word or phrase will be repeated, write it out once, and then establish an abbreviation for the rest of your notes. For example, if you are taking notes in a political science class on the search for weapons of mass destruction in Iraq, you might start by writing *weapons of mass destruction (WMD),* and then use WMD as you continue.

8. Write only what is essential. Include only the information nuggets you want to remember, even if your instructor says much more. Do this by paring down your writing. Say, for example, your instructor had this to say on the subject of hate crimes:

"After the terrorist attacks on September 11, 2001, law enforcement officials noted a dramatic shift in the nature of hate crimes. For the first time, replacing crimes motivated by race as the leading type of hate crime were crimes that targeted religious and ethnic groups and particularly Muslims."[6]

Your notes, which include some shorthand, might look something like this:

—After 9/11 HCs ⇄ ↑ focus & targeted religious and ethnic groups, esp. Muslims.

—Reduction of HC based on race.

Finally, remember that the primary goal of your note taking is to generate material that will help you learn and remember information. No matter how popular a note-taking strategy may be, it won't do you any good if it doesn't help you reach that goal. Keep a close eye on what works for you and stick to it.

If you find that your notes aren't comprehensible, legible, or focused, think critically about how you might improve them. Can't read your notes? You might have been sleepy, been careless in your handwriting, or used a leaky pen that smudged the page. Lots of confusing gaps? You might be distracted in class, have an instructor who goes off on tangents, or have holes in your knowledge base. Put your problem-solving skills to work to address your challenge, brainstorming solutions from the strategies in this chapter. With a little time and effort, your notes will become a helpful learning tool in school and beyond.

"The map is not the journey and the notes are not the course. Take notes, but don't try to be a stenographer."[7]

SCOTT WOELFEL,
graduate of the University of Missouri

Building Skill, Will, and Self-Management

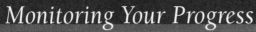

Monitoring Your Progress

Test Competence: Measure What You've Learned

MULTIPLE CHOICE. *Circle or highlight the answer that seems to fit best.*

1. You should consider using a formal or informal outline for note taking if
   A. your instructor tends to jump from point to point.
   B. your instructor tends to present material in an organized, logical manner.
   C. you learned to use an outline in high school and are comfortable with it.
   D. the other students around you are using an outline.

2. Guided notes are
   A. a complete set of class notes provided by the teacher.
   B. instructions on how to take effective notes.
   C. a basic outline of the key points an instructor plans to make in a lecture.
   D. another name for the course outline you receive at the beginning of the semester.

3. The Cornell note-taking system includes all of the following elements *except:*
   A. a space to record your notes from class.
   B. a space for any comments your instructor wants to make about your notes.
   C. a cue column to be used during review sessions.
   D. a summary area to summarize and reinforce the concepts on the page.

4. A think link is an especially effective note-taking system for
   A. visual learners.
   B. disorganized people.

270

C. students who are tired of using outlines.

D. students who want to make note taking a more creative process.

5. The benefits of taking notes include all of the following *except:*

A. helping you organize your study materials.

B. making you an active listener.

C. generating material to review for a test.

D. showing your instructor that you are busy.

6. As you prepare to take class notes, you should

A. sit next to another student who takes good notes.

B. hold off looking at the assigned reading material.

C. choose a note-taking system that suits the instructor's style, the course material, and your learning style.

D. choose a note-taking system you've used in other classes because you are familiar with it.

7. As you record information in your notes, you should

A. take down every word the instructor says.

B. avoid using shorthand because it may be difficult to read later on.

C. avoid leaving too much white space on the page.

D. record all key terms and definitions, especially those the instructor emphasizes.

8. It is a mistake to close your notebook during the question-and-answer period because

A. your instructor may assume you are not paying attention.

B. critical facts often emerge during this exchange.

C. the class is not officially over until you are dismissed.

D. you may need to rewrite your notes.

9. All of the following are true when you combine your class and text notes *except:*

A. Combining notes gives you a master set from which to study.

B. Combining notes engages you in active learning.

C. It is almost always a good idea to follow an outline form.

D. It is important to combine your notes when the material is fresh in your mind.

10. When you combine your class and text notes, your goal should be to

A. try to expand on what you have written.

B. copy your class and text notes verbatim.

C. reduce your combined notes so they contain only key terms and concepts.

D. avoid studying from your combined notes.

TRUE/FALSE. *Place a T or an F beside each statement to indicate whether you think it is true or false.*

_____ 1. The cue column in the Cornell note-taking system is a space for clarifying comments and questions, examples and ideas.

_____ 2. A table can be a helpful summary tool as you review your class notes.

_____ 3. There is one correct form of personal shorthand.

_____ 4. Critical thinking is an essential learning tool when combining class and text notes.

_____ 5. You only need to review your combined text and class notes once.

Target and Achieve a Goal

Commit to one specific note-taking strategy from this chapter to improve your study skills.

Name the strategy here: _____

_____

Describe your goal—what you want to gain by using this strategy. _____

_____

_____

Describe how you plan to use this strategy through the semester to achieve this goal.

_____

_____

Building Your Skills

Brain Power: Build Vocabulary Fitness

Here is a selection from the current media. Read the material, paying special attention to the context of the vocabulary words shown in bold type. Then choose the correct definition for each word in the table that follows. Use a dictionary to check your answers. Finally, on a separate sheet, use each vocabulary word in a sentence of your own to solidify your understanding.

Pat Tillman, a star defensive back for the Arizona Cardinals, was 25 years old when he joined the army in the wake of the September 11, 2001, terrorist attack that destroyed the World Trade Center. He was 27 when he died in combat in Afghanistan. Writing in the OpinionJournal.com, former presidential speechwriter Peggy Noonan describes what was behind Tillman's decision to serve his country.

Maybe he was thinking *Ask not what your country can do for you, ask what you can do for your country.* Maybe it was **visceral**, not so much thought as felt, and acted upon. We don't know because he won't say . . . Silence is the **refuge** of celebrities caught in scandal, not the usual response of those caught red-handed doing good.

All we know is that 25-year-old Pat Tillman, a rising pro football player (224 tackles in 2000 as a defensive back for the Arizona Cardinals, a team record) came back from his honeymoon . . . and told his coaches he would turn down a three-year, $3.6 million contract and instead join the U. S. Army . . .

Pat Tillman "came in like everyone else, on a bus from a processing station," according to a public information officer at Fort Benning, Ga., and received the outward signs of the leveling **anonymity** of the armed forces: a bad haircut, a good uniform, and physical testing to see if he is up to the **rigors** of being a soldier . . .

Those who know him say it's typical Tillman, a surprise decision based on his vision of what would be a good thing to do. When he was in college he sometimes climbed to the top of a stadium light tower to think and **meditate**. After his great 2000 season he was offered a $9 million five-year contract with the St. Louis Rams and said thanks but no, he was happy with the Cardinals.

But it was clear to those who knew Tillman that after September 11 something changed. The attack on America had prompted a rethinking. [Broadcaster] Len Pasquarelli reported . . . that the "free-spirited but **consummately** disciplined" starting strong safety told friends and relatives that, in Mr. Pasquarelli's words, "his conscience would not allow him to tackle opposition fullbacks where there is still a bigger enemy that needs to be stopped . . . " [Said his agent]: "This is something he feels he has to do. For him, it's a mindset, a duty."

Source: Peggy Noonan, "Privileged to Serve," *OpinionJournal*, July 15, 2002, www.opinion journal.com/columnists/pnoonan/?id=110001975. Reprinted with permission.

Circle the word or phrase that best defines each term as it is used in this excerpt.

VOCABULARY WORDS	A	B	C
1. visceral (adj.)	intuitive	superficial	intellectual
2. refuge (noun)	animal shelter	safe place	allure
3. anonymity (noun)	similarity	pride	state of being unknown
4. rigors (noun)	courage	disappointments	hardships
5. meditate (verb)	contemplate	intellectualize	feel
6. consummately (adv.)	anxiously	supremely able	usually

Get to the Root

Every time you learn a Greek or Latin root, you increase your ability to recognize English vocabulary words that include that root and to figure out

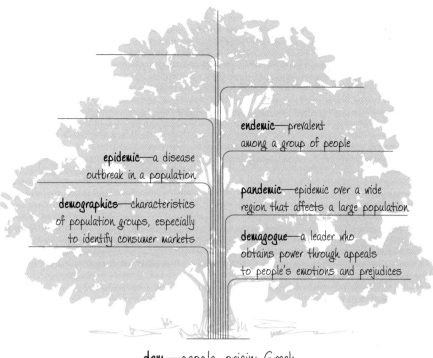

endemic—prevalent among a group of people

epidemic—a disease outbreak in a population

demographics—characteristics of population groups, especially to identify consumer markets

pandemic—epidemic over a wide region that affects a large population

demagogue—a leader who obtains power through appeals to people's emotions and prejudices

dem—people, origin: Greek

their meaning. Grow your vocabulary by studying this root and its related words, writing in two more words from the same root, and including definitions for both new words.

Investigate Using Research Navigator

Access Research Navigator using the Internet address shown on page 32. Then sign on to the service using your Login Name and Password. Scroll through the database titles listed for Content Select. Choose one and then enter a related keyword in a career area of interest for you. For example, if you are interested in early childhood education, you could choose the Education database and enter "kindergarten" as a keyword.

Then do the following:

- When the database generates a list of articles, choose one that seems interesting and open its full text.
- Read the article and take notes on it using strategies you have learned in this chapter.

Finally, read over your notes and, in writing, evaluate your experience of this article. What did you learn? Was the information useful? Have you gained any particular insight or idea from the article? Save the article on your computer if you found it valuable.

Building Will and Self-Awareness

Make Responsible Choices

Answer the following on a separate piece of paper or in a journal.

Taking effective notes is vital to business success. With this in mind, imagine that you are a business consultant who is getting ready for your first planning meeting with a new client. Your job is to take comprehensive notes as five executives tell you about the issues facing the company and why they need your help.

- Based on what you learned in this chapter, what steps would you take to prepare for the note-taking session?
- Describe also what you will do after the meeting to transform your notes from raw data into the building blocks of your report.
- What if you have trouble keeping up with the pace during the meeting and you are afraid that your notes will be incomplete? Are you likely

to ask the speaker to stop for a moment as you catch up, or will you find a way to get the missing information after the meeting?

- How is the above situation similar to—or different from—a classroom lecture in which you find yourself running behind the instructor's presentation and have to find a way to recapture what you missed?

Chapter Summary

As you use the summary on the following pages to review the concepts you learned in this chapter, focus also on its format—in this case the **Cornell system,** in other chapters a formal outline, and in still others a think link. As you become comfortable with the organization and style of these various formats, try using each of them to take class and reading notes, noting which approach works best for you in particular situations.

Chapter 7: Taking Lecture Notes

How will taking notes help you succeed in college?

- Taking notes makes you an active participant and provides you with study materials for tests.
- Use critical thinking to decide if something is important enough to write down

What note-taking system should you use?

- Two types of outlines show relationships among ideas:
  — Formal outlines use a prescribed organization, Roman numerals, capitalization, numbers, and indenting.
  — Informal outlines show the same associations but replace the formality with a system of consistent indentations and dashes.
- Guided notes, provided by instructors, are a bare-bones lesson, not complete notes.
- The Cornell note-taking system has three parts:
  — Section 1, the largest section on the right, is where you record information.
  — Section 2, the cue column, appears to the left of the notes and can be used for questions, keywords, comments, diagrams, and other helpful learning tools.
  — Section 3, which appears at the bottom of the page, provides space for a summary.
- Think links are visual note-taking forms that translate verbal concepts into diagrams that connect ideas and evidence.
- Other forms of note taking include timelines, tables, and hierarchy charts.

How can you make the most of class notes?

- To prepare for note taking, preview your reading material, review what you know, gather supplies, choose a good location, select the right note-taking system, and develop a buddy system in case you miss a class or want to compare notes.

- Recording information effectively in class requires that you are organized, that you develop a consistent system to indicate the importance of material and for marking difficult concepts, that you use diagrams, think links, and other creative approaches, and that you indicate material your instructor emphasizes or questions.
- Vital information is often passed on during class discussions, so pay attention to questions and student and instructor responses.

How do you combine class and text notes to create a master set?

- Study from a comprehensive set of notes that incorporates class and text presentations.
- Combining notes requires that you act quickly; that you reduce your combined notes to key terms and concepts; that you use the terms in your bare-bones notes as cues for reciting what you know; that you use critical-thinking questions to reflect as you learn; and that you review the material again by expounding on the keyword summary and critical-thinking questions until you demonstrate mastery.

What can you do to take notes faster?

- Use personal shorthand to speed up your in-class notes.

Class notes taken, often using personal shorthand, in the form of an outline, the Cornell system, or a think link actively engage you in learning. Note taking improves with practice as you focus on preparation, in-class recording, and review. Combined text and class notes that are reduced to key terms and concepts are an excellent study tool.

Endnotes

1. Walter Pauk, *How to Study in College*, 7th ed. Boston: Houghton Mifflin, 2001, pp. 236–241.

2. Eric Jensen, *Student Success Secrets*, 5th ed. Hauppauge, NY: Barron's Educational Services, 2003, p. 124.

3. John J. Macionis, *Sociology*, 10th ed. Upper Saddle River, NJ: Pearson/Prentice Hall, 2005, pp. 203–204.

4. Larry Berman and Bruce Allen Murphy, *Approaching Democracy: Portfolio Edition*. Upper Saddle River, NJ: Pearson/Prentice Hall, 2005, pp. 6–8.

5. James Deese and Ellin K. Deese, *How to Study and Other Skills for Success in College*, 4th ed. New York: McGraw-Hill, 1994, p. 28.

6. Information from Frank Schmalleger, *Criminal Justice Today*, 8th ed. Upper Saddle River, NJ: 2005, p. 71.

7. Mark W. Bernstein and Yadin Kaufmann, editors, *How to Survive Your Freshman Year*. Atlanta, GA: Hundreds of Heads Books, 2004, p. 84.

8

"How can I know what I think until I read what I write?"

NEW YORK TIMES COLUMNIST JAMES RESTON

DURING THE 1962 NEWSPAPER STRIKE

Effective Writing

COMMUNICATING YOUR MESSAGE

Words, shaped to present information and argue positions, have enormous power. Whether you write a research paper, a short essay, a memo to a supervisor, or an extensive report, words take ideas out of the realm of thought and give them a form that has an impact on others. In class or at work, writing well will help you understand what you take in and express what you learn, showing the potential of your mind.

Good writing depends on and reflects clear thinking. Good writing is also influenced by reading. Exposing yourself to the works of other writers introduces you to new concepts and perspectives as it helps you discover different ways to express ideas.

In this chapter you will explore answers to the following questions:

- ■ Why does good writing matter?
- ■ What are the elements of effective writing?
- ■ What is the writing process?

WHY DOES GOOD WRITING MATTER?

Learning to write effectively is crucial to academic and career success, as Key 8.1 shows. Your college almost certainly requires that you pass a semester- or yearlong writing course. This chapter will reinforce the skills you will learn in that course as it focuses on an important challenge—writing a research paper. Keep in mind that the approach to good writing outlined here applies to different writing situations, including responses to essay exams.

WHAT ARE THE ELEMENTS OF EFFECTIVE WRITING?

Every writing situation depends on three elements:

- **your purpose**—What do you want your work to accomplish?
- **your audience**—What do you need to know about your readers to meet your communication purposes and theirs?
- **your topic**—What is the subject about which you will write?

Consider purpose and audience even before you start planning your document. Then, consider topic during the early stage of planning.

Define Your Writing Purpose

Writing without a clear purpose is like driving without a destination. You'll get somewhere, but chances are it won't be the right place. Therefore, when you write, always decide what you want to accomplish before you start.

When you are assigned a research paper, your purpose is to uncover material others have written (see Key 8.2) and present your findings in one of two ways:

- as an *expository paper*, which presents information without arguing a viewpoint. Your work may include analyzing and synthesizing material from different sources and presenting it in a clear, unbiased way.
- as a *persuasive paper*, which presents and argues a point of view to prove a thesis. Your goal is to convince readers that your views and evidence are correct.

Identify Your Audience

As a writer, you speak to an audience of readers—a group or a single individual. Knowing who your readers are helps you communicate effectively.

Key 8.1 Make good writing a tool to achieve academic and career goals.

IN SCHOOL, GOOD WRITING MATTERS BECAUSE . . .	AT WORK, GOOD WRITING MATTERS BECAUSE . . .
. . . it demonstrates critical thinking as you question your thesis, weigh evidence, and choose words precisely.	. . . it shows your critical thinking, careful planning, hard work, and focus on the needs of your readers (supervisors, co-workers, vendors, or customers).
. . . planning, drafting, revising, and editing create good habits linked to time management and hard work.	. . . it influences how supervisors and co-workers judge your work and your ability to meet deadlines, especially in monthly and quarterly reports that summarize your accomplishments.
. . . it gives you tools for communicating your thoughts in class papers and essay exams.	. . . it enables you to produce effective business documents, including e-mails, letters, reports, and proposals.
. . . it forces you to focus on getting your message across to readers as you present and organize ideas.	. . . it communicates to prospective employers, on cover letters and resumes, that you understand their needs.
. . . it aids learning and helps you retain information when you rewrite and summarize class and reading notes.	. . . it helps you master details when working on projects that involve piecing together information from different sources.

Every writing situation is unique, depending on your purpose, topic, and audience. Your goal is to understand each element before you begin.

When you hand in a paper, your audience is usually an instructor who takes the role of either an *uninformed reader,* who knows little about your topic, or an *informed reader.* The following questions will help you determine how much information your reader needs:

- Who are my readers? Are they instructors or fellow students or both?
- How much do they know about my topic? Are they experts or beginners?
- Are they interested, or do I have to convince them to read my material?
- Can I expect readers to have open or closed minds about my topic?

Key 8.2   Research involves taking another look at the ideas of others.

re·search

re = again • **search**—from the Latin—to go around; definition—to look over carefully in order to find something.

Begin to Define Your Topic

Depending on your instructor, you may be assigned a *specific topic* for your paper ("Write a five-page paper describing the provisions of Federal Family and Medical Leave Act (FMLA), passed by Congress in 1993, guaranteeing workers 12 weeks of unpaid leave for family emergencies."), a *general topic* that gives you some choice ("Write a five-page paper on the impact of FMLA on working Americans."), or a *broad topic* ("Write a five-page paper on the difficulties workers are facing as they juggle career and family responsibilities.") The remainder of this chapter will look at writing assignments in which you are given a general topic and told to choose a specific aspect for your paper.

With a clear idea of purpose and audience and a sense of your topic's scope, you are ready to begin the writing process, which will give you the tools to craft this message.

WHAT IS THE WRITING PROCESS?

The writing process—planning, drafting, revising, and editing—allows you to express exactly what you want to say in the way you want to say it. Your goal is to produce a research paper that addresses your purpose, topic, and audience, comes in on schedule, and represents your best work.

Planning

When planning to write, use critical thinking to evaluate the assignment. Go over the logistics of the assignment, brainstorm for topic ideas, use prewriting strategies to define and narrow your topic, conduct research, write a thesis statement, and write a working outline. Although these steps are listed in sequence, in real life they often overlap.

Pay Attention to Logistics

Start planning by asking questions to determine the feasibility of different topics. Biting off more than you can chew is almost always a mistake, as student success expert Adam Robinson explains: "You will not impress your teacher by selecting an overly ambitious topic if the result is a [paper] that falls short. It's best to keep it manageable and do a terrific job."[1]Among the questions you should ask are:

While the library is still a major resource center, online research has become a significant source of information for many students.

1. **How much depth does my instructor expect?** Does she want a basic introduction or a more sophisticated, high-level presentation?

2. **How much time do I have to write the paper?** Consider your other course assignments as well as personal responsibilities, such as part-time work.

3. **How long should the paper be?** Much of the time, your instructor will give you a range—for example, 3–5 or 5–10 pages. Going too far above or below this range can count against you.

4. **What kind of research is needed?** Your topic and purpose may determine your research sources, and some sources are harder to get than others.

5. **Is it a team project or am I researching and writing alone?** If you are working with others, determine what each person will do and whether others can deliver their work on time.

6. **Am I interested enough in the topic to live and breathe it for an extended period?** Ask yourself whether the material will bring out the best in you or whether you will quickly tire of it. Understand, though, that lack of interest is no excuse for doing less than your best.

Answering questions like these will help you decide on a topic and depth of coverage.

Open Your Mind to Topic Ideas Through Brainstorming

Start the process of choosing a topic for an expository paper with *brainstorming*—a creative technique to generate ideas about a subject without making judgments about their worth (see Chapter 3):

- Begin by writing down anything on the assigned subject that comes to mind, in no particular order. To jump-start your thoughts, scan your textbook; look back at your notes; check general references at the library; or meet with your instructor to discuss ideas.
- Next, organize that list into a logical outline or think link that helps you see the possibilities more clearly.

Key 8.3 shows a portion of an outline constructed from a brainstorming list. The assignment for an introduction to business class is to choose an aspect of business ethics and write a short expository research paper on it. Since the student's research is only preliminary, many ideas are in question form.

Narrow Your Topic Through Prewriting Strategies

Prewriting strategies, including brainstorming, freewriting, and asking journalists' questions,[2] help you decide which possible topic you would most like to pursue. Use them to narrow your topic, focusing on the specific subideas and examples from your brainstorming session.

Brainstorming. The same process you used to generate ideas will help you narrow your topic. Write down your thoughts about one or more of the possibilities you have chosen, do more research, and then organize your thoughts into categories, noticing patterns that appear. See if any of the subideas or examples might make good topics.

Asking critical thinking questions can spark ideas and help you focus on what to write. Among the questions you may ask as you prepare for an expository paper are:

- What is the history of the topic? How has it developed over time?
- Are its effects on people and society good or bad?
- Does it raise broader issues?
- Can I think of anything similar in another context or culture?

Whether questions like these lead to productive topics or dead ends, it is important to keep questioning. Be open and objective, pursuing

Key 8.3   Brainstorming leads to topic ideas and sets the stage for organizing your thoughts.

Topic: Business Ethics

— What are business ethics?
— Recent scandals that raised ethical issues
   — Enron
   — WorldCom
— Who is responsible—the individual or the corporation?
— How do companies encourage ethical business practices?
   — Some companies have written codes of ethics
   — Codes are based on core ethical values that remain constant even as the environment changes
   — Codes of ethics only work if they are part of the corporate culture
— Why do people act unethically in business?
   — The bottom-line culture puts pressure on managers to show increasing profits every quarter.
   — Corporate cultures stress workers out to the point that they no longer ask whether actions are right or wrong.
   — People have such expensive lifestyles that they are willing to cut ethical corners to keep their jobs and earn large bonuses.

different directions, without judging possible topics as "silly" or "wrong."

Freewriting. When you *freewrite*, you jot down whatever comes to mind without censoring ideas or worrying about grammar, spelling, punctuation, or organization. Freewriting helps you think creatively and gives you an opportunity to piece together what you know about a subidea to see if you want to pursue it. The box on the next page shows a sample of freewriting for the business ethics paper.

Freewriting may seem like an extra step—especially since your instructor won't see your efforts—but this exercise is worthwhile in the long run, since it will help you produce a quality paper.

Dennis Kozlowski of Tyco, Ken Lay of Enron, and so many others give the impression that business is filled with greedy people willing to cheat and steal to get rich. It's hard to trust businesses when there are so many executives going to jail and so many companies engaged in out-right fraud. But all companies aren't bad. Many who are trying to do a good job use a code of ethics, based on core values. They help employees decide how to handle difficult situations. Examples: Texas Instruments and Johnson & Johnson. Both companies have had codes for decades and use them to respond to crises.

Asking journalists' questions. When journalists start working on a story, they ask themselves: Who? What? Where? When? Why? How? Asking these questions about subideas will help you choose a writing topic.

Who?   To whom do companies have an ethical responsibility? Who maintains ethical standards within corporations?

What?   What are business ethics? What is the difference between acting unethically and acting illegally, or are they the same? What is the impact of business codes of ethics on behavior? What companies have these codes, and what impact have they had on behavior? What role do core values play in business ethics?

When?   When is the best time for companies to address ethics problems—before or after they occur?

Where?   Do companies all over the country have ethics problems, or is the problem centered in certain geographic areas or industries?

Why?   Why do ethics problems surface? Why do companies make so many mistakes in handling ethics problems?

How?   How do companies train employees to act ethically? How do companies maintain their ethical standards in an ever-changing business environment?

Prewriting helps you develop a topic that is broad enough for investigation but narrow enough to be manageable. Prewriting also helps you see what you know and what you don't know, which is important because your instructor will judge your paper not on what you *feel* about the topic but on what you *think* about it. If your assignment requires more than you already know, you need to do research.

Go For It!   BUILDING YOUR SKILLS

ACTIVE THINKING

SKILL   WILL   SELF-MGMT.

USE PREWRITING STRATEGIES TO NARROW A TOPIC

Start here to apply prewriting strategies to a writing assignment from one of your courses:

- Define the assignment's general topic, the paper's purpose and audience (continue on a separate page, if necessary):

  _____

  _____

  _____

  _____

- Brainstorm to narrow your topic. (Remember that you may have to do some preliminary research.) Write down the results of your brainstorming session.

  _____

  _____

  _____

  _____

- Freewrite what you know and look for threads of an idea. (Begin here and continue on a separate page.)

  _____

  _____

  _____

  _____

  _____

- Ask the six journalists' questions to focus on possible writing topics:

Who? _____

What? _____

When? _____

Where? _____

Why? _____

How? _____

- Finally, considering everything you've written, come up with some potential paper topics. List one or two possibilities here:

Idea #1 _____

Idea #2 _____

Conduct Research and Make Notes

Your research will develop in stages as you narrow and refine your ideas. In the first brainstorming-for-ideas stage, look for an overview that can lead to a thesis statement. Follow the library search strategy suggested in the Research Appendix at the end of *Keys to College Studying*, starting with general books and articles that cover the topic. Use what you learn to answer your critical thinking questions and to help you choose a thesis.

In the second stage, go into more depth, tracking down information that fills in gaps. Use the Internet to investigate ideas, but avoid relying solely on electronic sources. Instructors expect you to get information from books, journals, and other library sources. Ultimately, you will reach a point where you have a "body" of information that you can evaluate to develop and implement a thesis.

As you research, create source notes and content notes to organize your work, keep track of sources, and avoid plagiarism. *Source notes* are the preliminary notes you take, usually on index cards, as you review research. They include vital bibliographic information, as well as a short summary and critical evaluation of the work. Write these notes when you consider a book or an article interesting enough to look at again. They do not signal that you have read a source carefully, only that you plan to review it later.

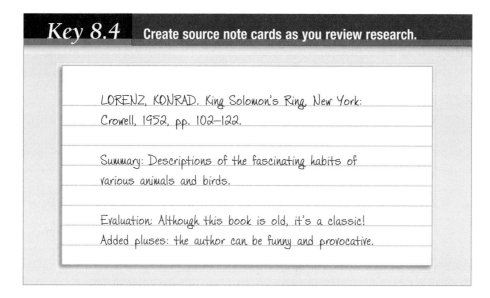

Key 8.4   **Create source note cards as you review research.**

> LORENZ, KONRAD. *King Solomon's Ring*, New York:
> Crowell, 1952, pp. 102–122.
>
> Summary: Descriptions of the fascinating habits of
> various animals and birds.
>
> Evaluation: Although this book is old, it's a classic!
> Added pluses: the author can be funny and provocative.

Each source note should include the author's full name; the title of the work; the edition (if any); the publisher, year, and city of publication; issue and/or volume number when applicable (such as for a magazine); and the page numbers you consulted. See Key 8.4 for an example of how you can write source notes on index cards.

Content notes, written on large index cards, in a notebook, or on your computer, provide an in-depth look at the source, taken during a thorough reading. Use them to record the information you need to write your draft. In addition to bibliographic information, content notes should paraphrase and summarize key concepts, cite quotations you want to use in your draft, and link the author's ideas to your thesis. It also helps to make notes directly on photocopies of sources—marginal notes, highlighting, and underlining—to supplement your content notes.

Write a Thesis Statement

Your next task is to organize your research and formulate a *thesis statement*, which declares your specific subject and point of view, reflects your writing purpose and audience, and acts as the organizing principle of your paper. In one or two sentences, it tells readers what to expect. If you are unsure whether your thesis meets the assignment's requirements, get your instructor's approval before you begin writing. The box on the next page shows an example from the paper on business ethics.

Although the thesis statement typically comes at the conclusion of an introductory paragraph, there is no hard and fast placement rule. Make your decision based on how your paper is organized and on instructor guidelines. Use your thesis statement to guide your writing, knowing that it may shift as ideas develop.

Topic   Business ethics
Purpose   To inform
Audience   Instructor who assumes the position of an uninformed reader

Thesis statement   In an environment where so many executives are behaving badly and where corporate reputations are being tarnished, companies are struggling with how to set expectations of ethical behavior. Most major corporations, including Texas Instruments and Johnson & Johnson, now believe that creating a corporate code of ethics is a critical first step in the process of sensitizing employees to how they should act under normal circumstances and during crises.

ACTIVE
THINKING

SKILL   WILL   SELF-MGMT.

Go For It!   BUILDING YOUR SKILLS

WRITE A THESIS STATEMENT

Continue your work on your paper by crafting a thesis statement that informs readers what the paper will accomplish. Link your thesis to your purpose, audience, and topic:

_____

_____

_____

_____

_____

Write a Working Outline or Think Link

The final planning step is creating a working outline or think link to use as a loose structural guide. As you draft, your ideas and direction may change, so be open to shifts that reflect new material and thoughts. As a way of organizing your research, consider keying your research to the outline so you know what sources to use at different points.

Introduction

— Corporate executives have abused the public trust at Enron, WorldCom, Tyco, Computer Associates, and other companies.

— At the same time many companies are defining themselves in ethical terms through a corporate code of ethics.

— Thesis: Companies like Texas Instruments and Johnson & Johnson use a code of ethics to sensitize employees to how to behave under normal circumstances and during crises.

Body of Paper

— Business ethics are based on values that define actions as right or wrong.

— When choices are ambiguous companies look to core values. The Josephson Institute of Ethics defines "six pillars of character" to help managers evaluate competing choices.

— Texas Instruments' code of ethics and "ethics test"

— Johnson and Johnson's credo and how it helped managers respond to the Tylenol crisis of 1982.

Conclusion

— Ethics codes are effective only if they are followed. Companies like TI and J & J show that it is possible to establish a corporate ethical climate that guides daily decisions and actions.

Create a Checklist

Use the checklist in Key 8.5 to make sure your preparation is complete and to avoid procrastination. Work backward from the assignment due date and estimate how long you need to complete each step. Keep in mind that you'll be moving back and forth among the tasks on the schedule.

Key 8.5   Use a preparation checklist to complete tasks and stay on schedule.

DATE YOU PLAN TO COMPLETE THIS STEP	TASK	IS IT COMPLETE?
	Appraise the assignment's logistics	
	Brainstorm for topic ideas	
	Use prewriting strategies to narrow your topic	
	Conduct research	
	Write a thesis statement	
	Write a working outline or think link	

Drafting

As its name implies, a first draft is the first of many versions of your paper. Each version moves you closer to saying exactly what you want in the way you want to say it. The main challenges you face at this stage are:

- defining an organizational structure
- integrating source material into the body of your paper to fit your structure
- finding additional sources to strengthen your presentation
- choosing the right words, phrases, and tone
- connecting ideas with logical transitions
- creating an effective introduction and conclusion
- checking for plagiarism
- creating a list of works cited

Some people aim for perfection when they write a first draft. They want to get every detail right. Do everything you can to resist this tendency because it may shut the door on ideas even before you know they are there.

Freewriting Your Rough Draft

Use everything that you developed in the planning stage as the raw material for freewriting a rough draft. For now, don't consciously think about your introduction, conclusion, or the structure within the paper's body. Simply focus on getting your ideas on paper. You can then start to shape it into something with a more definite form. Many people start with the introduction because it is the beginning of the paper, whereas others save the introduction for last to make sure it reflects the final product.

Writing an Introduction

The introduction tells readers what the paper contains and includes a thesis statement. The box below shows the introduction for the paper on business ethics. The thesis statement is underlined at the end of the paragraph.

> Open to the business section of any newspaper and you are likely to find at least one story of a corporate executive on trial and facing jail or a company paying huge fines or court settlements to the government, consumers, or investors. In the last few years, stories of alleged wrongdoing at Enron, WorldCom, Tyco International, Computer Associates, Sotheby's, and Adelphi Communications, to name just a few, have been front-page news. In an environment where so many executives are behaving badly and where corporate reputations are being tarnished, companies are struggling with how to set expectations of ethical behavior. Most major corporations, including Texas Instruments and Johnson & Johnson, now believe that creating a corporate code of ethics is a critical first step in the process of sensitizing employees to how they should act under normal circumstances and during crises.

Your instructor may specify how she wants the introduction to be written. Follow these guidelines, even if it is not the way you usually start a paper. Getting into the habit of meeting the specifications that the person in charge sets will help you succeed when you start your career.

Creating the Body of a Paper

The body of the paper contains your central ideas and supporting *evidence*, which supports your position with facts, statistics, examples, and expert opinions. Try to find a structure that helps you organize your ideas and evidence into a clear pattern. Several organizational options are presented in Key 8.6.

Writing the Conclusion

A conclusion brings your paper to a natural conclusion through the use of one or more of the following strategies:

- Summarize your main points (if material is longer than three pages).
- Show the significance of your thesis and how it relates to larger issues.
- Call the reader to action.
- Look to the future.

Key 8.6	Find the best way to organize the body of the paper.
ORGANIZATIONAL STRUCTURE	**WHAT TO DO**
Arrange ideas by time	Describe events in order or in reverse order.
Arrange ideas according to importance	Start with the idea that carries the most weight and move to less important ideas. Or move from the least to the most important ideas.
Arrange ideas by problem and solution	Start with a problem and then discuss solutions.
Arrange ideas to present an argument	Present one or both sides of an issue.
Arrange ideas in list form	Group a series of items.
Arrange ideas according to cause and effect	Show how events, situations, or ideas cause subsequent events, situations, or ideas.
Arrange ideas through the use of comparisons	Compare and contrast the characteristics of events, people, situations, ideas.
Arrange by process	Go through the steps in a process; a "how to" approach.
Arrange by category	Divide topics into categories and analyze each in order.

Avoid restating what your paper says. Instead, let the ideas in the body of the paper speak for themselves as you use your conclusion to wrap up.

Avoiding Plagiarism: Crediting Authors and Sources

When you incorporate ideas from other sources into your work, you are using other writers' *intellectual property*. Using another writer's words, content, unique approach, or illustrations without crediting the author is called *plagiarism* and is illegal and unethical. The following techniques will help you properly credit sources and avoid plagiarism:

Make source and content notes as you go. Plagiarism often begins accidentally during research; you may intend to cite or paraphrase a source, but forget to do so. To avoid this, write detailed source and content notes during research that indicate direct quotations.

Know the difference between a quotation and a paraphrase. A *quotation* repeats a source's exact words, which are set off from the rest of the text by quotation marks. A *paraphrase* is a restatement of the quotation in your own words. A restatement requires that you completely rewrite the idea, not just remove or replace a few words. As Key 8.7 illustrates, a paraphrase may not be acceptable if it is too close to the original.

Use a citation even for an acceptable paraphrase. Take care to credit any source that you quote, paraphrase, or use as evidence. To credit a source, write a footnote or endnote that describes it, using the format preferred by your instructor.

Understand that a paper that consists primarily of quoted material from other sources is not considered an original work. Even if you credit the sources for each quote, you are doing little more than stringing together a series of quotes, which is not acceptable scholarship. Your goal should be to use small sections of quoted material surrounded by your own explanations, evaluations, and conclusions.

Understand that lifting material off the Internet is plagiarism. Words in electronic form belong to the writer, just as words in print form do. If you cut and paste sections from a source document onto your draft, you are committing plagiarism.

Increasingly, instructors are being barraged with papers that are completely or partially plagiarized. Most instructors consider work to be plagiarized when a student

- submits a paper from a website that sells or gives away research papers.
- buys a paper from a non-Internet service.

Key 8.7   Avoid plagiarism by learning how to paraphrase.

QUOTATION

"The most common assumption that is made by persons who are communicating with one another is . . . that the other perceives, judges, thinks, and reasons the way he does. Identical twins communicate with ease. Persons from the same culture but with a different education, age, background, and experience often find communication difficult. American managers communicating with managers from other cultures experience greater difficulties in communication than with managers from their own culture."[3]

UNACCEPTABLE PARAPHRASE

(The underlined words are taken directly from the quoted source.)

When we communicate, we assume that the person to whom we are speaking perceives, judges, thinks, and reasons the way we do. This is not always the case. Although identical twins communicate with ease, persons from the same culture but with a different education, age, background, and experience often encounter communication problems. Communication problems are common among American managers as they attempt to communicate with managers from other cultures. They experience greater communication problems than when they communicate with managers from their own culture.

ACCEPTABLE PARAPHRASE

Many people fall into the trap of believing that everyone sees the world exactly as they do and that all people communicate according to the same assumptions. This belief is difficult to support even within our own culture as African-Americans, Hispanic-Americans, Asian-Americans, and others often attempt unsuccessfully to find common ground. When intercultural differences are thrown into the mix, such as when American managers working abroad attempt to communicate with managers from other cultures, clear communication becomes even harder.

- hands in a paper written by a fellow student or a family member.
- writes the paper collaboratively with one or more students without getting the instructor's approval.
- copies material in a paper directly from a source without proper quotation marks or source citation.
- paraphrases material in a paper from a source without proper source citation.

The risk to students who plagiarize is growing because cheating is now easier to discover. Make a commitment to hand in your own work and to uphold the highest standards of academic integrity.

Go For It!   **BUILDING YOUR SKILLS**

ACTIVE
THINKING

SKILL   WILL   SELF-MGMT.

AVOID PLAGIARISM

Think about plagiarism and explore your views on this growing problem.

Complete the following:

- Why is plagiarism considered an offense that involves both stealing and lying? Describe how you look at it.

  _____

  _____

  _____

- Citing sources indicates that you respect the ideas of others. List two additional ways that accurate source citation strengthens your writing and makes you a better student.

  1. _____

  2. _____

- What specific penalties for plagiarism are described in your college handbook? Explain whether you feel that these penalties are reasonable or excessive and whether they will keep students from plagiarizing.

  _____

  _____

  _____

- Many experts believe that researching on the Internet is behind many acts of plagiarism. Do you agree? Why or why not?

  _____

  _____

Solicit Feedback

Since it is difficult to be objective about your own work, asking for someone else's perspective can be very helpful. Talk with your instructor about your draft. Ask a classmate, a friend, or a coworker to take a look. Some classes include a peer-review process, and many schools have tutors in writing centers who also act as peer readers.

Another strategy is to ask a study partner to read your draft and answer specific questions like the following:

- Is my thesis clear and did my evidence back it up?
- Are the ideas logically connected?
- Are there places where my writing style, choice of words, paragraph structure, transitions, etc., detract from what I am trying to say?
- Am I missing anything?

Be open-minded about the comments you receive. Consider each carefully, and then make a decision about what to change.

Citing Sources

The bibliography cards you wrote while researching your topic should contain every source you used while writing. Your instructor may ask you to use this information to create different source lists:

- a *References List*, also called a *List of Works Cited*, includes only the sources you actually cited in your paper.

ACTIVE THINKING

Work Together BUILDING YOUR SKILLS

IMPROVE YOUR WORK THROUGH PEER REVIEW

Before handing in a paper, join with one of your classmates to review each other's drafts. Use the critical thinking questions in the *Solicit Feedback* section you just read to guide your analysis of your partner's work. Your goal is to give honest, thoughtful feedback and to be open to a different perspective when you receive feedback.

Respond in writing on a separate page: What did you learn from this partnership? How did your classmate's comments help you improve? What did you see—good or bad—in your classmate's paper that helped you improve your own work?

- a *Bibliography* includes all the sources you consulted, whether or not they were cited in the paper.
- an *Annotated Bibliography* includes all the sources you consulted as well as an explanation or critiques of each source.

Besides being the ethical thing to do, citing your sources according to the directions your instructor provides adds credibility to your work. When instructors scan your List of Works Cited, they will know that you did research to uncover information.

Your instructor will tell you what style to use to document your sources and whether to list footnotes at the end of the paper or the bottom of the page. The general styles of documentation are discipline specific:

- The Modern Language Association (MLA) format is generally used in the humanities, including history, literature, the arts, and philosophy. To learn more about MLA style, consult the official MLA Handbook (*The MLA Handbook for Writers of Research Papers*, 6th edition, by Joseph Gibaldi) or go to the MLA website: www.mla.org/style.

- The American Psychological Association (APA) style is the appropriate format in psychology, sociology, business, economics, nursing, criminology, and social work. For information on APA style, see the official APA Handbook (*Publication Manual of the American Psychological Association*, 5th edition) or visit the APA website: www.apastyle.org/previoustips.html.

- An alternate documentation style is found in the 15th edition of the *Chicago Manual of Style*, published by the University of Chicago Press. To learn more, go to www.press.uchicago.edu/Misc/Chicago/cmosfaq/cmosfaq.html.

- The Council of Biology Editors (CBE)—now called the Council of Science Editors—style is used to cite scientific sources. For information on this style, see the official CBE style manual (*Scientific Style and Format*) or the organization's website: www.councilscienceeditors.org/.

- The Columbia Online Style (COS) is often used to cite online sources. For information, see the official COS manual (*The Columbia Guide to Online Style* by Janice R. Walker and Todd Taylor) or click on www.columbia.edu/cu/cup/cgos/index.html.

Consult a college-level writers' handbook for an overview of these documentation styles.

Continue Your Checklist

Create a first-draft checklist (see Key 8.8), remembering that the elements of your draft do not have to be completed in this order.

Key 8.8   Update your checklist for the first draft.

DATE YOU PLAN TO COMPLETE THIS STEP	TASK	IS IT COMPLETE?
	Freewrite a draft	
	Plan and write the introduction	
	Organize the body of the paper	
	Include research evidence in the body	
	Plan and write the conclusion	
	Check for plagiarism and rewrite passages to avoid it	
	Credit your sources	
	Solicit feedback	

Meeting with your instructor to discuss your writing can be one of the best ways to get feedback as you work through preliminary drafts of a paper.

Revising

When you revise, you critically evaluate the content, organization, word choice, paragraph structure, and style of your first draft. You evaluate the strength of your evidence and whether there are gaps in continuity. You can do anything you want with your draft at this point to strengthen your work. You can turn things around, presenting information from the end of your paper up front, or even choose a totally different organizational structure.

If your instructor evaluates an early draft, be sure to incorporate his ideas into the final product. If you disagree with a point or don't understand the revision directions, schedule a conference to talk it over.

Your instructor will respect you more when you seek his feedback and take his comments seriously.

Revising as Self-Monitoring

Dr. Mel Levine, founder of All Kinds of Minds, a nonprofit institute for understanding learning differences, views revising as a time of self-monitoring in which you ask, "How am I doing?" and take a hard look at what you have written, making changes if you have gotten off track. Self-monitoring is a way of looking at the big picture (*Have I defended my thesis? Is my evidence strong enough and logically connected? Have I included information or made an argument that is irrelevant to my thesis?*) and the technicalities (*Am I using the right words? Is my grammar and spelling correct? Are my paragraphs well constructed? Are my transitions clear?*).

Levine believes that self-monitoring works best when you put the paper down for a day or even several days and come back to it with a fresh outlook. "The writing experience needs time to incubate," he explains. "With time, it is much easier to evaluate your own work, to detect and correct its flaws with some objectivity, and to deftly surmount the impasses that felt insurmountable while you were immersed in the act of writing."[4]

Key 8.9 on the following page shows a paragraph from the first draft of the business ethics paper, with revision comments added.

Use Critical Thinking Abilities as You Revise

Engage your critical thinking skills to evaluate the content and form of your paper. Ask yourself these questions as you revise:

- Does the paper fulfill the requirements of the assignment?
- Will my audience understand my thesis and how I've supported it?
- Does the introduction prepare the reader and capture attention?
- Is the body of the paper organized effectively?
- Does each paragraph have a *topic sentence* that is supported by the rest of the paragraph? (See Chapter 5 for an analysis of where to look for a topic sentence.)
- Have I effectively presented and supported my thesis?
- Is each idea and argument developed, explained, and supported by examples?
- Are my ideas connected to one another through logical transitions?
- Do I have a clear, concise, simple writing style?
- Does the conclusion provide a natural ending without introducing new ideas?

Key 8.9   **Incorporate revision comments to strengthen your paper.**

Like Texas Instruments, Johnson & Johnson developed a code of ethics that ~~written in plain English,~~

~~is a cornerstone of its corporate culture~~ ~~employees rely on to make decisions.~~ A simple one-page document that has

(add more detail here) been in place for more than 60 years, "Our Credo," as the code is called, states

                                                    customers, employees, communities, stockholders
J & J's ethical responsibilities to ~~everyone it does business with~~. It has been

translated into 36 languages for employees, customers, suppliers, governments,
                    to consult
and shareholders in every market in which it operates, from North America
                                                                      the
to the far reaches of Africa, Europe, Latin America, the Middle East, and

Asia/Pacific region (add footnote—Johnson & Johnson: Our Credo).

    When Johnson & Johnson updated its credo in the mid-1970s, executives
                                    it continued to represent company values.
examined every word and phrase to make sure ~~they still applied~~ "These meetings

infused the values in the minds of all of us managers," explained Bob Kniffin,
who was   at the time
Vice President of External Affairs, J & J's managers had no way of knowing that
                                            prepare them   one of the most
the exercise they were engaged in would ~~give them the skills~~ to handle a difficult
              s ever faced by an American company.
challenge. Only a few years later, many of the same executives who ~~examined~~ scrutinized the

company's credo struggled with how to protect consumers, company employees

and shareholders when bottles of Tylenol were poisoned on store shelves and

innocent people died.

Check for Clarity and Conciseness

Now check for sense, continuity, and clarity. Focus also on tightening your prose and eliminating wordy phrases. Examine once again how paragraphs flow into one another by evaluating the effectiveness of your

MULTIPLE INTELLIGENCE STRATEGIES FOR WRITING. The techniques below can help you uncover valuable research sources and clearly communicate what you want to say.

INTELLIGENCE	SUGGESTED STRATEGIES	WHAT WORKS FOR YOU? WRITE NEW IDEAS HERE
Verbal-Linguistic	■ Read many resources and take comprehensive notes on them. Summarize the main points from your resources. ■ Interview someone about the topic and take notes.	
Logical-Mathematical	■ Take notes on 3 × 5 cards and organize them according to topics and subtopics. ■ Create a detailed, sequential outline of your writing project. If your assignment requires persuasive writing, make sure that your argument is logical.	
Bodily-Kinesthetic	■ Visit places/sites that hold resources you need or that are related to your topic—businesses, libraries, etc. ■ After brainstorming ideas for an assignment, take a break involving physical activity. During the break, think about your top three ideas and see what insight occurs to you.	
Visual-Spatial	■ Create full-color charts as you read each resource or interview someone. ■ Use think link format or another visual organizer to map out your main topic, subtopics, and related ideas and examples. Use different colors for different subtopics.	
Interpersonal	■ As you gather resource material, discuss it with a fellow student. ■ Pair up with a classmate and become each other's peer editors. Read each other's first drafts and next-to-final drafts, offering constructive feedback.	
Intrapersonal	■ Take time to mull over any assigned paper topic. Think about what emotions it raises in you, and why. Let your inner instincts guide you as you begin to write. ■ Schedule as much research time as possible.	
Musical	■ Play your favorite relaxing music while you brainstorm topics for a writing assignment.	
Naturalistic	■ Pick a research topic that relates to nature. ■ Build confidence by envisioning your writing process as a successful climb to the top of a mountain.	

transitions—the words, phrases, or sentences that connect ideas. Make your transitions signal what comes next. For example:

- *also*, *in addition*, and *next* indicate that another idea is coming.
- *on the other hand* and *in contrast* indicate an opposing viewpoint.
- *finally*, *as a result*, and *in conclusion* signal that a summary is on the way.

Choose a Title

You can choose a title as you revise your paper or earlier after you develop a thesis. Your goal is to make sure the title reflects what the paper *actually* says rather than what you planned to write.

Editing

Editing involves correcting technical mistakes in spelling, grammar, and punctuation, as well as checking for consistency in such elements as abbreviations and capitalizations. Editing comes last, after you are satisfied with your ideas, organization, and writing style. If you use a computer, start with the grammar check and spell check to find errors, realizing that you still need to check your work manually. (For example, a spell checker won't pick up the mistake in the sentence, "They are not hear on Tuesdays.").

Look also for *sexist language*, which characterizes people according to gender stereotypes and often involves the male pronouns *he* or *his* or *him*. For example, "An executive often spends hours going through his electronic mail" implies that executives are always men. A simple change will eliminate the sexist language: "Executives often spend hours going through their electronic mail." Try also to be sensitive to words that leave out or slight women. Mail carrier, for example, is preferable to mailman.

Proofreading is the last editing stage and happens after your paper is in its final form. Proofreading means reading every word and sentence for accuracy. Look for technical mistakes, run-on sentences, and sentence fragments. Look for incorrect word usage and unclear references. A great way to check your work is to read it out loud. Consider teaming up with a classmate to proofread each other's work since, by this point, you may be too close to the material to catch even obvious errors.

A Final Checklist

You are now ready to complete your revising and editing checklist. All the tasks listed in Key 8.10 should be complete before you submit your paper.

Your final paper reflects all the hard work you put in during the writing process. Ideally, when you are finished, you have a piece of work that

Key 8.10   Create a revision and editing checklist.

DATE YOU PLAN TO COMPLETE THIS STEP	TASK	IS IT COMPLETE?
	Check the body of the paper for clear thinking and adequate support of ideas	
	Finalize introduction and conclusion	
	Check spelling, usage, and grammar	
	Check paragraph structure for clear topic sentences	
	Make sure language is clear and concise	
	Check punctuation and capitalization	
	Check transitions	
	Eliminate sexist language	
	Get feedback from peers and/or instructor	
	Title your paper	

shows your writing ability and clearly communicates and proves your thesis. Key 8.11, the final version of the business-ethics paper, is a product of this writing process.

As you complete this review of the writing process, keep in mind a point made earlier in Key 8.1—that the writing skills you develop in college will be reflected in the documents you give prospective employers, and these, in turn, will impact the success of your job search. June Brown, of Olive Harvey College, explains how good writing is at the center of your efforts: "The written documents you leave with a company may be your most lasting calling card. If your documents are incorrect, messy, or poorly organized, they will leave a negative impression. No matter how well you do in a face-to-face meeting, your cover letter, resume, and other work-related documents are a record that memorializes who you are. Make sure it is your best work."

Key 8.11   Following the writing process leads to a well-crafted paper.

CODES OF ETHICS ENCOURAGE COMPANIES TO DO WHAT IS RIGHT

Open to the business section of any newspaper and you are likely to find at least one story of a corporate executive on trial and facing jail or a company paying huge fines or court settlements to the government, consumers, or investors. In the last few years, stories of alleged wrongdoing at Enron, WorldCom, Tyco International, Computer Associates, Sotheby's, and Adelphi Communications, to name just a few, have been front-page news. In an environment where so many executives are behaving badly and where corporate reputations are being tarnished, companies are struggling with how to set expectations of ethical behavior. Most major corporations, including Texas Instruments and Johnson & Johnson, now believe that creating a corporate code of ethics is a critical first step in the process of sensitizing employees to how they should act under normal circumstances and during crises.

Business ethics, like personal ethics, are based on values that define actions as right or wrong, good or bad, proper or improper. Sometimes ethical decisions are clear—for example, almost no one would argue that it is acceptable for an automaker to hide a major safety defect in order to avoid the cost of recalling thousands of vehicles—but often they are not. (Should the same manufacturer issue the recall if the defect is likely to affect only 1 in 10,000 cars?) Business decisions in today's complex, competitive marketplace often involve choices that put a company's morals to the test.

The Josephson Institute of Ethics defines six key concepts to help managers evaluate competing choices (Josephson Institute of Ethics, "Six Pillars of Character," 2002). These are trustworthiness (honesty, integrity, promise-keeping, loyalty), respect (civility, courtesy and decency, dignity and autonomy, tolerance and acceptance), responsibility (accountability, pursuit of excellence, self-restraint), fairness (procedural fairness, impartiality, equity), caring (compassion, consideration, giving, sharing, kindness), and citizenship (law abiding, community service, protection of environment). These pillars are among the factors that underlie the ethics codes at Texas Instruments and Johnson & Johnson.

Texas Instruments places ethics at the core of its corporate culture. First published 45 years ago, TI's code sets ethical expectations, based on principles and values, for employees to consider every time they make a decision or take action. To encourage adherence to the highest ethical standards, TI gives each employee a business card sized "Ethics Test" to carry at all times (Texas Instruments, "The TI Ethics Quick Test," 1988). The test—with seven clear bullet points—is based on TI's core principles and on legal and societal values:

Key 8.11   Continued

- Is the action legal?
- Does it comply with our values?
- If you do it, will you feel bad?
- How will it look in the newspaper?
- If you know it's wrong, don't do it!
- If you're not sure, ask.
- Keep asking until you get an answer.

To support employees who face ethics-related challenges in an ever-changing and increasingly competitive business environment, TI established an ethics office in the late 1980s. The function of the office is to make sure business practices continue to reflect company values, to communicate and reinforce ethical expectations to every employee, and to give employees feedback on ethics-related problems (Texas Instruments, 1988).

Like Texas Instruments, Johnson & Johnson developed a code of ethics, written in plain English, that is a cornerstone of its corporate culture. A simple one-page document that has been in place for more than 60 years, "Our Credo," as the code is called, states J & J's ethical responsibilities to its customers, its employees, the communities in which it operates, and, its stockholders. It has been translated into 36 languages for employees, customers, suppliers, governments, and shareholders to consult in every market in which it operates, from North America to the far reaches of Africa, Europe, Latin America, the Middle East, and the Asia/Pacific region (Johnson & Johnson, "Our Credo," 2004).

McNamara (1999) describes Johnson & Johnson's updating of its credo in the mid-1970s along with subsequent events. Executives examined every word and phrase to make sure it continued to represent company values. "These meetings infused the values in the minds of all of us managers," explained Bob Kniffin, who was Vice President of External Affairs at the time. J & J's managers had no way of knowing that the exercise they were engaged in would prepare them to handle one of the most difficult challenges ever faced by an American company: Only a few years later, many of the same executives who scrutinized the company's credo struggled with how to protect consumers, company employees, and shareholders when bottles of Tylenol were poisoned on store shelves and innocent people died.

Experts inside and outside the company believed that the examination of the company's credo that had taken place in these meetings guided J & J's decision to recall every bottle of Tylenol and repackage the product at a cost of $100 million.

Key 8.11   Continued

According to Kniffin, who was a key player in the crisis, the ethical road was set before the crisis began. "In a crisis, there's no time for moral conclusions," he said. Those must be made beforehand (*Ethics Tools: Codes of Ethics, "About Codes of Ethics"*).

Corporate codes of ethics are effective only if they are followed. (Even Enron had a code of ethics that was set aside by the board of directors to allow the company to complete unscrupulous deals.) While products and marketing strategies change frequently to meet competitive pressures, core values never change, nor does the expectation (in companies like TI and J & J) that managers will weigh business decisions and actions against these values. The old joke about "business ethics" being a contradiction in terms does not apply at these companies—not only because they have taken the time to institutionalize a code of ethics and to use it to evaluate job candidates, but also because employees are expected to follow its guidelines, even when it hurts the bottom line. Taking the idea of a written ethics code to another dimension, financial services companies are considering adopting an industry-wide code to set uniform standards of right and wrong for every company (Berman, 2005). That would mean that even in the toughest competitive situations—where millions of dollars in commissions were up for grabs—everyone would be playing by the same ethical rules.

References

Berman, Dennis K. (2005, March 10). "Does Wall Street finally need an ethics code?" *The Wall Street Journal*, p. C1.

Johnson & Johnson (2004). Our Credo (last updated August 18, 2004). Retrieved February 16, 2005 from www.jnj.com/our_company/our_credo/index.htm

Josephson Institute of Ethics (2002). *Making Ethical Decisions: Introduction and Table of Contents* [Electronic version]. Retrieved February 22, 2005 from www.josephson institute.org/MED/MED-intro+toc.htm

McNamara, Carter. (1999). *Complete Guide to Ethics Management: An Ethics Toolkit for Managers* [Electronic version]. Retrieved February 16, 2005 from www.mapnp.org/library/ethics/ethxgde.htm

Texas Instruments (1988). "Ethics at TI." Retrieved March 4, 2005 from www.ti.com/corp/docs/company/citizen/ethics/quicktest.shtml

Building Skill, Will, and Self-Management

Monitoring Your Progress

ACTIVE THINKING

SKILL WILL SELF-MGMT.

Test Competence: Measure What You've Learned

MULTIPLE CHOICE. *Circle or highlight the answer that seems to fit best.*

1. Writing is considered a study skill for all of the following reasons *except:*
   A. Writing skills enable you to take effective notes.
   B. Writing skills give you the ability to effectively complete essay tests.
   C. Writing skills prepare you to write letters to friends.
   D. Writing skills help you solidify your knowledge as you prepare for tests.

2. Identifying your purpose for writing helps you
   A. choose a topic.
   B. understand your audience.
   C. write without grammatical mistakes.
   D. focus on what you want your document to accomplish.

3. Making a commitment to your audience enables you to
   A. provide the reader with the appropriate level of information to foster communication.
   B. exhibit an extensive and unique knowledge of your topic.
   C. focus on the needs of the reader instead of your purpose for writing.
   D. use your document as the basis for a speech.

4. The writing process includes all of the following *except:*
   A. planning.
   B. drafting.
   C. typing.
   D. revising and editing.

5. A creative technique that involves generating ideas about a topic, without judgment, is known as
   A. planning.
   B. drafting.
   C. brainstorming.
   D. evaluating.

6. A thesis statement does all of the following *except:*
   A. explain your writing style.
   B. tell readers what they should expect from your written presentation.
   C. link together your topic, purpose, and commitment to your audience.
   D. appear near the beginning of your document.

7. A first draft must
   A. have no spelling or punctuation errors.
   B. be ready to show to your instructor.
   C. have exactly the right tone.
   D. create the initial structure and content of your document.

8. Possible strategies for effectively organizing the body of a paper include all of the following *except:*
   A. arranging ideas as they occur to you.
   B. arranging ideas by time.
   C. arranging ideas according to importance.
   D. arranging ideas by problem and solution.

9. Citing your sources at the end of a paper
   A. is an ethical requirement when you use the ideas or words of other authors.
   B. should be done according to the rules of the source-citation style chosen by your instructor.
   C. adds credibility to your paper.
   D. all of the above.

10. Revising enables you to do all of the following *except:*
    A. fine-tune your first draft.
    B. finish the writing process and hand your document to your instructor.
    C. rewrite and strengthen sections of your draft.
    D. use critical thinking skills to evaluate your first draft.

TRUE/FALSE. *Place a T or an F beside each statement to indicate whether you think it is true or false.*

_____ 1. It is a mistake to have anyone read your paper before showing it to your instructor.

_____ 2. Editing involves identifying information gaps in your draft and conducting new research.

_____ 3. Checklists help you keep track of all the elements in the writing process.

_____ 4. Every document involves persuasive writing.

_____ 5. Freewriting is the time in the writing process to pay attention to grammar and spelling.

Target and Achieve a Goal

Commit to one specific writing strategy from this chapter to improve your study skills.

Name the strategy here:
_____

_____

Describe your goal—what you want to gain by using this strategy.
_____

_____

Describe how you plan to use this strategy through the semester to achieve this goal.
_____

_____

"The writing process gives you time to begin thinking about ideas and letting them float around in your mind for an hour or perhaps several days. If you write a paper the night before it is due, there is no time to reflect on your work, synthesize your ideas, or weave them in and out as you would a lovely tapestry. All you can do is just get it down and hand it in."

LYNN QUITMAN TROYKA,
author of Simon & Schuster's *Handbook for Writers*

Building Your Skills

Brain Power: Build Vocabulary Fitness

Here is a selection from the current media. Read the material, paying special attention to the context of the vocabulary words shown in bold type. Then choose the correct definition for each word in the table that follows. Use a dictionary to check your answers. Finally, on a separate sheet, use each vocabulary word in a sentence of your own to solidify your understanding.

In this editorial, the global news magazine The Economist *opines on the need to reform the world's patent systems so that inventors are properly rewarded. This reading is typical of what is found in the business press.*

Around the world, patent offices are being **inundated** with applications. In many cases, this represents the extraordinary inventiveness that is occurring in new fields such as the Internet. . . . But another, less-acceptable reason for the flood is that patent offices have been too **lax** in granting patents, encouraging many firms to rush to patent as many, often **dubious**, ideas as possible in an effort to erect legal obstacles to competitors. The result has been a series of messy and expensive court battles, and growing doubts about the effectiveness of patent systems as a **spur** to **innovation**. . . .

In 1998 America introduced so-called "business-method" patents, granting for the first time patent monopolies simply for new ways of doing business, many of which were not so new. This was a mistake. It not only **ushered in** a wave of new applications, but it is probably **inhibiting** rather than encouraging commercial innovation. . . .

There is an urgent need for patent offices to return to first principles. A patent is a government-granted temporary monopoly (patents in most countries are given about 20 years' protection) intended to reward innovators in exchange for a disclosure by the patent holder of how the invention works. . . . The qualifying tests for patents are straightforward—that an idea be useful, novel, and not obvious. Unfortunately most patent offices, swamped by applications that can run to thousands of pages and confronted by companies **wielding** teams of lawyers, are no longer applying these tests strictly or reliably. For example, in America many experts believe that dubious patents abound, such as the **notorious** one for a "sealed crustless sandwich." . . . Most of all, patent offices need to find ways of applying standards more strictly. This would make patents more difficult to obtain. But that is only right. Patents are, after all, government-enforced monopolies and so, as Jefferson had it, there should be some "embarrassment" (and hesitation) in granting them.

Source: "Monopolies of the Mind," *The Economist.* November 11, 2004, from Economist.com (http://economist.com/opinion/displayStory.cfm?story_id=3376181).

Circle the word or phrase that best defines each term as it is used in this excerpt.

VOCABULARY WORDS	A	B	C
1. **inundated** (verb)	rushed	coaxed	flooded
2. **lax** (adj.)	easy	slow	formal
3. **dubious** (adj.)	superior	doubtful	temporary
4. **spur** (noun)	incentive	drag	saddle
5. **innovation** (noun)	business	magic	creation
6. **ushered in** (verb)	announced	inaugurated	prevented
7. **inhibiting** (verb)	hindering	encouraging	ignoring
8. **wielding** (verb)	holding	hitting	controlling
9. **notorious** (adj.)	famous	infamous	silly

Get to the Root

Every time you learn a Greek or Latin root, you increase your ability to recognize English vocabulary words that include that root and to figure out their meaning. Grow your vocabulary by studying this root and its related words, writing in two more words from the same root, and including definitions for both new words.

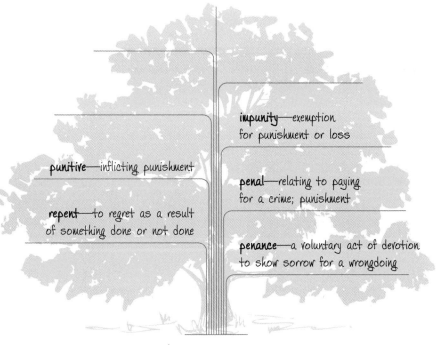

impunity—exemption for punishment or loss

punitive—inflicting punishment

penal—relating to paying for a crime; punishment

repent—to regret as a result of something done or not done

penance—a voluntary act of devotion to show sorrow for a wrongdoing

pen/punden—to pay, to compensate; origin: Latin

Investigate Using Research Navigator

Access Research Navigator using the Internet address shown on page 32. Then sign on to the service using your Login Name and Password. Scroll through the database titles listed for Content Select. Choose a database linked to a major you are interested in, and then enter a career-related keyword. For example, if you are taking a biology course, you could choose the Biology database and enter "medicine or physical therapy or nursing, etc." as a keyword.

- Using the database, find at least three sources that describe what someone involved in this career does and what a typical career ladder might be—i.e., how you might progress from an entry-level job to more advanced positions. Try to find specific descriptions of responsibilities and duties.

- Read the material you've found, and then write a two-page expository paper, to an uninformed reader, on the career opportunities in the field. Use the writing process to plan, draft, revise, and edit the paper.

- Finally, answer the following questions about your writing experience:

  -How did the writing process help you communicate effectively?
  -What was the most useful aspect of the process? The least useful?
  -How do you think the writing process will help improve your college writing?
  -After completing this exercise, how do you react to the question raised by former *New York Times* columnist James Reston, quoted at the beginning of the chapter, which asked: "How can I know what I think until I read what I write?"

Building Will and Self-Awareness

ACTIVE
THINKING

SKILL   WILL   SELF-MGMT.

Make Responsible Choices

Answer the following question on a separate piece of paper or in a journal.

Technology has changed the speed—and often the form—of communication. Even in business, e-mail and instant messages are filled with telescoped shorthand that bears little resemblance to standard English. With this in mind. . . .

- analyze whether you think writing "according to the rules" is becoming outmoded. How do you think technology will change the need to communicate according to universally accepted standards?

- analyze whether the writing process (planning, drafting, revising, editing) is an anachronism—a relic of another, simpler time—in the world of high-speed communication. Once again, consider the necessity to communicate complex ideas effectively to others.

- analyze your responsibility to write effectively to avoid misrepresenting facts or opinions. When you get a job, is the pressure to write well likely to come from within yourself or from others?

- analyze the effect on you and on your employer if your coworkers are poor writers.

Chapter Summary

As you use the following summary to review the concepts you learned in this chapter, focus also on its format—in this case the **Cornell system**, in other chapters a formal outline, and in still others a think link. As you become comfortable with the organization and style of these various formats, try using each of them to take class and reading notes, noting which approach works best for you in particular situations.

Chapter 8: Effective Writing

Why does good writing matter?	• Strong writing skills lead to academic and career success.
What are the elements of effective writing?	• Writing purpose: When you write a research paper, your purpose is to present information without arguing a viewpoint (an expository paper) or to present and argue a point of view to prove a thesis (a persuasive paper). —Audience: Clarify whether you are writing for informed or uninformed readers. —Topic: Your instructor may assign a specific, general, or broad topic.
What is the writing process?	• During the planning stage, pay attention to logistics, brainstorm topic ideas, use prewriting strategies to narrow your topic, conduct research, write a thesis statement, and create a writing checklist that will keep you on schedule. • The drafting stage allows you to put ideas on paper and create an organizational structure. Drafting involves freewriting a rough draft, writing an introduction, creating the body of the paper with ideas and supporting evidence within an effective organization, writing the conclusion, and crediting sources. For best results, share your first draft with others and incorporate their feedback. • During the revision stage, you critically evaluate content, organization, word choice, paragraph structure, and style of your first draft, focusing also on the strength of the evidence, logic, clarity and conciseness, among other things. • During the editing phase, you correct technical mistakes in spelling, grammar, and punctuation. Proofreading involves rereading every word for accuracy and consistency.

Academic and career success depends on good writing. The basic elements of writing are purpose, audience, and topic. The writing process involves planning, drafting, revision, and editing. A checklist will help you stay on schedule as you write.

Endnotes

1. Adam Robinson, *What Smart Students Know*. New York: Three Rivers Press, 1993, p. 210.
2. Analysis based on Lynn Quitman Troyka, *Simon & Schuster Handbook for Writers*. Upper Saddle River, NJ: Prentice Hall, 1996, pp. 22–23.
3. *Source of quotation:* Lynn Quitman Troyka, *Simon & Schuster Handbook for Writers*.
4. Dr. Mel Levine, *The Myth of Laziness*. New York: Simon & Schuster, 2003, pp. 183–185.

9

"Mathematics, even in its present and most abstract state, is not detached from life. It is just the ideal handling of the problems of life."

Quantitative Learning

BECOMING COMFORTABLE WITH MATH AND SCIENCE

As you might expect, quantitative thinking skills are critical for success in math and science. It may surprise you to know, however, that these skills will help you achieve other academic goals as well. Working with numbers helps train your mind to solve problems as it builds your ability to think actively and work through processes logically. In addition, quantitative skills are increasingly valuable in a workplace dominated by technology and the exchange of information.

This chapter will give you an overview of quantitative thinking and offer basic problem-solving strategies. You will also explore how to approach math and science in an open-minded, positive way, both in your coursework and during tests. Many students experience math anxiety, and a positive attitude is crucial to building a successful relationship with numbers. Finally, you will expand your understanding of the value of math and science learning in today's workplace.

In this chapter you will explore answers to the following questions:

- How are math and science part of your daily life?
- How can you master math and science basics?
- How can you overcome math anxiety?
- Why should math and science learning be an important part of your future?

HOW ARE MATH AND SCIENCE PART OF YOUR DAILY LIFE?

Numbers are a part of life. You use aspects of *quantitative thinking* often—basic calculations in your checkbook, geometrical thinking for how to pack a collection of items into the trunk of your car, figuring ratios for allowable deductions on a tax return, and so forth. Everyday functioning requires a certain level of comfort and competence in quantitative skills. These skills can be broken down into the following broad areas.

Arithmetic. Many everyday tasks, especially those involving money, require arithmetic (numerical computations such as addition, subtraction, multiplication, and division, plus the use of fractions, percentages, and other ratios). You are using arithmetic when you calculate how much tuition you can cover in a semester or figure how much to tip in a restaurant. You also use arithmetic when you interpret ingredient amounts and percentages on food labels in the effort to eat more healthily.

Algebra. A knowledge of *algebra*—a generalization of arithmetic in which letters representing unknown quantities are combined, often with other numbers, into equations according to mathematical rules—is needed almost as frequently as arithmetic. Algebra involves determining an unknown value using known values. You use algebra when you figure out the interest on a loan or compute what score you need on an exam or paper in order to achieve a particular final grade in a course.

Geometry. The most common uses of *geometry*—the mathematics of the properties, measurement, and relationships of points, lines, angles, surfaces, and solids—occur in determining areas and volumes. However, geometric ideas occur in many other forms. You make use of geometric principles without even thinking about it when, for example, you determine how closely you can pass a car or pack a suitcase so that it can close.

Probability and statistics. A knowledge of basic *probability* (the study of the chance that a given event will occur) and *statistics* (collection, analysis, and interpretation of numerical data) is needed for understanding the relevance and importance of the overwhelming amount of statistical information you encounter. For example, a woman's knowledge of probability can help her determine her risk of getting breast cancer; a student's understanding of statistics can help him analyze his chances of getting into a particular college as a transfer student.

Sciences. Biology, anatomy, and other sciences directly related to the human body can help you to better manage your health through a greater understanding of how your body works. Chemistry can help you figure out how to substitute ingredients in a recipe or become aware of possible inter-actions between medications you are taking. A knowledge of physics can help you load items safely on the roof of a car to minimize wind resistance and increase gas mileage.

Ultimately, both math and science are relevant to your other subjects because they aid problem solving and critical thinking as they move you from questions to solutions. When you put your brain through the paces of mathematical and scientific problem solving, you are building the kind of critical thinking ability that you can apply to problem solving in any subject. You use a similar analytical process when you write an essay on the causes of a historical event or reconcile different perspectives in a philosophy course.

HOW CAN YOU MASTER MATH AND SCIENCE BASICS?

Math and science are interrelated. Sciences such as chemistry, physics, and astronomy are quite often problem-solving courses. Classes in geology, anthropology, and biology also can fall into this category. You can apply the strategies you work with in your math courses to these sciences. "Math is the empowering skill that underlies all science," says Don Pierce, executive director of education at Heald College. "Without it, you can't succeed as a scientist. The scientific process depends on your ability to analyze, interpret, and attach meaning to data, so math and science are intrinsically linked."[1]

For example, in beginning chemistry, you will usually have to balance chemical equations. This may involve writing an equation, drawing a diagram, or perhaps working backward. In physics, the study of forces involves applying problem-solving strategies developed from vector calculus. In fact, the most common strategy to solve force problems involves drawing a diagram called a force diagram. The key thing to remember is that although these strategies are listed as mathematical strategies, the actual process of applying them is far more wide ranging, helping you to develop into a more adept critical thinker and problem solver.

Certain thinking strategies will help improve your ability to think quantitatively. Mastering math and science basics is easier when you take a critical approach to the classroom, the textbook, studying and homework, and word problems.

Classroom Strategies

When you are taking a math or science class, there are two primary ingredients for success:

Be prepared. Before class, read the material that will be covered that day. This allows you to build a base of knowledge, providing a context in which to ask questions about the material. Another way to focus your questions when in class is to review homework problems and mark any that gave you trouble. Noted scientist Louis Pasteur said that "Chance favors only the prepared mind"; with your "prepared mind" you will be as ready as possible to retain and understand what you hear and see in class.

Be in class. Take notes, focusing on the central ideas and connecting supporting examples (especially sample problems) to those ideas. Highlight items or examples that confuse you so that you can go back and focus on them later. Also, take responsibility for addressing any confusion you have: *ask questions*. Participating actively through questioning will help you clarify, retain, and use what you are learning. Finally, immediately after class, briefly review the information you just learned.

College math and science are quite different from high school courses—and the differences require you to be more focused and diligent about attending class and keeping up with homework. Among the differences you may notice are the following:

- Courses are faster paced.
- Assignments are crucial (although they may not always be collected).
- Class time may be more focused on theories and ideas than on problem solving.
- Class size might be considerably larger, with smaller lab sections. (If this is the case, you will most likely be working directly on problems only in your lab section.)
- Technological proficiency may be important; for example, you may need to know how to use a graphic calculator for your work in a particular course.

How to Approach Your Textbook

Math and science textbooks move sequentially (later chapters build on concepts and information introduced in previous chapters). Your command of later material depends on how well you learned material in earlier chapters. Use these strategies to get the most from your textbooks:

Interact with math material actively through writing. Math textbooks are problem-and-solution based. As you read, highlight important information and take notes of examples on a pad of paper. If problem steps are left out, as they often are, work them out on your pad or right in the book if there is room. Draw sketches as you read to help visualize the material. Try not to move on until you understand the example and how it relates to the central ideas. Write down questions you want to ask your instructor or fellow students.

Pay attention to formulas. In any math or science textbook, note the *formulas*—general facts, rules, or principles usually expressed in mathematical symbols—that are given. Evaluate whether these formulas are important and recall whether the instructor emphasized them. In some classes you are responsible for gathering all formulas through your reading; in others, the instructors will provide them. Either way, make sure you understand the formulas clearly and know how to apply them. Read the assigned material to prepare for homework.

Use memory skills with science material. Science textbooks are often packed with vocabulary specific to that particular science (for example, a chapter in a psychobiology course may give medical names for the parts of the brain). To remember what you read, use

Success in science courses means combining hands-on experience with a knowledge of vocabulary and formulas.

mnemonic devices, test yourself with flash cards, and rehearse aloud or silently (see Chapter 6). Selective highlighting and writing summaries of your readings, perhaps in table format, will also help.

Because many sciences rely on a base of mathematical knowledge, your math reading strategies will help you understand and remember the formulas that may appear in your science reading. As with math, make sure you understand the principles behind each formula, and do as many problems as you can to solidify your knowledge.

Studying and Homework

When it comes to studying and doing homework in math and science courses, action gets results. The exercise and strategies on pages 326–328 will help you work efficiently.

GET THE MOST FROM YOUR TEXTBOOK

From a textbook in a math or science course you are now taking, choose a chapter that you are about to cover in class. Do the following to maximize your understanding of the material:

1. Read the chapter now, before its material is covered in class. Take notes. Check this box when you have read it through. ☐

2. Identify and work through two difficult concepts or formulas. Develop a game plan to understand and learn each concept, basing your plan on what will help most—memory techniques, study groups, practice with problems, asking your instructor for help, and so forth.

Note the first concept or formula here: _____

Briefly describe your game plan. _____

_____

_____

Check the box when you have put your plan into action, and indicate whether it helped. Work done? ☐ How did it help? _____

_____

_____

_____

Note the second concept or formula here: _____

Briefly describe your game plan. _____

_____

_____

Check the box when you have put your plan into action, and indicate whether it helped. Work done? ☐ How did it help? _____

_____

_____

_____

Review materials. Review your class notes as soon as possible after each class. Have the textbook alongside and compare the lecture information to the book. Fill in missing steps in the instructor's examples before you forget them. You may want to write instructors' examples in the book by the corresponding topics.

Do problems, problems, and more problems. Working through problems is critical for math courses, as well as math-based science courses such as chemistry and astronomy, because it provides examples that will help you understand concepts and formulas. Plus, becoming familiar with a group of problems and related formulas will help you apply what you know to similar problems on other assignments and tests.

Fight frustration with action. Do not expect to complete every problem without effort. If you are stuck on a problem, go on to another one. If you repeatedly get a wrong answer, look at the steps you've taken and see if anything doesn't make sense. If you hit a wall, take a break to clear your head. If you have done the assigned homework but still don't feel secure, do additional problems.

Work with others. Even if your math and science classes have lab sessions, try to set up study groups outside of class. Do as much of your homework as you can and then meet to discuss the homework and work through additional problems. Be open to other perspectives, and don't hesitate to ask other students to explain their thought processes in detail. Sometimes students will do a problem differently but get the same correct answer; looking at alternative approaches to problems helps broaden your perspective on how the problems work. As you explain problems to one another, everyone builds understanding.

Focus on learning styles. Use strategies that activate your strengths. For example, a visual learner might draw pictures to illustrate problems, and an interpersonal learner might organize a study group. Musical learners might even make up songs describing math concepts—Barbara Aaker wrote 40 of them for her students at the Community College of Denver, and they have helped musical learners retain difficult concepts. Key 9.1 gives one of her algebra songs. The Multiple Intelligence grid on page 344 offers more ideas.

Strive for accuracy and precision. Although accuracy and precision are important in many different subjects, they have particular value in math and science. Complete a step of an algebra problem inaccurately, and your answer will be incorrect. Complete a step of a biology lab project imprecisely, and your results will be off. In class, of course, the consequences of inaccuracy are reflected in low grades; in life, the consequences could show

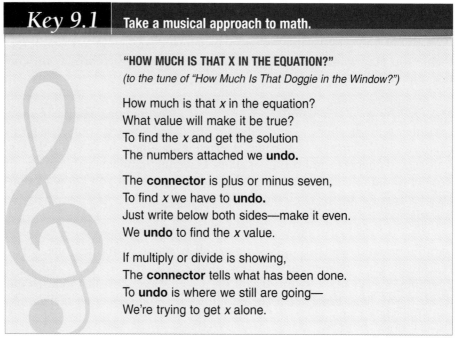

Key 9.1 | **Take a musical approach to math.**

"HOW MUCH IS THAT X IN THE EQUATION?"
(to the tune of "How Much Is That Doggie in the Window?")

How much is that x in the equation?
What value will make it be true?
To find the x and get the solution
The numbers attached we **undo.**

The **connector** is plus or minus seven,
To find x we have to **undo.**
Just write below both sides—make it even.
We **undo** to find the x value.

If multiply or divide is showing,
The **connector** tells what has been done.
To **undo** is where we still are going—
We're trying to get x alone.

Source: Reprinted with permission. Barbara Aaker, *Mathematics: The Musical.* Denver: Crazy Broad Publishing, 1999.

in more profound ways such as in a patient's health, in the strength of a bridge, or in the calculation of widely used data such as jobless rates. Check over the details of your work and strive for the right answers.

Word Problems

Because word problems are the most common way you will encounter quantitative thinking throughout your life, being able to solve them is crucial. Word problems can be tough, however, because they force you to translate between two languages—one expressed in words, and one expressed in numbers and symbols. Although math is a precise language, English and other living languages tend to leave more room for interpretation. This difference in precision makes the process of translating difficult.

Steps to Solving Word Problems

Translating English or any other language into math takes a lot of practice. George Polya, in his 1945 classic *How to Solve It,* devised a four-step method for attacking word problems.[2] The basic steps reflect the general problem-solving process you explored in Chapter 3, and they will work for any word problem, whether in a math or science course.

1. **Understand the individual elements of the problem.** Read the problem carefully. Understand what it is asking. Know what information you have. Know what information is missing. Draw a picture, if possible. Translate the given information from words into mathematical language (e.g., numbers, symbols, formulas).

2. **Name and explore potential solution paths.** Think about similar problems that you understand and how those were solved. Consider whether this problem is an example of a mathematical idea that you know. In your head, try out different ways to solve the problem to see which may work best.

3. **Choose a solution path and solve the problem.** As you carry out your plan, check each of your steps.

4. **Review your result.** Check your answer, if possible. Make sure you've answered the question the problem is asking. Does your result seem logical in the context of the problem? Are there other ways to do the problem?

Different problem-solving strategies will be useful to you when solving word problems. Evaluate which strategy will work best on a given problem and then apply the strategy. The following section outlines several problem-solving strategies by working through word problem examples.[3]

Problem-Solving Strategies

Strategy 1. Look for a pattern. G. H. Hardy (1877–1947), an eminent British mathematician, described mathematicians as makers of patterns and ideas. The search for patterns is one of the best strategies in problem solving. When you look for a pattern, you think inductively, observing a series of examples and determining the general idea that links the examples together.

Example: Find the next three entries in the following:

1. 1, 2, 4, _____, _____, _____
2. O, T, T, F, F, S, S, _____, _____, _____

Solutions to example:

1. When trying to identify patterns, you may find a different pattern than someone else. This doesn't mean yours is wrong. Example 1 actually has several possible answers. Here are two:

   - Each succeeding term of the sequence is twice the previous term. In that case, the next three values would be 8, 16, 32.
   - The second term is 1 more than the first term and the third term is 2 more than the second. This might lead you to guess the fourth

term is 3 more than the third term, the fifth term is 4 more than the fourth term, and so on. In that case, the next three terms are 7, 11, 16.

2. Example 2 is a famous pattern that often appears in puzzle magazines. The key to it is that "O" is the first letter of one, "T" is the first letter of two, and so on. Therefore, the next three terms would be E, N, and T for eight, nine, and ten.

Strategy 2. Make a table. A table can help you organize and summarize information. This may enable you to see how examples form a pattern that leads you to an idea and a solution.

Example: How many ways can you make change for a half dollar using only quarters, dimes, nickels, and pennies?

Solutions to example: You might construct several tables and go through every possible case. You could start by seeing how many ways you can make change for a half dollar without using a quarter, which would produce the following tables:

Quarters	0	0	0	0	0	0	0	0	0	0	0	0	0	0	0	0	0	0
Dimes	0	0	0	0	0	0	0	0	0	0	0	1	1	1	1	1	1	1
Nickels	0	1	2	3	4	5	6	7	8	9	10	0	1	2	3	4	5	6
Pennies	50	45	40	35	30	25	20	15	10	5	0	40	35	30	25	20	15	10

Quarters	0	0	0	0	0	0	0	0	0	0	0	0	0	0	0	0	0	0
Dimes	1	1	2	2	2	2	2	2	2	3	3	3	3	3	4	4	4	5
Nickels	7	8	0	1	2	3	4	5	6	0	1	2	3	4	0	1	2	0
Pennies	5	0	30	25	20	15	10	5	0	20	15	10	5	0	10	5	0	0

There are 36 ways to make change for a half dollar without using a quarter. Using one quarter results in this table:

Quarters	1	1	1	1	1	1	1	1	1	1	1	1
Dimes	0	0	0	0	0	0	1	1	1	1	2	2
Nickels	0	1	2	3	4	5	0	1	2	3	0	1
Pennies	25	20	15	10	5	0	15	10	5	0	5	0

Using one quarter, you get 12 different ways to make change for a half dollar. Finally, using two quarters, there's only one way to make change for a half dollar. Therefore, the solution to the problem is that there are 36 + 12 + 1 = 49 ways to make change for a half dollar using only quarters, dimes, nickels, and pennies.

Strategy 3. Identify a subgoal. Breaking the original problem into smaller and possibly easier problems may lead to a solution to the original problem. This is often the case in writing a computer program.

Example: Arrange the nine numbers 1, 2, 3, . . . , 9 into a square subdivided into nine sections in such a way that the sum of every row, column, and main diagonal is the same. This is called a magic square.

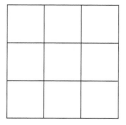

Solution to example: The sum of any individual row, column, or main diagonal has to be one-third the sum of all nine numbers (or else they wouldn't be the same). The sum of $1 + 2 + 3 + 4 + 5 + 6 + 7 + 8 + 9 = 45$. Therefore, each row, column, and main diagonal needs to sum to $45 \div 3 = 15$. Now, you need to see how many ways you can add three of the numbers from 1 to 9 and get 15. When you do this, you should get:

$9 + 1 + 5 = 15$	$8 + 3 + 4 = 15$
$9 + 2 + 4 = 15$	$7 + 2 + 6 = 15$
$8 + 1 + 6 = 15$	$7 + 3 + 5 = 15$
$8 + 2 + 5 = 15$	$6 + 4 + 5 = 15$

Now, looking at your magic square, notice that the center position will be part of four sums (a row, a column, and the two main diagonals). Looking back at your sums, you see that 5 appears in four different sums; therefore, 5 is in the center square.

	5	

Now, in each corner, the number there appears in three sums (row, column, and a diagonal). Looking through your sums, you find that 2, 4, 6, and 8 each appear in three sums. Now, you need to place them in the corners in such a way that your diagonals add up to 15.

2		6
	5	
4		8

Then, to finish, all you need to do is fill in the remaining squares so that 15 is the sum of each row, column, and main diagonal. The completed square is as follows:

2	7	6
9	5	1
4	3	8

Strategy 4. Examine a similar problem. Sometimes a problem you are working on has similarities to a problem you've already read about or solved. In that case, it is often possible to use a similar approach to solve the new problem.

Example: Find a magic square using the numbers 3, 5, 7, 9, 11, 13, 15, 17, and 19.

Solution to example: This problem is very similar to the example for Strategy 3. Approaching it in the same fashion, you find that the row, column, and main diagonal sum is 33. Writing down all the possible sums of three numbers to get 33, you find that 11 is the number that appears four times, so it is in the center.

	11	

The numbers that appear three times in the sums and will go in the corners are 5, 9, 13, and 17. This now gives you:

13		17
	11	
5		9

Finally, completing the magic square gives you:

13	3	17
15	11	7
5	19	9

Strategy 5. Work backward. With some problems, you may find it easier to start with the perceived final result and work backward.

Example: In the game of "Life," Carol had to pay $1,500 when she was married. Then, she lost half the money she had left. Next, she paid half the money she had for a house. Then, the game was stopped, and she had $3,000 left. With how much money did she start?

Solution to example: Carol ended up with $3,000. Right before that she paid half her money to buy a house. Because her $3,000 was half of what she had before her purchase, she had 2 × $3,000 = $6,000 before buying the house. Prior to buying the house, Carol lost half her money. This means that the $6,000 is the half she didn't lose. So, before losing half her money, Carol had 2 × $6,000 = $12,000. Prior to losing half her money, Carol had to pay $1,500 to get married. This means she had $12,000 + $1,500 = $13,500 before getting married. Because this was the start of the game, Carol began with $13,500.

Strategy 6. Draw a diagram. Drawing a picture is often an aid to solving problems, especially for visual learners. Although pictures are especially useful for geometrical problems, they can be helpful for other types of problems as well.

Example: There were 20 women at a round table for dinner. Each woman shook hands with the woman to her immediate right and left. At the end of the dinner, each woman got up and shook hands with everybody except those who sat on her immediate right and left. How many handshakes took place after dinner?

Solution to example: To solve this with a diagram, it might be a good idea to examine several simpler cases to see if you can determine a pattern of any kind that might help. Starting with two or three people, you can see there are no handshakes after dinner because everyone is adjacent to everyone else.

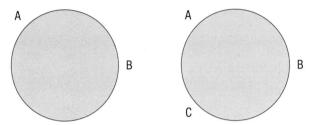

Now, in the case of four people, we get the following diagram, connecting those people who shake hands after dinner:

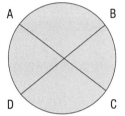

In this situation, you see there are two handshakes after dinner, AC and BD. In the case of five people, you get this picture:

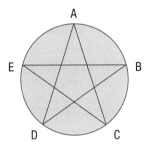

In this case, you have five after-dinner handshakes: AC, AD, BD, BE, and CE. Six people seated around a circle gives the following diagram:

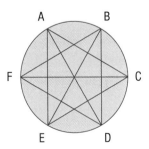

In this diagram, there are now a total of nine after-dinner handshakes: AC, AD, AE, BD, BE, BF, CE, CF, and DF. By studying the diagrams, you realize that if there are N people, each person would shake N − 3 people's hands after dinner. (They don't shake their own hands or the hands of the two people adjacent to them.) Because there are N people that would lead to N(N − 3) after-dinner handshakes. However, this would double-count every handshake, because AD would also be counted as DA. Therefore, there are only half as many actual handshakes. So, the correct number of handshakes is [N(N − 3)]÷2. So finally, if there are 20 women, there would be 20(17)÷2 = 170 after-dinner handshakes.

Strategy 7. Translate words into an equation. This strategy is often used in algebra.

Example: A farmer needs to fence a rectangular piece of land. He wants the length of the field to be 80 feet longer than the width. If he has 1,080 feet of fencing available, what should the length and width of the field be?

Solution to example: The best way to start this problem is to draw a picture of the situation and label the sides.

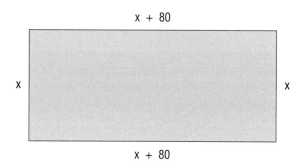

Let x represent the width of the field and x + 80 represent the length of the field. The farmer has 1,080 feet of fencing and he will need 2x + 2(x + 80) feet of fencing to fence his field. This gives you the equation: 2x + 2(x + 80) = 1080.

Multiplying out: 2x + 2x + 160 = 1080

Simplifying and subtracting 160:   4x = 920

Dividing by 4:   x = 230

Therefore,   x + 80 = 310

As a check, you find that   2(230) + 2(310) = 1080

TACKLE A WORD PROBLEM

Read this word problem:

When using a stair climber, Eric burns 9.6 calories per minute. When he walks on the treadmill, he burns 5.3 calories per minute. If Eric has 50 minutes to exercise and wants to burn 350 calories, how many minutes should he spend on each machine?

Work through the problem here, and use additional pages if you need to. Indicate the equation you came up with. Finally, name the strategy or strategies that you used.

_____

_____

_____

_____

_____

_____

_____

_____

_____

_____

_____

[The answer can be found on page 356.]

Adapted from The Math Forum @ Drexel, an online community for mathematics education (http://mathforum.org/).

These sample problems are designed to boost your ability to think critically through some basic math strategies. If these or other quantitative problems make you feel anxious, however, you may benefit from some information about math anxiety.

HOW CAN YOU OVERCOME MATH ANXIETY?

Math anxiety refers to any kind of uncomfortable, high-stress feeling that appears in relation to quantitative thinking. It occurs most commonly right before or during an exam. A student getting ready to take a test, or reading a particular problem on a test, experiences rising anxiety or even what can be described as "blanking out." Math anxiety also plagues people in class or lab sessions, if they have to work through a problem in front of others or with others, or even when doing math and science homework outside of the classroom.

Understand Myths and Facts About Math

Math anxiety stems in large part from misconceptions about math. Such assumptions are untrue as well as damaging to the thought processes of students who might otherwise succeed in math and science courses. Here are some common beliefs:

Myth: *People are born with or without an ability to think quantitatively; in other words, you either have it or you don't.*

Fact: *Quantitative thinking skills can be improved.*
Everyone is born with a unique set of natural talents; some people will naturally have more aptitude or interest in math and science than others. However, anyone can take their own aptitude and improve on it. As with critical thinking or other intellectual skills, quantitative thinking skills can be increased with hard work and practice. Working with numbers in a personal area of interest may also build aptitude; for example, students pursuing degrees in medicine or computers may find that they are more motivated in quantitative courses that relate to their career pursuits.

Myth: *Everyone is either a words person or a numbers person; you can't excel in both areas.*

Fact: *People can and do excel in both quantitative and verbal areas of study.* As mathematician and math anxiety expert Sheila Tobias reports, "No evidence exists, whatsoever, that writing ability and mathematics ability are mutually exclusive. In fact, people who show high capability on both the mathematical and verbal sections of the SAT are more likely to succeed in math than those who have a severely skewed score, strong only in quantitative skills."[4]

Myth: *Women aren't as capable as men of succeeding in math and science.*

Fact: *Gender does not determine quantitative aptitude.*
The ability to succeed in math and science does not rely on gender. "Scientists are made, not born," say economist W. Michael Cox and economics writer Richard Alm. "Scientific knowledge requires years of education at the college

level and beyond . . . what matters are the choices and opportunities open to young women at our universities."[5] In the past 30 years, such opportunities have grown, and women have increasingly taken advantage of them. For example, in 1971, only 0.8 percent of undergraduate women earned a bachelor's degree in engineering; in 2001, women made up 18.9 percent of those graduating with a bachelor's in engineering. In 1971, 16.5 percent of the recipients of doctoral degrees in the health sciences were women; by 2001–2002, the percentage jumped to 63.3 percent.[6]

Key 9.2 details how many women are now receiving degrees in math and science.

The stereotype that women do poorly in math, even if it is false, can cause damage. Women who believe in the stereotype may create a self-fulfilling prophecy that harms their ability to perform successfully in math and science courses. All students should combat this stereotype by taking an honest look at their relationship to math and science independent of gender.

One final assumption that many make about math is that it is boring or scary. Some of this attitude stems from the way in which math and science are taught, especially in the younger years. Sheila Tobias points out that, first of all, math skills have to be practiced extensively in the grade school years so that students can develop the level of proficiency needed to be more creative about math. Such practice, usually involving problems for which there is one right answer, most often leave no room for subjective debate such as one might find in an English or history class. This can frustrate students. In addition, teachers have to present a series of math rules to students and rarely offer opportunities to question such rules and formulas; some students react to this by turning off.[7]

Key 9.2   Women are taking advantage of math and science opportunities in college.

Of graduates receiving degrees in math and science, academic year 2001–2002, percentages who are women.

	BACHELOR'S	MASTER'S	DOCTORATES
Health Sciences	85.5%	77.5%	63.3%
Biological Sciences	60.8%	57.8%	44.3%
Mathematics	46.7%	42.4%	29.0%
Computer Science	27.6%	33.2%	22.8%
Engineering	18.9%	21.4%	17.3%

Source: Adapted from "Scientists Are Made, Not Born," W. Michael Cox and Richard Alm, *New York Times,* February 28, 2005, p. A19.

Finally, the fear that people feel can be real. "Few people can think clearly and well with a clock ticking away," says Tobias. "It is hard to perform at the blackboard with thirty sets of eyes watching you. No one likes a subject that is presented rigidly and uncompromisingly. And most people do not do well when they are scared. Some years ago, my colleagues and I came to suspect that math inability may not be the result of a failure of intellect but rather of nerve."[8]

Negative feelings stemming from any of these assumptions become "static," as Tobias calls it, interfering with the brain's ability to work. Emotional static can clog the mental pathways that a person uses to reason through a problem and come to a conclusion. Even though the static is often the primary issue, many people interpret their difficulties to a lack of brain power instead. As a result, confidence dwindles and students stop trying.[9] Many students carry negative feelings about math and science from experiences back in high school or even earlier.

Think about your attitude toward quantitative learning. If it has been affected by these false assumptions, or any other negative ideas, you may experience some level of math anxiety. Read on to discover what you can do about it.

Use Strategies to Combat Math Anxiety

Strategies that help include building self-knowledge, practice, using your resources, taking responsibility for your quantitative learning, understanding your rights as a quantitative learner, and taking your time.

Know yourself as a quantitative learner. Self-knowledge is essential to working through math anxiety. Which subjects make sense to you—and which give you trouble? Which strategies help you—and which don't help you? Which processes can you do more easily—and which require increased focus? What events, courses, instructors, or other people have influenced what you think of your math and science abilities, and how? You may want to put your thoughts in writing. The more you know about yourself as a quantitative learner, the more you will be able to identify—and deactivate—your emotional static. Your goal is to remove static from your creative and analytical brain pathways, giving your brain a chance to do good work.

Practice. The best way to overcome test-time anxiety and increase your confidence is to practice quantitative thinking. Keeping up with your homework, attending class, preparing well for tests, and doing extra problems alone and with others will help you feel confident because they increase your familiarity with the material. Key 9.3 shows additional ways to reduce math anxiety.

Key 9.3   Ten ways to reduce math anxiety.

1. Overcome your negative self-image about math.

2. Ask questions of your teachers and your friends, and seek outside assistance.

3. Math is a foreign language—practice it often.

4. Don't study mathematics by trying to memorize information and formulas.

5. READ your math textbook.

6. Study math according to your personal learning style.

7. Get help the same day you don't understand something.

8. Be relaxed and comfortable while studying math.

9. "TALK" mathematics. Discuss it with people in your class. Form a study group.

10. Develop a sense of responsibility for your own successes and failures.

Source: Ellen Freedman (March 1997). *Ten Ways to Reduce Math Anxiety* [online]. Available http://fc.whyy.org/ccc/alg1/reduce.htm (March 1998).

Use resources. Most schools have math or science learning labs, tutors, or computer programs that can help you practice difficult quantitative processes. Visit your instructor during office hours or ask a lab assistant or TA questions. Sometimes you will have an extra review session set up by an instructor or TA so that students can ask questions before a major test. You can even find help online; for example, you can submit a question to "Dr. Math" through the question-and-answer service on the website www.mathforum.org. Don't hesitate to make the most of any and all helpful resources available to you.

Take responsibility. Even though math anxiety is a real problem, students must take some responsibility for their responses to quantitative thinking. You can't change the math experiences you have had in the past, but you can make choices about how to respond to quantitative material from here on out. The following responsibilities are worded as intention statements; use them for focus and motivation.[10]

- I will attend all classes and do my homework.
- I will seek extra help when necessary, from an instructor, a tutor, or a fellow student.
- I will speak up in class when I have questions.

ASSESS YOUR LEVEL OF MATH ANXIETY

Answer the following statements by marking a number from 1 (Disagree) to 5 (Agree).

_____ 1. I don't like math classes, and haven't since high school.

_____ 2. I do okay at the beginning of a math class, but I always feel it will get to the point where it is impossible to understand.

_____ 3. I can't seem to concentrate in math classes. I try, but I get nervous and distracted and think about other things.

_____ 4. I don't like asking questions in math class. I'm afraid that the teachers or the other students will think I'm stupid.

_____ 5. I stress out when I'm called on in math class. I seem to forget even the easiest answers.

_____ 6. Math exams scare me far more than any of my other exams.

_____ 7. I can't wait to finish my math requirement so that I'll never have to do any math again.

SCORING KEY

28–35: You suffer from full-blown math anxiety.

21–27: You are coping, but you're not happy about mathematics.

14–20: You're doing okay.

7–13: So what's the big deal about math? You have very little problem with anxiety.

Now, combine the results of this assessment with what you know about yourself as a quantitative learner. On a separate sheet of paper, create a portrait of yourself as a quantitative learner in a journal entry. Include thoughts about your attitude toward math and science, your level of success in those areas through your educational career, events and people that have influenced you, how math and science might be (or are) part of your working life, and how you want to approach math and science in the future.

Source for assessment: Ellen Freedman (March 1997). *Test Your Math Anxiety* (online). Available: http://fc.whyy.org/CCC/alg1anxtest.htm (May 2005). Used with permission.

- I will be realistic about my abilities and will work to improve them.
- I will approach quantitative thinking with an open mind, not assuming the worst.

Know your rights. Along with being a responsible student, you also have rights regarding your mathematical learning. These include:[11]

- the right to learn at your own pace
- the right to ask questions
- the right not to understand
- the right to be treated as a competent person
- the right to believe you are capable of thinking quantitatively

Be persistent and take your time. Do not expect that you will be able to solve every problem in the wink of an eye. Speed does not necessarily translate into success when it comes to working with numbers. In fact, says Tobias, successful quantitative learners "never quit because they recognized long ago that progress in mathematics very often involves making just a little headway, one step at a time. They do not judge themselves as harshly as we judge ourselves when answers do not come out right. They are patient, tenacious, and rarely very fast."[12]

Beyond working to control your math anxiety, several other techniques will help you do your very best when you are tested on your math skills.

Reduce Math Anxiety at Test Time

In addition to the general strategies for test taking that you will explore in Chapters 10 and 11, here are several additional actions that can help you achieve better results on math and science exams.

- **Put key information in front of you.** Before you open the exam, write down any formulas or theorums that you just studied and don't want to forget (writing down formulas after a test is given out is *not* cheating). Use the back of the test if you don't have scrap paper.
- **Read through the exam first.** When you first get an exam, read through every problem quickly. Make notes on how you might attempt to solve the problem, if something occurs to you immediately.
- **Analyze problems carefully.** Categorize problems according to type. Take all the "givens" into account, and write down any formulas, *theorems* (mathematical statements proposed or accepted as demonstrable truth), or definitions that apply before you begin your calculations. Focus on what you want to find or prove, and take your time—precision demands concentration. If some problems seem easier than others, do them first in order to boost your confidence.

- **Estimate before you begin to come up with an approximate solution.** To *estimate* means to make a rough or preliminary calculation. After you estimate, work the problem and check the solution against your guess. The two answers should be close. If they're not, recheck your calculations. You may have made a simple calculation error.

- **Break the calculation into the smallest possible pieces.** Go step by step and don't move on to the next step until you are clear about what you've done so far. Focus only on the information you need to solve the problem.

- **Recall how you solved similar problems.** Past experience can give you valuable clues to how a particular problem should be handled.

- **Draw a picture to help you see the problem.** This can be a diagram, a chart, a probability tree, a geometric figure, or any other visual image that relates to the problem at hand.

- **Be neat.** When it comes to numbers, mistaken identity can mean the difference between a right and a wrong answer. A 4 that looks like a 9, for example, can mean trouble.

- **Use the opposite operation to check your work.** When you come up with an answer, work backward to see if you are right. Use subtraction to check your addition; use division to check multiplication; and so on.

- **Look back at the questions to be sure you did everything that was asked.** Did you answer every part of the question? Did you show all the required work? Be as complete as you possibly can. If you have time, rework problems on a scrap piece of paper and see if you arrive at the same answers.

Work Together BUILDING YOUR SKILLS

ACTIVE THINKING

SKILL   WILL   SELF-MGMT.

TAKE A STUDY GROUP APPROACH TO QUANTITATIVE LEARNING

Choose one or two people from one of your math or science classes—fellow students with whom you feel comfortable working. Use problems from your assigned text.

1. Choose one problem. Each of you work on the same problem separately. After finishing the problem, come together to share your methods. Discuss how each of you approached the problem. What steps did you each take in solving the problem? What strategies did you use? How did you check to see if your procedures were correct?

2. Now pick a different problem on which to work together. After solving it, discuss your problem-solving process. Did you learn more or less by working together as compared to working separately? Were you able to solve the problem faster by working together than when you worked alone? Did you gain a better understanding of the problem by working together?

MULTIPLE INTELLIGENCE STRATEGIES FOR WORKING WITH NUMBERS. When math and science get tough, look to your strongest multiple intelligences to figure out ways to cope.

INTELLIGENCE	SUGGESTED STRATEGIES	WHAT WORKS FOR YOU? WRITE NEW IDEAS HERE
Verbal-Linguistic	▪ Whenever possible, write out word problem versions of numerical problems and formulas. ▪ When you have word problems, convert them into numbers to help solidify the relationship between words and the numbers they signify.	
Logical-Mathematical	▪ Practice using math games and puzzles. ▪ Focus on process. Make sure you understand any formula you use; then, carefully work through each step of the problem-solving process.	
Bodily-Kinesthetic	▪ Find physical representations of problems. Use pennies; cut up an apple; measure lengths; drive distances. ▪ For hands-on experience, look for science classes with a strong laboratory component. ▪ When several instructors teach sections of the course, find out who is best at concrete examples.	
Visual-Spatial	▪ Draw visual representations of problems—geometrical shapes, grids, charts, matrices—and use plenty of space. ▪ Circle important items in the description of the problem. ▪ Write out formulas when working word problems.	
Interpersonal	▪ Go over homework problems with a study group each week. Pass around your solutions and discuss them. ▪ Take advantage of your instructor's office hours. Schedule a time to talk about concepts that are giving you trouble.	
Intrapersonal	▪ Find a solitary spot to do your reading or homework. ▪ Take quiet breaks when you hit a roadblock. Take a walk or a nap; see if this helps you think of a new approach.	
Musical	▪ Listen to, and study, music whenever possible. The rhythms and notes of music are based in mathematics; musical experience can enhance quantitative abilities.	
Naturalistic	▪ When you need science credits, look for courses in biological sciences and/or botany. ▪ Find patterns and categorize the information whenever possible.	

WHY SHOULD MATH AND SCIENCE LEARNING BE AN IMPORTANT PART OF YOUR FUTURE?

In a workplace increasingly dominated by statistics and information technology, people in nearly every profession need some level of skill in math and science. "Mathematics is no longer just an entry-level prerequisite for engineering, the physical sciences, and statistics," says Sheila Tobias. "Its principles and techniques, along with computers, have become part of almost all areas of work, and its logic is used in thinking about almost everything."[13]

The Mathematical Association of America has defined the level of *quantitative literacy* that every college graduate should have in order to succeed on the job (see Key 9.4). With competence in these areas, you will be able to tackle quantitative challenges at work and in your personal life.

Following are some specifics about the role of math and science in workplace success.

Certain careers require study in specific math and science disciplines. Careers such as actuarial or genetic science demand a strong background in probability and statistics, and some areas of business, economics, and engineering require strong skills as well. Medical careers require study in biology,

---

Key 9.4   **Know and build the skills that constitute quantitative literacy.**

"A quantitatively literate college graduate should be able to:

- Interpret mathematical models such as formulas, graphs, tables, and schematics, and draw inferences from them.

- Represent mathematical information symbolically, visually, numerically, and verbally. Use arithmetical, algebraic, geometric, and statistical methods to solve problems.

- Estimate and check answers to mathematical problems in order to determine reasonableness, identify alternatives, and select optimal results.

- Recognize that mathematical and statistical methods have limits.

In addition, college students should be expected to go beyond routine problem solving to handle problem situations of greater complexity and diversity, and to connect ideas and procedures more readily with other topics both within and outside mathematics."

Source: http://academic.bowdoin.edu/qskills/

Math and science open the door to a multitude of career opportunities. While attending a conference on alternative medicine, this group visits the New York Botanical Garden.

chemistry, anatomy, and other sciences. Calculus and differential equations are needed for most engineering fields, business and economics, physics, and astronomy. "One of the chief problems for students who opt out of mathematics too early is that they foreclose certain careers," says Evelyn Hu-DeHart of the University of Colorado at Boulder. "If a student doesn't continue in mathematics through calculus or precalculus while still in high school—perhaps for lack of early interest in pursuing a career in science or engineering—that student will need to do a lot of catching up if he or she discovers later on that indeed, science and engineering are interesting after all."[14]

Modern businesses demand quantitatively literate workers. To succeed in business, prospective employees need to be competent in two areas: use of numbers and problem solving.

- **Numbers.** People who work in any business, large or small, perform mathematical functions to budget income and expenses. For example, a corporate lawyer in charge of a five-person staff must submit a yearly budget that includes salaries, benefits, building overhead, and other expenses. "Business wants new employees from the educational system who can do mathematics accurately, within benchmark time periods, and frequently with the use of a calculator," says C. J. Shroll of the National Coalition for Advanced Manufacturing.[15]

- **Problem solving.** In business, the ability to set up and analyze a problem is even more important than performing the calculations that emerge from that analysis. Shroll says, "In the world of work [problem solving] means dealing with real, unpredictable, and unorganized situations where the first task is to organize the information and only then calculate to find an answer . . . organizing the information is the most important aspect."[16]

Quantitatively based visuals play a crucial role in the workplace. Due to the increased need for communication across language and cultural lines, visuals are becoming more and more important. "Charts, graphs, diagrams, etc., are the evolving language of business, made necessary because of the significant problems associated with communication based only on words, written or oral," reports Shroll. "The ideal situation is when someone has the ability to communicate in many different ways including charts, graphs, words, symbols, and more. Employees are most likely to understand a complex idea when it is presented in different ways. This is true for all people—in life as well as in work. Employers are often frustrated that many people coming to them have only learned to communicate with words."[17]

Even artists need math. If you are pursuing a degree in fine or performing arts and are fond of presenting yourself as someone who has no need to work with numbers, think again. "Quantitative literacy sneaks into many aspects of the arts and is a key to realizing expression of what is in the mind's eye," says Pamela Paulson of the Minnesota Center for Arts Education. "Measurement comes into play in every art form. Fractions are important in technical theater, music, visual arts, and dance. New computer programs have encouraged many new ways to connect the arts and mathematics. Any time you are mounting an arts production you are involved in basic mathematical computations for ordering materials and supplies, dealing with budgets, sewing costumes, angles for sets and lighting, etc. Artists definitely need basic mathematical literacy."[18]

Most important is the way math and science learning build critical thinking power, which is crucial to success in any job or career area. As Tobias states, "Just as college students' ability to think more complex thoughts is enhanced every time they learn a new word or phrase, so their ability to understand abstract concepts will be enriched when they master such mathematical constructs as 'limits,' 'nonlinear,' and 'exponential growth.'"[19]

"I advise my students to listen carefully the moment they decide to take no more mathematics courses. They might be able to hear the sound of closing doors."

JAMES CABALLERO
mathematician

Building Skill, Will, and Self-Management

Monitoring Your Progress

Test Competence: Measure What You've Learned

MULTIPLE CHOICE. *Circle or highlight the answer that seems to fit best.*

1. When studying a math or science textbook, note formulas and
   A. speed-read the text.
   B. prioritize summaries.
   C. scan for highlights.
   D. work through problems.

2. The first step in solving word problems is to
   A. carry out a plan.
   B. name and explore potential solution paths.
   C. understand the individual elements of the problem.
   D. review your results.

3. Typical problem-solving strategies include all of the following *except*:
   A. making a table.
   B. knowing you have the right to ask for help.
   C. looking for a pattern.
   D. examining a similar problem.

4. Drawing a diagram as a strategy for mathematical problem solving can be especially helpful to
   A. interpersonal learners.
   B. intrapersonal learners.
   C. musical–rhythmic learners.
   D. visual learners.

5. Myths and misconceptions about math include all of the following *except:*

   A. People are good at either words or numbers but not both.

   B. Math and science skills can be improved with practice.

   C. People are born with—or without—math skills.

   D. Women are less proficient at math and science than men are.

6. Attending classes, doing homework, seeking help, and approaching math with an open mind are part of

   A. taking responsibility for how you respond to math and science learning.

   B. the rights of a math learner.

   C. a typical math class syllabus.

   D. problem solving.

7. To make a rough or preliminary calculation when working a problem is called

   A. quantitative learning.

   B. a formula.

   C. rechecking.

   D. estimating.

8. Math test strategies include all of the following *except:*

   A. doing the easiest problems first.

   B. careful analysis of problems.

   C. drawing a magic square.

   D. noting key formulas and information on scrap paper.

9. A quantitatively literate college graduate should be able to do all of the following *except:*

   A. put mathematical information into visual, numerical, verbal, or symbolic format.

   B. interpret graphs and tables.

   C. estimate and check answers to problems.

   D. perform statistical and trigonometric calculations.

10. The most wide-ranging and important workplace skill that math and science learning builds is the ability to

    A. estimate a budget.

    B. work through and solve a problem.

    C. make mathematical calculations.

    D. create graphs.

TRUE/FALSE. *Place a T or an F beside each statement to indicate whether you think it is true or false.*

_____ 1. Probability refers to the study of the chance that a given event will occur.

_____ 2. When approaching a word problem, you should avoid thinking about similar problems you have encountered in the past.

_____ 3. By helping to organize and summarize problem information, tables help you see how examples form a pattern, and this may lead you to the solution.

_____ 4. Difficulty with math can be attributed to "emotional static" that clouds your ability to think through a problem.

_____ 5. When you finish all the problems on a math test, resist the temptation to check your answers because you may introduce new errors.

Target and Achieve a Goal

Commit to one specific quantitative learning strategy from this chapter to improve your study skills.

Name the strategy here: _____

_____

Describe your goal—what you want to gain by using this strategy.

_____

Describe how you plan to use this strategy through the semester to achieve this goal.

_____

_____

_____

Building Your Skills

Brain Power: Build Vocabulary Fitness

Here is a selection from the current media. Read the material, paying special attention to the context of the vocabulary words shown in bold type. Then choose the correct definition for each word in the table that follows. Use a dictionary to check your answers. Finally, on a separate sheet, use each vocabulary word in a sentence of your own to solidify your understanding.

In this excerpt from Newsweek, *George F. Will describes and supports his view that the nation's courts, with the involvement of public interest groups, are often going beyond their level of expertise in how they determine a law should be interpreted.*

In 2003 two professors at the New York Law School, Ross Sandler and David Schoenbrod, published "Democracy by Decree: What Happens When Courts Run Government" (Yale), perhaps one of this decade's most important books on governance. They explain how federal standards are attached to federal money by Congress's heroically **transmuting aspirations** into rights—enforceable claims. Congress has become a **bestower** of mass-produced rights—to "healthy" air, to "appropriate" education for the handicapped, etc.

These are what Sandler and Schoenbrod call "soft rights": "Traditional common law rights, such as the right against trespass, are typically negative. They tell government what it cannot do. Soft rights, such as the right to healthy air, are typically positive. They tell government what it must do." In practice, judges—unelected, unaccountable and inexpert—often **dictate** what it must do.

Some political activists have decided that the **dismantling** of segregation proved that the primary means of social improvement should be through judicially enforceable rights. And many liberals, frustrated by the public's increasing conservatism, are unwilling to have the patience required by democracy—the politics of persuasion. They know that rights claims can **truncate** debate and **trump** policy considerations about the community's conflicting **imperatives** and priorities. . . . All of which confirms Sandler and Schoenbrod's central point: Not all that lawyers do in their various venues amounts to the rule of law, as a democracy ought to understand that.

Source: George F. Will, "Judges and 'Soft Rights.'" *Newsweek,* 28 February 2005: 70. Reprinted with permission.

Circle the word or phrase that best defines each term as it is used in the excerpt.

VOCABULARY WORDS	A	B	C
1. transmuting (verb)	moving	changing	upgrading
2. aspirations (n. pl.)	procedures	desires	breaths
3. bestower (noun)	complimenter	seller	giver
4. dictate (verb)	prescribe	read aloud	establish
5. dismantling (noun)	separating	putting together	taking apart
6. truncate (verb)	shape	shorten	extend
7. trump (verb)	erase	support	get the better of
8. imperatives (n. pl.)	duties	issues	rules

Get to the Root

Every time you learn a Greek or Latin root, you increase your ability to recognize English vocabulary words that include that root and to figure out their meaning. Grow your vocabulary by studying this root and its related words, writing in two more words from the same root, and including definitions for both new words.

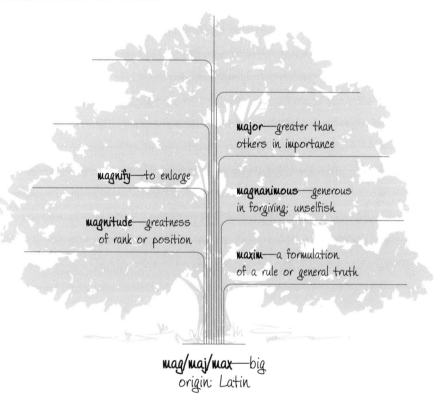

major—greater than others in importance

magnify—to enlarge

magnanimous—generous in forgiving; unselfish

magnitude—greatness of rank or position

maxim—a formulation of a rule or general truth

mag/maj/max—big
origin: Latin

Investigate Using Research Navigator

Do some research on a math- and/or science-related profession that interests you. First, access Research Navigator using the Internet address shown on page 32. Then sign on to the service using your Login Name and Password. Scroll through the subjects for New York Times Online. Choose subjects linked to this profession, and then enter keywords that are likely to call up articles with current information about it. Read at least two articles and take notes. Look for information such as the following:

- math/science education requirements for this profession
- what kinds of math or science someone in this profession might use on the job
- estimated salary and growth prospects for this career area
- technology knowledge required for this profession

Building Will and Self-Awareness

Make Responsible Choices

Answer the following question on a separate piece of paper or in a journal.

Consider your relationship to numbers and to math and science learning by responding to the following questions:

- What is your big-picture attitude toward math and science? In other words, if someone were to ask you if you were "into" math or the sciences, how would you answer?
- What is your reaction when you are unable to solve a quantitative problem? How do you feel when you make an error on a problem?
- How do you react when you solve a difficult problem successfully? What do you enjoy about working with numbers?
- Imagine that you are strongly interested in a profession that requires significant math and science competence—competence that you don't currently have. Using an example of a particular profession that holds some level of interest for you, describe what course of action you would choose. Would you find a way to develop the level of competence required? How? Would you abandon this profession for one less math-and-science oriented? What might be the pros and cons of your decision?

Chapter Summary

As you use the summary on the following pages to review the concepts you learned in this chapter, focus also on its format—in this case the **Cornell**

Chapter 9: Quantitative Learning

Numbers and math are part of every day functioning.

— Broad areas of quantitative skills:

How are math
and science part
of your life?

→ Arithmetic   → Probability and statistics

→ Algebra   → Sciences

→ Geometry

☆ Key skill useful
across the board:
PROBLEM
SOLVING

Math & science build problem-solving ability—useful in any subject and
in life

Math and science are interrelated

How can you master
math and science
basics?

Basic math and science strategies

— In the classroom: Be prepared, be in class, participate,
review right after class

Be highly involved
☆ and active student

— With your textbook: Interact with the material through
writing, pay attention to formulas, focus on memory skills

— Studying and homework: Review ASAP, do lots of problems,
work with others, consider learning styles, be precise

Word problems—
approach similar
to critical thinking
problem-solving plan

Word problems—Use Polya's 4-step method

① Understand elements of the problem

② Name and explore potential solution paths

③ Choose a solution and solve the problem

④ Review your result

Helpful word problem strategies:

— Look for a pattern   — Work backward

— Make a table   — Draw a diagram

— Identify a subgoal   — Translate into an equation

— Examine a similar problem

Math and science are part of everyone's life and build problem-solving skill which is useful in
any course, work, or life situation. Being successful as a quantitative learner demands involvement, responsibility, and hard work. Word problems are a big part of math courses and you
can tackle them using specific strategies.

How can you overcome math anxiety?	Math anxiety—high stress feeling that occurs when having to think quantitatively
	—"blanking out" and other physical reactions
	—can't perform in class
	—sources: misconceptions about math. Here are some key facts:

Bust the myths!
⭐ You <u>can</u> improve math skills.
⭐ You <u>can</u> be good at math if you are a words person.
⭐ Women <u>can</u> excel in math and science.

→ Quantitative thinking skills <u>can</u> be improved
   (Myth: you're born with it or you're not)
→ People can be verbal and also do well in math
   (Myth: You're either a numbers or words person)
→ Gender does not determine quantitative aptitude
   (Myth: men are better at math than women)

"Emotional static" comes from feeling that numbers are boring or scary & interferes with brain's ability to work

Fight math anxiety by:
— Knowing yourself as a quantitative learner
— Use resources
— Take responsibility
— Practice
— Persist and take your time

At test time:
— Put key info in front of you
— Read through exam first
— Recall similar problems
— Analyze problems
— Draw pictures
— Estimate
— Be neat
— Break calculations into pieces
— Look back at your work

Why should math and science learning be an important part of your future?

Math & science key for <u>everyone's</u> future
— Workplace dominated by information technology, statistics
— Math logic is used in thinking through any problem
— Workers need basic "quantitative literacy" (interpret numbers, represent numbers, estimate)
— Certain careers demand math & science
— Math-based visuals play work roles

The stress and physical reactions caused by math anxiety can be fought by dispelling myths and using focused strategies. The goal is to free the brain from "emotional static" so it can work. With basic quantitative literacy, numbers can help propel you to success in coursework and the workplace. Above all, numbers build your ability to solve problems.

system, in other chapters a formal outline, and in still others a think link. As you become comfortable with the organization and style of these various formats, try using each of them to take class and reading notes, noting which approach works best for you in particular situations.

> Here is the solution to the word problem on page 336:
>
> 20 minutes on the stair climber and 30 minutes on the treadmill.

Endnotes

1. *Keys to Lifelong Learning Telecourse.* Dir. Mary Jane Bradbury. Videocassette. Intrepid Films, 2000.

2. George Polya, *How to Solve It.* London: Penguin, 1990.

3. Rick Billstein, Shlomo Libeskind, and Johnny W. Lott, *A Problem Solving Approach to Mathematics for Elementary School Teachers.* Example 1–1 (p. 5); problem 2 (pp. 21–22); problem 3 (pp. 22–24); problem 4 (pp. 26–27); and problem set 1–2, #21 (p. 35). Copyright © 1993 by Addison-Wesley Publishing Company, Inc. Reprinted by permission of Pearson Education, Inc.

4. Sheila Tobias, "Math Anxiety: Author's Update," Spring 1990 [online]. Available: www.mathanxiety.net (May 2005).

5. Richard Alm and W. Michael Cox, "Scientists Are Made, Not Born," *New York Times,* February 28, 2005, p. A19.

6. Ibid.

7. Sheila Tobias, "Math Anxiety."

8. Ibid.

9. Ibid.

10. Adapted from Kathy Acker (March 1997). Math Anxiety Code of Responsibilities [online]. Available: http://fc.whyy.org/CCC/alg1/code.htm (March 1998).

11. Sheila Tobias, *Overcoming Math Anxiety.* New York: W. W. Norton & Company, 1993, pp. 226–227.

12. Sheila Tobias, "Math Anxiety."

13. Ibid.

14. College Board Online, "Interviews About Quantitative Literacy," June 22, 1999 [online]. Available: http://www.stolaf.edu/other/ql/intv.html (March 2005).

15. Ibid.

16. Ibid.

17. Ibid.

18. Ibid.

19. Sheila Tobias.

Active Thinking

Build Active Thinking: Make Connections

The following multiple-choice, true/false, fill-in-the-blank, matching, and essay questions reinforce the concepts you learned in the three chapters that make up Part III, *Notes, Writing, and Math: Building Active Study Skills.* These questions differ from the end-of-chapter objective quizzes in an important way: Instead of focusing on concepts in individual chapters, they encourage you to compare and integrate material from *different* chapters as you find ways to connect ideas. Recognizing relationships among ideas is essential to active learning because it builds critical thinking skills, adds meaning to information, and makes it more likely that you will retain what you learn.

MULTIPLE CHOICE. *Circle or highlight the answer that seems to fit best.*

1. Skills employed by effective note takers include all of the following *except:*
   A. arriving on time and with the necessary supplies ready.
   B. using the same note-taking system in every situation.
   C. reviewing notes as soon as possible after a lecture.
   D. taking notes on relevant comments made during discussions.

2. Of these aspects of the planning process for writing, which involves the least amount of critical thinking?
   A. Researching.
   B. Asking journalists' questions.
   C. Freewriting.
   D. Writing a thesis statement.

3. Careful reading is essential to solving word problems because

    A. word problems make up over half of the math problems you will encounter.

    B. you must understand exactly what the question is asking in order to translate it into an equation.

    C. word problems are written out and therefore depend more on reading skills than on math skills.

    D. you must translate numbers back into words when you answer the question.

4. One similarity between writing skills and math and science skills is that

    A. both involve asking and answering questions, the primary aspect of critical thinking.

    B. both require you to solve a problem.

    C. both are equally necessary for post-college success in any job.

    D. both involve an evaluation of perspective and assumption.

5. Effective note-taking skills are

    A. unrelated to the writing process.

    B. important to writing a clear thesis statement and supporting it with examples.

    C. essential when researching for a writing project.

    D. most important during the editing stage.

TRUE/FALSE. *Place a T or an F beside each statement to indicate whether you think it is true or false.*

_____ 1. You cannot develop the ability to work well with numbers—either you have it from birth or you don't.

_____ 2. The main advantage of receiving guided notes from your instructor is that you do not have to take your own class notes.

_____ 3. When you review your notes, you should enhance their effectiveness by adding clarifying information and comparing them to your text material.

_____ 4. You are not likely to use the math and science skills you are learning in college after you graduate.

_____ 5. How you present your ideas in writing may have a major influence on your ability to win and keep a job.

FILL-IN-THE-BLANK.   *Complete the following sentences with the appropriate word(s) or phrase(s) that best reflect what you learned in Part III. Choose from the items that follow each sentence.*

1. Like having a clear purpose for reading, having a clear purpose for writing gives _____ to your work. (understanding, interest, direction)

2. The most important way to prepare for taking notes successfully during a class period is to _____ that day's assigned course materials. (check out, preread, gather)

3. Reviewing class notes in a systematic way will help you _____ the information in your memory. (disregard, find fault with, solidify)

4. A knowledge of _____ and _____ will help you understand and interpret the numerical data you will encounter in work and life. (algebra/geometry, math/science, probability/statistics)

5. Writing without an understanding of your _____ will almost always lead to _____. (topic/writing success, audience/poor communication, research/a disorganized presentation)

6. Two types of notes you will take while doing research in preparation for a paper are _____ notes and _____ notes. (source/content, lecture/guided, outline/Cornell)

7. Part of being a successful word problem solver is to make sure to _____ —the important last step of the word problem–solving process. (name potential solutions, review your result, write an equation)

8. Two useful strategies for combating math anxiety are to know your _____ and to fulfill your _____. (limits/tasks, problems/equations, rights/responsibilities)

9. The act of using someone else's exact words, figures, unique approach, or specific reasoning without giving appropriate credit is known as _____. (cheating, dishonesty, plagiarism)

10. When you correct technical mistakes in spelling, grammar, and punctuation, you are _____ your document. (revising, editing, planning)

MATCHING. *Match each item in the left-hand column to an item in the right-hand column by writing the letter from the right that corresponds best to the number on the left.*

_____	1. emotional static	A. restatement of a quotation in your own words
_____	2. informal outline	B. central message you want to communicate in a written document
_____	3. Cornell note-taking system	C. the mathematics of lines, solids, points, angles, and surfaces
_____	4. think link	D. T-note system
_____	5. quantitative literacy	E. negative feelings that interfere with the brain's ability to work
_____	6. geometry	F. notes that combine information from both class notes and text notes
_____	7. master set	G. mind map
_____	8. thesis statement	H. the ability to understand and use mathematical models and information
_____	9. first draft	I. first, unpolished attempt to put your ideas on paper
_____	10. paraphrase	J. an organizational tool that shows a hierarchy of ideas through a system of consistent indenting and dashes

ESSAY QUESTION.   *Carefully read the following excerpt from* Society: The Basics, *5th ed., by John J. Macionis, a college textbook published by Prentice Hall, and then answer the essay question that follows. This exercise will help you focus on the meaning of the selection, apply your personal knowledge and experiences to the reading, organize your ideas, and communicate your thoughts effectively in writing.*

Before you begin writing your essay, it is a good idea to spend a few minutes planning. Try brainstorming possible approaches, writing a thesis statement, and jotting down your main thoughts in the form of an outline or think link. Because most essay tests are timed, limit the time you take to write your response to no more than one-half hour. This will force you to write quickly and effectively as it prepares you for actual test conditions.

SEEING INDIVIDUALITY IN SOCIAL CONTEXT

Perhaps the most compelling evidence of how social forces affect human behavior comes from the study of suicide. What could be a more personal "choice" than taking one's own life? But Emile Durkheim (1858–1917), a pioneer of sociology, showed that social forces are at work even in an isolated act of self-destruction.

From official records in and around his native France, Durkheim found some categories of people were more likely than others to take their own lives. Specifically, he found that men, Protestants, wealthy people, and the unmarried each had higher suicide rates than women, Catholics and Jews, the poor, and married people. Durkheim explained the differences in terms of social integration. Categories of people with strong social ties had low suicide rates while more individualistic people had high suicide rates.

In the male-dominated societies studied by Durkheim, men certainly had more autonomy than women. But whatever its advantages, autonomy also contributed to social isolation and a higher suicide rate. Likewise, individualistic Protestants were more prone to suicide than traditional Catholics and Jews whose rituals foster stronger social ties. The wealthy had more freedom than the poor but, once again, at the cost of a higher suicide rate. Finally, can you see why single people, compared to married people, were also at greater risk?

A century later, statistical evidence still supports Durkheim's analysis. . . . In 1995, there were 12.9 recorded suicides for every 100,000 white people, almost twice the rate for African Americans (6.7). For both races, suicide is more common among men than among women. White men (21.4) are four times more likely than white women (4.8) to take their own lives. Among African Americans, the rate for men (11.9) is six times that for women (2.0). Following Durkheim's logic, the higher suicide rate among white people and men reflects their greater wealth and freedom. Conversely, the lower rate among women and people of color follows from their limited social choices. Just as in Durkheim's day, we can see social patterns in suicide, the most personal of actions.

Source: Excerpted from John J. Macionis, *Society: The Basics,* 5th ed. Upper Saddle River, NJ: Prentice Hall, 2000, pp. 3–4. Reprinted with permission.

YOUR QUESTION. What you have just read illustrates a sociological perspective—the ability of sociologists to see general patterns in the behavior of particular individuals. Using your personal background as a point of reference, name and discuss two social forces, broad or narrow, that affect the way you and your family live. Then, analyze whether the effect of social forces on your behavior gives you a greater or lesser sense of personal power and control.

Be Accountable for Your Goals from Part III

Look back at the goals you set in the *Target and Achieve a Goal* exercises at the ends of Chapters 7, 8, and 9. In the space provided, write a short journal entry in which you assess your progress (use or continue on a separate piece of paper if you need more room). In your discussion, consider questions such as the following:

- Have you used the strategies you intended to use?
- What effect have these strategies had on your work?
- Have you achieved the goals you set? Why or why not?
- What is your plan going forward for these strategies and goals?

BECOMING A BETTER TEST TAKER AND CREATING YOUR FUTURE

IV

CHOOSING SUCCESS

10

"Whether it's boxing, basketball or badminton, one must be ready to succeed before entering the arena . . . long before the lights come up."

Test Taking

DEVELOPING A WINNING STRATEGY

For a runner, a race is equivalent to a test because it measures ability at a given moment. The best runners—and test takers—understand that they train not just for the race or test, but to achieve a level of competence that they will use elsewhere. When you successfully show what you know on tests, you develop the will and skill to perform well again and again. Exams also help you gauge your progress and, if necessary, improve or adjust your efforts. Most important, the test-preparation, test-taking, and test-evaluation skills you acquire today are tools for success throughout life.

Doing well on tests requires that you make a commitment to studying and to following through. The world of work values people who prepare well and get the job done. So, cultivating these habits as a student will give you a leg up in the workplace, whether you are there now or plan to enter after you graduate.

As you will see in this chapter, test taking is about preparation, persistence, and strategy. It is also about conquering fears, focusing on details, and learning from mistakes.

In this chapter you will explore answers to the following questions:

- How can preparation improve test performance?
- How can you work through test anxiety?
- What general strategies can help you succeed on tests?
- How can you learn from test mistakes?

HOW CAN PREPARATION IMPROVE TEST PERFORMANCE?

You prepare for exams every day of the semester—by attending class; staying on top of assignments; completing readings, papers, and projects; and participating in class discussions. You are actively learning and retaining the knowledge you need to do well on exams. The following additional measures will aid your preparation.

Identify Test Type and Material Covered

Before you begin studying, find out as much as you can about the test, including:

- **Topics that will be covered.** Will it cover everything since the semester began or will it be limited to a narrow topic?

- **Material you will be tested on.** Will the test cover only what you learned in class and in the text, or will it also include outside readings? Will you be given material to work with—for example, will you be asked to analyze a poem?

- **Types of questions.** Objective (multiple choice, true/false, sentence completion), subjective (essay), or a combination?

- **How the test will be graded.** Will partial credit be given for short-answer questions? Do you need to show your thought processes in order to get full credit? What sections of the exam are worth more—the essay or the multiple choice, for example?

- **Importance of the test in your final grade.** Is the test a midterm, a final, or a weekly quiz?

Your instructors may answer many of these questions. They may tell you the question format and the topics that will be on the test. Some instructors may even drop hints about possible questions, either directly ("I might ask a question on this subject on your next exam") or more subtly ("One of my favorite theories is . . . "). Do your best to be in class and alert so that you can benefit from these vital hints when you begin studying.

As you begin thinking about the test, remember that not all tests are created equal—a quiz is not as important as a midterm or a final. Prioritize your study time and energy based on the test's value, keeping in mind that the accumulated grades you get on small quizzes add up and can make a difference in your final grade.

Here are other practical strategies for predicting what may be on a test. As you prepare combine these with the strategies you learned in Chapters 4–7.

Use SQ3R to identify what's important. Often, the questions you write and ask yourself when you read assigned materials may be part of the test. Textbook study questions—or variations of them—are also good candidates.

Listen for clues at review sessions. Many instructors offer review sessions before midterms and finals in order to answer last-minute questions. Make every effort to be there, and keep your ears open for hints about what will be on the exam. Bring your own questions to these sessions and listen to the questions others ask. They may cover material you thought you knew, but actually need to review or learn more about.

Make an appointment to see your instructor. Spending a few minutes talking about the test one-on-one may clarify misunderstandings and help you focus on what to study.

Talk to people who already took the course. Try to get a sense of test difficulty, whether tests focus primarily on assigned readings or class notes, what materials are usually covered, and what types of questions are asked. If you learn that the instructor pays close attention to specific facts, for example, use flash cards to drill yourself on details. If she emphasizes a global overview, focus on concepts.

Examine old tests, if the instructor makes them available. You may find old tests in class, online, or on reserve in the library. (Make sure you have the instructor's permission to consult them.) Old tests will help you answer questions like:

- Do tests focus on examples and details, general ideas and themes, or a combination?
- Are the questions straightforward or confusing and sometimes tricky?
- Will you be asked to integrate facts from different areas in order to draw conclusions?
- Will you be asked to apply principles to new situations and problems?

After taking the first exam in a course, you will have a better idea of what to expect.

Create a Study Schedule and Checklist

Now choose what you will study. Go through your notes, texts, related primary sources, and handouts, and set aside anything you don't need. Then prioritize the remaining materials. Your goal is to focus on information that is most likely to be on the exam.

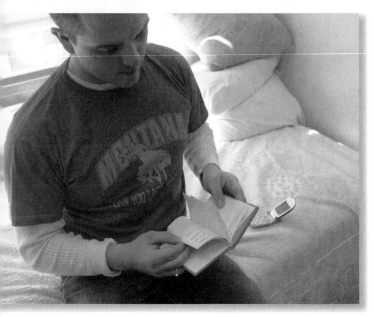

Using time management skills to schedule individual review sessions and study group meetings is part of successful test preparation.

Next, use the time-management and goal-setting skills from Chapter 1 to prepare a schedule. Consider all of the relevant factors—your study materials, the number of days until the test, your ongoing responsibilities, and the time you can study each day. If you establish your schedule ahead of time and write it in a planner, you are more likely to follow it.

Use a checklist to assign specific tasks to particular study times and sessions. That way, not only do you know when you have time to study, but you also have defined goals for each study session.

Try to build flexibility into your schedule. If it takes longer to study than you originally planned, you may have to rearrange your priorities to get everything done.

Studying for final exams is a big commitment that requires careful time management. Your college may schedule study days, sometimes known as "reading period" or "dead days," between the end of classes and the beginning of finals. Lasting from a day or two to several weeks, this period gives you uninterrupted hours to prepare for exams and finish papers. Use checklists to schedule this time wisely so that you accomplish your goals.

Prepare Through Careful Review

A thorough, *active* review is the best way to master material for an exam. As you learned in Chapters 5 and 7, rereading your notes and the text is a passive activity that may fool you into thinking that you know the material when you actually have a limited command. Instead of just rereading, ensure an active preparation with the following strategies:

Use SQ3R. The reading method you studied in Chapter 5 provides an excellent structure for reviewing your reading materials.

- *Surveying* reminds you of the topic overview.
- *Questioning* helps you focus, once again, on important ideas.

ORGANIZE FOR TEST SUCCESS

Complete the following checklist for each exam to define your study goals, get organized, and stay on track:

Course: _____ Instructor: _____

Date, time, and place of test: _____

Type of test (Is it a midterm or a minor quiz?): _____

What instructor said about the test, including types of test questions, test length, and how much the test counts toward your final grade: _____

_____

_____

Topics to be covered on the test, in order of importance:

1. _____

2. _____

3. _____

4. _____

5. _____

Study schedule, including materials you plan to study (texts, class notes, homework problems, and so forth) and dates you plan to complete each:

Material   **Completion Date**

1. _____   _____

2. _____   _____

3. _____   _____

4. _____   _____

5. _____   _____

Materials you are expected to bring to the test (textbook, sourcebook, calculator, etc.):

_____

_____

Special study arrangements (for example: study group meetings, meeting with the instructor, outside tutoring), including scheduled times:

_____

_____

*Life-management issues (such as rearranging work hours):*_____

_____

Make extra copies of the checklist so that they're ready to fill out as soon as an exam is announced.

Source: Adapted from Ron Fry, *"Ace" Any Test,* 3rd ed. Franklin Lakes, NJ: Career Press, 1996, pp. 123–124.

- *Reading* (or, in this case, rereading) reminds you of concepts and supporting information. Pay special attention to the material you have highlighted.
- *Reciting* helps to anchor the concepts in memory.
- *Reviewing,* such as quizzing yourself on the Q-stage questions, summarizing highlighted sections, making key-concept flash cards, and outlining chapters, helps solidify learning.

Actively review your combined class and text notes. As you learned in Chapter 7, one of the best ways to review for an exam is to combine and condense your text and class notes—a process that gets you actively involved with the material. Work with this combined note set to prepare for exams:

- **As exam time nears, go through your key terms and concepts outline and recite everything you know about a topic.** Remember that reading your notes is not enough. Learning will only take place if you express content in your own words and apply it to problems.
- **Use critical thinking to increase active involvement.** As you review, think about examples that illustrate concepts, ideas from outside readings and personal experiences that demonstrate points, and divergent ideas and opinions. Finally, use what you know to solve problems.
- **Continue to actively review until you demonstrate a solid knowledge of every topic.** Use varied techniques that get you involved with the material—take a practice test, have your study

partner question you, answer your SQ3R questions in writing one more time. Don't stop until you are sure of your knowledge and your ability to apply concepts to new material.

Take a Pretest

Use end-of-chapter text questions to create your own pretest. Or tap into any technology that accompanies your text, especially CD-ROMs and text websites that include quizzes. If your course doesn't have an assigned text, develop questions from your notes and assigned outside readings. Old homework problems will also help you target topics. The best questions integrate different topics in ways that make you think. When you are able to answer them correctly, you establish that you understand the material and can apply it in different ways. Take pretests under test-like conditions—in a quiet place, with no books or notes to help you (unless the exam is open book), and with a clock to tell you when time is up.

Go For It!   **BUILDING YOUR SKILLS**

WRITE YOUR OWN PRETEST

Prepare for an upcoming exam using a pretest you create.

Start thinking about an upcoming exam. Use the tips in this chapter to predict the material that will be covered, the types of questions that will be asked (multiple choice, essay, etc.), and the nature of the questions (a broad overview of the material or specific details).

Then be creative. Your goal is to write questions that your instructor is likely to ask—interesting questions that tap what you have learned, make you think about the material in different ways, and apply it to problems. Go through the following steps:

1. Write the questions you come up with on a separate sheet of paper. (You can also work with a study partner and answer each other's questions.)

2. Use what you created as a pretest. Set up test-like conditions—a quiet, timed environment—and see how well you do. Avoid looking at your text or notes unless your instructor gives open-book tests.

3. Evaluate your pretest answers against your notes and the text. How did you do?

_____

_____

(Continued)

4. Finally, after you take your instructor's exam, evaluate whether this exercise improved your performance on the actual exam. Would you use this technique again when you study for another exam? Why or why not?

_____

_____

_____

Prepare Physically

Most tests ask you to work at your best under pressure, so a good night's sleep will leave you rested and alert. It will also improve your ability to remember what you studied the night before. Studies have shown that going to sleep as soon as you finish studying actually aids recall. The best advice is not to study anything else, read the newspaper, watch television, or even talk with friends! Just shut off the lights and go to bed.

Eating a light, well-balanced meal is also important. Avoid high-calorie carbohydrates, such as candy and cakes, and focus on protein instead (eggs, milk and yogurt, meat and fish, nuts, and peanut butter). When time is short, grab a quick-energy snack such as a banana, orange juice, or a high-protein granola bar.

Finally, on exam day, dress comfortably, but avoid pajamas, since they may send the subconscious message that it is time for bed.

Make the Most of Last-Minute Cramming

Cramming—studying intensively and around the clock right before an exam—often results in information going into your head and popping right back out shortly after the exam is over. If learning is your goal, cramming is not a good idea. The reality, however, is that nearly every student crams during college, especially during midterms and finals. Use these hints to make the most of this intensive study time:

- **Focus on crucial concepts.** Summarize the most important points and try to resist reviewing notes or texts page by page.
- **Create a last-minute study sheet.** On a single sheet of paper, write down key facts, definitions, formulas, and so on. If you prefer visual notes, use think links to map out ideas and supporting examples. You can also put these items on flash cards and review them right before the test.
- **Arrive early.** Study your study sheet until you are asked to clear your desk.

A practical warning about cramming: Thousands of well-meaning students who study until four in the morning sleep through the sound of their alarm clocks and miss their exams. To prevent this from happening to you, try this: Set two or three clocks on alarm-wake rather than music-wake, and place them on distant tables. This will force you to get out of bed to stop the noise. Or ask a friend to call you to make sure you are up and running.

After your exam, evaluate how cramming affected your performance. Did it help, or did it load your mind with disconnected details? Did it increase or decrease your anxiety when the test began? Then evaluate how cramming affected your recall. Within a few days, you will probably remember very little—a reality that will work against you in advanced courses that build on this knowledge and in careers that require it. Think ahead about how you can start studying earlier to prepare for your next exam.

Whether you cram or not, you may experience anxiety on test day. Following are some ideas for handling test anxiety when it strikes.

HOW CAN YOU WORK THROUGH TEST ANXIETY?

A certain amount of stress can be a good thing. Your body is alert, and your energy motivates you to do your best. Some students, however, experience incapacitating stress before and during exams, especially midterms and finals.

Test anxiety can cause sweating, nausea, dizziness, headaches, and fatigue. It can reduce your ability to concentrate, make you feel overwhelmed, and cause you to "blank out." As a result, test anxiety often results in lower grades that may not reflect what you really know. To minimize anxiety, prepare thoroughly and build a positive attitude.

As you read this section, remember that it is perfectly normal to be nervous for a test, especially the first one of the semester, because you do not know what to expect. Reminding yourself that most students are feeling similar anxiety may help you relax.

Preparation

The more you know, the better you will perform on test day. In this sense, consider all the preparation and study information in *Keys to College Studying* as test-anxiety assistance. Two points in particular will help you combat anxiety:

- Finding out what to expect on the exam will add to your sense of control. Seek out information about the material that will be covered, the question format, the length of the exam, and the points assigned to each question.

- Creating and following a detailed study plan build knowledge and a sense of mastery. Divide the plan into small tasks. As you finish each, you will gain an increased sense of accomplishment, confidence, and control.

Attitude

Here are ways to maintain an attitude that will help you succeed.

See tests as opportunities to learn. Instead of thinking of tests as contests that you either "win" or "lose," think of them as signposts along the way to mastering material. Learning is far more important than "winning."

Understand that tests measure performance, not personal value. Your grade does not reflect your ability to succeed or your self-worth. Whether you get an A or an F, you are the same person.

Appreciate that instructors are on your side. Your instructors want you to do well, even when they give challenging tests, so contact them during office hours or via e-mail. Use them as a resource to clarify difficult concepts before an exam.

Seek study partners who challenge you. Find study partners who inspire you to do your best. Try to avoid people who are also anxious, because you may pick up on one another's fears and negativity. (For more on study groups, see Chapter 1.)

Be convinced that your work will make a difference. If you believe that your efforts will pay off, they are more likely to do just that. Students who think that their intelligence is fixed—that no matter how much they study, they will not appreciably change their academic performance—are not very resilient when they do poorly on tests. On the other hand, people who believe that intelligence is flexible and can be improved through hard work are more likely to put time and effort into studying and to bounce back and improve after a poor grade. Use this insight to take responsibility for creating success through your work and attitude.[1]

Practice relaxation. When you feel test anxiety mounting, breathe deeply, close your eyes, and visualize positive mental images such as getting a good grade and finishing with time to spare. Try to ease muscle tension—stretch your neck, tighten and then release your muscles.

Shut out negative vibrations. If you arrive at the testing room early for a last-minute review, pick a seat far away from others who are discussing the test. The last thing you want is to be distracted or pick up anxiety from classmates who are unsure of the material or who are quizzing each other about possible questions.

Practice positive self-talk. Tell yourself that you can do well and that it is normal to feel anxious, particularly before an important exam. As you walk into the testing room, give yourself a pep talk that builds confidence—something like, "I know this stuff, and I'm going to show what I know." Also, slay your perfection monster by telling yourself, "I don't have to get a perfect grade."

Remind yourself of your goals. Connecting the test to what you're working toward will help you calm down as you focus on what's important. For example, when you get jittery because of the upcoming test, refocus on the internship you had last summer and your goal of getting a full-time job after you graduate.

Math exams are a special problem for many students. Dealing with the anxieties associated with these exams was examined on pages 336–343.

A good attitude involves being prepared for different test-taking challenges than you experienced in high school. The exams that you take in college may ask you to critically analyze and apply material in ways that you never did before. For example, your English instructor may ask you to apply principles of poetry analysis to a poem you've never read, or your history instructor may give you a new primary source and ask you to place it in its historical context. Prepare for these challenges as you study by continually asking critical thinking questions (see Chapter 3).

Test Anxiety and the Returning Student

If you're returning to school after years away, you may wonder how well you will handle exams. To deal with these feelings, focus on what you have learned through life experience, including the ability to handle work and family pressures. Without even knowing it, you may have developed the time-management, planning, organizational, and communication skills necessary for college success.

In addition, your life experiences will give real meaning to abstract classroom ideas. For example, workplace relationships may help you understand social psychology concepts, and refinancing your home mortgage may help you grasp the importance of interest-rate swings—a key concept in economics.

MULTIPLE INTELLIGENCE STRATEGIES FOR TEST PREPARATION. If the topic or format of a test challenges your stronger or weaker intelligences, these tips will help you make the most of your time and abilities.

INTELLIGENCE	SUGGESTED STRATEGIES	WHAT WORKS FOR YOU? WRITE NEW IDEAS HERE
Verbal-Linguistic	■ Think of and write out questions your instructor may ask on a test. Answer the questions and then try rewriting them in a different format (essay, true/false, and so on). ■ Underline important words in review questions or practice questions.	
Logical-Mathematical	■ Make diagrams of review or practice questions. ■ Outline the key steps involved in topics on which you may be tested.	
Bodily-Kinesthetic	■ Review out loud. Recite concepts, terms and definitions, important lists, dates, and so on. ■ Create a sculpture, model, or skit to depict a tough concept that will be on your test.	
Visual-Spatial	■ Create a think link to map out an important topic and its connections to other topics in the material. Study it and redraw it from memory a day before the test. ■ Make drawings related to possible test topics.	
Interpersonal	■ Develop a study group and encourage each other. ■ In your group, come up with as many possible test questions as you can. Ask each other these questions in an oral exam–type format.	
Intrapersonal	■ Brainstorm test questions. Then, come back to them after a break or even a day's time. On your own, take the sample "test" you developed. ■ Make time to review in a solitary setting.	
Musical	■ Play music while you read if it does not distract you. ■ Study concepts by reciting them to rhythms you create or to music.	
Naturalistic	■ Bring your text, lecture notes, and other pertinent information to an outdoor spot that inspires you and helps you to feel confident, and review your material there.	

Parents who have to juggle child care with study time can find the challenge especially difficult before a test. Here are some suggestions that might help:

- **Find help.** This is especially important with younger children.
- **Plan activities.** If you have younger children, have a supply of games, books, and videos on hand to use while you study.
- **Explain the time frame.** Tell school-aged children your study schedule and the test date. Plan a reward after your test.

Preparing for an exam sets the stage for taking the exam. You are now ready to focus on methods to help you succeed when the test begins.

WHAT GENERAL STRATEGIES CAN HELP YOU SUCCEED ON TESTS?

Even though every test is different, there are general strategies that will help you handle almost all tests, including short-answer and essay exams.

Choose the Right Seat

Your goal is to choose a seat that will put you in the right frame of mind and minimize distractions. Finding a seat near a window, next to a wall, or in the front row will enable you to look off into the distance without being suspected of looking at another paper. To maximize your ability to focus, avoid sitting near friends during an exam.

Write Down Key Facts

Before you even look at the test, write down key information, including formulas, rules, and definitions, that you studied recently and don't want to forget. Use the back of the question sheet or some scrap paper for your notes. (Be sure your instructor knows that you made these notes after the test began.)

Begin with an Overview

Although exam time is precious, spend a few minutes at the start of the test gathering information about the questions—how many there are in each section, what types, and their point values. Use this information to schedule your time. For example, if a two-hour test is divided into two sections of equal value—an essay section with 4 questions and a short-answer section with 60 questions—you might spend an hour on the essays (15 minutes per question) and an hour on the short answers (1 minute per question).

Take level of difficulty into account as you parcel out your time. For example, if you think you can get through the short-answer questions in 45 minutes and sense that the writing section will take longer, you can budget an hour and a quarter for the essays.

Read Test Directions

Reading test directions carefully can save you trouble. For example, although a history test of 100 true/false questions and one essay may look straightforward, the directions may tell you to answer 80 of the 100 questions or that the essay is optional. If the directions indicate that you are penalized for incorrect answers—meaning that you lose points instead of simply not gaining points—avoid guessing unless you're fairly certain.

When you read directions, you may learn that some questions or sections are weighted more heavily than others. For example, the short-answer questions may be worth 30 points, whereas the essays may be worth 70. In this case, it's smart to spend more time on the essays than the short answers. To stay aware of the specifics of the directions, circle or underline key information.

Mark Up the Questions

Mark up instructions and keywords to avoid careless errors. Circle qualifiers, such as *always, never, all, none, sometimes,* and *every;* verbs that communicate specific instructions; and concepts that are tricky or need special attention. Another technique is to use a ruler as a guide as you read each line and underline keywords.

Marking up your question sheet exam may help you process the questions and avoid mistakes. On multiple-choice exams, for example, write one or two words next to the choices you reject indicating why they are wrong, circle the correct answer, and finally mark it in the specified place.

Work Together   BUILDING YOUR SKILLS

FOCUS ON QUALIFIERS

Work with a study partner in one of your courses to reinforce the importance of focusing on qualifying words in test questions. To do this:

- Read an assigned chapter in your text so that you are prepared to answer the end-of-chapter questions.

- Working together, look at these questions and identify the qualifiers that modify what the question is asking. List the qualifiers for each question and discuss their impact on the way you will answer the question.

- Answer each question as it is written in the text and compare answers with your partner. Discuss how the qualifier helped you formulate your answer.

- Finally, in the lines below, evaluate how this exercise has affected the way you will answer test quesions.

_____

_____

_____

_____

Take Special Care on Machine-Scored Tests

Use the right pencil (usually a #2) on machine-scored tests, and mark your answer in the correct space, filling it completely. (Use a ruler or your pencil as a straight edge to focus on the correct line for each question.) Periodically, check the answer number against the question number to make sure they match. If you mark the answer to question 4 in the space for question 5, not only will your response to question 4 be wrong, but also your responses to all subsequent questions will be off by a line. When you plan to return to a question and leave a space black, put a small dot next to the number on the answer sheet.

Neatness counts on these tests because the computer may misread stray pencil marks or partially erased answers. If you mark two answers to a question and partially erase one, the computer will read both responses and charge you with a wrong answer.

Work from Easy to Hard

Begin with the easiest questions, and answer them as quickly as you can without sacrificing accuracy. This will boost your confidence and leave more time for questions that require greater focus and effort. Mark tough questions as you reach them, and return to them after answering the questions you know.

According to study-skills expert Adam Robinson, a common mistake students make is spending the most time trying to answer questions about which they know the least instead of spending more time on the questions they can ace. When you know material well, expecially on an essay test, explains Robinson, "the favorable impression your answer will make in your teacher's mind will earn you the benefit of the doubt on the other questions."[2]

While it's tempting to rush through a test to get it over with, taking time to think when you need to will help you be more sure of your answers and may even help you stay calm.

Watch the Clock

Keep track of how much time is left and how you are progressing. (Wear a watch, since every class-room may not have a working wall clock.) Some students are so concerned about time that they rush through the test and have time left over. If this happens to you, spend the remaining time refining and checking your work instead of leaving early. (Being the last person in the room is not a bad thing if you use your time wisely.) You may be able to correct mistakes, change answers, or add informa-tion to an essay. If, on the other hand, midway through the test you realize that you are falling behind, reevaluate to determine the best use of the remaining time. Remaining flexible will help you during a time crunch.

Take a Strategic Approach to Questions You Cannot Answer

Even if you are a diligent student, you may face questions you do not under-stand or cannot answer. What do you do in this situation?

- If your instructor is proctoring the exam, ask for clarification. Sometimes a simple rewording will make you realize that you really know the material.
- If this doesn't work, skip the question and return to it later. Letting your subconscious mind work on the question sometimes makes a difference.
- Use what you do know about the topic to build logical connections that may lead you to the answer.

- Try to remember where the material was covered in your notes and text. Creating this kind of visual picture may jog your memory about content as well.

- Start writing—even if you think you're going in the wrong direction and not answering the question that was asked. The act of writing about related material may help you recall the targeted information. You may want to do this kind of "freewriting" on a spare scrap of paper. Then, think about what you've written, and then write your final answer on the test paper or booklet.

- If you think of an answer at the last minute but are short on time, write on the paper that you only have minutes left to answer the question, so you are putting your answer in outline form. While most instructors will deduct points for this approach, they may also give you partial credit because you showed that you know the material.

Master the Art of Intelligent Guessing

When you are unsure of an answer on a short-answer test, you can leave it blank or guess. As long as you are not penalized for incorrect answers, guessing sometimes helps. "Intelligent guessing," writes Steven Frank, an authority on student studying and test taking, "means taking advantage of what you do know in order to try to figure out what you don't. If you guess intelligently, you have a decent shot at getting the answer right."[3]

When you check your work at the end of the test, decide whether you would make the same guesses again. Because your first instincts are usually the best, chances are that you will leave your answers alone, but you may notice something that changes your mind—a qualifier that affects meaning, a miscalculation in a math problem. Or you may recall information that you couldn't remember the first time around. Use common sense and sound logic in all your guesses—they usually steer you in the right direction.

Maintain Academic Integrity

Cheating as a strategy to pass a test or get a better grade robs you of the opportunity to learn, which is ultimately your loss. Cheating also jeopardizes your future if you are caught. You may be seriously reprimanded—or even expelled—if you violate your school's code of academic integrity. Furthermore, employers don't hire, promote, or reward cheaters, expecially in the post-Enron era, when companies have become more vigilant than ever.

In recent years, cheating has become high-tech, with students using their cell phones, personal digital assistants (PDAs), graphing calculators, and Internet-connected laptops to share information with other test takers through text messaging or to search the Internet or other databases. Because high-tech cheating can be difficult to uncover when exams are administered in large lecture halls, some instructors ban all electronic devices from the room. At the University of Maryland at College Park, for example, students who have a cell phone or PDA in their possession during exams receive an automatic failure. Other instructors hand out multiple versions of the same test—with each version having multiple-choice questions in a different order so that no two students receive the same exam. This prevents students from passing answers back and forth electronically.[4]

The purpose of a test is to see how much you know, not merely to get a grade. Embrace this attitude so that you can learn from your mistakes.

HOW CAN YOU LEARN FROM TEST MISTAKES?

As painful as test mistakes can be, they are valuable learning tools if you approach them with an open mind. With exam in hand, use the following strategies to reduce the likelihood of repeating the same errors. (If your instructor posts grades but does not hand exams back, ask to see your paper.)

Ask yourself global questions that may help you identify correctable patterns.

- Can you generalize about your biggest problems on the test? Did you get nervous; did you misread the question; did you fail to study enough; did you study incorrectly; did you focus on memorizing material instead of understanding and applying it?

- Did your instructor's comments clarify what you failed to do? Did your answer lack specificity; did you fail to support your thesis with concrete examples; was your analysis weak?

- Were you surprised by the questions? For example, did you expect them all to be from the text instead of coming from the text and a supplemental reading?

- Did you make careless errors? Did you misread the question or directions, blacken the wrong box on the answer sheet, skip a question, write illegibly?

- Did you make conceptual or factual errors? Did you misunderstand a concept; did you fail to master facts or concepts; did you skip part of the text or miss classes in which ideas were covered?

Your answers to these questions will help you change the way you study for the next exam.

Rework the questions you got wrong. Based on instructor feedback, try to rewrite an essay, recalculate a math problem from the original question, or redo questions following a reading selection. If you discover a pattern of careless errors, redouble your efforts to be more careful and save time to double-check your work.

After reviewing your mistakes, fill in your knowledge gaps. If you made mistakes because of a lack of understanding, develop a plan to learn the material. Solidifying your knowledge can help you on future exams and in work and life situations that involve the subject you're studying.

Talk to your instructor. Talk with your instructor about specific mistakes on short-answer questions or about a weak essay. The fact that you care enough to review your errors will leave a positive lasting impression. If you are not sure why you were marked down on an essay, ask what you could have done to improve your grade. If you feel that an essay was unfairly graded, ask your instructor to reread it.

Rethink the way you studied. Make changes to avoid repeating your errors. Use the varied techniques in *Keys to College Studying* to study more effectively so that you can show yourself and your instructor what you are really capable of doing. For obvious reasons, the earlier in the semester you can make positive adjustments the better, so working hard to learn from early mistakes will help you throughout the semester.

If you fail a test, don't throw it away. Use it as a way to review troublesome material, especially if you will be tested on it again. Keep it as a reminder that you can improve if you have the will to succeed. When you compare a failure to later successes, you'll see how far you've come.

The willingness to learn from test mistakes is critical for all students, including those with reading-related learning disabilities. When researcher Roxanne Ruzic examined how learning-disabled students prepare for tests, she found that successful students applied what they learned from their mistakes on one test to their preparation for others. Students who dismissed this feedback did not excel.

Jack is a case in point, as Ruzic explains: "When Jack received his graded midterm exam [in introduction to international business], he discounted some of what the instructor wrote in his blue book, claiming she was wrong, rather than trying to figure out how to ensure that he knew the material and she knew that he knew it. While Jack did not do as well on the midterm as he would have liked, he used the same study techniques to prepare for the final exam as he had used for the midterm. Had Jack talked more to other people (including instructors) regularly to assess his understanding of content and expectations and worked in study groups, he would have been much more successful in his courses." Jack's final course grade was a C+—not where he could have been had he made the effort to learn from earlier setbacks.[5]

LEARN FROM YOUR MISTAKES

Examine what went wrong on a recent exam and build knowledge for next time.

Look at an exam on which your performance fell short of expectations. If possible, choose one that contains different types of objective and subjective questions. With the test and answer sheet in hand, use critical thinking to answer the following questions:

- Identify the types of questions on which you got the most correct answers (for example, matching, essay, multiple choice).

  _____

- Identify the types of questions on which you made the greatest number of errors.

  _____

- Analyze your errors to identify patterns—for example, did you misread test instructions, or did you ignore qualifiers that changed the questions' meaning? What did you find?

  _____

  _____

- Finally, list two practical steps you are prepared to take during your next exam to avoid the same problems:

  Action 1: _____

  Action 2: _____

"It is time for us all to stand and cheer for the doer, the achiever—the one who recognizes the challenge and does something about it."

VINCE LOMBARDI
football coach

Building Skill, Will, and Self-Management

Monitoring Your Progress

ACTIVE THINKING

SKILL WILL SELF-MGMT.

Test Competence: Measure What You've Learned

MULTIPLE CHOICE: *Circle or highlight the answer that seems to fit best.*

1. A typical test given in one of your courses measures
   A. your self-worth.
   B. how much you will ever know about a topic.
   C. your proficiency at a moment in time.
   D. general IQ.

2. To predict what will be on a test you can use the following strategy:
   A. Listen for clues during instructor-run review sessions.
   B. Use SQ3R to identify important ideas and facts.
   C. Try to find out what the test will be like from people who took the course before.
   D. All of the above.

3. Which of the following is *not* a good source to use when developing pretest questions?
   A. your textbook
   B. your class notes
   C. assigned outside readings
   D. the course description you received at the start of the semester

4. Cramming includes *all but which* of the following?
   A. Plagiarizing during an open-book test.
   B. Reviewing flash cards.
   C. Creating a last-minute study sheet.
   D. Writing helpful information on a piece of scrap paper at the start of the test.

5. Test anxiety refers to
   A. the uncertainty you feel when you haven't studied for a test.
   B. the uncertainty you feel when you have to take a test with a teacher you don't like.
   C. the uncertainty you feel when you don't like the coursework on which the test is based.
   D. the mental and physical symptoms of stress that appear before a test.

6. To achieve a positive attitude before a test, you should
   A. see the test as an opportunity to learn and experience success.
   B. tell yourself that the grade you get doesn't matter.
   C. get yourself keyed up for the test by cramming and drinking a lot of coffee.
   D. realize that once you take a test the results are final and you can't do anything about them.

7. Test anxiety may be especially difficult for returning students because
   A. they often see themselves as less prepared because they have taken a break.
   B. the study methods they learned years ago no longer work.
   C. they tend to be less committed than students who didn't take a break.
   D. they have already earned money, so they no longer need to focus on taking tests.

8. It is important to pay attention to qualifiers in test questions, including:
   A. always, sometimes.
   B. never, rarely.
   C. all, none.
   D. all of the above.

9. Spending a few minutes at the start of a test getting an overview is important because
   A. you're certain to have plenty of time to complete the exam.
   B. you can get a general sense of whether you will probably pass or fail.
   C. you can get an idea of the type of questions you face and how to approach them.
   D. you can decide which questions you have no hope of answering.

10. To identify patterns in your mistakes on a test, keep an eye out for
    A. questions that you have time to rework.
    B. subjective and objective questions.
    C. evidence that the test was incorrectly graded.
    D. both careless and conceptual errors.

TRUE/FALSE: *Place a T or an F beside each statement to indicate whether you think it is true or false.*

_____ 1. Since study schedules shift so often, it's a waste of time to create one before an exam.

_____ 2. The reading method SQ3R will help you study for tests.

_____ 3. Most instructors will allow you to bring your last minute study sheet into the testing room.

_____ 4. Colleges tend to ignore cheating on tests since so many students do it.

_____ 5. It is a mistake ever to guess on an objective test.

Target and Achieve a Goal

Commit to one specific test-taking strategy from this chapter to improve your study skills.

Name the strategy here: _____

_____

Describe your goal—what you want to gain by using this strategy. ____

_____

Describe how you plan to use this strategy through the semester to achieve this goal.

_____

_____

_____

Building Your Skills

Brain Power: Build Vocabulary Fitness

Here is a selection from the current media. Read the material, paying special attention to the context of the vocabulary words shown in bold type. Then choose the correct definition for each word in the table that follows. Use a dictionary to check your answers. Finally, on a separate sheet, use each vocabulary word in a sentence of your own to solidify your understanding.

Students are under pressure to do well on exams, especially on standardized tests that influence their admission to professional and graduate schools. As a result, reports Nicholas Zamiska of the Wall Street Journal, *some students are taking prescription drugs in the belief that they are performance enhancers. This practice raises important ethical and medical concerns.*

Students have long taken stimulants—ranging from caffeine to cocaine—to help them stay up all night writing papers and cramming for exams. Now, some high school and college kids are using prescription drugs in hopes of improving their performance on standardized admissions tests for college and graduate school. . . . "It used to be on the **fringes** completely, but now it's seeping into the mainstream," said, . . . an admissions consultant. . . . "If you're one of hundreds of kids fighting for one of 10 spots, you'll do everything you can to get the extra edge." [For example, a recent college graduate is] **wrestling** with whether to use a stimulant before he takes the Law School Admission Test. . . . "I really can't fail," he says, "because it's not just me that's failing. I fail for my parents and my entire family. Even if it bumps my score up an extra point, it's worth it."

The current drug of choice for many students is [the fast-acting amphetamine] Adderall . . . [often] prescribed for ADHD. . . . Amphetamines act on the brain by **mimicking** the neurotransmitter dopamine, which increases alertness and concentration. Studies . . . [have] found that low-dose stimulants increase concentration and alertness in everyone, not just people with attention disorders. Side effects of Adderall can include loss of appetite, **insomnia**, weight loss [and possible addiction]. . . .

It isn't hard to **scrounge** a pill from a sibling or schoolmate, or even to get a prescription of your own. Overall, prescriptions for stimulants have risen to 2.6 million a month in 2004, from 1.6 million in 2000. . . . Under federal law, it's illegal to knowingly possess a "**schedule** II" drug, such as Adderall, without a prescription. But prosecutions for possession are rare. . . .

[Although some students are convinced that taking Adderall improved their scores, others believe that it actually reduced their ability to concentrate.]

"I ended up focusing on the texture of my pencil, . . ." [said a student]. . . . "It made me feel much more jittery and 10 times more nervous than I would have been." [Later,] she retook the test . . . without the amphetamine. . . .

An online discussion group for people preparing for the law-school admissions test was recently abuzz with stories of students popping pills to improve scores. An argument broke out over whether that is proper. "Are you looking for a . . . easy way out, or what?" wrote someone. . . . "Am I the only one that feels that taking prescription drugs that are unnecessary for your health and the doctors that write these scrips are very unethical?"

Source: Nicholas Zamiska, "Pressed to Do Well on Admissions Tests, Students Take Drugs," *Wall Street Journal,* November 8, 2004, p. A1. Reprinted with permission.

Circle the word or phrase that best defines each term as it is used in this excerpt.

VOCABULARY WORDS	A	B	C
1. fringes (noun)	periphery	lace edges	political right
2. wrestling (verb)	struggling	engaging in a fist fight	arguing
3. mimicking (verb)	making fun of	imitating	ridiculing
4. insomnia (noun)	rapid heart beats	fainting	sleeplessness
5. scrounge (verb)	find	beg or borrow	ask politely
6. schedule (noun)	time-released	part of a list of items	list of controlled substances

Get to the Root

Every time you learn a Greek or Latin root, you increase your ability to recognize English vocabulary words that include that root and to figure out their meaning. Grow your vocabulary by studying the root on the following page and its related words, writing in two more words from the same root, and including definitions for both new words.

Investigate Using Research Navigator

Access Research Navigator using the Internet address shown on page 32. Then sign on to the service using your Login Name and Password. Using the *New York Times* archives, conduct a search for the keyword "cheating" on all the databases listed. Scan the article titles and descriptions and choose three to read in full that capture your interest, whether or not they

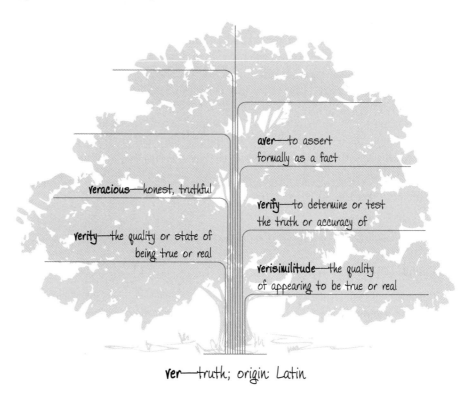

aver—to assert formally as a fact

veracious—honest, truthful

verify—to determine or test the truth or accuracy of

verity—the quality or state of being true or real

verisimilitude—the quality of appearing to be true or real

ver—truth; origin: Latin

are related to the issue of academic integrity discussed in this chapter. Then answer these questions on a separate page:

- No matter its form, cheating often has serious consequences on offenders. What did you learn from these articles that will make you rethink whether cheating on exams is worth the risk?

- Cheating also has serious consequences on others who are innocent of any infractions. What did you learn from these articles that will make you rethink whether cheating on exams is a "victimless crime"?

- If you found one or more articles on people who cheated in the work-place or their personal lives, speculate on whether you think these people cheated on exams while they were in school. Do you think that cheating on tests sets up a pattern for cheating at work and in relationships?

- How has this critical analysis changed your perspective on cheating, if at all?

Building Will and Self-Awareness

ACTIVE
THINKING
SKILL   WILL   SELF-MGMT.

Make Responsible Choices

Answer the following question on a separate piece of paper or in a journal.

Feelings similar to test anxiety can come up in all kinds of life and work situations. With this chapter's advice on how to overcome test anxiety in mind . . .

- Describe future situations, perhaps on the job or in an interview or audition, in which these strategies might come in handy.

- Describe the steps you will take to feel less anxious the next time you are preparing for a major exam. If you have never experienced test anxiety, analyze what you believe are the major reasons why you have escaped it.

- Read the previous Brain Power excerpt from the *Wall Street Journal*, and then discuss your views on taking amphetamines to improve test performance. Do you consider it an ethical choice?

Chapter Summary

As you use the summary on the following pages to review the concepts you learned in this chapter, focus also on its format—in this case a **think link**, in other chapters the Cornell system, and in still others a formal outline. As you become comfortable with the organization and style of these various formats, try using each of them to take class and reading notes, noting which approach works best for you in particular situations.

Endnotes

1. David Glenn, "Students' Performance on Tests Is Tied to Their Views of Their Innate Intelligence, Researchers Say," *The Chronicle of Higher Education*, June 1, 2004 (http://chronicle.com/daily/2004/06/2004060103n.htm).

2. Adam Robinson, *What Smart Students Know: Maximum Grades, Optimum Learning. Minimum Time.* New York: Three Rivers Press, 1993, p. 189.

3. Steven Frank, *The Everything Study Book.* Holbrook, MA: Adams Media Corporation, 1996, p. 208.

4. Brock Read, "Wired for Cheating," *The Chronicle of Higher Education*, July 16, 2004, p. A27.

5. Roxanne Ruzic. "Lessons for Everyone: How Students with Reading-Related Learning Disabilities Survive and Excel in College Courses with Heavy Reading Requirements." Paper presented at the Annual Meeting of the American Educational Research Association, April 13, 2001 [online]. Available: www.cast.org/udl/index.cfm?i=1540 (March 2004).

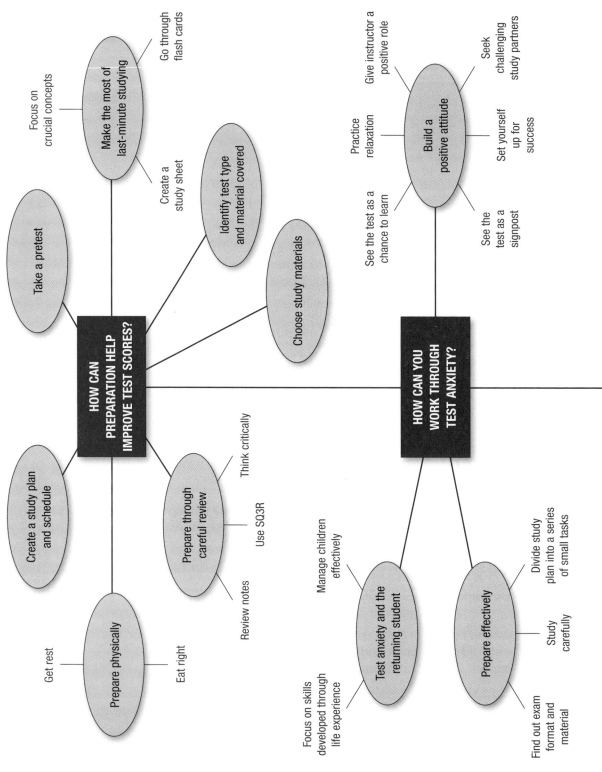

HOW CAN PREPARATION HELP IMPROVE TEST SCORES?

Make the most of last-minute studying
- Go through flash cards
- Focus on crucial concepts
- Create a study sheet

Take a pretest

Identify test type and material covered

Choose study materials

Create a study plan and schedule

Prepare physically
- Get rest
- Eat right

Prepare through careful review
- Think critically
- Use SQ3R
- Review notes

HOW CAN YOU WORK THROUGH TEST ANXIETY?

Build a positive attitude
- Give instructor a positive role
- Practice relaxation
- Seek challenging study partners
- Set yourself up for success
- See the test as a chance to learn
- See the test as a signpost

Test anxiety and the returning student
- Manage children effectively
- Focus on skills developed through life experience

Prepare effectively
- Divide study plan into a series of small tasks
- Study carefully
- Find out exam format and material

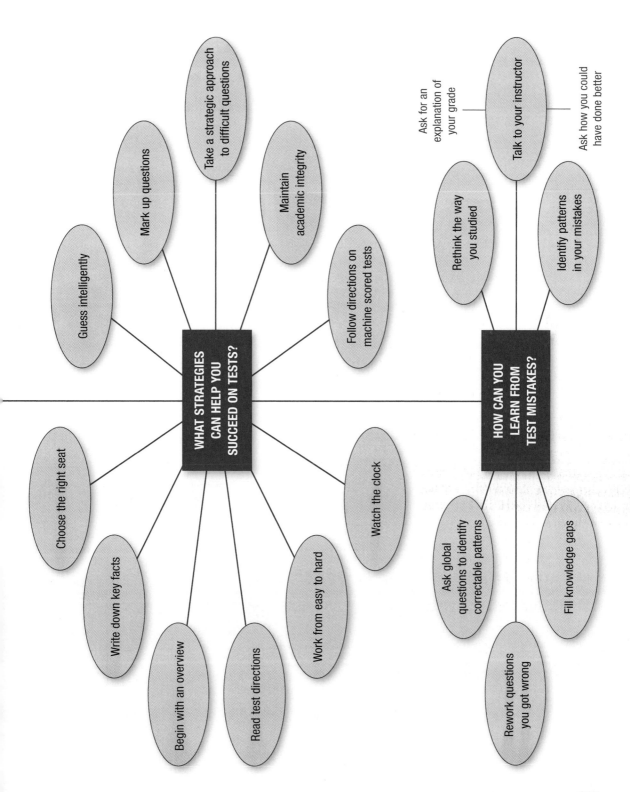

WHAT STRATEGIES CAN HELP YOU SUCCEED ON TESTS?

- Take a strategic approach to difficult questions
- Maintain academic integrity
- Mark up questions
- Guess intelligently
- Follow directions on machine scored tests
- Choose the right seat
- Write down key facts
- Begin with an overview
- Read test directions
- Work from easy to hard
- Watch the clock

HOW CAN YOU LEARN FROM TEST MISTAKES?

- Talk to your instructor
  - Ask for an explanation of your grade
  - Ask how you could have done better
- Rethink the way you studied
- Identify patterns in your mistakes
- Ask global questions to identify correctable patterns
- Rework questions you got wrong
- Fill knowledge gaps

11

"I wrote my name at the top of the page. I wrote down the number of the question '1.' After much reflection, I put a bracket round it thus '(1).' But thereafter I could not think of anything with it that was either relevant or true."

WINSTON CHURCHILL, BRITISH PRIME MINISTER, WORLD LEADER, AND AUTHOR DURING WORLD WAR II

Taking Objective, Essay, and Oral Exams

SHOWING WHAT YOU KNOW

Exams are preparation for life. When you get a job, volunteer to serve your community, or even work through your family budget, you'll put knowledge and skills into action—just as you do when you take an academic test.

As a student, your challenge is to build on the test-preparation strategies you learned in Chapter 10—and in all of *Keys to College Studying*—to answer objective, essay, and oral examination questions. The more comfortable you are with a variety of techniques for handling different questions the more likely you are to come up with the right answers.

The techniques you will learn in this chapter help ensure that you will be able to show what you know and avoid pitfalls. As you practice these techniques, the success that you experience will help you gain confidence in your ability to succeed.

In this chapter you will explore answers to the following questions:

- What kinds of test questions should you expect?
- How can you master objective tests?
- How can you master essay questions?
- How can you master oral exams?

WHAT KINDS OF TEST QUESTIONS SHOULD YOU EXPECT?

Every type of test question has a different way of finding out how much you know about a subject. For *objective questions*, you choose or write a short answer, often making a selection from a limited number of choices. Multiple-choice, fill-in-the-blank, matching, and true/false questions fall into this category. *Subjective questions* demand the same information recall as objective questions, but they also require you to plan, organize, draft, and refine a response. All essay questions are subjective.

Key 11.1 shows samples of real test questions from Western civilization, macroeconomics, Spanish, and biology college texts published by Pearson Education. Included are multiple-choice, true/false, fill-in-the-blank, matching, and essay questions, including a short-answer essay. Analyzing the types, formats, and complexity of these questions will help you gauge what to expect when you take your exams.

ACTIVE THINKING

SKILL WILL SELF-MGMT.

Work Together   BUILDING YOUR SKILLS

BENCHMARK TO IMPROVE YOUR TEST-PREPARATION HABITS

Benchmarking is a business practice that involves assessing how other companies do something and adopting the best practices. You can use benchmarking right now to learn how others prepare for exams—and to adopt what will work for you. Here's how:

Step 1. Form a study group with two or three other students in one of your academic courses, setting a meeting time that fits into each student's schedule. Ask each group member to record everything he or she does to prepare for the next exam. Among the items on the lists may be:

- making a study checklist and posting it on my bulletin board
- spending two hours a day studying at the library in the week before the exam
- learning what to expect on the test (topics and material that will be covered, types of questions that will be asked)
- getting a partner to drill me on multiple-choice questions from old tests
- using SQ3R to review material
- recording information on an iPod and listening to it between classes

- having a pretest breakfast with a study group
- getting to sleep by midnight the night before the exam

Step 2. After the exam, come together to compare preparation regimens. What important differences can you identify in routines? How might different routines have affected test performance and outcome?

Step 3. On a separate piece of paper, for your own reference, write down what you learned from the habits of your study mates that may help you as you prepare for upcoming exams.

Objective questions are a major part of classroom and standardized tests. As you will see next, answering these questions is part science and part art.

HOW CAN YOU MASTER OBJECTIVE TESTS?

You have taken objective tests throughout your years of school and you may continue to take them after graduation—at work, in certifying exams for different professions, even to qualify as a U. S. citizen if you come from another country. Doing well on objective exams depends on your knowledge of the test material and on your use of strategies to make the right choices.

Multiple-Choice Questions

Multiple-choice questions are the most popular type of question on standardized tests. Using the following strategies will help you answer them:

Read the directions carefully. Directions tell you precisely what to do. For example, whereas most test items ask for a single correct answer, some give you the option of marking several choices that are correct. For some tests, you might be required to answer only a certain number of questions.

Read each question thoroughly and try to think of the answer before looking at the choices. Then read the choices and make your selection. When the answer you thought of matches one of the choices, it is most likely correct. Do not second guess!

Professors are often valuable resources for information on the type of tests you will take for your courses. Don't hesitate to ask questions.

Key 11.1   Real test questions from real college texts.

From Chapter 29, "The End of Imperialism," in *Western Civilization: A Social and Cultural History,* 2nd edition.[1]

- **MULTIPLE-CHOICE QUESTION**

  India's first leader after independence was:

  A. Gandhi   B. Bose   C. Nehru   D. Sukharno   *(answer: C)*

- **FILL-IN-THE-BLANK QUESTION**

  East Pakistan became the country of _____ in 1971.

  A. Burma   B. East India   C. Sukharno   D. Bangladesh   *(answer: D)*

- **TRUE/FALSE QUESTION**

  The United States initially supported Vietnamese independence.   T   F   *(answer: false)*

- **ESSAY QUESTION**

  Answer one of the following:

  1. What led to Irish independence? What conflicts continued to exist after independence?
  2. How did Gandhi work to rid India of British control? What methods did he use?

From Chapter 6, "Unemployment and Inflation," in *Macroeconomics: Principles and Tools,* 3rd edition.[2]

- **MULTIPLE-CHOICE QUESTION**

  If the labor force is 250,000 and the total population 16 years of age or older is 300,000, the labor-force participation rate is

  A. 79.5%   B. 83.3%   C. 75.6%   D. 80.9%   *(answer: B)*

- **FILL-IN-THE-BLANK QUESTION**

  Mike has just graduated from college and is now looking for a job, but has not yet found one. This causes the employment rate to _____ and the labor-force participation rate to _____.

  A. increase; decrease   C. stay the same; stay the same

  B. increase; increase   D. increase; stay the same   *(answer: C)*

- **TRUE/FALSE QUESTION**

  The Consumer Price Index somewhat overstates changes in the cost of living because it does not allow for substitutions that consumers might make in response to price changes.   T   F   *(answer: true)*

- **ESSAY QUESTION**

  During a press conference, the Secretary of Employment notes that the unemployment rate is 7.0%. As a political opponent, how might you criticize this figure as an underestimate? In rebuttal, how might the Secretary argue that the reported rate is an overestimate of unemployment?

  (Possible answer: The unemployment rate given by the secretary might be considered an underestimate because discouraged workers, who have given up the job search in frustration, are not counted as unemployed. In addition, full-time workers may have been forced to work part-time. In rebuttal, the secretary might note that a portion of the unemployed have voluntarily left their jobs. Most workers are unemployed only briefly and leave the ranks of the unemployed by gaining better jobs than they had previously held.)

Key 11.1   Continued

From *Mosaicos: Spanish as a World Language,* 3rd edition.[3]

- **MATCHING QUESTION**

  You are learning new words and your teacher asks you to think of an object similar to or related to the words he says. His words are listed below. Next to each word, write a related word from the list below.

el reloj	el cuaderno	el pupitre	una computadora
el televisor	la tiza	el lápis	la mochila

  1. el escritorio _____
  2. el bolígrafo _____
  3. la videocasetera _____
  4. la pizarra _____
  5. el libro _____

  (answers: 1. el pupitre; 2. el lápis;
  3. el televisor; 4. la tiza; 5. el cuaderno)

- **ESSAY QUESTION**

  Your mother always worries about you and wants to know what you are doing with your time in Granada. Write a short letter to her describing your experience in Spain. In your letter, you should address the following points:

  1. What classes you take
  2. When and where you study
  3. How long you study every day
  4. What you do with your time (mention three activities)
  5. Where you go during your free time (mention two places)

From Chapter 13, "DNA Structure and Replication," in *Biology: A Guide to the Natural World,* 2nd edition.[4]

- **MULTIPLE-CHOICE QUESTION**

  What units are bonded together to make a strand of DNA?

  A. chromatids   B. cells   C. enzymes   D. nucleotides   E. proteins   *(answer: D)*

- **TRUE/FALSE QUESTION**

  Errors never occur in DNA replication, because the DNA polymerases edit out mistakes.   T   F

  (answer: false)

- **FILL-IN-THE-BLANK QUESTION**

  In a normal DNA molecule, adenine always pairs with _____ and cytosine always pairs with _____.

  (answers: thymine; guanine)

- **MATCHING QUESTION**

  Match the scientist and the approximate time frames (decades of their work) with their achievements.

Column 1	Column 2
_____ 1. Modeled the molecular structure of DNA	_____ A. George Beadle and Edward Tatum, 1930s and 1940s
_____ 2. Generated X-ray crystallography images of DNA	_____ B. James Watson and Francis Crick, 1950s
_____ 3. Correlated the production of one enzyme with one gene	_____ C. Rosalind Franklin and Maurice Wilkins, 1950s

  (answers: 1–B; 2–C; 3–A)

Underline keywords and phrases. If the question is complicated, try to break it down into small sections that are easy to understand.

Make sure you read every word of every answer. Instructors have been known to include answers that are right except for a single word. Focus especially on qualifying words such as *always, never, tend to, most, often,* and *frequently.* Look also for negatives in a question ("Which of the following is *not* . . . ").

Once you read every word, take the question on face value. Don't spend time reading "between the lines" to figure out what the instructor is *really* asking.

If you don't know the answer, eliminate answers that you know or suspect are wrong. If you can leave yourself with two possible answers, you will have a 50–50 chance of making the right choice. To narrow down, ask questions about each of the choices:

- **Is the choice accurate on its own terms?** If there's an error in the choice—for example, a term that is incorrectly defined—the answer is wrong.
- **Is the choice relevant?** An answer may be accurate, but unrelated to the question.
- **Are there any qualifiers?** Absolute qualifiers like *always, never, all, none,* or *every* often signal an exception that makes a choice incorrect. For example, the statement "Normal children *always* begin talking before the age of two" is untrue (most normal children begin talking before age two, but some start later). Analysis has shown that choices containing conservative qualifiers like *often, most, rarely,* or *may sometimes be* are often correct.
- **Do the choices give clues?** Does a puzzling word remind you of a word you know? Do any parts of an unfamiliar word—its prefix, suffix, or root—ring a bell?

Make an educated guess by looking for patterns. Certain patterns tend to appear in multiple-choice questions and may help you make smart guesses. Although these patterns may not apply to the specific test questions you encounter, they're important to keep in mind. Experts advise you to:

- consider the possibility that a choice that is *more general than the others* is the right answer.
- consider the possibility that a choice that is *longer than the others* is the right answer.

- look for a choice that has a *middle value in a range* and avoids extremes (the range can be from small to large or from old to recent). It is more likely to be the right answer.
- look for *two choices that have similar meanings*. One of these answers has a greater possibility of being correct.
- look for answers that *agree grammatically* with the question. For example, a fill-in-the-blank question that has *a* or *an* before the blank gives you a clue to the correct answer.

When questions are linked to a reading passage, read the questions first. This will help you focus on the information you need to answer the questions.

Here are examples of the kinds of multiple-choice questions you might encounter in a psychology course[5] (the correct answer follows each question):

1. Arnold is at the company party and has had too much to drink. He releases all of his pent-up aggression by yelling at his boss, who promptly fires him. Arnold normally would not have yelled at his boss, but after drinking heavily he yelled because
   a. parties are places where employees are supposed to be able to "loosen up."
   b. alcohol is a stimulant.
   c. alcohol makes people less concerned with the negative consequences of their behavior.
   d. alcohol inhibits brain centers that control the perception of loudness.

   (answer: C)

2. Which of the following has not been shown to be a probable cause of or influence in the development of alcoholism in our society?
   a. Intelligence   c. Personality
   b. Culture   d. Genetic vulnerability   *(answer: A)*

3. Geraldine is a heavy coffee drinker who has become addicted to caffeine. If she completely ceases her intake of caffeine over the next few days, she is likely to experience each of the following *except:*
   a. depression.   c. insomnia.
   b. lethargy.   d. headaches.   *(answer: C)*

True/False Questions

Read true/false questions carefully to evaluate what they are asking. If you're stumped, guess (unless you're penalized for wrong answers).

Look for qualifiers in true/false questions—such as *all, only,* and *always* (the absolutes that often make a statement false) and *generally, often, usually,* and *sometimes* (the conservatives that often make a statement true)—that can turn a true statement into a false one or vice versa. For example, "The grammar rule 'I before E except after C' is *always* true" is false, whereas "The grammar rule 'I before E except after C' is *usually* true" is true. The qualifier makes the difference.

Here are some examples of the kinds of true/false questions you might encounter in an introduction to psychology course.[6] The correct answer follows each question:

Are the following questions true or false?

1. Alcohol use is clearly related to increases in hostility, aggression, violence, and abusive behavior. *(True)*

2. Marijuana is harmless. *(False)*

3. Simply expecting a drug to produce an effect is often enough to produce the effect. *(True)*

4. Alcohol is a stimulant. *(False)*

Matching Questions

Matching questions ask you to match the terms in one list with the terms in another list, according to the directions. For example, the directions may tell you to match a communicable disease with the microorganism that usually causes it. The following strategies will help you handle these questions.

Make sure you understand the directions. The directions tell you whether each answer can be used only once or more than once.

Work from the column with the longest entries. The left-hand column usually contains terms to be defined or questions to be answered, whereas the right-hand column contains definitions or answers. As a result, entries in the right-hand column are usually longer than those on the left. Reading the items on the right only once will save time as you work to match them with the shorter phrases on the left.

Start with the matches you know. On your first run-through, mark these matches with a penciled line, waiting to finalize your choices after you've completed all the items. Keep in mind that if you can use an answer only once, you may have to change answers if you reconsider a choice.

Finally, tackle the matches you're not sure of. On your next run-through, focus on the more difficult matches. Look for clues and relationships you might not have considered. Think back to your class lectures, text notes, and study sessions as you try to visualize the correct response.

If one or more phrases seem to have no correct answer, look back at your easy matches to be sure that you did not jump too quickly. Consider the possibility that one of your sure-thing answers is wrong.

Fill-in-the-Blank Questions

Fill-in-the-blank questions, also known as sentence-completion questions, ask you to supply one or more words or phrases with missing information that completes the sentence. These strategies will help you make successful choices.

Be logical. Insert your answer; then reread the sentence from beginning to end to be sure it makes sense and is factually and grammatically correct. Consider thinking of the right answer *before* looking at the choices, then finding the choice that most closely matches.

Note the length and number of the blanks. These are important clues but not absolute guideposts. If two blanks appear right after one another, the instructor is probably looking for a two-word answer. If a blank is longer than usual, the correct response may require additional space. However, if you are certain of an answer that doesn't seem to fit the blanks, trust your knowledge and instincts.

Pay attention to how blanks are separated. If there is more than one blank in a sentence and the blanks are widely separated, treat each one separately. Answering each as if it were a separate sentence-completion question increases the likelihood that you will get at least one answer correct. Here is an example:

When Toni Morrison was awarded the _____ Prize for Literature, she was a professor at _____ University.

(Answer: Morrison received the **Nobel** *Prize and is a professor at* **Princeton** *University.)*

Think outside the box. If you can think of more than one correct answer, put them both down. Your instructor may be impressed by your assertiveness and creativity.

If you are uncertain of an answer, make an educated guess. Have faith that after hours of studying, the correct answer is somewhere in your subconscious and that your guess is not completely random.

Here are examples of fill-in-the-blank questions you might encounter in an introductory to astronomy course[7] (correct answers follow questions):

1. A _____ is a collection of hundreds of billions of stars. *(galaxy)*

2. Rotation is the term used to describe the motion of a body around some _____. *(axis)*

3. The solar day is measured relative to the sun; the sidereal day is measured relative to the _____. *(stars)*

4. On December 21, known as the _____ _____, the sun is at its _____ _____. *(winter solstice; southernmost point)*

ACTIVE
THINKING

SKILL **WILL** **SELF-MGMT.**

Go For It!   BUILDING YOUR SKILLS

DEVELOP HABITS FOR TEST SUCCESS

You have just studied strategies for taking objective tests. Think about five that will help improve your performance on upcoming tests. Write these strategies here:

1. _____
2. _____
3. _____
4. _____
5. _____

Over the next month, evaluate whether these strategies worked well, whether they had no impact, or whether they actually caused problems. Write your evaluation here:

_____

_____

_____

For the strategies that worked, name three actions you will take to transform them into habits:

Action 1: _____

Action 2: _____

Action 3: _____

HOW CAN YOU MASTER ESSAY QUESTIONS?

Essay questions ask you to express your knowledge and views in a less structured way than short-answer questions. With freedom of thought and expression comes the challenge to organize your ideas and write well under time pressure.

Strategies for Answering Essay Questions

Seven steps follow that will help you improve your responses to essay questions. Many of these guidelines reflect the methods for effective writing you learned in Chapter 8. The difference here is that you are writing under time pressure and working from memory.

1. Start by Reading the Questions

Decide which to tackle (if there's a choice). Use critical thinking to identify exactly what the question is asking.

2. Map Out Your Time

Use the techniques you learned in Chapter 10 to schedule your time, remembering that things don't always go as planned. Try to remain flexible if an answer takes longer than expected.

3. Watch for Action Verbs

Action verbs, like those in Key 11.2 on the next page, tell you what your instructor wants you to do as you answer the question. Underline these words as you read and use them to guide your writing.

According to Kim Flachmann, professor of English at California State University at Bakersfield, answering essay questions effectively depends on understanding action verbs: "Read every essay question very carefully," she advises students. "Look for performance words, especially action verbs that tell you how to approach the question. It may help to copy these words in the margin. Between the performance words are the content words—what you're being asked about."[8]

4. Plan

Think carefully about what the question is asking and what you know about the topic. On a piece of scrap paper, create an informal outline or a think link to map your ideas and supporting evidence. Then come up with

Key 11.2   Focus on action verbs on essay tests.

ANALYZE—Break into parts and discuss each part separately.

COMPARE—Explain similarities and differences.

CONTRAST—Distinguish between items being compared by focusing on differences.

CRITICIZE—Evaluate the issue, focusing on its problems or deficiencies.

DEFINE—State the essential quality or meaning.

DESCRIBE—Paint a complete picture, provide the details of a story or the main characteristics of a situation.

DIAGRAM—Present a drawing, chart, or other visual.

DISCUSS—Examine completely, using evidence and often presenting both sides of an issue.

ELABORATE ON—Start with information presented in the question, and then add new material.

ENUMERATE/LIST/IDENTIFY—Specify items in the form of a list.

EVALUATE—Give your opinion about the value or worth of something, usually by weighing positive and negative effects, and justify your conclusion.

EXPLAIN—Make the meaning of something clear, often by discussing causes and consequences.

ILLUSTRATE—Supply examples.

INTERPRET—Explain your personal views and judgments.

JUSTIFY—Discuss the reasons for your conclusions or for the question's premise.

OUTLINE—Organize and present main and subordinate points.

PROVE—Use evidence and logic to show that something is true.

REFUTE—Use evidence and logic to show that something is not true or how you disagree with it.

RELATE—Connect items mentioned in the question, showing, for example, how one item influenced the other.

REVIEW—Provide an overview of ideas and establish their merits and features.

STATE—Explain clearly, simply, and concisely.

SUMMARIZE—Give the important ideas in brief, without comments.

TRACE—Present a history of the way something developed, often by showing cause and effect.

a thesis statement that defines your content and point of view. If necessary—
and if you have the time—reorganize your outline or think link into an
exact writing roadmap.

When you are asked to apply concepts or principles to new ideas and
situations, take a deep breath and brainstorm the relationships between
what you know and what you are being asked. You might also go a step further, says Professor Flachmann. "I always tell students to try to find a
unique way into the question that not everybody is going to use. For example, if you are asked the causes of World War II, you may want to state and
compare them to the causes of World War I. That's the way to get a higher
grade and use your best critical thinking skills."[9]

The biggest mistake students make is to skip the planning stage and
start writing without thinking through or organizing their answers. Not
only does planning result in a better essay, but it also reduces stress. Instead
of scrambling for ideas as you write, you are in the position of carrying out
an organized plan.

To answer the third essay question in the box on page 408, one student
created the planning outline shown in Key 11.3 below. Notice how abbreviations and shorthand help the student write quickly. Writing "Role of BL in IC"
is much faster than "Role of body language in interpersonal communication"
(see Chapter 7 for shorthand note strategies).

Key 11.3   Create an informal outline during essay tests.

Roles of BL in IC
1. To contradict or reinforce words
   — e.g., friend says "I'm fine"
2. To add shades of meaning
   — saying the same sentence in 3 diff. ways
3. To make lasting 1st impression
   — impact of nv cues and voice tone greater than words
   — we assume things abt person based on posture, eye contact, etc.

Here are some examples of essay questions you might encounter in an interpersonal communication course. In each case, notice the action verbs from Key 11.2.

1. Summarize the role of the self-concept as a key to interpersonal relationships and communication.

2. Explain how internal and external noise affects the ability to listen effectively.

3. Describe three ways that body language affects interpersonal communication.

5. Draft

Unlike writing a paper, in which you can go through a series of drafts before your final version, your first draft on an exam is usually the one you hand in. If you take enough time and effort in the planning stage, you will have enough material to construct a suitable answer.

Use the following guidelines as you draft your answer:

- Start by stating your thesis, and then get right to the evidence that backs it up. You won't have time to write an extensive introduction, and your instructor won't expect one.
- Pay close attention to how you organize your ideas and how well you support them with evidence. Try to structure your essay so that each paragraph presents an idea that supports the thesis.
- Use clear language and tight logic to link ideas to your thesis and to create transitions between paragraphs.
- Look back at your outline periodically to make sure you cover everything.
- Wrap it up with a short, to-the-point conclusion.

Spend the bulk of your time developing your thesis and supporting evidence and logic. As instructors mark test essays, they generally do not look for fully developed introductions or conclusions.

Pay attention to the test directions when drafting your answer. Your essay may need to be of a certain length, for example, or may need to take a certain form (for example, a particular format such as a business letter). Finally, write on only one side of the page to give the grader the best chance of reading your response.

6. Revise

Take a few moments to evaluate your word choice, paragraph structure, and style. Although you may not have the time or opportunity to rewrite your entire answer, you can certainly improve it with minor deletions or additions in the margin. If you find a hole in your work—an idea without support, for example, or some unnecessary information—add the new material in the margins and cross out what you don't need. When adding material, you can indicate with an arrow where it fits or note that inserts can be found on separate pages. If you have more than one insert, label each to avoid confusion (for example, Insert #1, Insert #2, etc.). Be neat as you make changes.

As you check over your essay, ask yourself these questions:

- Have I answered the question?
- Does my essay begin with a clear thesis statement, and does each paragraph start with a strong topic sentence that supports the thesis?
- Have I provided the support necessary in the form of examples, statistics, and relevant facts to prove my argument?
- Is my logic sound and convincing?
- Have I covered all the points in my original outline?
- Is my conclusion an effective wrap-up?
- Does every sentence effectively communicate my point?

7. *Edit*

Check for mistakes in grammar, spelling, punctuation, and usage. No matter your topic, the correct use of language leaves a positive impression and eliminates problems that could lower your grade.

Go For It!   BUILDING YOUR SKILLS

ACTIVE THINKING

SKILL   WILL   SELF-MGMT.

WRITE TO THE VERB

Focusing on the action verbs in essay test instructions can mean the difference between giving instructors what they want and answering off the mark.

- Start by choosing a topic you learned about in this text—for example, the internal and external barriers to listening. Write your topic here:

  _____

  _____

- Put yourself in the role of instructor. Write an essay question on this topic, using one of the action verbs listed in Key 11.2 to frame the question. For example, "Analyze the classroom-based challenges associated with internal barriers to listening."

_____

_____

■ Now choose three other action verbs from Key 11.2. Use each one to rewrite your original question.

1. _____

2. _____

3. _____

■ Finally, analyze how each new verb changes the focus of the essay question. Describe the change here for each of the three new questions.

1. _____

_____

2. _____

_____

3. _____

_____

Key 11.4 shows the student's completed response to the essay on body language, including the word changes and inserts she made while revising the draft.

Neatness is a crucial factor in essay writing. No matter how good your ideas are, if your instructor can't read them, your grade will suffer. If your handwriting is a problem, try printing or skipping every other line, and be sure to write on only one side of the page. Students with illegible handwriting might ask to take the test on a computer.

Some instructors give essay exams in oral form. Handling these exams presents a special challenge.

HOW CAN YOU MASTER ORAL EXAMS?

In an oral exam, your instructor asks you to present verbal responses to exam questions or to discuss a pre-assigned topic. Exam questions may be similar to essay questions on written exams. They may be broad and general or focused on a narrow topic, which you are expected to explore in depth.

Key 11.4   Response to an essay question with revision marks.

QUESTION: Describe three ways that body language affects interpersonal communication.

Body language plays an important role in interpersonal communication and helps shape the impression you make. Two of the most important functions of body language are to contradict and reinforce verbal statements. When body language contradicts verbal language, the message ~~conveyed~~ delivered by the body is dominant. For example, if a friend tells you that she is feeling "fine," but her posture is slumped, and her facial expression troubled, you have every reason to wonder whether she is telling the truth. If the same friend tells you that she is feeling fine and is smiling, walking with a bounce in her step, and has direct eye contact, her body language is ~~telling the truth.~~

    The nonverbal cues that make up body language also have the power to add shades of meaning. Consider this statement: "This is the best idea I've heard all day." If you were to say this three different ways—in a loud voice while standing up; quietly while sitting with arms and legs crossed and looking away; and while ~~maintening~~ maintaining eye contact and taking the receiver's hand—you might send three different messages.

    Finally, the impact of nonverbal cues can be greatest when you meet someone for the first time. When you meet someone, you tend to make assumptions based on nonverbal behavior such as posture, eye contact, gestures, and speed and style of movement.

    In summary, nonverbal communication plays a ~~crusial~~ crucial role in interpersonal relationships. It has the power to send an accurate message that may ~~destroy~~ belie the speaker's words, offer shades of meaning, and set the tone of a first meeting.

Margin revision marks:

, especially when you meet someone for the first time

her eye contact minimal,

accurately reflecting and reinforcing her words.

Although first impressions emerge from a combination of nonverbal cues, tone of voice, and choice of words, nonverbal elements (cues and tone) usually come across first and strongest.

MULTIPLE INTELLIGENCE STRATEGIES FOR TAKING OBJECTIVE, ESSAY, AND ORAL EXAMS. These tips will help you handle different types of test questions and situations.

INTELLIGENCE	SUGGESTED STRATEGIES	WHAT WORKS FOR YOU? WRITE NEW IDEAS HERE
Verbal-Linguistic	■ Read carefully to understand every word of every question. ■ Do language-oriented questions first, saving extra time for questions involving visual or quantitative elements.	
Logical-Mathematical	■ Focus on quantitative and/or objective questions first, saving extra time for more subjective work such as essays. ■ Use logic to narrow choices in multiple choice and matching questions.	
Bodily-Kinesthetic	■ Select an area and/or a seat in the testing location where you feel comfortable. Take brief breaks to stretch your muscles at your seat. ■ Use the podium, table, chair, and whiteboard as props during oral exams.	
Visual-Spatial	■ Focus on the length and number of the blanks in fill-in-the-blank questions. ■ Create think links to map out responses to ssay questions.	
Interpersonal	■ Replay study group conversations in your mind to remember key facts. ■ Look your instructor in the eye and talk directly to her during an oral exam.	
Intrapersonal	■ If you encounter a difficult question, take a deep breath and focus on what you know about the topic. ■ Visualize answering every question correctly.	
Musical	■ Remember the rhymes and tunes you created to help you learn material. Recite them to yourself to recall an answer.	
Naturalistic	■ Instructor and weather permitting, take your exam outdoors.	

Students with learning disabilities that affect their writing may need to take all their exams orally. If you have a disability that fits into this category, speak with your advisor and instructors to set up an examination system that works for you.

Benefits of Presenting Effectively

You may never have taken an oral exam in college—and you may never have one. Nevertheless, mastering oral-exam skills will help you feel more comfortable answering questions in class and taking part in class discussions. (Some instructors consider your class participation when determining course grades.) There are other benefits as well that extend beyond the classroom:

Oral skills are essential for communication. Whether you address your class with a presentation, your coworkers with guidelines for next year's budget, or a community group with a message about local safety issues, you need the ability to get your point across clearly as well as concisely, and in a manner that grabs and holds attention.

Oral skills are crucial to career success. In the workplace, employees are often asked to present information in meetings and through public speaking to members of their work teams, clients, and other business associates. The more comfortable you are speaking with ease and thinking on your feet, the more successfully you will handle a supervisor dropping by for a business trip debriefing or an unexpected phone call in which you are asked to talk about a research project.

Oral skills are important even before you are employed, because the ability to communicate effectively during job interviews is key to getting the job you want. Your grades and accomplishments may not matter if you are not able to interact successfully with your interviewer. Employers are searching for people who can inform and persuade with ease and self-assurance, and they look for evidence of this at your interview.

Communication skills are becoming even more important in the modern information-oriented workplace—and, ironically, harder to find in today's job applicants. According to the National Association of Colleges and Employers, fewer and fewer job seekers are prepared with effective communication skills. Paul Baruda, an employment expert for the jobs website Monster.com, explains: "You can be the best physicist in the world, but if you can't tell people what you do or communicate it to your coworkers, what good is all of that knowledge? I can't think of an occupation, short of living in a cave, where being able to say what you think cogently . . . . isn't going to be important."[10]

An obstacle to effective interpersonal communication is technology, says Debra Vargulish, a college recruiter for Kennametal Inc. Recent graduates "are so used to using a BlackBerry, instant messaging their friends, that a lot of them don't understand how to . . . use the telephone . . . It's not so much the technology as knowing *what* to say."[11]

The message from employers is clear: You can differentiate yourself from others—and get the job you want—by being comfortable and effective while communicating with others and being able to inform and persuade under pressure. Becoming proficient at taking oral exams will help you achieve these workplace goals.

Preparation Strategies

Because oral exams require that you speak logically and succinctly with little time to organize your thoughts, some instructors will give you the exam topic in advance and may even allow you to bring your notes to the exam room. Other instructors may ask you to study a specified topic and then ask you directed questions during the exam. Your challenge is to prepare effectively, just as you would for a written exam, as you practice your oral presentation skills.

Speaking in front of others—even an audience of one, your instructor—involves developing a presentation strategy before you enter the exam room:

One important part of preparing for an oral presentation is to get organized by writing out your thoughts.

- **Learn your topic.** Study for the exam until you have mastered the material. Nothing can replace subject mastery as a confidence booster.

- **Plan your presentation.** Dive into the details. Brainstorm your topic if it is preassigned, narrow it with the prewriting strategies you learned in Chapter 8, determine your central idea or argument, and write an outline that will be the basis of your talk. If the exam uses a question-and-answer format, make a list of the most likely questions the instructor will ask and formulate the key points of your responses.

- **Use clear thinking.** Illustrate concepts with evidence, and use clear logic to link your thoughts. Try to formulate an effective beginning and ending that focus on the exam topic.

- **Draft your thoughts.** To get your thoughts organized for the exam, make a keyword draft, using "trigger" words or phrases that will remind you of what you want to say. Use bullets to separate and set off your points.

Practice Your Presentation

The element of performance distinguishes speaking from writing. As in any performance, practice is essential. Use the following strategies to guide your efforts:

- **Know the parameters.** How long do you have to present your topic? Make sure you stick to the guidelines your instructor gives you. Where will you be speaking? Be aware of the physical setting—where your instructor will be sitting, and what you may have around you to use, such as a podium, table, chair, or whiteboard.

- **Use index cards or notes.** If your instructor doesn't object, bring note cards to the presentation. However, keep them out of your face; it's tempting to hide behind them.

- **Pay attention to the physical.** Your body position, your voice, and what you wear contribute to the impression you make. Look good and sound good. Walk around if you like to talk that way, and try to make eye contact with your instructor. Never forget that you are speaking to your instructor, so use nonverbal cues to acknowledge his presence and engage him in your talk.

- **Do a test run with friends or alone.** If possible, audiotape a practice session and evaluate how you did. Make a special effort to eliminate filler words and expressions such as *uh, like, you know,* and *um.*

- **Time your practice sessions.** This will help you determine whether to add or cut material. If you are given your exam topic in advance, make sure you can say everything you want to say in the allotted time. During the exam, monitor your rate of speech to make sure it is not too rapid. Nervous speakers have a tendency to race through a presentation, which minimizes its effectiveness.

- **Try to be natural.** Use words you are comfortable with to express concepts you know. Don't try to impress your instructor with big words that sound stiff and formal, but do include specialized vocabulary about your topic that you learned in class and in the text. Your goal is to demonstrate your knowledge and enthusiasm for the topic.

Be Prepared for Questions

After your formal presentation, your instructor may ask you questions about the exam topic. Your responses and the way you handle the questions will affect your grade. Here are some strategies for answering questions effectively:

- **Take the questions seriously.** The exam is not over until the question-and-answer period ends.

- **Jot down keywords from the questions.** This is especially important if the question has several parts and you intend to address one part at a time.

- **Ask for clarification.** If you don't understand a question, ask the instructor to rephrase it. Your goal is to answer the question the instructor asks.

- **Think before you speak.** Take a moment to organize your thoughts and to write down keywords for the points you want to cover.

- **Answer only part of a question if that's all you can do.** Emphasize what you know best and impress the instructor with your depth of knowledge.

- **Be calm if you don't know an answer.** Although you may take it for granted that you may not be able to answer all the questions on a written exam, you may panic when a question you can't answer comes your way on an oral exam. Simply tell the instructor that you don't know the answer to the question and move on to the next.

Handling Your Nerves During an Exam

Taking an oral exam is similar to giving a speech or business presentation. All eyes are on you as you communicate your message. If you respond with a bad case of nerves—also known as *speech tension*—there are things you can do to help yourself:

- **Keep your mind on your presentation, not on yourself.** Focus on what you want to say and how you want to say it, not on yourself.

- **Take deep breaths right before you begin, and have a bottle of water handy.** Deep breathing will calm you and the water will quench your thirst.

- **Visualize your own success.** Create a powerful mental picture of yourself acing the exam. Then, visualize yourself speaking with knowledge, confidence, and poise.

- **Establish eye contact with your instructor.** Realize that he wants you to succeed. You'll relax when you feel that your instructor is on your side.

You can help yourself before the exam begins by getting a good night's sleep and arriving early so you can begin to focus on what you have to accomplish.

Whatever type of exam you take during college, knowing what to expect from different types of questions and developing strategies for doing well will help you feel in control. It is then up to you to see the test as an opportunity to show what you know.

"Do, or do not. There is no 'try.'"

YODA
The Empire Strikes Back

Building Skill, Will, and Self-Management

Monitoring Your Progress

Test Competence: Measure What You've Learned

MULTIPLE CHOICE. *Circle or highlight the answer that seems to fit best.*

1. An example of an objective question is one that
   A. measures your ability to differentiate one object from another.
   B. allows the use of open-book materials during the test.
   C. asks you to select from a limited number of choices.
   D. requires you to plan, organize, draft, and refine a written response.

2. A strategy that is *not* advised for making an educated guess on a multiple-choice question is to
   A. look for a choice with a middle value in a range.
   B. look for a shorter choice.
   C. look for a choice that agrees grammatically.
   D. look for a more general choice.

3. Which of the following is an example of an absolute qualifier?
   A. Always
   B. Seldom
   C. Frequently
   D. Almost

4. When working through a matching question, you should
   A. work from the column that has the shortest entries.
   B. start with the matches you do not know.
   C. resist the temptation, after you make a choice, to change your answer at the end of the test.
   D. tackle the matches you're not sure of after you mark the matches you know.

5. Essay questions fall into all the following categories *except:*

    A. objective questions.

    B. subjective questions.

    C. important questions.

    D. critical thinking questions.

6. When answering an essay question, you should

    A. spend most of your time on the introduction because the grader will see it first.

    B. skip the planning steps if your time runs short.

    C. use the four steps of the writing process but take less time for each step.

    D. write your essay and then rewrite it on another sheet or booklet.

7. Good writing skills on essay tests depend on all of the following factors *except:*

    A. clear ideas and thinking.

    B. writing quickly so that you have time for several revisions.

    C. having an organized approach.

    D. critical thinking.

8. The one activity you probably *will not* have time for during an essay test is

    A. planning your essay.

    B. drafting your essay.

    C. drafting an alternate essay as a backup.

    D. revising and editing your essay.

9. One way in which oral examination skills will prove useful after graduation is that

    A. you will often take oral exams on the job.

    B. you need to be prepared to speak in front of people at any time.

    C. many jobs require you to make presentations to work teams, clients, and others.

    D. planning is essential to any profession.

10. Which of the following *is not* a useful oral exam strategy?

    A. Jotting down keywords from the questions.

    B. Answering only those questions you feel like answering.

    C. If you don't understand a question, asking for clarification.

    D. Answering only part of a question if that's all you can do.

TRUE/FALSE. *Place a T or an F beside each statement to indicate whether you think it is true or false.*

_____ 1. Fill-in-the-blank questions are also known as sentence completion questions.

_____ 2. The verbs *define, describe, discuss,* and *explain* all have the same meaning on essay tests.

_____ 3. Brainstorming and freewriting are two important planning tools during an essay test.

_____ 4. During an oral exam, focus exclusively on your subject and ignore your presentation method.

_____ 5. It is unusual for students to get nervous before and during an oral exam.

Target and Achieve a Goal

Commit to one specific test-taking strategy from this chapter to improve your study skills.

Name the strategy here: _____

_____

Describe your goal—what you want to gain by using this strategy. _____

_____

_____

Describe how you plan to use this strategy through the semester to achieve this goal.

_____

_____

_____

Building Your Skills

Brain Power: Build Vocabulary Fitness

Here is a selection from the current media. Read the material, paying special attention to the context of the vocabulary words shown in bold type. Then choose the correct definition for each word in the table that follows. Use a dictionary to check your answers. Finally, on a separate sheet, use each vocabulary word in a sentence of your own to solidify your understanding.

Testing is a worldwide phenomenon as is the conviction by many that students are overtested. The following article looks at testing trends in Japan and Great Britain.

Countries around the globe have been grappling with the **ramifications** of [standardized testing] for years. . . .

[In Japan,] students take fewer tests than American students. The consequences, however, are higher. Tests determine the high school, university, and sometimes which elementary and junior high schools they attend. Even after graduation, many government agencies and corporations test applicants before placing them in jobs. "If you have **aspirations**. . . , you're cramming all the way from your youngest age to university," said a . . . sociology professor.

Many students attend private after-school programs called "juku" that help students study for exams. "They learn a lot more than [American] kids do," said [the professor]. "Their heads are crammed with information by the time they finish high school. The bad part is . . . it **stifles** creativity and flexibility in learning. You've got a whole lot of kids who know a whole lot of facts and figures, but they're not good at critical thinking. . . . "

As in the United States, England's high-stakes testing system has spurred debate. . . . "One of the things you are seeing in the United Kingdom, because they've been at it so long, is reaction from the teachers union and parent groups, who have been doing things like **boycott** tests," said a [professor of education at the] University of Washington. "It continues to be **contentious** mostly because of the large amount of time taken for testing. . . . "

England's 10-year-old school **accountability** system is similar to America's. . . . it includes high-stakes testing and school inspections similar to our **accreditation** system. Similar to U.S. exams, England's tests focus on reading, math, and science. . . .

Source: "Beyond A-B-C: What Testing Doesn't Measure—Other Places, Other Tests," Dailybulletin.com. *The Sun* and *Inland Valley Daily Bulletin*, Los Angeles Newspaper Group, (http://lang.sbsun.com/socal/beyondabc/part_5/other_places.asp) 2004. Reprinted with permission.

Circle the word or phrase that best defines each term as it is used in this excerpt.

VOCABULARY WORDS	A	B	C
1. ramifications (noun)	pressures	complicating developments	need for
2. aspirations (noun)	ambitions	breathing problems	talents
3. stifles (verb)	encourages	belittles	represses
4. boycott (verb)	protests	refuses to deal with as a sign of disapproval	ignore
5. contentious (adj.)	provoking angry debate	agreeable	mystifying
6. accountability (adj.)	bookkeeping	answerability	education
7. accreditation (adj.)	granting credit or recognition that sets standards	giving course credits for	penal

Get to the Root

Every time you learn a Greek or Latin root, you increase your ability to recognize English vocabulary words that include that root and to figure out

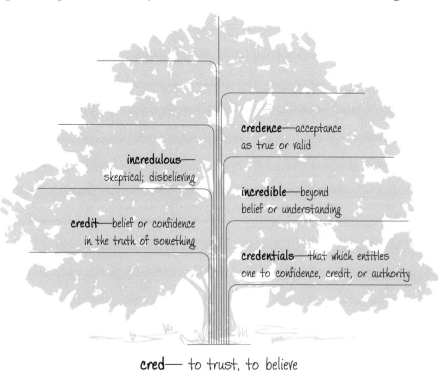

credence—acceptance as true or valid

incredulous—skeptical; disbelieving

incredible—beyond belief or understanding

credit—belief or confidence in the truth of something

credentials—that which entitles one to confidence, credit, or authority

cred— to trust, to believe
origin: Latin

their meaning. Grow your vocabulary by studying this root and its related words, writing in two more words from the same root, and including definitions for both new words.

Investigate Using Research Navigator

Access Research Navigator using the Internet address shown on page 32. Then sign on to the service using your Login Name and Password. Scroll through the database titles listed for Content Select. Choose 5 to 10 databases linked to careers you might be interested in. For each one, enter the keyword "continuing education."

- Search through the articles in each content area for information on continuing education requirements. Continuing education consists of courses you must take while you are working in a field to keep abreast of new information and technologies. Describe what you learned for each content area.

- Do more research—either on Research Navigator or on the Internet— to find out if students must pass an exam to get continuing education credit. What did you learn?

- What if you learned that a career that interests you requires that you pass certification exams at different stages in your career? Medicine and actuarial science are two examples. How do you think this information would affect your decision to pursue this career?

Building Will and Self-Awareness

Make Responsible Choices

Answer the following question on a separate piece of paper or in a journal.

Your success as a test taker depends, in large part, on your attitude. Do you take tests seriously, viewing them as an opportunity to learn and demonstrate mastery, or do you consider them as intrusions that mean little in the real world? Use these questions to evaluate your attitude:

- If you were in charge of a college, would you test students on course material or trust them to be responsible for their own learning? Explain.

- Do you believe that a positive attitude toward tests is important for learning? For doing well in a career?

- What do you think the connection is between test taking and handling unforeseen challenges at work?

Chapter Summary

As you use the summary below to review the concepts you learned in this chapter, focus also on its format—in this case a **formal outline,** in other chapters a think link, and in still others the Cornell system. As you become comfortable with the organization and style of these various formats, try using each of them to take class and reading notes, noting which approach works best for you in particular situations.

CHAPTER 11

I. Tests generally take two forms.

   A. Objective tests ask you to choose the correct answer from a limited number of choices.

   B. Subjective tests require you to formulate a response, usually in essay form.

II. Test-taking strategies can improve your performance on objective tests.

   A. Multiple-choice questions require that you carefully read test directions, understand what the question is asking before you proceed, and underline keywords. If you aren't certain of an answer, narrow your choices by eliminating possibilities and looking for patterns.

   B. True/false questions sometimes include qualifiers that can change meaning. Paying attention to qualifiers will increase your chance of making the right choice.

   C. Matching questions ask you to match terms in one list with terms in another. To increase the likelihood that you will choose correctly read the directions carefully, work from the column with the longest entries, start with the matches you know, and leave difficult matches to the end.

   D. Fill-in-the-blank questions ask you to complete sentences with missing information. Use logic to focus on the nature of the blank spaces.

III. Essay questions allow you freedom of thought and expression but can be an organizational and writing challenge.

   A. Carefully read the question so that you know exactly what you are being asked, paying special attention to action verbs. Then schedule your time so that you have enough time for all the questions.

   B. Take a few minutes to plan your response. Map out your ideas and supporting evidence and craft a thesis statement.

   C. Draft answers based on your plans, knowing that your first draft is the one you will hand in. Center each answer on your thesis statement.

D. Revise to improve the content and organization of your response, making sure that your additions and deletions can be read.

E. Edit your essay for grammatical, spelling, punctuation, and usage mistakes.

IV. Oral exams, which require that you present verbal responses to exam questions or to discuss a pre-assigned topic, involve content and presentation.

A. To do well, study just as you would for an essay test. Then take steps to practice your presentation.

B. Be prepared for questions at the end of your presentation.

C. It is not unusual to experience speech tension during an exam. Combat symptoms by using breathing and visualization techniques.

Endnotes

1. Margaret L. King, *Western Civilization: A Social and Cultural History*, 2nd ed. Upper Saddle River, NJ: Pearson Education, 2003. Questions from *Instructor's Manual and Test Item File* by Dolores Davison Peterson. Used with permission.

2. Arthur O'Sullivan and Steven M. Sheffrin, *Macroeconomics: Principles and Tools*, 3rd ed. Upper Saddle River, NJ: Pearson Education, 2003. Questions from *Test Item File 2* by Linda Ghent. Used with permission.

3. Matilde Olivella de Castells, Elizabeth Guzmán, Paloma Lupuerta, and Carmen García, *Mosaicos: Spanish as a World Language*, 3rd ed. Upper Saddle River, NJ: Prentice Hall, 2002. Questions from *Testing Program* by Mark Harpring. Used with permission.

4. David Krogh, *Biology: A Guide to the Natural World*, 2nd ed. Upper Saddle River, NJ: Prentice Hall, 2002. Questions from *Test Item File* edited by Dan Wivagg. Used with permission.

5. Gary W. Piggrem and Charles G. Morris, *Test Item File for Understanding Psychology*, 3rd ed. Reprinted by permission of Pearson Education, Upper Saddle River, NJ, 1996.

6. Ibid.

7. Eric Chaisson and Steve McMillan, *Astronomy Today*, 3rd ed. Reprinted by permission of Pearson Education, Upper Saddle River, NJ, 1999.

8. *Keys to Lifelong Learning Telecourse*. Dir. Mary Jane Bradbury. Videocassette. Intrepid Films, 2000.

9. Ibid.

10. Jim McKay, "Employers Complain About Communication Skills," *Pittsburgh Post-Gazette*, February 6, 2005 [online]. Available www.shapiroandduncan.com (March 1, 2005).

11. Ibid.

12

"Education is not the filling of a pail,
but the lighting of a fire."

WILLIAM BUTLER YEATS, IRISH POET

Moving Ahead

MAKING TODAY'S STUDY SKILLS THE FOUNDATION FOR TOMORROW'S SUCCESS

By its very nature, college tests your endurance and willingness to work as you study for tests, write papers, and meet all the requirements to graduate. The experience of college can lead you to believe in the power of dreams and hard work to achieve life goals even if these goals are years in the making. When you graduate, the knowledge and accomplishments you have built will give you more power to handle the ups and downs of life and to continue on toward your future.

This final chapter of *Keys to College Studying* encourages you to step back and focus on where all your hard work is leading. With an active thinker's skills, self-awareness, motivation to learn, and self-management, you can build the life you envision.

In this chapter you will explore answers to the following questions:

- How will what you've learned bring academic and life success?
- How can you handle failure and success?
- How can you live your mission?

HOW WILL WHAT YOU'VE LEARNED BRING ACADEMIC AND LIFE SUCCESS?

You leave this course with far more than a final grade, a notebook full of work, and a credit hour or three on your transcript. You have grown as an active, responsible thinker in these and other ways:

- You have built important study skills that will promote success in college, on the job, and in life.
- You have strengthened your will to learn because of your understanding of the value of your education, and you have become aware of who you are as a learner, which will help make knowledge accessible and open the door to lifelong learning.
- You have developed ways to manage your learning and monitor your progress, resulting in greater personal responsibility and the flexibility to adapt to change.

Skills Prepare You to Succeed

The skills you gained this semester are your keys to success now and in the future (see Key 12.1). As you move through your college years, keep motivation high by reminding yourself that these tools will benefit you in everything you do.

Will and Self-Awareness Open the Door to Lifelong Learning

Throughout the semester, you've explored a range of strategies that you can use when working toward academic success. As you've applied these strategies by completing the text exercises, you've begun to figure out what works for you—and what doesn't. Your self-awareness, combined with an understanding of your learning style and the strategies that suit that style best, will help you work toward your academic goals in ways that prove most effective for you.

Even more important, knowing yourself in this way will help you continue to learn about both yourself and the world around you—a crucial life skill for the modern world. Knowledge in many fields is doubling every two to three years, and your personal interests and needs are changing constantly. Being a motivated lifelong learner will allow you to ride the waves of change, remaining able to manage and achieve your evolving career and personal goals.

Key 12.1   **The skills you acquire in college are lifelong tools for success.**

ACQUIRED SKILL	IN COLLEGE, YOU'LL USE IT TO . . .	IN CAREER AND LIFE, YOU'LL USE IT TO . . .
Setting goals	. . . map out, work toward, and achieve academic goals such as completing assignments and doing well on tests	. . . accomplish work tasks; map out, work toward, and achieve job and personal goals
Managing time	. . . get to classes on time, juggle school and work, turn in assignments when they are due, plan study time	. . . finish work tasks on or before they are due, balance duties on the job and at home
Knowing and using your learning styles	. . . select study strategies that make the most of your learning styles; function effectively in a study group	. . . select jobs, career areas, and other pursuits that suit what you do best; function effectively in a work team
Critical and creative thinking	. . . analyze academic readings and class discussions, think through writing assignments, solve math problems, brainstorm paper topics, work through academic issues, work effectively on team projects	. . . find ways both on the job and in your personal life to perform responsibilities at peak levels, analyze relationships that affect you, communicate effectively to reach your goals, and take actions that move you forward
Reading	. . . read course texts and other materials	. . . read workplace materials (operating manuals, memos, guidebooks, current information in your field); read for practical purposes, for learning, and for pleasure at home
Note taking	. . . take notes in class, in study groups, during studying, and during research	. . . take notes in work and community meetings and during important phone calls
Test taking	. . . perform effectively on quizzes, tests, and final exams	. . . take tests for certification in particular work skills and for continuing education courses; perform well under any kind of pressure
Writing	. . . write essays and research papers	. . . write work-related documents, including e-mails, reports, proposals, and speeches; write personal letters and journal entries
Quantitative learning	. . . understand concepts and work through problems in math and science courses and in courses such as business and economics that have a mathematical component	. . . apply quantitative principles to situations involving numbers (finances, statistics, projections, and so on), use problem-solving skills, and use visuals (charts and graphs) to communicate
Establishing and maintaining a personal mission	. . . develop a big-picture idea of what you want from your education, and make choices that guide you toward those goals	. . . develop a big-picture idea of what you want to accomplish in your career and life, and make choices that guide you toward those goals

To feed your will to learn and continue to develop your self-knowledge, ask questions and be open to new ideas in ways like the following:

Investigate new interests. When information and events catch your attention, take your interest one step further and find out more. Instead of dreaming about it, just do it.

Read, read, read. Reading expert Jim Trelease says that people who don't read "base their future decisions on what they used to know. If you don't read much, you really don't know much" as the world continually changes.[1] Read about a passion, be it basketball or knitting, then read more about it and more. Ask friends which books changed their lives. Reread books that you hurried through in school, savoring the ideas and language. Keep up with local, national, and world news through newspapers, magazines, and the Internet.

Pursue improvement in your studies and career. After graduation, stay on top of ideas, developments, and new technology in your field by seeking out *continuing education* courses. Sign up for career-related seminars. Take single courses at a local college or community learning center. Some companies offer on-the-job training or pay employees to take courses that will strengthen their skills.

Find a mentor. A *mentor* is a trusted advisor who will help you make academic and career decisions. Your mentor may be a teacher or even a friend with valuable life experience and a desire to help you reach your goals. A mentor may point you to important information and courses, introduce you to people, or be a sounding board for your hopes, dreams, and plans. Finding a mentor and nurturing the mentoring relationship may be among the most important things you do in your life, because you never know who may turn out to be an important guide as your life develops. Start now to be open to meeting people who might fill this role.

Break out of your box. Grab the opportunity to debate classmates with different political views. Take courses that force you out of your comfort zone and listen carefully to other perspectives on society, culture, religion, marriage, and work. Attend an after-class lecture *because* the speaker is controversial. Build relationships with people who, on the surface, have little in common with you, and who may be much older or younger. Travel internationally and locally.

The willingness—and eagerness—to learn throughout life is the master key that unlocks the doors you encounter on your journey. If you keep this key firmly in your hand, you will discover worlds of knowledge and places for yourself within them.

Being Responsible and Flexible as You Monitor Your Progress Helps You Adapt to Change

In the years ahead you may experience significant school, work, and personal changes that will affect your progress toward your goals (see Key 12.2 for examples). How you react to these changes, especially if they are unexpected or difficult, is almost as important as the changes themselves in determining your future success. The ability to "make lemonade from lemons" is the hallmark of people who land on their feet.

Active thinkers find ways to adapt to and benefit from changes both personal and environmental. Flexibility will help you re-evaluate—and, if necessary, modify—your goals so that you can continue to progress. Combine flexibility with an active sense of responsibility and you can adapt to the loss of a job or an exciting job offer, a personal health crisis or a

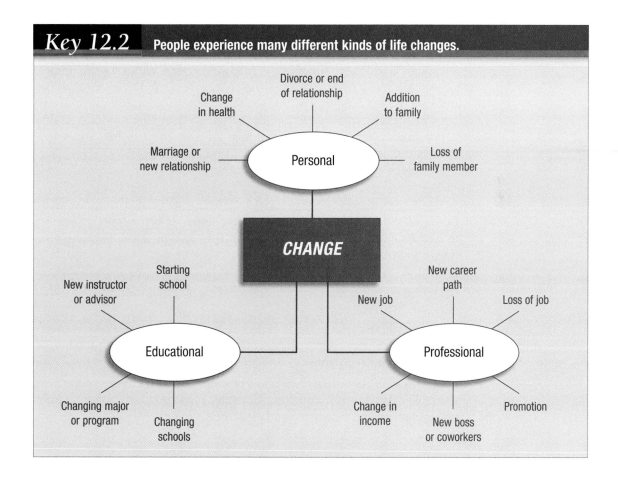

Key 12.2   **People experience many different kinds of life changes.**

happy change in family status, failing a course or winning an academic scholarship. Here's how:

Step one: Re-evaluate. First, determine whether your goals still work in the context of the change. For example, if you become dissatisfied with your major, you may want to rethink your academic path and even your career. Look also at your progress. If you haven't gotten as far as you planned, determine whether the goal is out of your range or simply requires more stamina—and patience—than you anticipated.

Step two: Modify. Based on your re-evaluation, you can modify a goal in two ways: You can adjust the existing goal (change its time frame or the steps leading to the goal), or you can replace it with a more compatible goal. For example, a student having trouble completing requirements for a major might choose to spend an extra semester in school (a change of time frame), complete a course or two in summer school (a change of interim steps), or switch to a major for which he has completed more required courses (a replacement with a more compatible goal).

Although sudden changes may throw you off balance, the unpredictability of life can open new horizons. Margaret J. Wheatley and Myron Kellner-Rogers, leadership and community experts and founders of the Berkana Institute, explain that people "often look at this unpredictability with resentment, but . . . unpredictability gives us the freedom to experiment. It is this unpredictability that welcomes our creativity."[2] Here are some strategies they recommend for making the most of unpredictable changes:

- **Look for what happens when you meet someone or experience something new.** Be aware of new feelings or insights that arise. See where they lead you.
- **Be willing to be surprised.** Great creative energies can come from the force of a surprise. Instead of turning back to familiar patterns, see what you can discover.
- **Use your planning as a guide rather than a rule.** If you allow yourself to follow new paths when changes occur, you are able to grow from what life presents to you.
- **Focus on what is rather than what is supposed to be.** Stay aware of the reality of what is happening. Consider plans you have made in light of that reality and be open to adaptation.

REVISIT YOUR LEARNING READINESS

In Chapter 1 you performed a preliminary assessment of your learning skills. Now answer the following to see how you perceive you have grown as a student and thinker. For each statement, circle the number that feels right to you, from 1 for "not true at all for me" to 5 for "absolutely true for me."

1. I see the connection between the effective study skills I learn today and my future academic, career, and life success.　① ② ③ ④ ⑤

2. I set effective short- and long-term study goals that will help me manage my workload.　① ② ③ ④ ⑤

3. I manage my time effectively and control any tendency to procrastinate.　① ② ③ ④ ⑤

4. I am aware of what causes me stress and I take steps to reduce it.　① ② ③ ④ ⑤

5. I am aware of my personal learning style, and I choose study strategies that take advantage of my strengths and minimize my weaknesses.　① ② ③ ④ ⑤

6. I understand the components of critical thinking and use critical thinking skills to get the most from my work.　① ② ③ ④ ⑤

7. I take a systematic approach to reading and studying.　① ② ③ ④ ⑤

8. I am aware of various note-taking styles and techniques and use the ones that help me to best take down and retain information.　① ② ③ ④ ⑤

9. I use listening and memory techniques that work best for me.　① ② ③ ④ ⑤

10. I approach writing assignments with a plan and with enough time to carry it out.　① ② ③ ④ ⑤

11. I know and use the strategies that help me do my best on tests.　① ② ③ ④ ⑤

12. I understand and use a research strategy when doing library or Internet research.　① ② ③ ④ ⑤

Total your answers here: _____

If your total ranges from *12 to 27*, you consider your academic readiness/awareness to be *low*.

If your total ranges from *28 to 44*, you consider your academic readiness/awareness to be *average*.

If your total ranges from *45 to 60*, you consider your academic readiness/awareness to be *strong*.

Take a moment to look back at the assessment in Chapter 1 on page 9. Compare how you scored yourself then with how you score yourself here (you may even want to write your old scores for each question in parentheses next to the new ones). Where have you grown the most? Where do you still want to develop? Of what development are you most proud?

Examining your changing views of yourself helps you gauge your progress toward your learning goals. Seeing how far you've come can also inspire you to look ahead and set new goals for the future.

The course of your life, and your progress toward goals, is often unpredictable. Instead of resisting this unpredictability, let it bring out the explorer in you as you focus on handling what *is* rather than fixating on what is *supposed to be*. Taking things as they come will also help you manage the success and failure that are both a natural part of your life journey.

HOW CAN YOU HANDLE FAILURE AND SUCCESS?

No matter how smart or accomplished you are, you will make mistakes and fail in ways big and small throughout your life. You will also succeed in ways you never imagined possible. How you respond to both your failures and successes—and what you learn from them—will have a major impact on your life.

Failure, especially, is one of the greatest teachers. What you gain when you take responsibility for learning from a failure may stay with you more intensely and guide you more effectively than almost anything else you learn.

Learn from Failure

You have choices when deciding how to view a failure or mistake. Pretending it didn't happen can deny you valuable lessons and may create more serious problems. Blaming someone else falsely assigns responsibility, stifling opportunities to learn. Blaming yourself can result in feeling incapable of success and perhaps becoming afraid to try.

By far the best way to survive a failure is to take responsibility for it and see what you can learn. Mistakes are natural, and your value as a human being does not diminish when you make one. Expect that you will do the best that you can within the circumstances of your life, knowing that getting through another day as a student, an employee, or a parent is a success in itself.

Learning from your failures and mistakes involves active thinking and problem solving.

Analyze what happened. For example, imagine that after a long night of studying for a chemistry test, you forgot to complete an American history paper due the next day. Your focus on the test caused you to overlook other tasks. Now you may face a lower grade on your paper if you turn it in late, plus you may be inclined to rush it and turn in a paper that isn't as good as it could be.

Come up with creative ways to change. You can make a commitment to note deadlines in a bright color in your planner and to check due dates more often. You can also try arranging your study schedule so that it is more organized and less last-minute.

Put your plan into action and keep an eye on how it is working. If you rearrange your study schedule, for example, look carefully at whether it is improving your ability to stay on top of your responsibilities. Keep this in mind for the future: Even if you receive a good grade after your stressful all-nighter, this does not mean that you should call the experience a success. Stick to your plan for change and you will find that you earn a much greater benefit from continuing to learn from your mistake.

Sometimes you can't get motivated to turn things around. Here are some ways to boost your outlook when failure gets you down:

- **Believe you are a capable person.** Focus your energy on your strengths and know that you can try again.
- **Share your disappointment with others.** Blow off steam and exchange creative ideas that can help you learn from what happened.
- **Look on the bright side.** At worst, you got a lower grade because your paper was late. At best, you learned lessons that will help avoid the same mistake in the future.

People who learn to manage failure demonstrate to themselves and others that they have the courage to take risks and learn. Employers often value risk takers more than people who always play it safe.

Celebrate Success

Acknowledging your successes is as important as learning from your mistakes. Success is a process. Although you may not feel successful until you reach an important goal, just moving ahead (however fast or slow the movement) equals success. Earning a B on a paper after you had received a C on the previous one, for example, is worth celebrating.

How can you make the most of your successes?

- **Appreciate yourself.** You deserve it. Take time to acknowledge what you have accomplished, whether it is a good grade, an important step

When you work hard, the confidence you gain can help you stay motivated to succeed again.

in learning a new language, a job offer, a promotion, or graduation. Reward yourself in a way that you enjoy—take a break, see a movie, take a night off to visit with friends.

- **Stay sensitive to others who are less successful.** Remember that you have been in their place and they in yours, and the positions may change many times in the future. Appreciate and build on what you have while supporting others as they need it.

- **Take your confidence on the road.** This victory can lead to other accomplishments. Let your success motivate you to work even harder as you set new goals.

There are many day-to-day ways to promote success. For example, you can set up a schedule that builds confidence. Rob Stevens, financial analyst and entrepreneur, recommends that you start every day by doing the hardest things right off the bat. "One of Thomas Jefferson's rules for success was to do the worst things first. Go after the things that you're afraid to do, that you don't like to do, that you'd rather not do. Do them the first thing in the morning, if you can. You'll boost your self-image for the rest of the day, and you'll have a lot more pleasure from that point on."[3]

ACTIVE THINKING

SKILL WILL SELF-MGMT.

Go For It!   **BUILDING YOUR SKILLS**

LEARN FROM A MISTAKE

Analyze what happened when you made a mistake in order to avoid the same mistake next time.

Describe an academic situation where you made a mistake—for example, you didn't study enough for a test, you didn't complete an assignment on time, you didn't listen carefully enough to a lecture and missed important information. What happened? _____

_____

_____

What were the consequences of the mistake?

What, if anything, did you learn from your mistake that you will use in similar situations?

HOW CAN YOU LIVE YOUR MISSION?

You've set short- and long-term goals and put your motivation into high gear to reach them. You're on your way, but where are you going? Think about the big picture that is broader than any individual goal you're pursuing. Your thoughts about who you want to be, what you want to do, and what principles you want to live by will help you set a direction for your life that is your *personal mission*.

Dr. Stephen Covey, author of *The Seven Habits of Highly Effective People*, believes that it is up to each of us to set a personal mission and then put it in writing to make it real and to be more likely to put it into action. The *personal mission statement* then becomes, says Covey, "a personal constitution, the basis for making major, life-directing decisions."[4]

Here is a mission statement written by Carol Carter, one of the authors of *Keys to College Studying:*

> My mission is to use my talents and abilities to help people of all ages, stages, backgrounds, and economic levels achieve their human potential through fully developing their minds and talents. I aim to create opportunities for others through work, service, and family. I also aim to balance the time I spend working with time spent with family and friends, since my personal relationships are a priority above all else.

How can you start formulating a mission statement? Try using Covey's three aspects of personal mission as a guide. Think through the following:

- **Character.** What aspects of character do you think are most valuable? When you consider the people you admire most, which of their qualities stand out?
- **Contributions and achievements.** What do you want to accomplish in your life? Where do you want to make a difference?

- **Values.** How do your values inform your life goals and the steps you take to reach them? What in your mission reflects what you value highly? For example, if you value community service, your mission may be to hold elected office in your state. Running for student-body president next semester shows that you are being true to your values and mission as it gives you the experience to achieve your dream.

If you frame your mission statement carefully so that it truly reflects what you want out of life, it can be your guide even as circumstances change. When life throws you a curveball, the key is not to change your mission—if that is what you continue to want—but to find new ways to adapt and succeed.

Consider anchoring your personal mission on the following four commitments: to live with integrity, to create personal change, to broaden your perspective, and to work to achieve your personal best.

Live with Integrity

You've spent time exploring who you are, how you learn, and what you value. When you live with integrity, you are true to yourself while considering the needs of others.

Having integrity puts your sense of what is right into day-to-day action as you demonstrate honesty, trust, fairness, respect, and responsibility—the pillars of integrity from Chapter 1. When you act with integrity, you earn trust and respect from yourself and from those around you. If people can trust you to be honest, to be sincere in what you say and do, and to consider the needs of others, they will be more likely to encourage you, support your goals, and reward your work. Integrity is a must for both academic and workplace success.

No matter who you are, where you come from, and what challenges you face, you can live your mission and aim for your personal best. After having a stroke, this student learned how to write with her feet using a special device.

Think of situations in which a decision made with integrity has had a positive effect. Have you ever confessed to an instructor that your paper is late without a good excuse, only to find that despite your mistake you earned the instructor's respect? Have extra efforts in the workplace ever helped you gain a promotion or a raise? Have your kindnesses toward a friend or spouse moved the relationship to a deeper level? When you act with integrity, you have the power to improve your life and the lives of others.

Most important, living with integrity helps you believe in yourself and in your ability to make good choices. A person of integrity isn't a perfect person but one who makes the effort to live according to values and principles, continually striving to learn from mistakes and to improve. Take responsibility for making the right moves, and you will follow your mission with strength and conviction.

Create Personal Change

How has your idea of who you are and where you want to be changed since you first opened this book? What have you learned about your values, your goals, and your styles of communication and learning? Consider how your goals have changed. As you continue to grow and develop, keep adjusting your goals to your changes and discoveries.

Stephen Covey says, "Change—real change—comes from the inside out. It doesn't come from hacking at the leaves of attitude and behavior with quick fix personality ethic techniques. It comes from striking at the root— the fabric of our thought, the fundamental essential paradigms which give definition to our character and create the lens through which we see the world."[5]

Examining yourself deeply in that way is a real risk, demanding courage and strength of will. Questioning your established beliefs and facing the unknown are much more difficult than staying with how things are. When you face the consequences of trying something unfamiliar, admitting failure, or challenging what you thought you knew, you open yourself to learning opportunities. When you foster personal changes and make new choices based on those changes, you grow.

Work Together   BUILDING YOUR SKILLS

STUDY SKILLS TOP 10

In groups of three or four, develop a "Top 10" list of most important study strategies that you've built in this course. First, group members should take a few minutes on their own to brainstorm their personal "most important strategies" lists (these can have any number of items). Then join as a group and look at your lists together. If there are strategies that all or most of you have listed in common, put those on your Top 10. Then discuss and come to agreement on what the rest should be, adding them to the list. Finally, prioritize your list, with the most important strategy coming first and then descending in order of importance.

Write your list here. You may want to make copies and share them with your class.

1. _____
2. _____
3. _____
4. _____
5. _____
6. _____
7. _____
8. _____
9. _____
10. _____

Broaden Your Perspective

Look wide, beyond the scope of your daily life. You are part of an international community and a global economy. In today's economically interconnected world, people all over are dependent on each other for products and services that are the necessities of life. For example, what happens to the Japanese economy may affect the prices of automobiles and electronic equipment sold in your neighborhood. The North American Free Trade Agreement (NAFTA) makes Mexico our special trading partner and affects the price of produce sold at your local market.

Globalization may change the course of your career. If you take a job with a multinational corporation, you may find yourself working in Europe or Asia or the Middle East. Even if you never leave the United States, you will probably be doing business with people all over the world. You are an important link in the worldwide chain of human connection, communication, and interdependence that is creating a better world.

The previous century was marked by intense change. The industrial revolution transformed the face of farming, and inventions such as the telephone and television fostered greater communication. Labor unions organized, the civil rights movement struggled against inequality, and women fought for the right to vote.

Now, in the early years of this century, major shifts are continuing at an even faster pace. Computer and Internet technologies are transforming every industry and changing the skill set workers need to be of value in a global marketplace. The Internet and cable news networks spread information rapidly to the global community. Many people continue to strive for equal rights, on the one hand, as medical science makes strides to eradicate disease and improve the quality of life, on the other. You are part of a world that is responsible for making the most of these developments. When you choose to achieve your potential, you also choose to make the world a better place.

Aim for Your Personal Best

Your personal best is simply the best that you can do, in any situation. It may not be the best you have ever done. It may include mistakes, for nothing significant is ever accomplished without making mistakes and taking risks. It may shift from situation to situation. As long as you aim to do your best, though, you are inviting growth and success.

Aim for your personal best in everything you do. As an active thinker, you will always have a new direction in which to grow and a new challenge to face. Continually seek improvement in your personal, educational, and professional life, knowing that you are capable of such improvement. Enjoy the richness of life by living each day to the fullest, developing your talents and potential into the achievement of your most valued goals.

"In a world that is constantly changing, there is no one subject or set of subjects that will serve you for the foreseeable future, let alone for the rest of your life. The most important skill to acquire now is learning how to learn."

JOHN NAISBITT
author and futurist

Test Competence: Measure What You've Learned

MULTIPLE CHOICE. *Circle or highlight the answer that seems to fit best.*

1. Lifelong learning involves all of the following *except*:
    A. keeping up with advancements in your chosen field.
    B. focusing your energy on what you know you do best.
    C. reading to stay informed and broaden your perspective.
    D. developing a relationship with a mentor.

2. Being flexible in the face of change involves
    A. changing your direction when you encounter obstacles in your life and work.
    B. acknowledging the change and assessing whether your goals need to be modified.
    C. reacting in a way that you have seen work for others.
    D. focusing on an aspect of your life not affected by the change.

3. When you need to modify a goal, you can change
    A. the goal itself.
    B. the goal's time frame.
    C. the goal's interim steps.
    D. any of the above.

4. The best way to survive and benefit from a failure is to
    A. ignore that it ever happened and move on.
    B. determine if someone else is responsible for what happened.
    C. take responsibility and see what you can learn.
    D. resolve not to try again to do what you failed to do.

5. Developing self-confidence that you can build on in other situations is one of the key elements associated with

   A. making the most of your successes.

   B. accepting your failures.

   C. getting an A in every course.

   D. maintaining consistent life goals.

6. One of Thomas Jefferson's rules for success was:

   A. Save the most difficult things for last.

   B. Delegate the most difficult things.

   C. Talk about the things that you are afraid to do.

   D. Do the most difficult things first.

7. According to Stephen Covey, a "personal constitution" and "basis for making major, life-directing decisions" refers to a

   A. personal goal.

   B. lifelong learning plan.

   C. personal mission.

   D. long-term goal.

8. A person of integrity

   A. makes the effort to live according to values and principles.

   B. never makes a wrong move.

   C. is always confident in the ability to do the right thing.

   D. is able to come up with a good explanation in the face of failure.

9. Workplace change in the modern world is especially rapid for all of the following reasons *except:*

   A. People feel it will be beneficial to start the century with new goals and attitudes.

   B. Computer technology is transforming the workplace and changing the way companies do business.

   C. The world has a global economy that increases competition and innovation.

   D. Women and minorities have greater opportunities than ever before to be agents of success.

10. Trying to achieve your personal best implies

    A. being perfect at everything you do.

    B. choosing goals and sticking with them no matter what happens.

C. basing your belief in yourself on what others think of you.

D. continually seeking improvement in your personal, educational, and professional life.

TRUE/FALSE. *Place a T or an F beside each statement to indicate whether you think it is true or false.*

_____ 1. Critical thinking is important for academic success but doesn't have much use beyond college.

_____ 2. When facing the unpredictability of life, stick tightly to what you've planned.

_____ 3. The process of handling a failure involves analyzing what happened, coming up with ways to change, and putting your plan into action.

_____ 4. The three primary aspects of a personal mission are character, contributions and achievements, and values.

_____ 5. The events of your life have no connection to what goes on in the rest of the world.

Target and Achieve a Goal

Commit to one specific strategy from this chapter to improve your study skills.

Name the strategy here: _____

_____

Describe your goal—what you want to gain by using this strategy. _____

_____

_____

_____

Describe how you plan to use this strategy through the semester to achieve this goal.

_____

_____

_____

Building Your Skills

Brain Power: Build Vocabulary Fitness

Here is a selection from the current media. Read the material, paying special attention to the context of the vocabulary words shown in bold type. Then choose the correct definition for each word in the table that follows. Use a dictionary to check your answers. Finally, on a separate sheet, use each vocabulary word in a sentence of your own to solidify your understanding.

This excerpt from the New York Times *describes some ways that students can reduce educational debt through good works.*

Abraham Lo, a 23-year-old University of Pennsylvania graduate who teaches at a Philadelphia charter school, has a **staggering** debt—$48,000, mostly in federal loans. But because high school science teachers are relatively scarce, the government will forgive $10,000 of that debt if Mr. Lo teaches for five years . . .

Loan forgiveness programs are not new. The Peace Corps and other federal good-works agencies have long helped out volunteers with college debt. But like college loans themselves, the programs are growing rapidly. At a time when the average student graduates with more than $10,000 in debt and when graduate student indebtedness can climb into the six figures, more loan help is coming from the public and private **sectors**.

According to a recent study by the nonprofit American Institutes for Research, the number of on-the-job programs—in which graduates get help repaying their loans because they work in **designated** areas—more than doubled from 1998 to 2002. Most programs, provided by the federal or state governments, offer **incentives** for teachers (ed.gov) and health care professionals (nhsc.bhpr.hrsa.gov) to work in underserved areas—Indian reservations, inner cities, rural **outposts**.

A host of state programs are also designed to **channel** students into specific fields. Pennsylvania, for example, forgives up to $2,000 a year on loans for graduates who go into veterinary medicine or family farming.

Source: Sandra Salmans, "Good Works Can Lighten the Loan." *The New York Times* April 25, 2004, Education Life, p. 8. Reprinted with permission.

Circle the word or phrase that best defines each term as it is used in the excerpt.

VOCABULARY WORDS	A	B	C
1. staggering (adj.)	overwhelming	overactive	unsteady
2. sectors (noun)	divisions	segments	fragments
3. designated (adj.)	difficult	special	selected
4. incentives (noun)	motivators	prizes	rewards

| 5. outposts (noun) | commercial districts | outlying settlements | small towns |
| 6. channel (verb) | inspire | force | guide |

Get to the Root

Every time you learn a Greek or Latin root, you increase your ability to recognize English vocabulary words that include that root and to figure out their meaning. Grow your vocabulary by studying this root and its related words, writing in two more words from the same root, and including definitions for both new words.

gradual—progressing by continuous degrees

digress—to turn aside from the main subject

retrograde—moving backward

transgress—to exceed a boundary; overstep

aggressive—inclined to behave in a bold or even hostile fashion

grad/gress—to step, origin: Latin

Investigate Using Research Navigator

Look back through your work on previous Research Navigator questions throughout the text. You have researched topics using each of the available databases—ContentSelect, Link Library, and the New York Times on the Web. Write a summary of your research experience with each database, including answers to the following questions:

- Characterize each database briefly. What is the focus or specialty of each? What is a researcher most likely to find on each database?

- How would you describe your experience using each database? Consider ease of use, availability of material in full-text format, currency of material, and scope of material indexed.

- Which database seemed to have the most information you requested?

- Overall, which database would you be most likely to return to for future research?

Building Will and Self-Awareness

Make Responsible Choices

Answer the following question on a separate piece of paper or in a journal.

The following questions ask you to imagine the near future. Choose one or more questions and freewrite some answers on a separate piece of paper.

- You are at your graduation dinner. Your best friend or favorite relative stands up and talks about your five most significant strengths that contributed to your successful graduation from college. What do you think they are?

- You are preparing your post-graduation resume and need to list your college contributions and achievements. What would you like them to be?

- You are prepping for an interview for a job in a field in which you have had no training or experience whatsoever. You decide to list for yourself five items—qualities, life events, or achievements—that will indicate to the interviewer that you are prepared to succeed in any field. What are they?

What do your answers say about the life choices and personal goals that are most important to you? Thinking about your answers, draft a personal mission statement on a separate sheet of paper, up to a few sentences long. Make sure that it reflects who you want to be and what you want to achieve in school and beyond.

Chapter Summary

As you use the following summary to review the concepts you learned in this chapter, focus also on its format—in this case the **Cornell system,** in other chapters a formal outline, and in still others a think link. As you become comfortable with the organization and style of these various formats, try using each of them to take class and reading notes, noting which approach works best for you in particular situations.

Chapter 12: Moving Ahead

How do study	Academic skills promote life success

How do study
skills connect
to life success?

Academic skills promote life success
—Skills prepare you to succeed on the job
   → thinking, goal setting, managing time
   → reading, writing, note & test taking

—Will and self-awareness promote lifelong learning
   → Lifelong learning is necessary in a knowledge-based workplace
   → To keep learning: investigate interests, read, find a mentor,
      pursue career development
—Being responsible and flexible as you monitor your progress
   helps you adapt to change
   → How to adapt: ① Re-evaluate goals
                ② Modify goals

How can you
handle failure
and success?

☆ Failure is
   a learning
   opportunity

Handling failure and success
—Failure: take responsibility for it and see what you can learn
   → Analyze what happened
   → Come up with ways to change
   → Activate your plan and monitor how it's working
—Celebrate success
   → Appreciate yourself
   → Stay sensitive to others
   → Take your confidence on the road

Your academic work will continue to serve you in life as you use specific skills on the job, stay on top of new knowledge by continuing to learn, and monitor your progress toward goals so that you can be aware of and adapt to change.

    Everyone experiences failure and success. When you fail, analyze what happened, make a new plan, and implement it. Make sure that you also celebrate your successes.

How can you live
your mission?

★ Character
★ Contributions
   & achievements
★ Values

Personal mission—a statement of who you want to be, what you
want to do, and what principles you want to live by.
— Covey's three aspects of personal mission:
   → Character
   → Contributions and achievements
   → Values

Anchor your mission through 4 commitments
— Live with integrity—demonstrate honesty, trust, fairness,
   respect, and responsibility
— Create personal change—stay aware of your development
   and promote it
— Broaden your perspective—know how you connect to
   community and world
— Aim for your personal best—invite growth continually
   by seeking improvement

Set a course for life by defining your personal mission—who you are, what you do,
and what you value. Activate that mission by living with integrity, creating personal
change, broadening your perspective, and aiming for your personal best.

Endnotes

1. Linton Weeks, "The No-Book Report: Skim It and Weep." *Washington Post*, May 14, 2001, p. C8.

2. Margaret J. Wheatley and Myron Kellner-Rogers, "A Simpler Way." *Weight Watchers Magazine* 30.3 (1977), pp. 42–44.

3. *Keys to Lifelong Learning Telecourse*. Dir. Mary Jane Bradbury. Videocassette. Intrepid Films, 2000.

4. Stephen Covey, *The Seven Habits of Highly Effective People*. New York: Simon & Schuster, 1989, pp. 70–144, 309–318.

5. Ibid.

Active Thinking

Build Active Thinking: Make Connections

The following multiple-choice, true/false, fill-in-the-blank, matching, and essay questions reinforce the concepts you learned in the three chapters that make up Part IV, *Becoming a Better Test Taker and Creating Your Future: Choosing Success.* These questions differ from the end-of-chapter objective quizzes in an important way: Instead of focusing on concepts in individual chapters, the questions encourage you to compare and integrate material from *different* chapters as you find ways to connect ideas. Recognizing relationships among ideas is essential to active learning because it builds critical thinking skills, adds meaning to information, and makes it more likely that you will retain what you learn.

MULTIPLE CHOICE. *Circle or highlight the answer that seems to fit best.*

1. Stress reduction prior to a test is important for all of the following reasons *except:*
   A. It reduces memory interference when you study.
   B. It enables you to effectively organize your study time.
   C. It gives you time to go to a movie or see friends.
   D. It clears your mind so you are receptive to the input from study group members.

2. You are more likely to suffer from test anxiety if you are
   A. unaware of your learning style.
   B. well prepared.
   C. on good terms with your instructor.
   D. a graduating senior.

3. One positive effect resulting from being both a student and a parent is
   A. a legitimate explanation for less-than-ideal performance.
   B. developing the skill to juggle multiple responsibilities.
   C. study assistance from school-age children.
   D. sympathy from instructors who are also parents.

4. You can improve your awareness and understanding of qualifiers on tests (words like *often, may,* and *sometimes*) by increasing your
   A. reading and goal setting.
   B. reading and math.
   C. reading and writing.
   D. writing and time management.

5. Actively reviewing your combined class and text notes helps you prepare for exams for *all but one* of the following reasons:
   A. The critical thinking you do during your review encourages active involvement with the material.
   B. Because your key-term combined outline is short, you will have time to study other topics.
   C. You maximize your study time because you have all your notes in one place.
   D. Your key-term summary will give you cues to recite what you know about the material.

TRUE/FALSE. *Place a T or an F beside each statement to indicate whether you think it is true or false.*

_____ 1. Students should devote as much time studying for a quiz as they do a final exam.

_____ 2. An effective study schedule never includes breaks.

_____ 3. Marking up test questions will help you focus on directions and key terms.

_____ 4. After setting your long-term goals, it is a sign of weakness to adjust them.

_____ 5. Few people experience a major failure in their lives.

FILL-IN-THE-BLANK. *Complete the following sentences with the appropriate word(s) or phrase(s) that best reflect what you learned in Part IV. Choose from the items that follow each sentence.*

1. A trusted personal advisor who will help you make important academic and career decisions is known as a _____. (supervisor, mentor, friend)

2. A _____ person is likely to adjust his _____ in response to changing circumstances. (flexible/goals, inflexible/outlook, flexible/major)

3. Planning your response to an essay question involves creating a _____ that includes _____. (final draft/supporting evidence, planning outline/footnotes, planning outline/supporting evidence)

4. When you review your test mistakes, try to identify _____. (failures, handwriting problems, correctable patterns)

5. Taking a _____ will help prepare intellectually and _____ for the actual test. (review course/physically, course outline/psychologically, pretest/psychologically)

6. When dealing with matching questions, working from the column with the _____ entries will save _____. (shortest/time, longest/time, shortest/mistakes)

7. It is important to be sensitive to _____ verbs on essay tests. (action, passive, static)

8. _____ exams require a thorough knowledge of a subject as well as effective _____ skills. (Written/oral presentation, True-false/written presentation, Oral/oral presentation)

9. When you draft a response to an essay question, get right to your _____ and minimize your _____. (evidence/introduction, thesis/evidence, thesis/introduction).

10. When editing your response to an essay question, focus on _____, _____, and _____. (grammar/spelling/usage, evidence/thesis/logic, grammar/thesis/logic)

MATCHING. *Match each item in the left-hand column to an item in the right-hand column by writing the letter from the right that corresponds best to the number on the left.*

_____ 1. intelligent guessing

_____ 2. personal mission

_____ 3. academic integrity

_____ 4. cramming

_____ 5. test anxiety

_____ 6. qualifiers

_____ 7. subjective questions

_____ 8. objective questions

_____ 9. study schedule

_____ 10. inflexibility

A. last-minute studying

B. stress related to test taking

C. using what you know to figure out what you don't know on a test

D. failure to acknowledge a shift in life circumstances

E. short-answer test questions

F. your college's standards of right and wrong that guide student behavior

G. broad picture of what you want to accomplish in your life

H. a time line of what you want to accomplish before an exam and when you want to accomplish it

I. test questions that allow you to express your answers in essay form

J. words that have the potential to change the meaning of test questions

ESSAY QUESTION. *Carefully read the following excerpt from* Life on Earth, *2nd ed., by Teresa Audesirk, Gerald Audesirk, and Bruce E. Byers, a college textbook published by Prentice Hall, and then answer the essay question that follows. This exercise will help you focus on the meaning of the selection, apply your personal knowledge and experiences to the reading, organize your ideas, and communicate your thoughts effectively in writing.*

Before you begin writing your essay, it is a good idea to spend a few minutes planning. Try brainstorming possible approaches, writing a thesis statement, and jotting down your main thoughts in the form of an outline or think link. Because most essay tests are timed, limit the time you take to write your response to no more than one-half hour. This will force you to write quickly and effectively as it prepares you for actual test conditions.

LIVING THINGS REPRODUCE THEMSELVES

The *continuity of life* occurs because organisms reproduce, giving rise to off-spring of the same type. The processes for producing offspring are varied, but the result—the perpetuation of the parents' genetic materials—is the same. The *diversity of life* occurs in part because offspring, although arising from the genetic material provided by their parents, are normally somewhat different from their parents. . . . The mechanism by which traits are passed from one generation to the next, through a "genetic blueprint," produces these variable offspring.

DNA Is the Molecule of Heredity

All known forms of life use a molecule called **deoxyribonucleic acid**, or **DNA**, as the repository of hereditary information. Genes are segments of the DNA molecule. . . . An organism's DNA is its genetic blueprint or molecular instruction manual, a guide to both the construction and, at least in part, the operation of its body. When an organism reproduces, it passes a copy of its DNA to its offspring. The accuracy of the DNA copying process is astonishingly high: Only about one mistake occurs for every billion bits of information contained in the DNA molecule. But chance accidents to the genetic material also bring about changes in the DNA. The occasional errors and accidental changes, called **mutations**, are crucial. Without mutations, all life-forms might be identical. Indeed, there is reason to believe that, without mutations, there would be no life. Mutations in DNA are the ultimate source of genetic variations. These variations, superimposed on a background of overall genetic fidelity, make possible the final property of life, the capacity to evolve.

Source: Excerpted from Teresa Audesirk, Gerald Audesirk, and Bruce E. Byers, *Life on Earth*, 2nd ed. Upper Saddle River, NJ: Prentice Hall, 2000, pp. 5–6.

YOUR QUESTION. Analyze and discuss why adaptive traits (traits that help the species cope with a difficult environment) that are the result of genetic mutations are likely to be passed on to the next generation while non-adaptive traits are not likely to be passed on.

Be Accountable for Your Goals from Part IV

Look back at the goals you set in the *Target and Achieve a Goal* exercises at the ends of Chapters 10, 11, and 12. In the space provided, write a short journal entry in which you assess your progress (use or continue on a separate piece of paper if you need more room). In your discussion, consider questions such as the following:

- Have you used the strategies you intended to use?
- What effect have these strategies had on your work?
- Have you achieved the goals you set? Why or why not?
- What is your plan going forward for these strategies and goals?

Appendix

CONDUCTING RESEARCH

TAPPING INTO THE WORLD OF INFORMATION

The strategies in this appendix will help you find reliable, accurate information from the library and the Internet as you conduct research for your courses. More detailed information about Internet research can be found in *The Prentice Hall Guide to Evaluating Online Resources with Research Navigator* and through online access at www.researchnavigator.com, both of which accompany the purchase of this text.

CONDUCTING RESEARCH AT THE COLLEGE LIBRARY

Consider the library to be the "brain" of your college. The library is and will continue to be your most reliable information source—so much so that instructors expect to see library research citations in your work.

Start with a Road Map

The better you know the "road map" of your library, the less time you'll spend searching for elusive materials. Here are some key resources.

Circulation desk. All publications are checked out at the circulation desk, which is usually near the library entrance.

Reference area. Here you'll find reference books, including encyclopedias, directories, dictionaries, almanacs, and atlases. You'll also find library employees who can direct you to information. Computer terminals, containing the library's catalog of holdings, as well as online bibliographic and full-text databases, are usually part of the reference area.

Book area. Books—and, in many libraries, magazines and journals in bound or boxed volumes—are stored in the *stacks*. A library with *open stacks* allows you to search for materials. In a *closed-stack* system, a staff member retrieves materials for you.

Periodicals area. Here you'll find recent issues of popular and scholarly magazines, journals, and newspapers.

Audio-visual materials areas. Many libraries have special locations where you can study non-print materials including video, art and photography, and recorded music collections.

Electronic library resources. Computer terminals, linked to college databases and the Internet, may be scattered throughout the library or clustered in specific areas. Most schools have network systems or library websites that allow access to online library materials via personal computer.

Almost all college libraries offer orientation sessions on how to find what you need. If you need help, take a real or virtual tour and sign up for training.

Information Search Basics

The most successful and time-saving method for information retrieval involves a practical, step-by-step search that takes you from general to specific sources. At any point in your search, you can conduct a *keyword* search—a method for locating sources through the use of topic-related words and phrases. A keyword is any natural-language word or phrase that is used as a point of reference to locate other information. To narrow your topic and reduce the number of "hits" (resources pulled up by your search) add more keywords. For example, instead of searching through the broad category *art,* focus on *French art* or, more specifically, *nineteenth-century French art.*

Key A.1 provides tips for using the keyword system. The last three entries describe how to use "or," "and," and "not" to narrow searches with what is called *Boolean logic.*

Start with general reference works. These works cover topics in a broad, nondetailed way and are often available in print, online, or on CD-ROM. Examples of general reference works include encyclopedias, almanacs, dictionaries, biographical references (such as *Webster's Biographical Dictionary*), and bibliographies (such as *Books in Print*). Scan these sources for a topic overview and more specialized sources.

Search specialized reference works. Turn next to *specialized reference works* for more specific facts. Specialized reference works include encyclopedias

Key A.1	Perform an effective keyword search.	
IF YOU ARE SEARCHING FOR . . .	**DO THIS**	**EXAMPLE**
A word	Type the word normally.	Aid
A phrase	Type the phrase in its normal word order (use regular word spacing) or surround the phrase with quotation marks.	financial aid or "financial aid"
Two or more keywords without regard to word order	Type the words in any order, surrounding the words with quotation marks. Use *and* to separate the words.	"financial aid" and "scholarships"
Topic A or topic B	Type the words in any order, surrounding the words with quotation marks. Use *or* to separate the words.	"financial aid" or "scholarships"
Topic A but not topic B	Type topic A first within quotation marks, and then topic B within quotation marks. Use *not* to separate the words.	"financial aid" not "scholarships"

and dictionaries that focus on a narrow field (such as the *Encyclopedia of American History*). Although the entries in these volumes are short summaries, they focus on critical ideas and introduce keywords you can use to conduct additional research. Bibliographies that accompany the articles point to the works of recognized experts. Your library can help you access a *subject guide* that will direct you to lists of specialized reference works, organized by subject. A keyword search may help you find such works.

Browse through books and articles on your subject. Use the computerized library catalog or the results of your keyword search to find books and other materials on your topic. The catalog, searchable by author, title, and subject, tells you which publications the library owns. Each catalog listing refers to the library's classification system, which in turn tells you exactly where to find the publication.

Periodicals include journals, magazines, and newspapers. *Journals* are written for readers with specialized knowledge (while *Newsweek* magazine may run a general-interest article on AIDS research, for example, the *Journal of the American Medical Association* may print the original scientific study for an audience of doctors and scientists). Many libraries display periodicals that are up to a year or two old, and they usually convert older copies to microfilm or microfiche. Many full-text articles are also available online.

Periodical indexes such as *The Reader's Guide to Periodical Literature* lead you to specific articles and are generally available in print and on CD-ROM. Because there is no all-inclusive index for technical, medical, and scholarly journal articles, you'll have to search indexes that specialize in narrow subject areas.

Ask the librarian. Librarians can assist you in solving research problems, usually more quickly than you can on your own. They can help you locate unfamiliar or hard-to-find sources, navigate catalogs and databases, and uncover research shortcuts. To obtain the best guidance, focus on your specific topic. For instance, if you are researching how President Franklin D. Roosevelt's physical disability may have affected his leadership during World War II, let the librarian know instead of simply asking for information about Roosevelt. Librarians can also give you guidelines about the most useful sources for specific disciplines, such as periodicals or journals devoted to psychology research.

CONDUCTING RESEARCH ON THE INTERNET

The *Internet,* a computer network that links organizations and people around the world, can connect you to billions of information sources. Because of its widespread reach, the Internet is an essential research tool—if used wisely. Unlike your college library collection—evaluated and selected for usefulness and reliability by educated librarians—websites and Internet resources are not necessarily evaluated or overseen by anyone. As a result, Internet research depends on your critical judgment.

Most Internet information is displayed on *websites,* cyberspace locations developed by companies, government agencies, organizations, and individuals. Together, these sites make up the World Wide Web. Other information can be found on *newsgroup sites* (collections of messages from people interested in a particular topic), *FTP sites* (File Transfer Protocol sites that allow users to download files), and other *non-websites* (Gopher sites) that provide access to databases or electronic library holdings.

Start with General References: Subject Directories and Search Engines

Both subject directories and search engines are systems that help you wade through the innumerable bits of information found on the Internet. *Subject directories* are large lists of websites sorted by category, much as Yellow Pages directories organize business telephone numbers. Information is accessible through keyword searches. When searching, try a subject directory first, since the results may be more manageable than those provided by a search engine. Some of the most popular and effective subject directories include Yahoo! (www.yahoo.com), Go.network (www.go.com), and Lycos (www.lycos.com).

Commercial subject directories do not evaluate Web content in contrast to the growing number of academic subject directories that do. The advantage of using academic directories is that you know someone has screened the sites and listed only those that have been determined to be reliable, regularly updated, and reputable. Among the subject directories aimed at academic audiences are the Librarian's Index to the Internet (www.lii.org), INFOMINE (www.infomine.com), and Academic Info (www.academicinfo.com).

Slightly different from subject directories, *search engines* hunt for keywords through the entire Internet—newsgroups, websites, and other resources—instead of just websites. This gives you wider access but may yield an enormous list of "hits" unless you know how to limit your search effectively. Some useful search engines include Google (www.google.com), Alta Vista (www.altavista.com), HotBot (www.hotbot.com), Ask (www.ask.com), and Excite (www.excite.com). As with subject directories, each search engine includes helpful search tools and guides.

Use a Search Strategy

The World Wide Web has been called "the world's greatest library, with all its books on the floor." With no librarian in sight, you need to master a basic search strategy that will help you avoid becoming overwhelmed while researching online.

1. **Think carefully about what you want to locate.** University of Michigan professor Eliot Soloway recommends phrasing your search in the form of a question—for example, What vaccines are given to children before age five? Then he advises identifying the important words in the question (vaccines, children, before age five) as well as other related words (polio, shot, pediatrics, and so on). This will give you a collection of terms to use in different combinations as you search.[1]

2. **Use a subject directory to isolate sites under your desired topic or category.** Save the sites that look useful. Most Internet software programs have a "bookmark" or "favorites" feature for recording sites you want to find again.

3. **Explore these sites to get a general idea of what's out there.** Usually, in academic research, you will need to go beyond the subject directory's listings. Use what you find there to notice useful keywords and information locations.

4. **Move on to a search engine to narrow your search.** Use your keywords in a variety of ways to uncover more possibilities:

   - Vary word order if you are using more than one keyword (for example, search under *education, college, statistics* and *statistics, education, college*).
   - Limit your search through Boolean operators, such as "and," "not," and "or."

5. **Evaluate the number of links that appears.** If there are too many, narrow your search by using more, or more specific, keywords (*Broadway* could become *Broadway* AND "*fall season*" AND *2004*). If there are too few, broaden your search by using fewer or different keywords.

6. **When you think you are done, start over.** Choose another subject directory or search engine and search again. Different systems access different sites.

Use Critical Thinking to Evaluate Every Source

Since the Internet is largely an uncensored platform for free-flowing information, getting the most value from your time and effort requires you to carefully evaluate what you find. It takes time and experience to develop the instincts you need to make these evaluations, so talk to a librarian or instructor if you have questions about specific sources. Your research will only be as strong as your critical thinking.

Robert Harris, professor and author of *WebQuester: A Guidebook to the Web,* has come up with an easy-to-remember system for how to evaluate Internet information. He calls it the CARS test for information quality (Credibility, Accuracy, Reasonableness, Support). Use the information in Key A.2 to question any source you find as you conduct research.[2]

Educational and government sites are generally more likely to have been screened and selected by educated professionals than other sites. Look for URLs ending in .edu (these sites originate at an educational institution) and .gov (these sites originate at government agencies). A URL (Universal Resouce Locator) is the string of text and numbers that identifies an Internet site. All the sites listed in the Research Navigator databases have been selected to maximize reliability and credibility. Finally, if you are unsure of the credibility of a source, ask your instructor about its authenticity.

Be Prepared for Internet-Specific Problems

The nature of the Internet causes particular problems for researchers. Stay aware of the possibility of the following:

Key A.2   Use the CARS test to determine information quality on the Internet.

CREDIBILITY	ACCURACY	REASONABLENESS	SUPPORT
Examine whether a source is believable and trustworthy.	Examine whether information is correct— i.e., factual, comprehensive, detailed, and up-to-date (if necessary).	Examine whether material is fair, objective, moderate, and consistent.	Examine whether a source is adequately supported with citations.
What are the author's credentials? Look for education and experience; title or position of employment; membership in any known and respected organization; reliable contact information; biographical information; and reputation.	*Is it up-to-date, and is that important?* If you are searching for a work of literature, such as Shakespeare's play *Macbeth,* there is no "updated" version. However, if you want reviews of its latest productions in major theaters, you will need to note when material was created. For most scientific research, you will need to rely on the most updated information you can find.	*Does the source seem fair?* Look for a balanced argument, accurate claims, and a reasoned tone that does not appeal primarily to your emotions.	*Where does the information come from?* Look at the site, the sources used by the person or group who compiled the information, and the contact information. Make sure that the cited sources seem reliable and that statistics are documented.
Is there quality control? Look for ways in which the source may have been screened. For example, materials on an organization's website have most likely been reviewed and approved by several members; information coming from an academic journal has to be screened by several people before it is published.	*Is it comprehensive?* Does the material leave out any important facts or information? Does it neglect to consider alternative views or crucial consequences? Although no one source can contain all of the available information on a topic, it should still be as comprehensive as is possible within its scope.	*Does the source seem objective?* While there is a range of objectivity in writing, you want to favor authors and organizations who can control their bias. An author with a strong political or religious agenda or an intent to sell a product may not be a source of the most truthful material.	*Is the information corroborated?* Test information by looking for other sources that confirm the facts in this information— or, if the information is opinion, that share that opinion and back it up with their own citations. One good strategy is to find at least three sources that corroborate each other.

Key A.2   Continued

CREDIBILITY	ACCURACY	REASONABLENESS	SUPPORT
Is there any posted summary or evaluation of the source? You may find abstracts of sources (summary), or a recommendation, rating, or review from a person or organization (evaluation). Either of these—or, ideally, both—can give you an idea of credibility before you decide to examine a source in depth.	*For whom is the source written, and for what purpose?* Looking at what the author wants to accomplish will help you assess whether it has a bias. Sometimes biased information will not be useful for your purpose; sometimes your research will require that you note and evaluate bias (such as if you were to compare Civil War diaries from Union soldiers with those from Confederate soldiers).	*Does the source seem moderate?* Do claims seem possible, or does the information seem hard to believe? Does what you read make sense when compared to what you already know? While wild claims may turn out to be truthful, you are safest to check everything out.	*Is the source externally consistent?* Most material is a mix of both current and old information. External consistency refers to whether the old information agrees with what you already know. If a source contradicts something you know to be true, chances are higher that the information new to you may be inconsistent as well.
Signals of a potential lack of credibility: Anonymous materials, negative evaluations, little or no evidence of quality control, bad grammar or misspelled words	*Signals of a potential lack of accuracy:* Lack of date or old date, generalizations, one-sided views that do not acknowledge opposing arguments	*Signals of a potential lack of reasonableness:* Extreme or emotional language, sweeping statements, conflict of interest, inconsistencies or contraditions	*Signals of a potential lack of support:* Statistics without sources, lack of documentation, lack of corroboration using other reliable sources

Source: Robert Harris, "Evaluating Internet Research Sources," November 17, 1997, *VirtualSalt.* Available: www.virtualsalt.com/evalu8it.htm (April 8, 2005).

- **Information that may or may not be current.** If your particular research depends on having the most updated information available, pay attention to how (or whether) material is dated and use the latest material you can find.
- **Technology problems.** Websites may move, be deleted, or have technical problems that deny access. Try to budget extra time to allow for problems that may arise. Write out full citations for websites while you have them on your screen, or copy and paste into your word processing program for later reference and printout.

DECIDING WHEN TO USE THE LIBRARY
AND WHEN TO USE THE INTERNET

The Internet is indeed an incredible tool that can lead you to all kinds of useful information, and the ease of the Internet search has led many students to shift their focus from the library stacks to the computer terminal. However, the Internet has limitations that should lead any responsible researcher to think carefully about information found online and to combine Internet research with more reliable library research.

Some Limitations of the Internet

Focusing on Internet searches at the exclusion of traditional library searches may raise issues and problems that affect the quality of your research, because:

- **Search engines can't find everything.** As wide-reaching as they may be in scope, the method by which search engines like Google scan the Internet does not allow them to index particular academic books and papers catalogued by some library Web databases.

- **The Internet prioritizes current information.** Most Web pages have only been created in the last 10 years or so, and many of these pages focus on the latest and most popular information, placing a disadvantage on researchers looking for historical information.

- **Not all sources are in digital format.** Some information you are looking for may be available only to researchers who are willing to comb through library stacks.

- **Some digital sources cost money.** As a student, you have free access to all of the valuable materials collected for your library. As an independent Internet researcher, however, you may have to subscribe to read any number of publications online, including many respected academic journals.

When to Prioritize the Library

For certain situations the library is a better, or first, choice. Head to the library when:

- You are conducting in-depth research, requiring a historical perspective. Older information is more likely to be available at the library than on the Web.

- You want to verify the authenticity of what you discover on the Internet.

- You need personal, face-to-face help from a librarian.

- You feel more comfortable navigating the established library system than the tangle of Internet sites.

One of the clear advantages of using a library is the fact that librarians are there to help. Most good research is not a solo venture; researchers work in tandem with librarians and others who have specific knowledge of materials and where and how to find them. The Internet has no comparable component.

Finally, library materials have some clear practical advantages. The books you check out of the library are portable, cause less eyestrain than a computer screen, and don't shut down when the power goes out.

COMBINING LIBRARY AND INTERNET SEARCHES—THE WAVE OF THE FUTURE

The Internet is a modern reality—but it has not, as some predicted, replaced the printed word. Both sides are slowly learning to work together, ultimately to the benefit of researchers using materials from both sources.

Libraries are responding to the Internet boom in two ways: They are working to make scholarly material more available online, and they are overhauling physical layouts to combine electronic search stations with traditional print holdings. Companies that run subject directories and search engines are responding as well. For example, Google plans to digitize, through scanning, some of the holdings at a few of the world's major libraries—Stanford, Oxford, the University of Michigan, and the New York Public Library.

Your research and critical thinking skills give you the ability to collect information, weigh alternatives, and make decisions. Your need to use these skills doesn't stop at graduation—especially in a workplace dominated by information and media. "Work projects may involve interviewing people, researching on the Web, library research, taking a look at costs, providing input on support levels, and more . . . ," says Victor Yipp of Commonwealth Edison. "These basic skills—being inquisitive and using the library, the Internet, and other people to uncover information—will do well for you in school and later on in life."[3]

Endnotes

1. Lori Leibovich, "Choosing Quick Hits Over the Card Catalog." *New York Times,* August 10, 2001, p. 1.

2. Robert Harris, "Evaluating Internet Research Sources." *VirtualSalt,* 17 November 1997 [online]. Available: www.virtualsalt.com/evalu8it.htm (April 2005).

3. *Keys to Lifelong Learning Telecourse.* Dir. Mary Jane Bradbury. Videocassette. Intrepid Films, 2000.

Answer Key

ANSWERS FOR *BUILDING SKILL, WILL, AND SELF-MANAGEMENT*

CHAPTER 1

TEST COMPETENCE: MEASURE WHAT YOU'VE LEARNED

Multiple Choice

1. C   2. A   3. D   4. C   5. D   6. B   7. D   8. C   9. A   10. D

True/False

1. T   2. F   3. F   4. T   5. T

BRAIN POWER: BUILD VOCABULARY FITNESS

1. B   2. A   3. B   4. A   5. C   6. C   7. B

CHAPTER 2

TEST COMPETENCE: MEASURE WHAT YOU'VE LEARNED

Multiple Choice

1. D   2. C   3. B   4. D   5. B   6. A   7. A   8. B   9. C   10. A

True/False

1. F   2. F   3. T   4. T   5. F

BRAIN POWER: BUILD VOCABULARY FITNESS

1. A   2. B   3. C   4. B   5. A   6. B   7. B

CHAPTER 3

TEST COMPETENCE: MEASURE WHAT YOU'VE LEARNED

Multiple Choice

1. C   2. C   3. D   4. B   5. A   6. B   7. A   8. C   9. B   10. D

True/False

1. T　2. T　3. F　4. T　5. F

BRAIN POWER: BUILD VOCABULARY FITNESS

1. A　2. B　3. B　4. C　5. C　6. A

CHAPTER 4

TEST COMPETENCE: MEASURE WHAT YOU'VE LEARNED

Multiple Choice

1. B　2. D　3. A　4. B　5. B　6. A　7. C　8. D　9. A　10. B

True/False

1. T　2. F　3. T　4. F　5. T

BRAIN POWER: BUILD VOCABULARY FITNESS

1. C　2. B　3. A　4. C　5. A　6. B　7. C　8. C

CHAPTER 5

TEST COMPETENCE: MEASURE WHAT YOU'VE LEARNED

Multiple Choice

1. B　2. A　3. C　4. C　5. D　6. B　7. D　8. C　9. D　10. D

True/False

1. F　2. F　3. F　4. F　5. F

BRAIN POWER: BUILD VOCABULARY FITNESS

1. A　2. B　3. A　4. C　5. B　6. C　7. A　8. B

CHAPTER 6

TEST COMPETENCE: MEASURE WHAT YOU'VE LEARNED

Multiple Choice

1. C　2. D　3. A　4. D　5. A　6. A　7. A　8. D　9. A　10. A

True/False

1. F　2. F　3. F　4. F　5. T

BRAIN POWER: BUILD VOCABULARY FITNESS

1. B　2. C　3. B　4. A　5. C　6. B　7. A　8. A

CHAPTER 7

TEST COMPETENCE: MEASURE WHAT YOU'VE LEARNED

Multiple Choice

1. B   2. C   3. B   4. A   5. D   6. C   7. D   8. B   9. C   10. C

True/False

1. T   2. T   3. F   4. T   5. F

BRAIN POWER: BUILD VOCABULARY FITNESS

1. A   2. B   3. C   4. C   5. A   6. B

CHAPTER 8

TEST COMPETENCE: MEASURE WHAT YOU'VE LEARNED

Multiple Choice

1. C   2. D   3. A   4. C   5. C   6. A   7. D   8. A   9. D   10. B

True/False

1. F   2. F   3. T   4. F   5. F

BRAIN POWER: BUILD VOCABULARY FITNESS

1. C   2. A   3. B   4. A   5. C   6. B   7. A   8. C   9. B

CHAPTER 9

TEST COMPETENCE: MEASURE WHAT YOU'VE LEARNED

Multiple Choice

1. D   2. C   3. B   4. D   5. B   6. A   7. D   8. C   9. D   10. B

True/False

1. T   2. F   3. T   4. T   5. F

BRAIN POWER: BUILD VOCABULARY FITNESS

1. B   2. B   3. C   4. A   5. C   6. B   7. C   8. A

CHAPTER 10

TEST COMPETENCE: MEASURE WHAT YOU'VE LEARNED

Multiple Choice

1. C   2. D   3. D   4. A   5. D   6. A   7. A   8. D   9. C   10. D

True/False

1. F   2. T   3. F   4. F   5. F

BRAIN POWER: BUILD VOCABULARY FITNESS

1. A   2. A   3. B   4. C   5. B   6. C

CHAPTER 11

TEST COMPETENCE: MEASURE WHAT YOU'VE LEARNED

Multiple Choice

1. C   2. B   3. A   4. D   5. A   6. C   7. B   8. C   9. C   10. B

True/False

1. T   2. F   3. F   4. F   5. F

BRAIN POWER: BUILD VOCABULARY FITNESS

1. B   2. A   3. C   4. B   5. A   6. B   7. A

CHAPTER 12

TEST COMPETENCE: MEASURE WHAT YOU'VE LEARNED

Multiple Choice

1. B   2. B   3. D   4. C   5. A   6. D   7. C   8. A   9. A   10. D

True/False

1. F   2. F   3. T   4. T   5. F

BRAIN POWER: BUILD VOCABULARY FITNESS

1. A   2. A   3. C   4. A   5. B   6. C

ANSWERS FOR *ACTIVE THINKING: MONITORING YOUR PROGRESS* (END-OF-PART EXERCISES)

PART I: CHAPTERS 1–3

Multiple Choice

1. C   2. A   3. B   4. B   5. D

True/False

1. F   2. T   3. F   4. T   5. F

Fill-in-the-Blank

1. self-management
2. values
3. thinking positively
4. 8
5. diverse
6. long-term goals
7. time
8. questioning
9. assumptions/perspective
10. brainstorming

Matching

1. D   2. J   3. F   4. A   5. E   6. I   7. B   8. C   9. G   10. H

PART II: CHAPTERS 4–6

Multiple Choice

1. D   2. B   3. C   4. B   5. C

True/False

1. F   2. F   3. T   4. T   5. F

Fill-in-the-Blank

1. pace
2. mnemonic devices/flash cards
3. rhyming link word/humorous visual image
4. vocalizers/subvocalizers
5. critically
6. ask yourself what you know about a topic/write questions linked to chapter headings
7. highlighting/marginal notes
8. partial hearing loss/learning disabilities
9. verbal signposts
10. acronyms

Matching

1. D   2. G   3. E   4. B   5. I   6. J   7. C   8. A   9. F   10. H

PART III: CHAPTERS 7–9

Multiple Choice

1. B   2. C   3. B   4. A   5. C

True/False

1. F   2. F   3. T   4. F   5. T

Fill-in-the-Blank

1. direction
2. preread
3. solidify
4. probability/statistics
5. audience/poor communication
6. source/content
7. review your result
8. rights/responsibilities
9. plagiarism
10. editing

Matching

1. E   2. J   3. D   4. G   5. H   6. C   7. F   8. B   9. I   10. A

PART IV: CHAPTERS 10–12

Multiple Choice

1. C   2. A   3. B   4. C   5. B

True/False

1. F   2. F   3. T   4. F   5. F

Fill-in-the-Blank

1. mentor
2. flexible/goals
3. planning outline/supporting evidence
4. correctable patterns
5. pretest/psychologically
6. longest/time
7. action
8. oral/oral presentation
9. thesis/introduction
10. grammar, spelling, usage

Matching

1. C   2. G   3. F   4. A   5. B   6. J   7. I   8. E   9. H   10. D

Glossary of Definitions

Chapter 1

avian—of or relating to birds

pandemic—outbreak of disease spread over a wide geographic area and affecting a large proportion of the population

imminent—about to occur

evolution—a gradual process of development

gauge—to measure or evaluate

components—elements or parts

disassemble—to take apart

Chapter 2

commissions—groups of people officially authorized to perform certain duties or functions

nomenclature—the procedure of assigning names to the kinds and groups of organisms listed in a taxonomic classification

zoology—the branch of biology that deals with animals and animal life

universal—of, relating to, extending to, or affecting the entire world or all within the world; worldwide

mandatory—required or commanded by authority; obligatory

eliminate—to leave out or omit from consideration; reject

perennial—appearing again and again; recurrent

Chapter 3

neutral—belonging to neither side in a controversy

mediation—an attempt to bring about a peaceful settlement or compromise

entities—things that exist as particular or discrete units

transformative—characterized by a change in character or condition

chiefly—most importantly; principally

dialogue—a conversation involving an exchange of ideas and opinions

Chapter 4

prudential—proceeding with caution or circumspection as to danger or risk

intrinsically—belonging to the essential nature or constitution of a thing

whittle—to reduce, remove, or destroy gradually as if by cutting off bits with a knife

complaisant—marked by an inclination to please or oblige; tending to consent to others' wishes

regurgitating—to parrot; to throw or pour back out without thought or analysis

venture—to undertake the risks and dangers of; to brave

electrifies—to excite intensely or suddenly as if by electric shock

complements—fills up, completes, or makes perfect

Chapter 5

automated—a process that occurs automatically without human involvement

deploy—to arrange in an appropriate position; to extend, especially in width

dubious—doubtful; giving rise to uncertainty; questionable or suspect as to true nature or quality

contaminants—something that soils or makes impure; something that makes unfit for use by the introduction of undesirable elements

hexagonal—having six angles and six sides

fossilized—changed into a fossil with remnants of organisms of past geological ages

attributed—ascribed; explained by indicating a cause

harbinger—forerunner; precursor; something that foreshadows what is to become

Chapter 6

baffling—puzzling or confusing

discerned—came to know or recognize; showed insight

somnolent—drowsy, sleepy

interval—amount of time between two specified instants or events

circadian—occurring in a daily, rhythmic cycle

anecdotal—based on or consisting of reports of observations

gleaned—picked over in search of relevant material; gathered in a discriminating way

imminent—ready to occur; about to take place

Chapter 7

visceral—obtained through intuition rather than from reasoning or observation

refuge—a shelter from danger or hardship

anonymity—the state of being unknown and nameless

rigors—a harsh or trying circumstance; hardship

meditate—to reflect on; contemplate

consummately—with supreme ability or skill

Chapter 8

inundated—overwhelmed as if with a flood

lax—lacking in rigor or strictness; negligent

dubious—fraught with uncertainty or doubt

spur—something that serves as a goad or incentive

innovation—a creation (a new device or process), often resulting from study and experimentation

ushered in—preceded and introduced; inaugurated

inhibiting—holding back; restraining; hindering

wielding—regulating by influence or authority; controlling

notorious—generally known and talked of by the public, usually in an unfavorable way; infamous

Chapter 9

transmuting—changing from one form or state into another

aspirations—desires for achievement; ambitions

bestower—one who presents or gives

dictate—to prescribe with authority; impose

dismantling—a taking apart, a tearing down

truncate—to shorten by cutting off

trump—to get the better of, by using a crucial resource

imperatives—obligations or duties

Chapter 10

fringes—a marginal, peripheral, or secondary part, often characterized by extreme views

wrestling—contending or struggling

mimicking—copying or imitating closely

insomnia—sleeplessness

scrounge—to obtain by begging or borrowing with no intention of returning an item

schedule—federally regulated list of controlled substances, ranked in classes by potential for abuse

Chapter 11

ramifications—a development or consequence growing out of and sometimes complicating a problem

aspirations—a strong desire for high achievement; hopes and ambitions

stifles—represses; keeps in or holds back

boycott—refuses to have dealings with, usually to express disapproval or to force acceptance of certain conditions

contentious—given to angry debate; provoking dispute; quarrelsome

accountability—responsibility to someone or for some activity; answerability

accreditation—granting credit or recognition

Chapter 12

staggering—causing great astonishment, amazement, or dismay; overwhelming

sectors—parts or divisions, as of a city or a national economy

designated—selected and set aside for a duty, an office, or a purpose

incentives—things that induce action or motivate effort

outposts—outlying settlements

channel—to direct or guide along some desired course

Index